AFRO-DESCENDANTS, IDENTITY, AND THE STRUGGLE FOR DEVELOPMENT IN THE AMERICAS

Ruth Simms Hamilton
AFRICAN DIASPORA SERIES

Afro-Descendants, Identity, and the Struggle for Development in the Americas

Edited by

BERND REITER *and* KIMBERLY EISON SIMMONS

MICHIGAN STATE UNIVERSITY PRESS • *East Lansing*

⊖ The paper used in this publication meets the minimum requirements of
ANSI/NISO Z39.48-1992 (R 1997) (Permanence of Paper).

Michigan State University Press
East Lansing, Michigan 48823-5245

Printed and bound in the United States of America.

18   17   16   15   14   13   12   1   2   3   4   5   6   7   8   9   10

LIBRARY OF CONGRESS CATALOGING-IN-PUBLICATION DATA
Afro-descendants, identity, and the struggle for development in the Americas /
edited by Bernd Reiter and Kimberly Eison Simmons.
p. cm. — (Ruth Simms Hamilton African diaspora series)
Includes bibliographical references.
ISBN 978-1-61186-040-5 (pbk. : alk. paper) 1. Blacks—Race identity—Latin America.
2. Racially mixed people—Race identity—Latin America. 3. African Americans—Race
identity. 4. Racially mixed people—Race identity—United States. 5. Social integration—Latin
America. 6. Social integration—United States. 7. Latin America—Race relations. 8. United
States—Race relations. I. Reiter, Bernd, 1968– II. Simmons, Kimberly Eison.
E29.N3A56 2012
305.80098—dc23
2011036828

Cover and book design by Charlie Sharp, Sharp Des!gns, Lansing, Michigan
Cover art graciously provided by Jürgen Escher

Michigan State University Press is a member of the Green Press Initiative and is committed
to developing and encouraging ecologically responsible publishing practices. For more
information about the Green Press Initiative and the use of recycled paper in book
publishing, please visit *www.greenpressinitiative.org*.

Visit Michigan State University Press at *www.msupress.org*

Contents

Prologue

Bernd Reiter

From April 28 to April 30, 2010, the Institute for the Study of Latin America and the Caribbean (ISLAC) of the University of South Florida hosted an international conference entitled "Reexamining the Black Atlantic: Afro-Descendants Still at the Bottom?" The question was rhetorical, but the aim of asking it was not. As the organizer of the conference, I had long wanted to bring together scholars, activists, and funding-agency representatives committed to, and engaged in, the problems of Afro-descendant communities spread over the Americas. As an activist-turned-scholar, who had lived and worked in the Colombian Pacific (Chocó) and then in Salvador, Brazil, I was keenly aware of the many changes that had affected black communities in the Americas since I lived there (1989–90 in Colombia; mid to late '90s in Salvador), and I was equally aware that a new generation of scholars was producing new readings and interpretations about the situation of those diverse communities. From working first with the Catholic Church and later with local and international NGOs, I also knew that scholars were not the only ones knowledgeable about Afro-descendant communities in the region, which is why I decided to also invite local activists and funding-agency representatives to this conference. The conference thus was a "dream-come-true" for me—made possible by the unconditional support of the new director of our Institute, Dr. Rachel May. Under her leadership, ISLAC will continue to coordinate and support research and activism aimed at Afro-descendant communities in the Americas. The conference would also not have been possible without the active support and encouragement we received from the Inter-American Foundation, in particular Linda Borst-Kolko, vice president of operations, who not only facilitated the attendance of some activists, but also, through her own participation, ensured the participation of other funding-agency representatives engaged in these issues. I am indeed very grateful to Linda and the Inter-American Foundation for their participation in my conference and their unwavering support of Afro-Latin communities in different parts of the Americas.

The conference was a great success and allowed for many encounters and reencounters. Old and new faces met and interchanged their ideas and experiences, and as on so many other occasions, decided to "keep in touch" and continue working on this topic. At a final plenary session, entitled "Lessons Learned and Elaboration of an Action Plan," the participants not only decided to publish the papers presented at the conference, but also to find a way to make them available to a broader audience, especially to the very communities for which this knowledge would be helpful: Afro-descendants in the Americas. To achieve this goal, we hope to create and publish a Spanish translation of this book. Furthermore, we decided to continue our effort to bring together scholars, activists, and funding-agency representatives interested in Afro-descendants in hopes that well-informed funding decisions can be facilitated; that academic work can be grounded in real-life experience; and that local activism has a chance to put their daily work into a broader perspective. Finally, we decided to produce a "mapping" that brings together the different needs of local communities, expressed by activists and described by scholars, with the resources already available at universities and funding agencies in an effort to facilitate future action. We will continue our efforts to bring together activists, scholars, and funding-agency representatives to facilitate the circulation of knowledge, to add a real-life dimension to academic work, and to improve the livelihoods of Afro-descendants in the Americas. The University of South Florida Institute for the Study of Latin America and the Caribbean (ISLAC) was put in charge of coordinating this effort toward continuity.

Of crucial importance to the success—and continuity—of this project was Kimberly Eison Simmons, coeditor of this book, and book series editor of the African Diaspora Research Project Series of the Michigan State University Press. Kimberly facilitated contact with Julie Loehr, acquisitions editor of MSU Press, without whom this book would not have become a reality.

The original description of the conference read as follows:

Slavery has forever changed the face of the Americas and racism is a persistent problem, as well as a common element that unites the destinies of historically excluded groups across the different geographical and political unities that to-gether form the Americas. Over the last decade, most countries of the western hemisphere have not only recognized the continuing importance of colonial legacies and racism, some of them have also designed social policies that take explicit account of the far reaching effects of racism.

This recognition has produced a full-scale revision of national projects and official versions of imagining and presenting the nation to its own citizens and to the rest of the world. Countries that only ten years ago officially declared that racism did not affect them are now enacting affirmative-action policies.

In Brazil, for example, the myth of "racial democracy" has been steadily disman-tled over the last few years, and over the past five years, the Brazilian state has enacted several federal affirmative-action policies to actively address the deep inequalities characterizing this country. In the United States, to the contrary, the voices against such policies are growing stronger, and affirmative action might be on the verge of ending.

Comparing the Americas through the lenses of racism and exclusion has already produced very fruitful insights into the shortcomings of American and Caribbean democracies, and into the continuing importance of colonial legacies in the region. Regional comparison also adds significantly to our understanding of persistent poverty and provides insights into the effectiveness of different measures of targeted poverty reduction. In particular, inter-American dialogue among historically excluded groups promises to allow lessons learned in one country to inform affected groups in others.

AIM OF THE CONFERENCE

This international conference aimed at analyzing and comparing the causes and effects of racism in the Americas. Instead of stopping at this merely academic level, we also invited local activists and development practitioners, such as private foundations and international aid agencies, to join this discussion, in order to add a concrete policy component.

By facilitating a dialogue between scholars and development practitioners, we not only seek to stimulate an important dialogue that is grounded in real life experience, but also produce valuable policy suggestions.

This conference therefore actively embraced and promoted the University of South Florida's combination of research with real-life problem-solving agency. This interna-tional and cross-disciplinary conference facilitated cooperation among different USF scholars and research units, namely ISLAC, International Affairs, Africana Studies, and the Patel Center.

SPECIFIC QUESTIONS THAT WERE ADDRESSED IN THE CONFERENCE

Among the questions addressed in this conference were:

- What is the importance of international organizations in the dissemination of racial consciousness across national borders?
- Can the lessons learned in one country be readily applied in another?
- Is the application of North American racial categories to the analysis and crafting of social policies in countries like Brazil part of "imperialist reason" (Bourdieu, 1999), or of the inter-American dialogue among historically excluded groups and the agencies that support them?[1]
- At what stage are group-conscious public policies across the Americas?
- What positive and negative results have they produced so far?
- Is there a change in "racial consciousness" connected to these policies?

EXPECTED OUTCOMES

- The articles presented in this conference will be gathered, edited, and published.
- We will create a network of scholars, institutes, agencies, and local communities interested in analyzing and addressing the pressing problems of Afro-Latins.
- We will elaborate an action plan that involves scholars, local activists, and funding agencies.
- We will share and disseminate policy-relevant information about racism and its effects among scholars, practitioners, and funding agencies.
- A lasting working relation between ISLAC, the Patel Center, the Institute on Black Life, and the Department of Africana Studies will be initiated.

Not all questions have been successfully addressed, and we might not achieve all of the outlined outcomes. However, the book gives evidence of an ever-growing and expanding awareness of each other: communities of scholars, activists, and funders are listening, learning, and cooperating with each other more and more. Much more has to be done to make knowledge production relevant and available to those who can actually use it (other than to advance their own academic careers). Local activists are in dire need of knowledge; funders can and should listen more to local activists and engaged scholars who have acquired local and specialized knowledge. Conferences like the one held in Tampa in 2010, and books like these are but timid efforts to fight back against alienation, hopelessness, isolation, ivory tower arrogance, and self-serving funding projects—but hopefully they can be inspiring.

As the organizer of the conference and coeditor of this book, I want to thank all participants and ISLAC staff for organizing and participating in the conference that was the origin of this book. Special thanks go to all the panel chairs and discussants who provided very useful remarks, allowing the presenters and authors to challenge themselves and push their thoughts and works forward.

What follows is a list of all participants and ISLAC staff. I want to thank all of you!

- *ISLAC staff*: Yulliana Novoa, Nina Thompson
- *Panel chairs*: Kevin Yelvington, associate professor, Department of Anthropology, USF; Rachel May, associate professor, Department of Humanities, and director of the Institute for the Study of Latin America and the Caribbean, USF; and Cheryl Rodriguez, associate professor, Department of Africana Studies, and director of the Institute on Black Life, USF
- *Discussants*: Scott Ickes, assistant professor, Department of History, USF; Edward Kissi, associate professor, Department of Africana Studies, USF; Mark Amen, associate professor, Department of Government and International Affairs, and academic director of the Kiran C. Patel Center for Global Solutions; and Eric Duke, assistant professor, Department of Africana Studies, USF

Some participants were unable to contribute to this volume, due to their busy schedules as activists and scholars. Their contributions were nevertheless important and shall not be forgotten. Thank you! Participants whose presentation and work are not included are: Hon. George Martinez, activist and hip-hop ambassador; Todd A. Cox, deputy director and program officer for Advancing Racial Justice and Minority Rights at the Ford Foundation; Isnel Pierreval, youth ambassador, Haiti; Lorelei Williams, consultant; and Susan Greenbaum, professor, Department of Anthropology, USF.

My final thanks go to Dr. Faye V. Harrison for her gracious keynote address and thoughtful contribution to this book.

NOTE

1. Pierre Bourdieu and Lorie Wacquant, "On the Cunning of Imperialist Reason," *Theory, Culture, and Society* 16, no. 1 (1999): 41–58.

Introduction

Bernd Reiter

> Global Africa, the geographically and socio-culturally diverse peoples of Africa
> and its Diaspora, is linked through complex networks of social relationships
> and processes. Whether examined at the level of the household, neighborhood,
> village, city, province, state, or region, the experiences of these dispersed peoples
> are multilayered, interactively varied, and complex, and yet constituted of and
> mediated within a global and unequal social ordering system.
>
> —Ruth Simms Hamilton, *Routes of Passage*

SITUATING DEVELOPMENT IN THE CONTEXT
OF UNEQUAL SOCIAL ORDERING SYSTEMS

Development remains an elusive ideal. There is no agreement as to what development truly means and how generalizable some of its claims are. The most insightful
approach on development comes from Amartya Sen (1999), who argues that development cannot be reduced to economic growth, because economic growth is only
a means to an end—and that end is "living the kind of life one has reason to value"
(10). To Sen, freedom constitutes the core of development—the freedom to act, to
participate, to work, to have a voice, to be recognized and respected by one's peers
and community members, to pursue one's education, to participate in markets, and

at the most basic level, the freedom to live. This freedom depends crucially on one's capabilities—that is, one's potential to act, or one's agency. Most people of this world encounter barriers that restrict and limit their agency—while few people dispose of excessive agency, which intrudes on the lives of others.

This collection of papers focuses on one crucial factor limiting the agency of a particular group of people—namely, racism—and how it impacts the capabilities of people of African descent in the Americas. Racism, the way it is treated here by the scholars, activists, and funding-agency representatives contributing to this volume, is a structural phenomenon that works dialectically: by limiting the agency of some, it bestows extra-capabilities on others, thus providing them with unearned privileges and advantages—even with a sense of normalcy (Reiter 2009).

Racism has transformed black and indigenous people in the Americas into "others" and minorities—even in such countries and regions where they constitute numerical majorities. Racism has, at the same time, brought all those together that suffer under the same racial regime, thus forging a shared sense of destiny and a solidarity that reaches beyond national borders—in what Paul Gilroy (1993) has so famously termed "the Black Atlantic." It has allowed for the emergence of diasporic networks and connections of thought and action, where different people and groups in different countries are able to relate to each other's experiences and problems, offering insight and advice, and developing concerted action.

This sharing of experience and insight is what motivates this volume. It is based on the understanding that no knowledge is absolute and objective, but instead limited and situated. Furthermore, the contributors to this book acknowledge that scholarly approaches to understanding reality are limited, whereas other approaches, determined by different positionalities, have valuable contributions to make as well. While academic inquiry has the potential to be more reliable, nonacademic knowledge production is broader and more intuitive because it is not limited to the confinements of scientific methodology. Taken together, they can complement each other and jointly complete the jigsaw puzzle that constitutes the understanding of human reality.

The main goal that all the authors assembled here share is to facilitate a fruitful interchange of the different knowledges of scholars, activists, and funding-agency representatives, so that development can be rethought and reconstituted based on the informed input of the different specialists. After all, development has remained elusive to the populations this book is concerned with—African descendants. This is in part, so we argue, because not enough of those who design and execute development programs and strategies pay attention to the specific needs and problems of the Black Diaspora. Diaspora communities face specific problems and barriers in their quest for agency—and just as all knowledge is situated and limited, so all development strategies have to be specific, contextualized, and situated, if any success is truly desired.

However, even though the specific situations of African descendants in the Americas need further explanation, we do not have to start from zero. Especially, some of the broader context in which development is discussed is beyond much dispute, and some lessons must be accepted from the past—be that the past of a collapsing USSR, which demonstrated the lack of viability and undesirability of "real socialism," or the more recent past that showed us the impossibility and undesirability of "free" markets. This is what we all know, even if some of us do not want to admit it: Markets can provide great opportunities for people. However, it provides many more opportunities for those who enter markets with greater assets, be it people, groups (firms), or countries. Catching up is hard to do and might be altogether impossible under market conditions. We also know that markets do not emerge and develop spontaneously—states have always helped their own markets and made them possible. The same is true for individuals, groups, and firms. Without support from their states and governments, they have a diminished chance to enter and survive highly competitive markets, even more so when assets have already been distributed and are highly concentrated (Bowles and Gintis 1999). To enter markets with a true chance of success, as well as to establish the foundations for agency, historically excluded groups rely on their governments.

Furthermore, it is clear by now that firms and individuals cannot gain easy access to markets if the necessary conditions are not in place—such as access to information, capital, infrastructure, and an environment of law, order, and peace. Most black communities in the Americas—from Canada to Argentina—know these limitations, pitfalls, and limits all too well. They have remained at the bottom of social, political, and economic hierarchies despite their multigenerational efforts to move up. They have struggled long and hard, and they continue to believe and invest in education and different strategies aimed at securing a better life for their children. They have done the hardest, most menial jobs even after slavery ended—and although their life situations have improved together with those of the broader societies, their efforts have not made them equal.

At this point, we also know that politics matter. One of the strongest cases for how politics matter comes from Kerala, India, where the local government was able to change the social reality of Keralans—lifting their literacy, health, and thus life standards up to levels equal, sometimes even superior, to those of rich Western countries, despite the prevailing scarcity of resources and the below-average levels of income of Keralans (Heller 2000). Development is after all not simply a matter of economics— and all those who have tried to convince us of this dogma were either simply wrong or ill-intentioned. We have also learned that gender matters, and focusing development aid on women can make a difference, because women around the world tend to make many of the decisions that impact the lives of families and communities—and they are oftentimes the ones carrying out those policies aimed at improving families, neighborhoods, and overall lifestyles (Seligson and Passé-Smith 2008).

And although politics matter, we are now also well aware that government alone cannot bring about development if the people are not actively involved in the process of democratic governance. During the 1990s, development policies thus started focusing on strengthening civil society, based on the insight that successful development may result from strong civic organizing able to pressure governments and hold people accountable. Authors such as Judith Tendler (1997) went further and argued that successful development results when central states cooperate with local states and local civil society—creating a tripartite "state-civil synergy." Beyond the specifics of how much government and how much civil society is needed to achieve development, it is by now clear that states and civil societies both have important roles to play in development. Great attention thus needs to be paid to both state capacities and civil-society activism, measured through such complex indicators as social capital and civic-mindedness.

However, some questions and issues have not been successfully addressed, let alone resolved, especially with respect to people throughout the African Diaspora. The age-old discussion about the relationship between states and markets rages on—despite all the evidence that has long demonstrated that markets do not come about by themselves, that states can do much to further development, and that the real question thus is what smart government action is and what it would look like. Our analysis needs to go beyond the simple dichotomy of states versus markets and instead focus on what governments can do to help markets work more efficiently and more equitably. Hence, in our discussions about Afro-descendants, political economy retains an important space, and we have to ask how government action reaches different people who are differently positioned throughout society.

Again, Amartya Sen's work in *Development as Freedom* (1999) as well as Muhammad Yunus's (2003) work on microfinance offer important insights. Both these approaches share a focus on the importance of free agency. If people have the freedom to act, they will do so in their own benefit and thus achieve development for themselves and their communities. However, both these approaches are still somewhat undertheorized—especially the one offered by Yunus. Even though they point to the importance of agency, they do not offer a comprehensive framework that allows us to see and examine why and how agency works or can work, and under what conditions and limitations.[1] However, in all of this, it is clear that governments play important roles in "making markets work." Access to markets, in turn, is what most people on this planet want, as poverty is still the number one issue plaguing Afro-descendants and other historically marginalized groups. Economic welfare thus remains a central theme for the poor and excluded, and as such it is the theme of several contributions assembled here.

We also know now that investing in education is a crucial ingredient for achieving development. The history of South Korea has been analyzed to prove this point, and such agencies as the World Bank have learned this lesson some years back, thanks to the studies undertaken by World Bank economists such as George Psacharopoulos (1973). Education and development are tightly and causally related, where education is a necessary but not sufficient condition for development. Great attention thus needs to be paid to education and educational policies—leading some of the authors assembled here to focus entirely on education.

Despite all the shortcomings in understanding development, the history of development and developmental aid has taught us one undeniable fact: "The solutions to the world's problems have to be highly contextualized," in the words of Hans Rosling (2006).[2] There are no ready-made, one-size-fits-all, general solutions to the different, and very specific, problems people face in different parts of the world. This is especially the case in African diasporic contexts. Development discourse needs to become more grounded and situated—that is, more aware of local circumstances, the specific political forces at work, and the specific historical, cultural, and social factors that determine and limit the agency of different people and groups. Only if we are aware and understand exactly what limits people's agency, and thus what restricts their capabilities to live the kind of life they want to live—only then will we be able to support their own efforts towards a better life. If, on the other hand, rich countries and the organizations they control continue to ignore the circumstances and the voice of those they attempt to assist, then this assistance will continue to achieve very little and run the risk of undermining people's efforts towards emancipation by reproducing dependencies and lack of freedom.

This need to ground and situate development discourse and practice certainly poses great challenges—especially if such goals as the Millennium Development Goals are kept in mind, goals that aim to achieve a world without poverty and hunger by 2015. However, this same need also provides great opportunities for all those whose job it is to provide grounded and situated accounts and explanations about the lifeworlds of different peoples, namely, social scientists. Social scientists produce a myriad of extremely detailed accounts of the specific situations and problems of different groups suffering from a lack of access and development. Some social scientists are also specialists in the knowledge of local people and groups—groups whose voices by themselves have no chance to be heard, let alone respected and considered. Social scientists thus can be allies of, and transmitters for, all those whose voices are so readily discounted: the poor, the illiterate, the minorities, the marginalized, and the stigmatized.

Such diverse scholars as Karl Popper (2002), Donna Haraway (1988), and Sandra Harding (1993) have argued that truly reliable knowledge about "how reality really is" or "how things really are" might be entirely out of our reach. The best we seem to be able to do is to develop theoretical models that permit us to make inferences about reality that allow us to see and explain causal connections that we have previously overlooked, or simply not recognized as patterned and thus relevant. Relevant and engaged social science thus needs to be self-critical and humble in recognizing its own limits and, at the same time, seek ways to insert its findings into those spheres that are instrumental in the formulation and application of policies targeting the poor and the excluded. Such an attitude requires first and foremost recognition of findings produced in different academic disciplines, as well as recognition of the validity of knowledge held and produced outside of academia.

The Continued Importance of Racism

Accordingly, development must be discussed not merely at the macro level, by analyzing the state and its different strategies. If anything, Sen alerts us that development needs to start and end with concrete people. Transferred to the rest of the social sciences, this means providing situated analyses of different people and groups in specific places, dealing with specific historical conditions. Racism and sexism are concrete mechanisms limiting agency, and it is thus imperative to include an analysis of these mechanisms of exclusion in the development debate, and thus insert the voice of social scientists and local activists into the discussion currently dominated by bankers and economists.

People who have been stigmatized and marginalized for centuries face two types of obstacles: first, they are forced to compete in market systems from extremely skewed starting positions; that is, they have to compete with individuals and firms that have accumulated assets and carved out competitive advantages for themselves for centuries (Brown et al. 2005). As mentioned above, markets work best for those who can enter them with assets—and competitive advantages easily translate into even greater asset differences between those who started competing way ahead and those who started from zero, as Fred Hirsch (1976) has long ago demonstrated. To use a metaphor: no matter how fast you can run, you will never catch up with the guy who started running years before you. The second main obstacle historically excluded and racialized people face is the effect that racism has had on them. Persistent racism is in effect able to diminish the performance of those who are targeted, as many studies in education and psychology have shown (Ogbu and Davis 2003; Ogbu 2008).[3]

Recognizing the importance of racism as an extremely relevant factor limiting agency and diminishing the chances to succeed and "catch up" with those who not only do not face discrimination but actually benefit from it is thus central to the broader task of situating and grounding development and developmental discourse—especially in those parts of the world colonized by Europeans.

Postcolonial Conditions

As a result of these insights, we are once again forced to ask an old question: What is development? And how can it be achieved? The social sciences have sought to give answers to these questions at least since the 1960s, when most of Africa achieved independence and colonialism was slowly coming to an end. The new world that emerged after colonialism was one deeply structured by five hundred years of European domination—a domination that had set the framework not only for what the world would look like, but also how the solutions to the world's problems had to be presented. After colonialism thus came postcolonialism, that is, a world where the former colonizers still held all the power and controlled all the knowledge—at least the kind of knowledge the West had defined as worth our while.

Hence, the rich part of the world, after having become rich by exploiting the poor part of the world, now set out to define what needed to be done in the poor countries. During colonial times, they had trained locals, thus creating a new, local elite who soon would become the beacons and the spokespersons of this new movement towards "development." The poor countries, so was the verdict, had to "catch up." Western science produced exactly the kind of justifications needed to advance this project—a project that brought, now we know, more markets for Western firms, more debt to already impoverished countries, and in the end, more Western control over poor countries. Western developmental doctrine accomplished foremost one thing: it helped the West. In academia, this project was termed "modernization," and modernization theory emerged in different disciplines as a broader paradigm that had at its core the belief that development equaled modernity, where modernity simply meant to become Western.

To make matters worse, the available macro-approaches, focusing on state roles, modernization, or international structures of dependency, did not provide us with enough analytical tools to effectively understand the life situation of diverse peoples and countries facing very specific problems—let alone the very specific needs and problems of different groups within any given country. Although the usage of such terms as "Third World" has slowly faded, much analysis still seems to adhere to a First World/Third World mindset and, worse, analytical framework when thinking about poverty, ineffective government, corruption, lack of infrastructure, inequality, democracy, and quality of life.

The truth is that some marginalized groups face typical "Third World" problems in their "First World" countries, while most Third World countries have elites and upper-middle classes living at very high standards—comparable, and oftentimes superior, to those of First World elites, because they can rely on an abundance of cheap labor. In such countries, the privileged few count on a mass of poor people willing to take over almost all of the unpleasant daily tasks that middle classes in rich countries have to handle themselves (such as babysitting, carrying bags, cleaning, washing, and cooking). The structuring of most societies and the forging of those social hierarchies that determine who works as a maid and who is an employer are reflections of very ingrained colonial legacies. Colonial legacies need to be acknowledged and actively addressed if any real improvement towards equitable development is a true goal—and this cannot be achieved with reference to simple First World/Third World chauvinisms.

Education provides a good example. Situations like those in Baltimore, where 76 percent of African American males do not finish high school, do not live up to the idea of a First World country—especially if we consider the much higher educational requirements in the United States as compared to most South American or African countries, where achieving eleven years of formal education provides a graduate with much better chances in the job market than in the United States. This becomes even clearer when considering that most poor countries of the western hemisphere offer at least basic healthcare and education services to their populations, whereas in the richest country on the planet, the United States, 30 million Americans are not able to go to the doctor or hospital when they get sick, for lack of money. Amartya Sen (1999, 23) pointed out that African American males have a lower life expectancy than the average Bangladeshi—even though they have a much higher average income. Our discussions about development need to become more sophisticated, less biased, and more embracing of knowledge produced by non-economists, as the analytical frameworks of orthodox economists tend to be too abstract to capture the real-life problems affecting actual people and communities.

Individuals and communities—their life chances and capabilities—need to be moved to center stage of any discourse on development. This automatically implies a firm commitment to democracy—not because democracy is the most efficient means to achieve the ends of economic growth and modernization. It is not. Instead, democracy *is* the end—or formulated differently, the means and the ends need to overlap for "development" to retain any true meaning. The analysis assembled here points beyond instrumental approaches on how to best and most quickly achieve growth. In doing so, it reflects the historical learning that too many times aggregated economic growth has not improved the life situations of the historically excluded.

Lofty discourses—produced mostly by economists and political scientists working at American elite universities—about world systems, globalization, neoliberalism, dependency, modernization, state roles, and the importance of well-functioning bureaucracies have proven of little help for analyzing why some countries, and some groups within countries, continue to face poverty and exclusion. For a whole school of American scholars, development has remained a question of modernization, where countries need to first undergo a process of industrialization and produce the social forces able to press for political participation and democracy later. Even faced with all of the shortcomings of this model that have since become apparent in those countries that have actually undergone such a trajectory, these scholars have remained celebratory about the achievements of "the West." They also neglect to analyze the difficulties the West has imposed on the rest of the world, ruling out an easy "catching up." The bias of some analysts becomes obvious in such figures as the late Samuel Huntington, who expressed reservations about too much participation of the people, thus voicing what can only be interpreted as a deep-seated bias against the poor. Scholars like Huntington took their belief in the moderating power of the middle classes from Seymour Martin Lipset, perhaps the godfather of modernization theory. This entire school of thought was brilliantly proven wrong by Adam Przeworski and Fernando Limongi, who in 1997 published "Modernization: Theory and Facts," proving that industrialization and capitalism did not lead to democracy. But even if they did, modernization theory does not explain if industrialization is the only way to go, or even the most desirable path to follow, or how industrialization can be achieved—let alone how freedom from hunger, disease, illiteracy, exploitation, inadequate housing, inadequate education, and lack of political participation could be achieved by all those deprived of true development.

Latin American writers and thinkers such as Andre Gunder-Frank, Raul Prebish, and Fernando Henrique Cardoso developed a countertheory against modernization during the 1970s. These authors explained that the lack of development of a country was caused by the development of other, richer countries, as they controlled international markets, organizations, and institutions that reproduced poverty for the majority and wealth for the few. However, the application of dependency theory, and its offspring, world system theory, fairs no better when it comes to providing guidelines for all those suffering—especially as it became clear that revolution does not offer a promising way out of poverty. If knowledge is power, we should not be surprised that the powerful seek to defend their exclusive access to the domain of knowledge—limiting it to powerful organizations or to fancy and highly unpractical theories, legitimized by degrees given to them by club-like elite universities.

Such treatments, although intellectually interesting, leave us with very little, and they seem to help the academic careers of their authors more than all those in need of reliable analytical frameworks that would help them to understand the forces that hold them back, so they can devise strategies to overcome them. We have learned that well-functioning states and state apparatuses are important for achieving economic development; but the fact is that most states do not function well—not in poor countries and not even in rich ones. Political scandals, corruption, nepotism, the abuse of state power, and political representatives interested in anything but the common good and the welfare of the citizens they represent, have led to widespread disenchantment with politics—in poor and rich countries alike. In the United States the military-industrial complex and the power of huge media conglomerates have long taken over genuine political-will formation and deliberation and replaced them with a theater of politics, where internally incoherent platforms are packaged and sold only to allow political elites to stay in power by catering to the biggest lobbyists and all those in fear of nonwhites and foreigners (think of the notorious proposition to cut back government, while at the same time arguing for *more* military spending and *more* government interference in private lives—at least when unborn life is at stake).

To overcome such legacies, we are faced with the task of liberating ourselves from the patterns—political, economic, but also intellectual—that have long dominated the discourse and the practice of development. We need to reassess the value and importance of modernization, without risking the pitfall of romanticizing poverty. As proposed earlier, Amartya Sen's thinking about capabilities provides a starting point. For Sen, the ultimate goal of development must be the enlargement of the range of opportunities and concrete possibilities a person has to live the kind of life he or she deems worth living. This includes the freedom to participate in public life and to be considered a full member of a community, and to be able to participate in the public sphere without shame (Sen 1999). To achieve such a goal, social scientists, funding-agency representatives, local activists, and traditional knowledge-bearers need to communicate and respect each other's knowledge and wisdom. Elitism and exclusivity have to be attacked and overcome, as elites have never proven to advance anybody's agenda but their own. Racism has to be recognized, analyzed, and addressed effectively by making it a mainstream concern and an integral part of any serious analysis of social reality—not the exclusive domain of disenchanted minorities who, so goes the stereotype, complain too much. This also implies that the understanding of all those affected by injustice, exploitation, stigmatization, and racism has to be recognized and valued for what it truly is: expert knowledge.

Such a utopian agenda will of course not be achieved quickly, nor could it. However, something far less ambitious can be achieved, namely, taking concrete, even if small, steps in the right direction. Whenever bankers listen to social scientists; when academics communicate with activists; when academic work is done not just by elite universities but diverse sources—then we come one step closer to a more democratic reality and a less divided world. The works assembled here were put together in just this hope, namely, to facilitate the dissemination and cross-fertilization of different types of knowledge, produced by different types of stakeholders and participants in reproducing development discourse as it applies to the specific situation of people of African descent in the Americas.

Chapter Overview

Part 1, "The Black Atlantic Reexamined," brings together two essays. The first, written by cultural anthropologist Faye V. Harrison, entitled "Building Black Diaspora Networks and Meshworks for Knowledge, Justice, Peace, and Human Rights," addresses the part that transnational networks play in Afro-descendants' struggles for subsistence security, food sovereignty, sustainable environments, security, and, holistically understood, human rights, which encompass civil/political rights along with economic, social, and cultural rights. UN conferences and NGO forums, as well as world social forums, have been building Black Diaspora networks and meshworks for knowledge, justice, peace, and human rights, and legal instruments of the international human-rights regime into intelligible norms and strategies for mobilization. Under the best-case scenarios, once these transnationally negotiated norms and plans of action are taken home to local and regional struggles, they undergo a reinterpretation and, ultimately, an indigenization that resonates with the everyday practical consciousness and cultural logics of particular places and situations. Short of this outcome, the transnational exchange or circulation of information does not necessarily result in the production of politically enabling knowledge, free from the baggage of differential power that is mapped across the North/South axis. Consequently, across the dense field of Black Atlantic meshworks, all networks and network participants are not equal. Nonetheless, the more relatively privileged are not necessarily the more knowledgeable when it comes to solving problems, resolving conflicts, and imagining and putting into practice the most humane outcomes. Subaltern knowledge, enhanced through local and translocal activism, is, therefore, integral to decolonizing neoliberal globalization.

The second essay, jointly written by historian Darién J. Davis, sociologist Tianna S. Paschel, and Inter-American Bank representative Judith A. Morrison, is entitled "Pan-Afro-Latin African Americanism Revisited: Legacies and Lessons for Transnational Alliances in the New Millennium." It provides an overview and an interpretation of the different collaborations and interchanges among black communities of the western hemisphere. The authors also analyze the changing patterns of black organizing and their varying impact on states and governments, and they consider the importance and impact of international organizations for the development, change, and dissemination of black consciousness and transnational collaboration. The authors, all of whom have themselves played key roles in the processes they describe and analyze, conclude that "While Afro-Latin Americans will continue to face economic, political, and cultural challenges in a region plagued by inequalities, they have made advances over the last several decades. We argue that this is in part because they have constructed Pan-African alliances and transnational collaborations that have played a significant role in raising global awareness and influencing national policies."

Part 2, "Double-Consciousness and Black Identity—Globalized," unites the largest number of essays. This is in part due to the salience and problematic potential of black communities having to negotiate their identity vis-à-vis their own nation-state and other black communities of the African Diaspora to which they are more and more exposed. In her chapter, historian Lauren Derby challenges the view that anti-Haitianism is an ahistorical constant in Dominican history, contending that one must historicize its emergence as well as distinguish between popular and official discourses. She argues that anti-Haitianism is a form of racialized nationalism that emerged with plantation agriculture at the turn of the twentieth century as U.S. sugar firms imported Haitian labor resulting in a new subproletariat, rather than during the Haitian occupation of 1822; and that recent popular violence against Haitians is partly a result of the 2003 Dominican bank crisis, when rural employment plummeted over 50 percent and wage levels sank to the lowest in the Caribbean. Thus the current wave of Haitian-Dominican tension may represent popular scapegoating as Dominican salaries plummeted and jobs evaporated, as well as intrastate factionalism within the reigning Dominican Liberation Party due to the unstable coalition that brought Leonel Fernández to power.

Cultural anthropologist Kimberly Eison Simmons draws on the experiences of students who participated in the Council on International Educational Exchange

(CIEE) Program in Spanish Language and Caribbean Studies, in Santiago, Dominican Republic, from 2000 to 2004, to situate the seemingly conflicting racial projects of the Dominican Republic and the United States. She discusses how, for African Americans and Dominicans, the question of race is actually very similar when it becomes a question of color, as blackness and mixedness are situated processes that encompass ideas of ancestry as well as phenotypic expression in both countries. She argues that racial discourses, and the politics surrounding race and color, for Dominicans in the United States, and African Americans in the Dominican Republic, are very similar because of historical colorization—which she defines as intragroup racial and color-naming practices. She suggests that growing interaction between African Americans and Afro-Dominicans, and a growing understanding of race and the racial systems in both the United States and the Dominican Republic contribute to how identities are being reconstructed. Particularly, African Americans in the Dominican Republic and Dominicans in the United States encounter a racial dilemma—how one is racially defined within a new national context as categories are often based on the state's own definitions, series of laws, and informal ways of classifying people based on skin color.

In "Negotiating Blackness within the Multicultural State in Latin America: Creole Politics and Identity in Nicaragua," political scientist Juliet Hooker focuses her attention on a population often overlooked and forgotten, namely, Creoles living on the Caribbean coast of the country. The chapter explores the ways that Latin American Afro-descendants are remaking and reimagining their collective identities in the context of official multicultural policies that now recognize their existence and have endowed them with a certain measure of collective rights, through the lens of the contemporary mobilization of Afro-descendant Creoles from Nicaragua's Atlantic coast. The author traces changes in the ways English-speaking Creoles imagine and represent their identity within a Nicaraguan nation that has been portrayed as overwhelmingly mestizo or Indo-Hispanic, focusing in particular on the contemporary emphasis on a strong "black" racial group identity among many younger Creoles, one that is imagined in terms of transnational connections to the African Diaspora, including to an African past and Afro-Caribbean ancestry. Finally, Hooker analyzes the shifting conceptions of Creole identity in light of the connections between the current emphasis on blackness and changes to Nicaragua's model of multiculturalism that begin to recognize the existence of racial hierarchy, and to implement specific policies to combat racism and racial discrimination. In particular, she focuses on the impact of multicultural policies on the self-making strategies of Nicaraguan Creoles, and on the forms of activism that have emerged from current imaginings of Creole collective identity, and their effect, in turn, on the multicultural state.

Political scientist Leonardo Reales Jiménez shifts our attention to another often-forgotten group of Afro-descendants in the Americas, namely Afro-Colombians. He demonstrates how racial discrimination and social exclusion are complex structural problems that have affected the Afro-Colombian population for decades. Afro-Colombians experience the highest level of poverty, which is demonstrated by their extremely limited access to education, healthcare, and employment. In fact, most regions with Afro-Colombian presence endure the worst socioeconomic conditions, and the main victims of the armed conflict are Afro-Colombians. Racial discrimination and exclusionary practices, and other human-rights violations against people of African descent, have been committed by both state and nonstate actors. They are prohibited by the constitution and human-rights treaties ratified by the Colombian state. However, their noxious effects on the Afro-Colombian communities have not been extensively explored. This chapter thus describes the consequences of racist practices on Afro-Colombians, and the challenges of their struggle for human rights in the framework of armed conflict. The text represents one of the few works of its kind that explains the main aspects of the dramatic human-rights situation of Afro-Colombians throughout the nation's contemporary history.

Political scientist and criminologist Seth Racusen discusses what he calls "The Grammar of Color Identity in Brazil." In this chapter, which relies on a survey conducted by the Federal Fluminense University of Rio de Janeiro in 2002 (Pesquisa Nacional Brasileira, PESB), he finds that Brazilians use a "ranking grammar and a deracialization grammar," that is, a rather complex way of negotiating social hierarchies that makes reference to ethnic markers. To Racusen, Brazil thus is a thoroughly racialized society, which further debunks the myth of a raceless Brazil or Latin America. He also ponders the impact of these rather complex ways of self-identification on such public policies as affirmative action, as being to some degree of African descent does not and should not, according to Racusen, qualify one for affirmative action.

Racusen's essay leads to the next section of this book, Part 3: "Racism in 'Raceless' Societies and the State: The Difficulties of Addressing What Ought Not Exist."

Latin Americanist and economist Paula Lezama tackles the important problem of how to go beyond the mere comparison of incomes and life circumstances in order to assess—and quantify—the true life conditions of racialized groups and thus quantify the importance of racism. After developing a theoretical model that promises to achieve this goal, she applies her framework to the situation of Afro-Colombians. This chapter, then, analyzes welfare conditions of Afro-Colombians vis-à-vis non–Afro-Colombians, using Amartya Sen's Capability Approach as the theoretical framework, and the latent variable modeling as the empirical method. Applying Multiple Indicators Multiple Causes (MIMIC) models, Lezama is able to provide findings on two latent constructs: "knowledge" and "being adequately sheltered." She finds that after controlling statistically by a set of relevant exogenous "causes" of each capability dimension, ethnic background has a consistently negative influence. Therefore, the capability set, or the freedom an Afro-descendant enjoys in achieving the life he/ she wants in terms of "knowledge" and "shelter" is consistently lower in relation to non–Afro-descendants. This evidence points toward the proposition that Afro-Colombian deprived conditions are due to pervasive patterns of racial discrimination, and not just to low income levels or lower educational attainment as official discourse and academic dialogue have argued.

In "Racism in a Racialized Democracy and Support for Affirmative Action Policy in Salvador and São Paulo, Brazil," political scientist Gladys Mitchell-Walthour brings our attention back to the country with the largest black population in the Americas: Brazil. Mitchell-Walthour shows how affirmative-action policies were implemented in universities in Brazil beginning in 2001 yet remain a controversial topic for Brazilians. Much of the debate about affirmative action stems from scholars and activists. The opinions of potential beneficiaries are largely ignored in social-science literature on political opinion and racial attitudes. She finds that in a select sample of Afro-Brazilians from Salvador and São Paulo, age, income, city, and opinion about the major problem of blacks are all statistically significant variables for predicting support for affirmative action. As age decreases and income increases, the likelihood that a respondent will support affirmative-action policies for blacks and browns in employment and university admission increases. Respondents from São Paulo and those who admit that the major problem of blacks (*negros*) is racism or discrimination are more likely to support affirmative action than respondents from Salvador and respondents that blame the major problem of blacks on other social factors.

The final chapter in this section is coauthored by economist and Dominican activist Altagracia Balcácer Molina and Dorotea Wilson, former mayor of Puerto Cabezas, Nicaragua—one of the major cities on the Atlantic Coast—and a former member of the Nicaraguan parliament and the government of the Autonomous Region. Both authors participated in the conference that gave origin to this book as representatives of the Network of Afro-Latin-American and Afro-Caribbean Women—one of the largest and most influential networks of African-descendant women in the western hemisphere. In their paper, they provide data on the situation of black women in this region, and they point to their own activism as a way to address and one day overcome this situation. They focus on the Dominican Republic to demonstrate the profound and long-lasting effects of racism, arguing that "it was possible to establish the alleged superiority only through the use of force by the groups that unilaterally built a hierarchical social structure based on discriminatory criteria, such as poverty, ethnic-racial differences, sex, sexual orientation, and age, among others."

Part 4, "Migration, Diasporas, and the Importance of Local Knowledge," engages frontally with the theme elaborated above, namely, the need to produce and consider situated knowledge in order to be able to better understand the lifeworlds of poor and historically excluded groups. The chapters assembled under this section also highlight the importance of considering and respecting the knowledge of those who are true experts in their own lifeworlds: locals. Ecological and visual anthropologist Amanda D. Concha-Holmes highlights marginalized epistemologies in the academy by reframing Afro-Cuban ecological knowledge. She shows how African knowledges have often been understood within an evolutionary hierarchical model denoting inferiority (and even criminality) in conceptualization and practice. Currently, African-derived religions are identified as folklore—consumed by tourists, but not necessarily offering critical knowledge to the academy (e.g., religious studies, anthropology, or conservation). Yet, the global flow of people, ideas, and practices that is glossed as African Diaspora deserves improved attention. Concha-Holmes outlines some of the historical movements of Africans to the Caribbean, specifically Cuba, and delineates how scholarship and legislation have altered through time to create distinct images of Afro-Cubans. Specifically, by translating Osain, the Yoruba deity of healing herbs and the sacred forest, she hopes to expand the understanding of Yoruba Diaspora ecological knowledge.

In "Neoliberal Dilemmas: Diaspora, Displacement, and Development in Buenos Aires," cultural anthropologist Judith M. Anderson brings our attention to a country that has gone through great efforts to "whiten" its population—Argentina. Indeed, Anderson argues that the prevailing belief among scholars and the general public is that the anti-black racism that has come to characterize U.S. race relations does not exist in Latin America and the Caribbean. Furthermore, it is believed that ideologies about blackness are exclusively imported from outside the region. These ideas, combined with the mythology that Argentina does not have its own native black population, have created the presumption among Argentines that anti-black racism does not exist in their country. Anderson, however, shows that Argentina has a long history of discrimination towards several ethnic and racial minorities; Afro-Argentines in particular have been favored targets of many prejudiced policies and practices. Accompanying this violence are many hidden histories of resistance that are slowly being recovered, as well as a visible mobilization around black identities. These struggles for visibility against the backdrop of anti-black racism have led to coalition building among some members of black communities, and have especially strengthened a sense of black identity among foreigners. But this has not been a unified effort; many have chosen instead to retreat from public spaces rather than confront the trauma of discrimination. Recent immigration from Africa, Latin America, and the Caribbean has led to the heightening of multiple black identities in Argentina. The popular vision of

U.S. racial politics there is one in which blacks are extremely subordinated. However, blacks residing in Argentina recognize that they too have a racialized inferior status in the nation. This occurs to the extent that dominant society dismisses racism as an invention of the imagination of black people rather than a lived reality. The everyday experiences of black residents in Argentina serve as examples of the variety of ways that anti-black racism persists even in so called "racial democracies."

The final chapter in the section, as well as of this book, is written by sociologist Mamyrah Dougé-Prosper and entitled "Pluralizing Race." Dougé-Prosper focuses on a case study of Miami, Florida, to demonstrate how Haitians in the United States have developed their racial identity according to their social and economic positioning in the homeland and the host country. By analyzing the discourse and practice of the civic organization Take Back the Land, she shows how the racial identification process of Haitians is mitigated by factors such as color of skin, class, gender, and immigration status. The author discusses the importance of situating knowledge, of ensuring reflexivity in academic research, of problematizing representation in activist work, of pluralizing race, and of applying an intersectional understanding to the study of oppression.

Finally, in the conclusion, the editors seek to bring the findings presented in the different chapters together and present some of the combining and overarching themes—and learnings—that can be drawn from the individual chapters.

NOTES

1. In fairness, we should add that Sen has recently sought to address this shortcoming in another book on the subject, namely, *The Idea of Justice* (Belknap Press, 2009).

2. Hans Rosling said this in his talk "Debunking Third-World Myths with the Best Stats You've Ever Seen," available online at http://www.youtube.com/watch?v=RUwS1uAdUcI.

3. The case of the Japanese Burakumin is interesting in this regard: although ethnically the same as dominant Japanese, they perform consistently worse in standardized tests and assessments of intelligence; see, for example, Neisser 1986, 29.

REFERENCES

Bowles, Samuel, and Herbert Gintis. 1999. *Recasting Egalitarianism.* New York: Verso.

Brown, Michael, Martin Carnoy, Elliot Currie, Troy Duster, David Oppenheimer, Majorie Schultz, and David Wellman, eds. 2005. *Whitewashing Race.* Berkeley: University of California Press.

Evans, Peter. 1995. *Embedded Autonomy.* Princeton, NJ: Princeton University Press.

Gilroy, Paul. 1993. *The Black Atlantic*. Cambridge, MA: Harvard University Press.

Hamilton, Ruth Simms. 2007. *Routes of Passage: Rethinking the African Diaspora*, vol. 1, part 2. East Lansing: Michigan State University Press.

Haraway, Donna. 1988. "Situated Knowledge." *Feminist Studies* 14(3):575–599.

Harding, Sandra. 1993. *The Racial Economy of Science*. Indianapolis: University of Indiana Press.

Heller, Patrick. 2000. *The Labor of Development*. Ithaca, NY: Cornell University Press.

Hirsch, Fred. 1976. *Social Limits to Growth*. Cambridge, MA: Harvard University Press.

Kohli, Atul. 2004. *State-Directed Development*. Princeton, NJ: Princeton University Press.

Kuhn, Thomas. 2009. *The Structure of Scientific Revolutions*. Chicago: University of Chicago Press.

Neisser, Ulric. 1986. *The School Achievement of Minority Children: New Perspectives*. New York: Routledge.

Nussbaum, Martha. 2003. "Capabilities as Fundamental Entitlements: Sen and Social Justice." *Feminist Economics* 9(2–3):33–59.

Ogbu, John, ed. 2008. *Minority Status, Oppositional Culture, and Schooling*. New York: Routledge.

Ogbu, John, and A. Davis. 2003. *Black American Students in an Affluent Suburb: A Study of Academic Disengagement*. Mahwah, NJ: Lawrence Erlbaum Publishers.

Polanyi, Karl. 2001. *The Great Transformation*. Boston: Beacon Press.

Popper, Karl. 2002. *The Logic of Scientific Discovery*. New York: Routledge.

Przeworski, Adam, and Fernando Limongi. 1997. "Modernization: Theory and Facts." *World Politics* 49(2):155–183.

Psacharopoulos, George. 1973. *Returns to Education: An International Comparison*. San Francisco: Jossey-Bass.

Reiter, Bernd. 2009. *Negotiating Democracy in Brazil*. Boulder, CO: First Forum Press.

Seligson, Mitchell A., and John T. Passé-Smith. 2008. *Development and Underdevelopment: The Political Economy of Global Inequality*. Boulder, CO: Lynne Rienner Publishers.

Sen, Amartya. 1999. *Development as Freedom*. New York: Anchor Books.

Tendler, Judith. 1997. *Good Government in the Tropics*. Baltimore: Johns Hopkins University Press.

Yunus, Muhammad. 2003. *Banker of the Poor*. Washington, DC: Public Affairs.

PART 1

The Black Atlantic Reexamined

Building Black Diaspora Networks and Meshworks for Knowledge, Justice, Peace, and Human Rights

Faye V. Harrison

I f intellectuals, especially those based within academic settings, attempt to align their scholarship with the dismantling of racism in its multiple modalities and entanglements with other inequalities, then it is imperative that they collaborate in building alliances. Grassroots activists, practitioners within nongovernmental organizations, philanthropists, and other parties with varying stakes in racial justice can potentially work together in coalitions of knowledge and mobilization promoting human rights and patterns of development based on principles of economic and environmental justice. Scholarship for transformations of this sort cannot be limited to conversations in which academics talk mainly to themselves, invoking the most recent theoretical trends in endogamous and, largely, elitist terms. Appropriating a language of power and change when largely disengaged from the high-stakes, life-and-death struggles around the world does nothing to bring about substantive change. The particular struggles with which this chapter as well as the others in this book are most immediately concerned are those among people of African descent in Latin America and the Caribbean. The cultural and political-economic geography of this part of the Americas is a dynamic zone of historicity, pluriculturality, power, and intellectual engagement that informs our thinking about both the usefulness and the limitations of "Diaspora" and "Black Atlantic" (Gilroy 1993) as conceptual and intercommunity organizing tools.

EXEMPLARS OF ACTIVIST-ACADEMIC PARTNERSHIPS

In spring 2010, the University of South Florida's Institute for the Study of Latin America and the Caribbean hosted the international conference "Reexamining the Black Atlantic: Afro Descendants Still at the Bottom?" That dynamic meeting was organized around the participation of activists, development practitioners, and philanthropists. It emphasized the importance of developing a sustainable academic–community partnership through which research would service the capacity-building needs and objectives of grassroots communities, organizations, and movements. This approach to concerted action speaking louder than words alone made the conference and its follow-up activities somewhat akin to participatory activist scholarship projects, such as the following exemplars:

- The Global Afro-Latino and Caribbean Initiative (GALCI), based at Hunter College and the Caribbean Cultural Center in New York and organized "to foster cross-border Afro-Latino initiatives . . . and facilitate contact with multilateral agencies and progressive private foundations" (Turner 2002, 32).
- The Caribbean Central American Research Council (CCARC), an interdisciplinary consultancy nonprofit organization linked to the University of Texas, Austin's activist anthropology program, specifically the collaborative, activist research that Edmund T. Gordon, Charles R. Hale, and their interdisciplinary associates have undertaken along the Atlantic/circum-Caribbean coasts of Nicaragua and Honduras among indigenous, Afro-indigenous Garifuna, and (Afro-descendant) Creole organizations to document and gain "legal recognition of" their communal land claims (e.g., Gordon, Gurdián, and Hale 2003).
- The collaborative "decolonial" and "undisciplinary" framework-building work that has emerged from the approach to development and social movements in which University of North Carolina, Chapel Hill's Arturo Escobar (2008) is a pivotal figure—exemplary of a critical mode of knowledge production and application with significant epistemological as well as practical implications.

A leading proponent of "world anthropologies" (Ribeiro and Escobar 2006) that are not subjugated or marginalized by the North Atlantic metropolitan regime of social sciences, Escobar has partnered activist research with Pacific Coast ethnic groups, notably Afro-Colombians. This paradigm-shifting project has placed subaltern, Afro-diasporic ontologies and epistemologies in the foreground as legitimate and necessary sources of knowledge that can inform interventions against the assaults of state, corporate, and insurgent-sanctioned violence; and against unjustly conceived and implemented mega-development projects. Mismanagement and environmental degradation are not uncommonly integral to these profits-over-people enterprises. In those exploitative contexts, the rights to free enterprise and free markets by any means necessary are effectively elevated over the purportedly universal rights of human beings. When the people targeted are racialized as black, and, hence, have been subjected to a historically deep regime of radical alterity or "otherness," their lives, cultures, and knowledges are too often devalued in terms of a categorical infrahumanity (Bogues 2006; Wynter 2002, 2003). Moreover, their lives are subjected to the realpolitik of what João Costa Vargas, drawing on Nancy Scheper-Hughes's thinking on the everyday expressions of violence and genocide, has described as the *genocidal continuum* characterizing Black diasporic predicaments (Vargas 2008; Scheper-Hughes 2000, 2002; Bourgois and Scheper-Hughes 2004).

All three of these projects, exemplars of sorts, draw upon skills and resources within universities, but beyond these, they are organized around epistemological and political partnerships designed to further the objectives of Afro-descendant (and in some cases indigenous) social movements. Although projects such as these are not altogether new, within the past decade or so they have assumed greater salience and urgency. Race-conscious identities, social action, and political mobilization have proliferated and intensified throughout the Americas, and, in fact, all over the world (Harrison 1995, 2005; Mullings 2005). This is in large part an outcome of deepening human-rights crises around the globe—a trend, I have argued (Harrison 2002), that stems from the negative, disjunctive impact that global restructuring under its neoliberal guise has had in many parts of the world, both in the North and the South. I acknowledge, however, that globalization should not be seen monolithically, and that some of its dimensions have created important new opportunities for some Afro-descendant sectors (e.g., see Ulysse 2007 on Jamaican informal commercial importers [ICIs]). Nonetheless, substantive human rights, understood in the most robust, holistic terms, appear to be in increased jeopardy at this moment of deregulated marketization, privatization, and capital accumulation—a moment when disparities of wealth, health, life expectancy, and military power are growing both at the global level and within nations. Feminist activists and scholars often point out how women and girls suffer the brunt of this vulnerability to deepening poverty, and its implications for education, health, and political participation (Gunewardena and Kingsolver 2007). I have also made a version of this argument in some of my own writings (Harrison 2004, 2009). Intellectuals concerned with race and racism must demonstrate how—in gender-varied ways—racially subjugated peoples, the majority of whom face structural obstacles to accumulating net assets (i.e., wealth) and to securing the means of subsistence to meet basic needs, also bear the brunt of these forces, which subject them to multiple modalities and assaults of structural violence (Harrison 1997, 2008; Farmer 2003, 2004; Bourgois and Scheper-Hughes 2004). In view of these conditions, racially subordinated peoples have been compelled to take collective action in their defense and in affirmation of their dignity as human beings. They are claiming their rights as full citizens of nation-states and, beyond the limits of national location, as agents of change and public well-being who have risen to the challenge and imperative of operating on a global terrain.

Antiracism, Human Rights, and International Conferences

International and regional conferences have also contributed to Afro-descendants' recent trends in activism. The United Nations has especially played a catalytic role by providing transnational and global spaces for dialogue and concerted action. UN-facilitated discourse and action have fostered the development of networks, as well as inspired the more "self-organizing, decentralized, and nonhierarchical 'meshworks'" (Escobar 2008, 11) among activists, and the extra-academic partnerships in support of their struggles.

The activities within these arenas have given greater international visibility and legitimacy to local and regional grievances. Through these activities, strategies and plans of action for promoting justice, peace, and human rights are devised that give antiracist activists the moral leverage and organizational capacity to more effectively lobby states and multinational agencies, holding them accountable to the norms and standards set by international law and reinforced by the declarations and plans of action that come out of UN prepcoms (preparatory conferences), world conferences, and, in their wake, post-conference review sessions.

There are many UN conferences and parallel nongovernment organizational (NGO) forums that have been relevant to the lives and struggles of Afro-descendants, but the main ones to which I am referring are those related to the Third World Conference against Racism, Racial Discrimination, Xenophobia and Related Intolerance (WCAR) held in Durban, South Africa, in 2001. The 2000 Santiago Declaration (officially titled the Draft Declaration and Plan of Action at the Regional Conference of the Americas), drafted in preparation for the WCAR Declaration and Plan of Action, was historic for recognizing the transatlantic slave trade and enslavement as a crime against humanity whose legacy persists in the "widespread poverty and marginalization" (Turner 2002, 32) that peoples of African descent suffer throughout the hemisphere today. The accord reached in Santiago also led to the acceptance of the umbrella terms "Afro-descendant" and "Afro-Latino" as political categories for denoting all people of African descent, no matter the degree of admixture or their position in the color continuum or complex "racial calculus" (Harris 1970). As Lovell and Wood's research (1998), among that of many others, has shown, statistical data on life expectancy, employment distribution, income, educational attainment, health, and criminal (in)justice status indicate that mulattos have more in common with blacks than with whites, who, on average, are more advantaged along these indices. The data show that even middle-class blacks and mulattos face discrimination, causing them to fall behind whites in many of these indices. This evidence belies the "mulatto escape hatch" (Degler 1971) accepted by earlier generations of scholars.

For purposes of political expediency and for the sake of building a united front for combating racism and related intolerances, an Afro-descendant consciousness and solidarity assumed a central position on the hemispheric and global stage for anti-racist human rights. At the June 2001 prepcom in Geneva right before the Durban WCAR, Afro-descendants joined forces with African delegates to form the African and African Descendants Caucus (Turner 2002, 32). The strength of the caucus led to the final NGO and conference documents characterizing slavery as a crime against humanity and recommending that reparations be seriously considered.

In its vision and praxis, African descendants' antiracism has both discursively and politically shifted the boundaries of human rights beyond the limits of mainstream liberal democratic notions of rights, which frequently upstage and sometimes even deny economic, social, and cultural rights as universal human rights, or as rights at all. This is so despite the fact that, along with the Universal Declaration of Human Rights, the International Bill of Rights includes the International Covenant on Civil and Political Rights and the International Covenant on Economic, Social and Cultural Rights, both of which are treaties of which many nation-states are signatories. But *de jure* agreements and legalities do not necessarily translate into substantive realities protected by compliance with and enforcement of the law, be it national or international. If we confuse or conflate the *de jure* with the *de facto*, we can easily buy into the argument that we have already achieved an Obama-era "postracial" society in the United States, and progressive multicultural orders in those Latin American countries in which the ethnic distinctiveness of indigenous and African-descended peoples have come to be recognized constitutionally and legislatively.

The 1993 passage of Law 70 in Colombia granted Afro-Colombian communities collective land titles and the right to manage the resources found within those biodiversity-rich territories, but unfortunately, it has not effectively protected Afro-Colombian communities in the Pacific region from the encroachment of mega-development projects, and from the violence of the military, paramilitary forces, insurgent guerrillas, and narco-traffickers, resulting in mass displacement of the population, declining subsistence security, and declining health, with women, children, and the elderly being especially vulnerable (Escobar 2008; Wade 1993, 357; Jordan 2008; TransAfrica Forum 2008).

Paradoxically, the desperate economic marginality of these communities has led many young adults to seek the resources that come from joining the army, the paramilitias, and drug traffickers. In opposition to this self-defeating dependence, peace communities that refuse to take sides with any of the armed encroachers have been mobilized (Angel-Ajani 2008). Women's activism has been central to this political project. Unfortunately, this heroic movement of nonviolence has not received as much exposure in global media circuits as the Civil Rights Movement did fifty years ago. However, a greater degree of visibility has started to emerge.

The 2000 Santiago prepcom, the 2001 WCAR, and most recently the Durban Review in April 2009, along with all the research and lobbying done by the Working Group of Experts on People of African Descent and the Special Rapporteur on Contemporary Forms of Racism, have helped to create more of a climate of support for African-descended people's initiatives at home and across transnational fields of engagement, solidarity, and visibility. As J. Michael Turner (2002) has pointed out, Afro-Latinos probably gained more from WCAR-related events and activities than any other African or Afro-descendant group.

From the vantage point of U.S. foreign policy, the relative effectiveness of their engagements is reflected in the increased visibility and higher priority that Afro-Latin Americans have achieved in the lobbying of the TransAfrica Forum African American lobby, the advocacy of the Black Congressional Caucus, and the reformulation of policy in the U.S. Congress. For example, the Congressional Research Service (CRS 2008) has produced a major report for members of Congress who provide input into foreign policy, determining USAID and Peace Corps objectives and defining the agenda of multilateral development banks (e.g., Inter-American Development Bank, World Bank). Although the United States has never officially participated in any of the three WCARs, the report contains a section on the impact of Durban and regional conferences, acknowledging their international sociopolitical significance. Despite its demonstrated ambivalence toward hemispheric and world antiracisms, the U.S. government has had to make adjustments in response to what has, in effect, become a "racial report card" for monitoring multilateral development agencies such as the World Bank and Inter-American Development Bank (Turner 2002, 33). This new trend came out of the lobbying efforts of solidarity networks facilitated by GALCI, which strongly recommended that development projects within Afro-descendant communities be closely evaluated, critiqued, and, when necessary, redesigned in ways that promote those communities' general well-being and seriously take into account gender equity and child/youth development. The 2008 Congressional Review Service (CRS) report, in anticipation of the UN Durban Review Conference, includes a brief description of the Inter-Agency Consultation on Race in Latin America, a donor consortium with representation from the World Bank, the Inter-American Development Bank, Inter-American Foundation, the British Department for International Development, the Pan American Health Organization (PAHO), OAS Commission on Human Rights, and Ford Foundation. The work of the Inter-Agency Consultancy, founded in 2000 and operative until 2009 (personal communication, Linda Borst Kolko, 29 April 2010), demonstrates that Afro-Latin Americans are no longer invisible, as Minority Rights Group International demonstrated quite a while ago (Minority Rights Group 1995). Afro-Latin Americans have made their way into the agenda of U.S. foreign policy, which has historically been driven by what international-relations scholar Robert Vitalis (2000) characterizes as a longstanding, unspoken "norm against noticing race" (Harrison 2002, 56). The insistence among Afro-Latin Americans that race seriously matters and that racism exists in their societies can no longer be ignored. However, there is still the need to be critically vigilant of what the new foreign and national policies actually mean, what the effects of neoliberal multicultural regimes are on the ground, and whether these legislative and developmental reforms are sufficient for Afro-descendant well-being and empowerment. My sense, based on critiques of the new multiculturalisms with their double-edged sword of expanding the space for citizenship while sustaining the overall nexus of power (Hale 2005, 2006), is that they are absolutely necessary but insufficient. This is especially true if the goal of restructured governance is to achieve social, economic, and environmental justice that is wedded to expanded, substantive forms and expressions of citizenship and human rights.

THE STRUGGLE OVER WHAT IT MEANS TO BE HUMAN

African-descended activists in the United States, both indigenized and immigrant, as well as those struggling throughout the Diaspora, have long struggled over what it means to be human, to enjoy human dignity, and to have racially subjugated people's claims to citizenship seriously acknowledged and respected. The debate over persistent black dehumanization and struggles for *re*humanization has, therefore, played a central role in social and political thought among African Diaspora thinkers. In my view, Afro-diasporic struggles for political, economic, sociocultural, and, more recently, environmental and development rights have helped to stretch the boundaries of rights discourses and practices internationally. There is a need to rethink and rework the terms of the international human-rights discourse to adequately address and account for the experiences and struggles of subaltern people, particularly Afro-descendants. Afro-descendants have been active conversants in these debates; yet this role has been underappreciated, both politically and theoretically.

João Costa Vargas (2008) and Sylvia Wynter (2003) are two African-descended intellectuals who are interrogating and theorizing the parameters of key human-rights categories. Based on his research in both the United States and Brazil, Vargas argues that we are witnessing nothing less than a "genocidal continuum" in contemporary Black Diaspora communities. The life-threatening severity of the cumulative effect of "quotidian acts and representations of discrimination, de-humanization, and ultimate exclusion" (Vargas 2008, 10) is underreported and undertheorized in the social analysis of African-descended peoples, whose lives are still profoundly devalued and assaulted by symbolic violence, incarceration, police brutality, high infant mortality, shortened life expectancies, deficient health care and discriminatory medical treatment, substandard schooling and miseducation, declining economic opportunities, mass internal displacement because of civil unrest and unnatural disasters—such as Hurricane Katrina and the post-catastrophe neglect in the wake of the 2007 earthquake on Peru's southern Pacific coast—everyday violence in ghettoes and favelas, post-traumatic stress, chronic depression, and self-hatred (11). In studies of genocide and other human-rights abuse, where the legal definitions underscore deliberate intentionality rather than the structural violence that ensues well beyond the evil motivations of individuals, Afro-diasporic communities are largely absent, despite ample evidence of the destruction, in whole or in part, "caused by bodily or mental harm" inflicted on a racialized population (xx).

The contemporary devaluation of black lives and the categorical "infrahumanity" (Gilroy 2002) experienced by considerable segments of Afro-diasporic communities is part of the troubled legacy that Jamaican postcolonial theorist Sylvia Wynter (2002, 2003) has interrogated in her provocative, no-holds-barred call for an "after-man" formulation of the terms of what it should mean to be and to become fully human. She advocates an ontology and epistemology premised on conceptual grounds other than those established in the image, and within the parameters of the legacy, of the Western Enlightenment. She argues that the model of man and mankind derived from that universalism-claiming trajectory presumes the radical "othering" and inferiorization of the African and African-derived (Bogues 2006). In other words, Africans and Afro-descendants are calibrated as less than fully human. Despite the globally accepted regime of universal human rights as a category of "soft law," this template remains imprinted on contemporary discourses about intelligence, academic achievement, economic development, poverty, criminality, cultural competence, and cultural capital. Wynter insists that as a consequence of this dominant regime of knowledge, full humanity cannot be achieved without the fundamental reconstruction of the very terms, presuppositions, and material conditions of what is human. In my view, this conceptualization has implications for thinking critically about the historical development of, and epistemological struggles over, the philosophical, legal, and political constitution of the presently existing human-rights system.

Besides the intellectual work of university-based scholars, there are also the meaningful intellectual activities, including cultural production, grounded in the everyday life, social action, and political mobilization of ordinary women and men who are, ultimately, the constituents of community-based organizations and social movements. This is the locus of what Sally Engle Merry (2006) refers to as vernacularization. This process involves the translation of transnational discourses such as that of universal human rights into accessible ideas and meanings that resonate with daily life and locally embodied knowledge. When it occurs, vernacularization is achieved unevenly; it does not entail the simple transplantation of ideas that circulate through the circuits of the UN (charter- and treaty-based bodies), international human-rights NGOs (e.g., Amnesty International, Human Rights Watch, Minority Rights Group International), and regional bodies (e.g., Inter-American Commission on Human Rights, Inter-American Court of Human Rights, both autonomous organs of the Organization of American States). It results from a dialogic process of cross-fertilization. Hence, to the extent that human-rights knowledge can be vernacularized within African Diaspora contexts, it must become grounded in the ontological and epistemological sediment of Afro-descendants' lived experiences. These collective experiences may potentially teach decolonizing lessons about the pluricultural and racially stratified "socionatural world" (Escobar 2008, 5), its patterns of unequal development, and the modernity aligned with the "imperial globality" that defends "white privilege worldwide" (20). Insightfully, Escobar explains that

> *White privilege* . . . [is] not so much [about phenotypical whiteness] but the defense of a Eurocentric way of life that worldwide has historically privileged white peoples (and particularly since the 1950s, those elites and middle classes around the world who abide by this outlook) at the expense of non-European and colored peoples. This is global coloniality at its most material. (20)

Escobar suggests that vernacular knowledge within Afro-diasporic communities may yield models of culture, political ecology, and economic transformation that illuminate possibilities beyond the presently constituted modernity of the colonial legacy. For these local models to weigh into strategic debates that inform policies and their implementation, a process of translation must occur to facilitate the flow of ideas from communities, social movements, and sites of population displacement to the national, regional, and transnational arenas where interventions might potentially disrupt the prevailing pattern of belief, knowledge, and practice. Can this translation take place outside of coalitions of knowledge and the sociopolitical practices with which they are linked?

TOWARD BUILDING TRANSNATIONAL, ACTIVIST-ACADEMIC SOLIDARITIES

For the past decade, I have belonged to an international network of colleagues comprising the Commission on the Anthropology of Women within the International Union of Anthropological and Ethnological Sciences (IUAES). We have worked to keep afloat and, to the extent possible, develop the commission in ways that insert our voices into anthropology's international congresses and into other world conferences, such as UN NGO forums. At the NGO forums parallel to the Fourth World Conference for Women in 1995, and more recently the 2001 WCAR, we attempted to facilitate and frame conversations between social scientists and intellectuals based outside of universities in community-based organizations, NGOs, and, in some instances, government. We have taken this approach because we believe that "at least some of our theory and practice as scholars, educators, and social critics [should] be informed and challenged by our having an ongoing dialogue [and interaction] with ... activists and advocates for human rights" (Harrison 2005, 1).

It is imperative that we come to understand the dialogic relationship and tensions among various kinds of knowledge claims, from ethnographic and statistical, to the official reports of governments and UN bodies, to expressions grounded in vernacular epistemologies. As I have argued before: "When anthropologists and other social scientists understand how different modes of inquiry interact within this larger web of knowledge claims, they are better able to invest their energies in building cooperation and a mutually beneficial coalition among various knowledges and those who produce them" (Harrison 2000, 62).

Can we help to build coalitions of knowledge and mobilization for the African Diaspora and its allied sites that give us the basis for imagining and modeling a potentially viable alternative to the existing imperial world order (Harrison 2008, 306–307)—or as Escobar (2008) would likely phrase it, the world order "otherwise"?

This is the kind of question many of us attempt to address in our research and teaching. Although we can certainly generate tentative, hypothetical perspectives, we cannot really come up with the best answer without positioning ourselves in nonhierarchical and decentralized meshworks rather than in conventional networks tending toward vertical relations of power.

Cristóbal Valencia Ramírez (2009) illuminates the wariness that some Afro-Venezuelan activists have expressed, because of the experience of having their local particularities and priorities subsumed within wider diasporic and (other) transnational solidarities that are too often organized hierarchically despite their invocation of sameness and equal positioning. This is the double-edged sword of transborder solidarity, which is needed but has its contradictions. While extra-academic projects are definitely important, it is also necessary that we remain self-critical enough to assess the extent to which our good intentions are inadequate for offsetting the dynamics that reproduce the privilege and power some members of networks and so-called partnerships have over others, especially those whom we aim to support. This is a risk and danger that we should be vigilant about and find effective ways to avoid or circumvent. The path ahead of us is full of complicated zigzags and detours, but no obstacle is impossible to overcome, and no problem is impossible to solve if we galvanize our collective will to act in genuine critical solidarity with Afro-descendants in Latin America and the Caribbean.

SOME FINAL THOUGHTS

The project of rethinking the Black Atlantic, the overarching theme that initially brought this book's contributors together as conference participants, and ascertaining the extent to which the historical marginality and infrahumanity of Afro-descendants continue to persist is an important one. It entails that we clarify the meanings we invest in our key terms and how our audiences make sense of the ideas we invoke. For instance, the mapping and remapping of a Black Atlantic or Afro-Atlantic (Yelvington 2006) has received considerable attention since Paul Gilroy's seminal intervention (Gilroy 1993). His Anglophone bias has been contested by scholars of Francophone, Lusophone, and Hispanophone settings within the African Diaspora; his peripheralization of Africa's ongoing agency in Diaspora developments has been addressed by Lorand Matory (2005, 2006) and others who argue for Africa's coeval role in transatlantic dialogues and interaction. More recently, scholars and activists working among Afro-descendants on the Pacific Coast of Columbia, Ecuador, and Peru have sometimes questioned whether a Black Atlantic cartography is an appropriate and sufficiently inclusive gloss. The analyses of Feldman (2006) and Escobar (2008) inspire us to ask, is there not a Black Pacific that, of course, has a relationship with the Black Atlantic? Moreover, taking the whole world into account, there is also a trans–Indian Ocean Diaspora (Jayasuriya and Pankhurst 2003) that places Afro-descendant minorities in Iraq (Zubyr) and India (Siddis), among other places, onto our Diaspora map.

The African Diaspora is indeed global, but the hemispheric mapping of Africanity, African descent, and blackness, which are interrelated but not necessarily the same (see Walker 2002), is, nonetheless, an important pursuit because lives, subsistence security, communal land rights, the stewardship of biodiversity, citizenship, and human rights are seriously at stake. It is, therefore, imperative that academic and extra-academic engagements offset the unfortunate tendency of so many people in the United States to be unaware of Afro-Latin America and its social movements (Mullings 2009). This learned and enforced ignorance was clearly reflected in the former president George W. Bush, who was completely unaware that Afro-Brazilians existed, and demonstrated his ignorance on a mass-mediated world stage. This socially constructed ignorance is also manifested most unfortunately among many black Americans programmed to be blind to their counterparts in Latin America, who are much more aware of their fellow Diaspora Africans in Anglo North America.

One of my students, a bright young Haitian American woman, reacted quite emotionally to a presentation I gave in one of my classes last year. The presentation was on the African Diaspora in Latin America, historical and contemporary background for readings I had assigned on Afro-Latina perspectives on race and gender in society. I showed several PowerPoint slides of a wide array of Afro-Latin American faces and scenarios. The most poignant were on Afro-Colombian displacement from the Chocó and other departments of Colombia. After class, the student came up to me with tears streaming down her checks. "Why didn't we know that these people—who look like us—exist and are affected by American policies? What can we do to make more people here aware?" Perhaps by her outrage and interest in continuing the discussion after class she had taken the first step toward finding a way to redress the marginal place that Afro-Latin Americans occupy in the consciousness of even some of the most educated black people in North America. I am glad I gave that presentation that day.

REFERENCES

Angel-Ajani, Asale. 2008. "Out of Chaos: Afro-Colombian Peace Communities and the Realities of War." In *Transnational Blackness: Navigating the Global Color Line*, ed. Manning Marable and Vanessa Agard-Jones, 281–300. New York: Palgrave Macmillan.

Bogues, Anthony, ed. 2006. *After Man, Towards the Human: Critical Essays on Sylvia Wynter*. Kingston, Jamaica: Ian Randle Publishers.

Bourgois, Philippe, and Nancy Scheper-Hughes. 2004. "Comment (on Paul Farmer's 'An Anthropology of Structural Violence')." *Current Anthropology* 45(3):317–318.

Congressional Research Service. 2008. *The 2009 U.N. Durban Review Conference: Follow-Up to the 2001 U.N. World Conference against Racism*. Report prepared for members and committees of Congress by Luisa Blanchfield, analyst in International Relations, Foreign Affairs, and Trade Division. November 20.

Degler, Carl N. 1971. *Neither Black nor White: Slavery and Race Relations in Brazil and the United States*. New York: Macmillan.

Escobar, Arturo. 2008. *Territories of Difference: Place, Movements, Life*, Redes. Durham, NC: Duke University Press.

Farmer, Paul. 2003. *Pathologies of Power: Health, Human Rights, and the New War on the Poor*. Berkeley: University of California Press.

———. 2004. Sidney W. Mintz Lecture for 2001: "An Anthropology of Structural Violence." *Current Anthropology* 45(3):305–325.

Feldman, Heidi Carolyn. 2006. *Black Rhythms of Peru: Reviving African Musical Heritage in the Black Pacific*. Middletown, CT: Wesleyan University Press.

Gilroy, Paul. 1993. *The Black Atlantic: Modernity and Double Consciousness*. Cambridge, MA: Harvard University Press.

———. 2002. *After Race: Imagining Political Culture beyond the Color Line*. Cambridge, MA: Belknap Press.

Gordon, Edmund T., Galio C. Gurdián, and Charles Hale. 2003. "Rights, Resources, and the Social Memory of Struggle: Reflections on a Study of Indigenous and Black Community Land Rights." *Human Organization* 62(4):369–381.

Gunewardena, Nandini, and Ann Kingsolver, eds. 2007. *The Gender of Globalization: Women Navigating Cultural and Economic Marginalities*. Santa Fe, NM: School of Advanced Research Press.

Hale, Charles. 2005. "Neoliberal Multiculturalism: The Remaking of Cultural Rights and Racial Dominance in Central America." *PoLAR: Political and Legal Anthropology Review* 28(1):10–28.

———. 2006. Más Que un Indio *(More Than an Indian): Racial Ambivalence and the Paradox of Neoliberal Multiculturalism in Guatemala*. Santa Fe, NM: School of Advanced Research Press.

Harris, Marvin. 1970. "Referential Ambiguity in the Calculus of Brazilian Racial Identity." *Southwestern Journal of Anthropology* 26:1–14.

Harrison, Faye V. 1995. "The Persistent Power of 'Race' in the Cultural and Political Economy of Racism." *Annual Review of Anthropology* 24:47–74.

———. 1997. "The Gendered Politics and Violence of Structural Adjustment: A View from Jamaica." In *Situated Lives: Gender and Culture in Everyday Life*, ed. Louise Lamphere, Helena Ragoné, and

Patricia Zavella, 451–468. New York: Routledge.

———. 2000. "Facing Racism and the Moral Responsibility of Human Rights Knowledge." *Annals of the New York Academy of Sciences* 925:45–69.

———. 2002. "Global Apartheid, Foreign Policy, and Human Rights." *Souls: A Critical Journal of Black Politics, Culture, and Society* 4(3):48–68.

———. 2004. "Global Apartheid, Environmental Degradation, and Women's Activism for Sustainable Well-Being: A Conceptual and Theoretical Overview." *Urban Anthropology and Studies of Cultural Systems and World Economic Development* 33(1):1–35.

———. 2005. "Introduction: Global Perspectives on Human Rights and Interlocking Inequalities of Race, Gender, and Related Dimensions of Power." In *Resisting Racism and Xenophobia: Global Perspectives on Race, Gender, and Human Rights*, ed. Faye V. Harrison, 1–31. Walnut Creek, CA: AltaMira Press.

———. 2008. *Outsider Within: Reworking Anthropology in the Global Age.* Urbana: University of Illinois Press.

———. 2009. "Building Solidarities for Human Rights: Diasporic Women as Agents of Transformation." In *Gendering Global Transformations: Gender, Culture, Race, and Identity*, eds. Chima J. Korieh and Philomina Okeke-Ihejirika, 17–28. New York: Routledge.

Jayasuriya, Shihan de S., and Richard Pankhurst, eds. 2003. *The African Diaspora in the Indian Ocean.* Trenton, NJ: Africa World Press.

Jordon, Joseph. 2008. "Afro-Colombia: A Case for Pan-African Analysis." In *Transnational Blackness: Navigating the Global Color Line*, ed. Manning Marable and Vanessa Agard-Jones, 87–98. New York: Palgrave Macmillan.

Lovell, Peggy, and Charles H. Wood. 1998. "Skin Color, Racial Identity, and Life Chances in Brazil." *Latin American Perspectives* 25(3):90–109.

Matory, J. Lorand. 2005. *Black Atlantic Religion: Tradition, Transnationalism, and Matriarchy in the Afro-Brazilian Candomblé.* Princeton, NJ: Princeton University Press.

———. 2006. "The 'New World' Surrounds an Ocean: Theorizing the Live Dialogue between African and African American Cultures." In *Afro-Atlantic Dialogues: Anthropology in the Diaspora*, ed. Kevin A. Yelvington, 151–192. Santa Fe, NM: School of American Research Press.

Merry, Sally Engle. 2006. *Human Rights and Gender Violence: Translating International Law into Local Justice.* Chicago: University of Chicago Press.

Minority Rights Group. 1995. *No Longer Invisible: Afro-Latin Americans Today.* London: Minority Rights Group International Publications.

Mullings, Leith. 2005. "Interrogating Racism: Toward an Antiracist Anthropology." *Annual Review of Anthropology* 34:667–693.

———, ed. 2009. *New Social Movements in the African Diaspora: Challenging Global Apartheid.* New York: Palgrave Macmillan.

Ramírez, Cristóbal Valencia. 2009. "Active Marooning: Confronting *Mi Negra* and the Bolivarian Revolution." *Radical History Review* 103(Winter):117–30.

Ribeiro, Gustavo Lins, and Arturo Escobar, eds. 2006. *World Anthropologies: Disciplinary Transformations in Systems of Power.* Oxford: Berg Publishers.

Scheper-Hughes, Nancy. 2000. "The Genocidal Continuum." In *Power and Self,* ed. Jeannette Mageo, 29–47. Cambridge, MA: Cambridge University Press.

———. 2002. "Coming to Our Senses: Anthropology and Genocide." In *Annihilating Difference: The Anthropology of Genocide*, ed. Alexander Laban Hinton, 348–381. Berkeley: University of California Press.

Scheper-Hughes, Nancy, and Philippe Bourgois, eds. 2004. *Violence in War and Peace: An Anthology.* Malden, MA: Blackwell Publishing.

TransAfrica Forum. 2008. Colombia: Law 70 of 1993. Fact sheet. Summer/Fall. Available at http://transafricaforum.org.

Turner, Michael J. 2002. "The Road to Durban—and Back." *North American Congress on Latin America (NACLA) Report on the Americas* 35(6):31–35.

Ulysse, Gina Athena. 2007. *Downtown Ladies: Informal Commercial Importers, A Haitian Anthropologist, and Self-Making in Jamaica.* Chicago: University of Chicago Press.

Vargas, João Costa. 2008. *Never Meant to Survive: Genocide and Utopias in Black Diaspora Communities.* Lanham, MD: Rowman and Littlefield.

Vitalis, Robert. 2000. "The Graceful and Liberal Gesture: Marking Racism Invisible in American International Relations." *Millennium* 29(2):331–356.

Wade, Peter. 1993. *Blackness and Race Mixture: The Dynamics of Racial Identity in Colombia.* Baltimore: Johns Hopkins University Press.

Walker, Sheila. 2002. "Africanity vs. Blackness: Race, Class, and Culture in Brazil." *NACLA Report on the Americas* 35(6):16–20.

Wynter, Sylvia. 2002. "After Man, Towards the Human: The Thought of Sylvia Wynter." Keynote response at conference in honor of Sylvia Wynter. Centre for Caribbean Thought, University of the West Indies, Mona Campus, June 14–15.

———. 2003. "Unsettling the Coloniality of Being/Power/Truth/Freedom: Towards the Human, After Man, Its Overrepresentation—An Argument." *CR: The New Centennial Review* 3(3):257–337.

Yelvington, Kevin, ed. 2006. *Afro-Atlantic Dialogues: Anthropology in the Diaspora.* Santa Fe, NM: School of Advanced Research Press.

Pan-Afro-Latin African Americanism Revisited: Legacies and Lessons for Transnational Alliances in the New Millennium

Darién J. Davis, Tianna S. Paschel, and Judith A. Morrison

Any survey of the literature on pan-Africanism reveals that works on Afro-Latin Americans are conspicuously absent. For much of the twentieth century, Afro-Latin Americans remained politically and culturally marginalized within their nation-states, and thus absent from international forums. The historical invisibility of Afro-Latin Americans in the world arena can also be directly traced to the dearth of cultural, political, and financial forums and institutions that encouraged or forged what Stuart Hall calls "imaginary coherence, across cultural, linguistic, and historical differences as response to dispersal and fragmentation" (Hall 1990, 52).

Early articulations of pan-African unity focused on Africa and the English- or French-speaking Black Atlantic, but these forums provided conceptual frameworks that black Latin Americans would later adopt and transform based on their own cultural realities. Latin American articulations of pan-African diasporic consciousness, coming after the independence movements of many African nations in the 1960s, focused on transnational connections to further their own political, economic, and other programs nationally (Walters 1993). Indeed, the decline of empire and the institutionalization of the nation-state at the beginning of the twentieth century encouraged black identification with nationhood rather than race. Moreover, Latin American nationalists have often tried to dismiss attempts to organize around race as mere foreign importations. Political and cultural organization around blackness in Latin American nations often caused violent backlashes against blacks, as the massacre of Afro-Cubans associated with the Partido Independiente de Color (PIC) clearly illustrate.[1] Nonetheless, across the diverse national discourses of race-nation, the struggles and strategies of peoples of African descent show many similarities. Brent Edwards argues that the only way to contemplate transnational black discourses is "by attending to the ways that discourses of internationalism travel, the ways they are translated, disseminated, reformulated, and debated in transnational contexts marked by difference" (Edwards 2003).

Attempts to understand the historical and present struggles of Latin Americans of African descent, who number up to 150 million,[2] must take into account economic and political conditions at the global, national, and local levels, whether in countries like Brazil, Venezuela, Colombia, and Cuba, where the population of African descent is significant, or in countries such as Argentina and Mexico, where they represent less than 5 percent of the population. At the same time, as a general rule, Afro-Latin Americans continue to face greater social and economic discrimination than their white counterparts. Socioeconomic status can often mitigate these pressures, but black Latin Americans are overrepresented among the poor, and many black Latin Americans continue to be denied development opportunities and basic access to education, healthcare, and housing, and a host of other rights as defined by the United Nations Declaration of Human Rights.[3]

In the face of endemic marginalization and exclusion over centuries, black Latin Americans have sought to forge transnational alliances to promote their national agendas. This paper examines how black Latin Americans have created and developed transnational alliances from the beginning of the twentieth century to the present day. We answer three broad questions that give us a window into cross-national collaboration in the Americas: (1) What obstacles and challenges have Afro-Latin Americans encountered as they forge transnational or pan-African alliances? (2) What have Afro-Latin Americans learned from these collaborations? and (3) What lessons can be gleaned and applied to future alliances in the new millennium? By highlighting the gains and shortcomings of regional and international alliances, we can more fully understand contemporary and future cross-national alliances in their proper historical context. We highlight the many achievements of Afro-Latin Americans and contextualize the still urgent challenges in the fight against marginalization and disenfranchisement as Latin Americans reach out and collaborate with organizations and individuals in more economically advanced countries with different cultural modes of organizing and social norms.

HISTORICAL COLLABORATIONS: FROM PAN-AFRICANISM
TO AMERICAN TRANSNATIONALISM, 1900–1980

Pan-Africanist conferences began in the early twentieth century to unite peoples of African descent on both sides of the Atlantic to secure their human rights in the face of a shared experience of oppression. Pan-Africanists aimed to provide a forum for dialogue among people of African descent across cultures, but the varied social experiences of peoples in the Americas constituted a formidable challenge to meaningful cross-national conversations (Walters 1993, 326). First, pan-Africanists tended to organize along linguistic lines: Anglophone, Francophone, and Spanish-speaking, for example. Due to political disenfranchisement and economic marginalization, Afro-Latin American participation in such forums prior to the 1980s was limited. Although race consciousness heightened in the post–World War II era, the onslaught of military dictatorships in many Latin America countries curtailed the possible emergence of black movements and Afro-Latin American participation in international forums until the development of representative democratic governments in the 1980s and 1990s.

Even among the pioneering pan-Africanists from the English-speaking black community, issues of community representation divided would-be leaders. Jamaican-born Marcus Garvey and his United Negro Improvement Association, first founded in Jamaica in 1914, claimed to have wide mass appeal and viewed other pan-Africanists such as W. E. B. Dubois elitist and ineffectual (Brisbane 1949, 261–262). Garvey's major success was in meeting the needs of many disenfranchised men and women of African descent to connect to a positive historical past, as his praise of the mythical Ethiopia indicated. Garveyites celebrated Ethiopia as a land of their ancestors. They carried the UNIA flag with them as they sang during marches with "[all] the splendor and pageantry of a medieval coronation . . . at this greatest of Negro shows" (Cronon 1955, 63). Garvey understood the power of performance for middle- and working-class blacks who were not gaining access to the middle class (Rudwick 1959, 428). He was less successful among Latin Americans—even in places like Panama, Cuba, and Costa Rica, where there were English-speaking Caribbean immigrants.[4] U.S.-based organizations such as the National Association for the Advancement of Colored People (NAACP) often made overtures to immigrants and to blacks in places such as Cuba and Puerto Rico in the first half of the twentieth century, but the focus and goals were hardly transnational (Davis 1998). From the 1930s to the 1950s, the Francophone Caribbean, Spanish-Caribbean, and Afro-Brazilians pursued agendas that emphasized the marginalization of people of African descent and celebrated blackness as essential to the national polity and to national culture. Aimé Césaire's focus on racism in France and Nicolas Guillén's specific interest in Cuban identity limited their transnational reach. Moreover, the issues of colonialism for the majority black French Caribbean were different from the issues of blacks in Cuba, not to mention the French tradition of the "mission civilisatrice" and Cuba's Martían rhetoric of national unity regardless of race.[5] Even Abdias do Nascimento's Teatro Experimental do Negro (TEN), which forged links with black American artists, first emerged as a cultural platform in the theater before branching out to address specific goals such as literacy (Davis and Williams 2006).

The Congresses on Black Culture in the Americas

Even before the return to democracies in many countries, the "Congresses on Black Culture in the Americas," organized between 1977 and 1984, represented a rare accomplishment in transnational organization around blackness, albeit with a focus on culture, cultural respect, and recognition. The Organization of American States in conjunction with the Fundación Colombiana de Investigaciones Folklóricas, for example, sponsored the 1977 meeting in Colombia, and issues such as the creation of Latin American culture and the support of liberation struggles in Africa were key to the agenda (Congreso de Cultura Negra de las Américas 1977). The Second Congress on Black Culture in the Americas—held in Panama City, Panama, in 1980—developed the theme of race and class. According to congress president Gerardo Maloney, two major achievements of the conference were the integration and incorporation of blacks from all regions of the Americas, and the conviction of all members of the inseparable relationship between ethnicity and class in the Americas (Congreso de Cultura Negra de las Américas 1989). The Third Congress, held in São Paulo, Brazil, in 1982 under the directorship of black leader Abdias do Nascimento, in conjunction with the Instituto de Pesquisa e Estudos Afro-Brasileiros (IPEAFRO) manifested a more defiant tone and indicated the desire to link cultural production, political awareness, and socioeconomic realities. The theme of this congress, "African Diaspora: Political Consciousness and African Culture," reflected the growing political consciousness of Afro-Latin American communities (Congreso de Cultura Negra de las Américas 1989, 85–89).

All four forums pursued similar goals: cultural or racial identity and consciousness, celebration of African roots, pursuit of self-esteem programs, denunciation of racism and marginalization, and the establishment of networks—but the task of setting specific social and economic agendas within a transnational context would not begin to materialize for at least another decade. As Afro-Latin American agendas shifted from the promotion of racialized identities and studying culture to the pursuit of economic and social goals, cross-alliance networks were better able to work collaboratively for specific outcomes. Indeed, the shift allowed for collaboration with international agencies, including private foundations and development banks, which became even more critical for the advancement of black movements in the region.

Cross-national tensions and differences hardly disappeared, however. Indeed, as international funds became available, and interested parties from around the Americas began to collaborate, national, linguistic, class, and other challenges, such as representation in international forums, seemed evident, even if they were not specifically articulated. Only when Afro-Latin Americans and their allies recognize these challenges will they be better prepared to pursue agendas that, as Juan de Dios Mosquera, from the Movimento Nacional Cimarrón Colombia, noted, "unite allies not because they are black people but because all those involved identify with the work to edify black people," and where black communities play a central role in the development of their own communities (Davis 1996).

THE EMERGENCE OF CONTEMPORARY REGIONAL AFRO-LATIN NETWORKS: THE 1990S AND BEYOND

Whereas many of the previous cross-border efforts that we describe above were explicitly pan-Africanist projects, aimed at providing forums for people in the African Diaspora to meet and exchange experiences, the 1990s marked the emergence of a number of regional political networks of Afro-Latin activists. We use the term "transnationalism" to talk about the broad range of cross-border alliances, organizations, and networks that Afro-Latin American activists have become increasingly involved in over time. While there is much debate in the literature on what transnationalism actually means, the nature of most of the transnational networks we analyze here fall into Keck and Sikkink's (1998) notion of "transnational advocacy networks," defined as "forms of organization characterized by voluntary, reciprocal, and horizontal patterns of communication and exchange . . . that defend a cause or proposition." They also contend that such networks typically have "shared values, a common discourse, and dense exchanges of information" (8). While we will show that the actual building of such networks among blacks in the Americas has been a complex, dynamic, and incomplete process, the intent behind many of these networks do mirror those outlined by Keck and Sikkink.

Women played a crucial role in this process. One of the most important efforts was the Red de Mujeres Afrolatinoamericanas y Caribeñas (Network of Afro-Latin American and Caribbean Women), which was created in 1992 with the aim of organizing black women activists across borders in the region. Organizing in response to the 500-year celebration of the "discovery of the Americas" in Santo Domingo, three hundred black women from thirty-two countries organized the "Primer Encuentro de Mujeres Negras Latinoamericanas y del Caribe," a gathering that gave birth to the network.[6] While the conference was open to all black women in Latin America and the Caribbean, the majority of women who became country representatives for the Red were black feminists affiliated with black women's organizations.

The patriarchal structure of many black organizations, the dominance of a single male leader, and concerns about how racism affected black women differently from black men, all contributed to the creation of black women's organizations and international networks such as the Red.[7] At the same time, women began to compare their experiences with others, both inside and outside of their organizations, creating logical transnational collaborations in which they were the protagonists in the struggle against racism, but also connected to issues that affected the black population as a whole (Vieira 1995, 19–46). Thus, the black women's organizations that began to emerge in the late 1980s were important for the development of transnational strategies in the Black Movement more generally. Some of the most active members of the Red would also go on to found later networks of Afro-Latin women and men, like Alianza.

Another important effort to bring black activists together to organize politically across borders occurred on 8–10 December 1994 in Montevideo, Uruguay. The Afro-Uruguayan NGO Organizaciones Mundo Afro (simply known as Mundo Afro), established in 1988, hosted "The First Seminar on Racism and Xenophobia: A Program for Afro-Americans." The gathering brought Uruguayans together to forge a platform of cooperation with black activists, scholars, and others associated with international donor organizations from throughout the Americas. Participants included advocates from many of the cultural and linguistic regions of the Americas, including Afro-Latin Americans from Brazil, Uruguay, Argentina, Honduras, the Dominican Republic, Colombia, Peru, Cuba, and activists and scholars from the United States. The absence of participants from past conferences and community activists from many other Latin American communities, including those from the Red, is an indication of the structural problems that have historically limited communication among Latin American nations. Regional gatherings such as the one organized by Mundo Afro also illustrate the need to address communication challenges. Although held in Uruguay, for example, many of the participants could not communicate in Spanish. While Brazilians and Spanish-speaking Latin Americans often "get by," communication of official international instruments may be compromised. When French or English speakers are present without translators or official interpreters, communication becomes even more complicated. Regional conference organizers often do not have the financial resources to hire translators or interpreters, or to acquire adequate systems and platforms for cross-language communications.[8]

While the Uruguay conference was a milestone in raising black consciousness in Uruguay and the Southern Cone, it also led to the eventual creation of a network of African-descendant organizations called La Alianza Estratégica de Afro descendientes, or "Alianza" (the Strategic Alliance of Afro-descendants).[9] Because few at the Uruguayan conference knew about the history of transnational networks, they could not draw on the similar experiences that preceded the conference; instead it served as a first encounter and opportunity to learn about the existence of other groups in the region. Many of the structural, linguistic, and even economic problems that have inhibited regional cooperation and the forging of an "imagined Afro-Latin American community," to paraphrase Benedict Anderson, have been addressed or at least recognized by subsequent transnational networks. Indeed networks and congresses that clearly articulate their goals, purposes, and desired outcomes seem to have reaped the most success (Anderson 1991). While cultural celebrations and affirmations of identity play an important role in Afro-diasporic congresses and collaboration, gatherings that only aim to reify black identity across national borders have not been as successful or sustainable.

CONTEMPORARY PAN-AFRICAN POLITICS AND THE ORGANIZATION OF AFRICANS IN THE AMERICAS

Since World War I, people of African descent have created Afro-diasporic forums and have organized international meetings; however, the nature of these encounters has varied, from academic meetings, to cultural events, to conferences that aim at influencing their respective governments and international institutions. These types of collaborations represent important transnational undertakings. Multinational academic associations such as the Latin American Studies Association (LASA), the Brazilian Studies Association (BRASA), the Association for the Study of the World-wide African Diaspora (ASWAD), as well as university-based conferences, such as the "African Diaspora and the Modern World" conference organized by Sheila Walker at the University of Texas–Austin in 1996, represent variations of these forums. The Tampa conference in 2010 also played an important role in raising awareness and in fostering knowledge that helps build transnational alliances. The innovative platform of the Tampa conference, which brought together activists, donors, and scholars, represents an important trend among allies who want to engage Afro-Latin Americans and have a meaningful impact on African-descendant communities from the halls of the ivory tower. In the last decade, LASA's "Otros saberes/Outros saberes" has assured the continued dialogue among scholars and activists on key race-related topics; this network funded by a consortium of donors, including the Ford Foundation, Open Society Institute, and others, has brought grassroots Latin American perspectives to North American universities and scholars. Finally, internationally sponsored meetings on racism and antiracism, such as the Durban conference as well as others sponsored by the Inter-American Development Bank, the World Bank, and the no-longer-operational donor network Inter-Agency Consultation on Race, have undoubtedly been important in transnational dialogue because of their ability to mobilize funds and governments as well as black participants from across the Americas.[10]

Despite all the advances, there is not one regional American or Latin American network that has been able to provide a forum or network space for the majority of Afro-Latin American organizations, nor is it clear that such a network is desirable. Nonetheless, current and future networks would be well served by assessing the knowledge of previous networks and the history of their triumphs and challenges. The history of the Organization of Africans in the Americas (OAA) warrants particular attention.

The idea for the OAA emerged in 1992 with the objective of forming "links among the African peoples of the West: to get to know each other, to share our concerns and experiences, and we hope, to collectively fight the problems of racism and marginalization which afflict us no matter where we reside." Although the OAA would depart from previous experiences of pan-African organizations in the Americas in important ways—including a shift away from a focus on black culture and toward the consolidation of a more explicitly political agenda—structural, linguistic, and economic challenges along with issues of North-South representation contributed to its eventual demise. As a lobbying group, the OAA played an important role in promoting greater visibility for Afro-Latin Americans among international organizations based in Washington, DC, and illustrated the potential of a hemispheric collaboration prior to Durban.

While internal disputes, North-South power relations, and issues related to leadership style eventually led to the organization's decline, OAA executive director Michael Franklin and others were directly involved in creating the new network dedicated to Afro-Latin Americans in Spanish-speaking countries: AfroAmérica XXI.

Despite the shortcomings of the OAA, AfroAmérica XXI benefited directly from the experience and historical knowledge of its participants, and succeeded in attracting many black NGOs and elected officials into the organization. In turn, AfroAmérica XXI became successful in pressuring multilateral institutions like the World Bank, the Inter-American Development Bank, and the Organization of American States (OAS) to adopt programs for black populations in Latin America. Michael Franklin also addressed the Permanent Council of the OAS in February of 1999 in one of the first formal presentations on African descendants in the General Assembly. Despite the OAA's aggressive lobbying style and harsh criticism of African-descendant leaders with whom OAA did not agree, or who were not direct participants in the OAA network, the OAA was effective in getting a number of donors to commit to specific projects to address the situation of black populations in the Americas. Its activities led to the 2000 World Bank meeting on race and development. This meeting was historic in that it served as the seed for what would become the Inter-Agency Consultation on Race in Latin America, a donor network housed at the Inter-American Dialogue.[11]

The creation of the OAA marked an important transition from pan-Africanist *encounters* focused on the celebration of culture, to the construction of regional political *organizations* whose ultimate goal was to affect the policies of Latin American governments and multilateral institutions. However, by 2000 the OAA itself became associated with internal conflict and discursive strategies that did not fit into the international policy arena, and was plagued by three other major problems. First, the organization lacked clear transnational short- and long-term policies and objectives. Second, the leadership could not sustain the transnational ties that emerged out of the 1996 meeting in Uruguay.[12] Finally, the organization fell prey to North-South power relations by concentrating power and decision making within the leadership in Washington, DC.[13] The fact that black activists and organizations gained greater visibility because of the work of the OAA cannot be denied.[14] As a result of this visibility, many black activists and NGOs would take advantage of one of the most important political openings that black activists in Latin America have had: the 2001 Third World Conference Against Racism.

THE SANTIAGO AND DURBAN CONFERENCES:
THE HEIGHT OF TRANSNATIONAL BLACK NETWORKS

The Third World Conference Against Racism (WCAR), held in Durban, South Africa, in 2001, served as a critical and defining moment for the further development of pan-Afro-Latin American alliances in the region. Unlike previous world conferences, this event had strong representation from Latin American civil-society organizations.

The Durban conference acted as a catalyst for the adoption of national and local-level policy reforms for black populations, and the creation of a number of national state entities charged with addressing racism, discrimination, and racial inequality. Organizations such as the Red de Mujeres, and other transnational relationships, such as the collaborations between Mundo Afro in Uruguay and a number of black NGOs in Brazil, attest to the importance of cross-national collaborations. Different networks drew on and appealed to different countries based on a series of factors including geography and historical relationships. The Andean region would be represented by the strongest and more organized members of AfroAmérica XXI, for example, while Alianza would draw from the experience of black activist-academics in the Caribbean, Central America, Brazil, and Uruguay, particularly those affiliated with black NGOs.

While Durban was important as a transnational encounter, it is also important to reiterate that it was the first time that black organizations from different countries throughout the hemisphere organized politically and were effective. Still, strategic action by black activists in Latin America around the Durban conference and preparatory meetings was unparalleled in its ability to pressure Latin American governments to officially recognize that racism (and racial inequality) existed in their countries, and served as the catalyst to begin formal state-sponsored efforts. Unlike the two previous world conferences against racism, which primarily sought to put diplomatic pressure on the apartheid regime in South Africa, this third conference was set to include the broad participation of civil society across the world. This shift in the format of the conference made it an even more important watershed event in the region, and activists in the region with expertise in strategizing around UN conferences reaped significant benefits. Black women activists, in particular, called upon their experiences from previous UN conferences, including the Cairo conference in 1994 and Beijing in 1995. In the end, their expertise was critical in leveraging national governments.[15] It also gave them experience in figuring out the possibilities and limitations of international conferences as spaces to make demands on governments.

Black activists in countries such as Brazil and Uruguay, which had more formal organizational structures, more contact with UN mechanisms, and thus more transnational experience, were better equipped to begin preparations for the Durban conference soon after the official United Nations announcement. The strategic leveraging of the Durban conference also required a particular kind of professionalization among black activists and their organizations, as well as large amounts of funding.[16]

In the early part of 2000, official preparatory meetings for the Durban conference were held in Geneva and in Latin America. Black activists who participated in these meetings worked on constructing strategies to pressure their governments before and during the conference. Concomitant to these official meetings, black and indigenous activists also attended conferences to coordinate their political position and intervention in the Durban conference. One of the most important of these was a regional meeting held in San Jose, Costa Rica, sponsored by the Instituto Interamericano de Derechos Humanos, and publicized by the OAS, OAA, and the media. As a result of this meeting, the Alianza attained greater visibility, and leaders such as Epsy Campbell, a member of the Red de Mujeres and a founding member of Alianza, came to the forefront.[17] The other representatives of Alianza represented strong national organizations in their respective countries, including Celeo Alvarez of the Organización Negra Centroamericana—ODECO (Honduras); Carlos Rosero of Proceso de Comunidades Negras—PCN (Colombia); Ivanir dos Santos of Centro de Articulação das Populações Marginalizadas—CEAP (Brazil); and a number of representatives of Mundo Afro (Uruguay).

While many of the regional efforts by black activists around Durban were certainly homegrown in the sense that black activists were the key initiators of such efforts, there were key moments where they formed alliances with actors in the United States. Some of these include the Washington-based TransAfrica Forum and the Global Afro-Latino Caribbean Initiative (GALCI),[18] as well as the International Human Rights Law Group,[19] which was important in facilitating dialogue between racial-justice lawyers in the region. One important North-South exchange was the Southern Education Foundation's project on comparative human relations, initiated in 1997, which was a series of seminars that included high-level government officials and civil-society representatives from the United States, Brazil, and South Africa. In the fourth seminar, held in Cape Town, South Africa, in May 2000, Afro-Brazilian activists began to play a key role in the project. At this meeting, longtime black activist Abdias do Nascimento directly confronted Brazilian diplomats and pressured their government to recognize racism within this UN forum—this was a milestone in international forum engagement for Brazil (Telles 2004).

In addition to the activists who participated in civil-society forums related to the Durban conferences, black activists from Latin American also acted as experts during the preparation for Durban. In October 2000, a meeting of experts was held in Santiago to assess the situation of groups that suffer from systematic discrimination. Edna Roland, of the black women's NGO Fala Preta, was responsible for writing the background paper on the situation of Afro-descendants in the Americas, and later became the eminent expert on African descendants for the process, and Ibsen Hernandez Valencia of the OAA served as an expert witness. Both women also had the chance to respond to statements made by government officials, allowing civil society to verify official claims.

Black activists were able to successfully pressure their governments precisely because of the local and international activism that preceded them. In the seminar of experts in Chile, for example, the deputy high commissioner for human rights, Mary Robinson, stated that while Latin America was a region of great racial and cultural diversity, "there was a need to acknowledge the legacy of inequality that had resulted from these events, particularly for indigenous peoples and Afro-Latin Americans."[20] This statement, and the general structure and tone of this meeting of experts emerged as a result of previous activism by Afro-Latin American organizations and their allies at various levels. The high commissioner, for instance, had met with a number of black NGO representatives during her visit in April to Brazil, when they presented her with documents outlining the situation of Afro-Brazilians. In many ways, because the preparations for the UN conference against racism created the space for transnational collaboration to reap results (allowing civil society to participate in more substantial ways than previous conferences), they also opened the door to critique and vigilance from sectors of civil society. In this way, the Durban conference became a stage upon which black organizations throughout Latin America could hold their governments accountable for inaction on issues of racism and racial inequality.

The Road from Santiago to Durban

In December 2000, government officials from thirty-five countries and as many as six hundred people representing civil-society organizations in the Americas met in Santiago de Chile to discuss racism, racial discrimination, and the need for targeted policies for black populations, indigenous peoples, and ethno-racial groups. The Santiago conference was the largest and most significant of the regional meetings held globally to prepare for Durban, and a model of transnational strategizing and collaboration. The majority of the civil-society representatives at this conference were from black political organizations from throughout Latin America and the Caribbean, some of whom had organized nationally in preparation for the conference, and some of whom represented Alianza and AfroAmérica XXI. Funding institutions also played a critical role in making the meetings possible, as many of the activists were funded by private foundations, including the Instituto Interamericano de Derechos Humanos and the Ford Foundation, although many were self-funded or received support from their governments.

The strategies used by civil-society representatives showcase the growth of black activists over the previous decade. In a context of increasingly professionalized NGOs in a number of countries, particularly those organizations affiliated with the Alianza network, leveraging and mobilizing around UN conferences had already emerged as a viable strategy to influence state policies. Black activists across Latin America broke through structural barriers, linguistic challenges, and competing interests to utilize institutional channels to seek outcomes that would benefit Afro-Latin Americans—including lobbying diplomats and writing the text that would eventually be included in the Santiago document, which was signed by the governments. By speaking as regional networks, as opposed to isolated activists from specific countries, black Latin American representatives were able to convince diplomats from different countries that the tide was moving toward the recognition of more rights and policies for black populations. In this sense, activists' effectiveness could be seen in their ability to leverage alliances and transnational networks, and raise funds to participate en masse in the conference; it could also be seen in the preparation and mobilizing that some activists did at the national level. The actual text of the Santiago document acted as a blueprint for the Durban Program of Action, and used explicit language concerning affirmative action, land rights, and reparations.[21] Perhaps most importantly, the Santiago conference gave Afro-Latin American activists a common language to talk about their struggles and their demands as exemplified in the famous statement made by Romero Rodríguez, one of the founding members of the Alianza and Mundo Afro in Uruguay: "We came as blacks and left as Afro-descendants,"[22] the latter being a term that was eventually incorporated into the Durban "Programme of Action" and has been used by multilateral and international donor agencies, and even national-level government policies adopted after Durban.[23]

Santiago also fostered other types of alliances that, in some countries, were not always easy to consolidate at the national level. One example was the alliance made with indigenous groups. A number of regional meetings, sponsored by different institutions, sought to further consolidate indigenous and black collaboration in preparation for Durban. This included a large regional meeting in Ecuador followed by a meeting in Arica, Chile, in June 2001, where the Mesa de Diálogo dos Pueblos Afrodescendientes e Indígenas de las Américas was formed. Finally, exactly one month before Durban, in a meeting essentially organized by the Alianza network and their allies, indigenous and black representatives from throughout the region met in Montevideo before traveling to South Africa. This meeting, and a corresponding document to governments, the *Carta de Montevideo*, would serve as a reminder to governments that they had already signed on to the Santiago document, and had an obligation to defend Santiago positions in Durban. It was also a reminder that black and indigenous organizations in the region would be a united front during the Durban conference and would not be relegated to participating only in the civil-society forum. Thus, by the time of the Durban conference, Latin American and Caribbean governments had officially recognized racism and government obligations to develop concrete policies aimed at black populations, indigenous peoples, and other groups.[24] The conference was not without controversy and problems, however, including internal tensions among the civil-society participants and the disengagement of the United States that threatened to overshadow the transnational achievements.[25]

While the Durban Plan of Action included many recommendations for the guarantee of specific rights for particular groups, including land rights and affirmative action, many countries did not follow up on many issues. Nonetheless, the Durban conference served as an important catalyst for the adoption of legislation aimed at addressing ethno-racial inequality for African descendants in some countries in Latin America. Among these specific acts are affirmative action policies and the creation of government agencies charged with designing inclusion policies. The conference also set a standard for movements to organize regionally. As Romero Jorge Rodríguez of Mundo Afro suggests:

> Santiago obliges the Afro-descendant movement in the Americas to frame development as a regional process of mobilization and as an expression of proposals with neighboring communities, developing from the dialectical process a new way of acting from what was historically determined as the African Diaspora in the World (Rodríguez 2004).

Post-Durban

The term "Afro-descendant" became a powerful symbol for constructing a collective identity and developing regional strategies to hold governments in Latin America accountable for addressing ethno-racial issues. For many activists, the Durban conference was also their first encounter with the African continent, an event they found empowering. The newfound awareness among many activists was evident in subsequent meetings, including the 2002 World Bank forum entitled "Durban Plus One: Opportunities and Challenges for Racial and Ethnic Inclusion in Development." Other regional conferences in Central America, Brazil, Chile, and the Caribbean have continued to discuss ways to meet local, regional, and international goals while sharing experiences internally and across national and ethnic borders. The 24–26 February 2004 convention that brought together Afro-Colombians and North American activists and politicians to discuss U.S. policy towards Colombia, and the challenges and opportunities for Afro-Colombians, is only one example. It is significant that the Organization of American States–based Inter-American Commission of Human Rights now includes the status of Afro-Latin Americans as a policy area and is working on formalizing concrete policies and actions. While the actors have changed, many of the challenges facing black communities in Latin America have persisted. Durban represented both a culmination of previous efforts by Afro-Latin Americans to organize regionally, and a new beginning, with unparalleled collaboration between the Black Movement, governments, and international agencies.[26]

GOVERNMENTS AND INTERNATIONAL INSTITUTIONS RESPOND

Latin American Governments

Immediately following the Durban conference, Honduras, Paraguay, and Venezuela ratified the 1965 UN Convention on the Elimination of Racial Discrimination, joining seventeen other Latin American nations. Although many countries did not make any legislative or substantial policy changes as a result of Durban, others—including Brazil, Argentina, and Mexico—created national government agencies to begin to implement policies to combat racial discrimination; the Peruvian government set up a national commission to consult the government on these issues.[27] Brazil was probably the most proactive—instituting affirmative action policies and implementing important pieces of legislation, including the creation of SEPPIR (Special Secretariat for the Promotion of Racial Equality); the adoption of Law 10.639, which mandates the teaching of Afro-Brazilian and African history throughout the school system in all grades; and affirmative-action policies at a number of public universities, among other reforms. Implementation and enforcement remain challenges, however. The presence of international agencies has also played a key role in maintaining government involvement in Brazil and elsewhere. Indeed, these agencies have become an integral part of transnational black alliances.

International Agencies and the Creation of the Inter-Agency Consultation on Race in Latin America (IAC)

On June 19, 2000, the World Bank convened members of civil society, donor agencies, think tanks, and governments for a historic discussion on race within the context of development, in an event that would later be called "Race and Poverty: Inter-Agency Consultations on Afro-Latin Americans." This was one of the first meetings to bring donors and experts together to discuss the issues facing Afro-Latin Americans, and it eventually gave rise to the Inter-Agency Consultation on Race in Latin America (IAC), comprised of the World Bank, Inter-American Development Bank, Ford Foundation, Inter-American Foundation, and the Kellogg Foundation.[28]

The initial motivation for creating an IAC was largely to enable donors to respond to the increasing demands by civil-society groups in preparation for the UN World Conference Against Racism. The OAA had actively lobbied the development institutions and had gained attention from members of Congress on these issues, particularly the Congressional Black Caucus. The level of personal commitment to advancing a race and equity agenda from a few key high-ranking managers at the World Bank and Inter-American Development Bank, coupled with a growing number of technical staff members interested in the topic (such as the conference organizer Jeanette Sutherland, who had previous contact with the OAA network prior to joining the World Bank) turned the space into a support network of donors advancing a challenging agenda within their respective institutions. Participating IAC institutions agreed to appoint two representatives to ensure continuity, thereby garnering a greater institutional commitment. In the beginning, representatives were high-level staff, typically managers who supervised divisions and large staffs. As the IAC developed, representatives became increasingly technical, with less access to decision makers, and therefore less access to financial resources for special projects or initiatives. Thanks to funding from the British Department for International Development (DFID), the IAC sustained its operations for many years.[29]

The official goals of the IAC were to keep participating donor institutions well informed about each others' programs and plans; allow participants to share information and analyses about the situation of Latin Americans of African descent; conduct joint activities of mutual interest; launch independent activities that reinforce and enrich the work of participating organizations; and maintain a dialogue with Afro-Latin American leaders and institutions in the region (IAC website 2006). The founding of the IAC facilitated greater collaboration between participating donor institutions and led to the development of a number of important regional conferences and policy initiatives.

One of the most significant projects to come out of the IAC was Todos Contamos, or Everyone Counts,[30] a collaborative effort between the Inter-American Development Bank and the World Bank to improve data collection through national institutes of statistics. Todos Contamos served as an initial opportunity for representatives from national statistics and census offices throughout Latin America to meet with civil-society representatives from African-descendant and indigenous organizations to begin a conversation on how to incorporate better information regarding race and ethnicity. Both banks have undertaken research efforts in the region, such as studies on African descendants.

Todos Contamos marked the first time that national statistical institutions in Latin America met with civil-society organizations representing racial and ethnic communities to discuss data collection. After the first Todos Contamos meeting, two country-level initiatives were funded in Ecuador by the banks. In 2001, the World Bank, the Inter-American Development Bank (IDB), and the Economic Commission for Latin America and the Caribbean (ECLAC) launched the Program for Improvement of Surveys and Measurements of Living Conditions in Latin America and the Caribbean (MECOVI) before Todos Contamos. Consequently the data generated was general, but Todos Contamos relied on the data as a first step for its more in-depth analysis.

Similarly, in 2002, the World Bank organized a forum entitled "Durban Plus One: Opportunities and Challenges for Racial and Ethnic Inclusion in Development." The bank's Office of Diversity Programs and the Latin America and Caribbean Regional Office (LCR) created the forum with the collaboration of other regional departments to assess the policies of the World Bank, the IDB, and the United Nations in light of the resolutions of Durban. Senior managers and staff from the World Bank, the IDB, and the Office of the High Commissioner for Human Rights, as well as outside academics, discussed lessons learned in bringing excluded people to the forefront of the development agenda, and ways to ensure that financial resources, knowledge, and empowerment opportunities reach excluded people. In an effort financed by the Inter-American Foundation, the IAC held a joint donor conference in La Ceiba, Honduras, in February 2004, focusing on youth leadership. Also, between 2001 and 2006, representatives of IAC-participating institutions met regularly, worked together on initiatives, hosted a number of roundtable sessions, and collaborated on publications—including the 2004 Conference Report from the La Ceiba conference, and the important series of World Bank country-level studies *Más Allá de los Promedios*, both published in 2004.

Participation in the IAC gave individual institutions the needed support to sustain their work on Afro-descendants within their own institutions. Moreover, donors could also utilize their access to governments, so that the act of having meetings at the banks helped maintain the visibility of Afro-Latin Americans. In February 2003 the Inter-American Development Bank established the multi-donor "Social Inclusion Trust Fund" to support African descendants and other target populations, including indigenous peoples, persons living with disabilities and/or HIV/AIDS, and low-income women. The fund had the goal of providing institutional support, raising awareness, and supporting IDB operations. Approximately one third of the fund's resources were to target African-descendant groups, and another third was designated to support crosscutting projects that worked with multiple target populations. A new version of this fund has been mobilized as the Gender and Diversity Fund.

The last regional meeting of the IAC was the "Race Counts: Policy Agenda for

Racial Equality in the Americas" roundtable held at the World Bank on February 28, 2006, with high-level political, media, and academia participation, and including a Hill reception cosponsored by then-senator Barack Obama's office, the Congressional Black Caucus, and the Brazil Information Center. Some of the speakers included Graciela Dixon, president of the Supreme Court of Panama; Claire Roberts, president of the Inter-American Commission on Human Rights; Carlos Alberto Reis, Brazilian justice minister; Benedita da Silva, former minister and governor from Brazil; Epsy Campbell, former Costa Rican political party president, and vice-presidential and presidential candidate; José "Netinho" de Paula Neto, owner of TV da Gente, television host, and entertainer; and academics such as Marcelo Paixão and Fernando Urrea.

The IAC was effective in garnering greater visibility for African-descendant issues, particularly in Washington; however, it also faced significant challenges raising funds. The donors were members of the IAC, but there was no expectation of payment of dues or concrete contributions to sustain the IAC, or of commitment to specific institutional programs. Donor members committed staff time to participating in meetings of the group and attending events organized by other donor agencies, and this in and of itself was viewed as a significant institutional commitment to the program.

Participating members of the IAC were effective at garnering resources for specific activities, and thereby directly affecting both national and transnational projects, but the bulk of these resources came from special funds or line items in executive offices, or were redirected from existing projects/programs in other fields. As a result, the activities were not institutionalized within the donor organizations. In addition, the World Bank, one of the most active members of the IAC, underwent a major restructuring in the mid-2000s. Social-sector specialists who had been responsible for operations in the Latin American Division began to have increasing responsibility for monitoring World Bank safeguards as integrated members of project teams. The idea behind this change was to mainstream race and ethnicity into the core operations of the bank, and have race and ethnicity become an integral part of project analysis. As a result it became increasingly difficult to create stand-alone programming for race and ethnicity. The Inter-American Development Bank also underwent restructuring in late 2000, leading to changes in the Social Development unit, where much of the work related to race and ethnicity was concentrated.

The Organization of American States has also begun to address the issue of racial discrimination and racism in Latin America and the Caribbean. The Inter-American Convention against Discrimination, under consideration by the Inter-American Court of Human Rights at the Organization of American States, provides African descendants with a regional body to redress human-rights violations throughout the Americas, a resource that might be absent from their own nations. In countries where national courts have been reluctant to address racial inequities, African descendants can use the court as a means for pressuring governments. Currently every Spanish- or Portuguese-speaking country in the Americas has officially yielded jurisdiction to the court over basic human-rights matters. African-descendant communities must continue to use the court as an instrument for asserting legal rights, as indigenous communities have successfully used the court to influence their governments to gain concessions they would not have otherwise been offered. African descendants benefit from filing suits with the court, because the act of filing creates a public record that African descendants consider themselves the victims of racism in their society.

International Foundations

Ford Foundation has been a leader in the field of race in Latin America. In the very early years, Ford made an institutional commitment to hire key program officers such as J. Michael Turner, an African American historian; Rebecca Reichmann, an academic working on issues of race and self-identification (1988–1993); and sociologist Edward Telles (1997–2000), to promote issues of racial justice. The first Ford Latin American offices opened in 1962. Ford provided seed capital to many Brazilian NGOs, and was also an initial sponsor of hemispheric organizing efforts, including preparation for the World Conference Against Racism. As the major funder for this conference, Ford Foundation received the bulk of the criticism after the event from the U.S. press. Ford then redirected funding to more neutral race topics, hired staff with more politically diverse backgrounds, and funded both sides of an affirmative-action debate in Brazil. Despite slight shifts in policy, Ford continues to be an important player in the field of African-descendant development in Latin America. The Ford Foundation's International Fellowships Program (IFP) focuses on training diverse candidates with an emphasis on Latin America, and has educated a significant cadre of new Latin American academics of African and indigenous origin. The program is scheduled to run until 2014.

The Kellogg Foundation had several key staff members in the late 1990s who were interested in funding projects to promote African descendants. Blas Santos, based in the Dominican Republic, was responsible for securing funding for several new NGO networks, including the OAA. In the mid-2000s, however, Kellogg made a commitment to limit funding in South America; but before leaving the region, Kellogg decided to leave an institutional legacy that could be self-supporting. In 2008, Kellogg Foundation launched a targeted endowment program to promote racial equality in Brazil, building on investments that the foundation had made over the previous decade. The endowment focuses on the large African-descendant population in the Brazilian semi-arid northeast region—where African descendants are highly represented and are disproportionately poor—offering another alternative to the historical transnational operations that have focused on the cities of the southeast, such as Rio de Janeiro and São Paulo.[31] Current activities of the endowment fund include mapping, generation of knowledge products related to Afro-Brazilian populations, board development, leadership development of partners for grant-making, generation of funding plans, staffing, and financial planning. Under the leadership of Athyade Motta, formerly of the Ford Foundation, the fund is beginning to explore possibilities for international grant-making.

The U.S. Government

Starting in the 1970s, the Inter-American Foundation (IAF) began funding African-descendant civil-society institutions. In 1977, the IAF assisted in purchasing the headquarters of the Instituto de Pesquisas da Cultura Negra (IPCN) in Lapa, but was asked to leave the country—in part because the IPCN's project description called Brazil a racist country (Pereira 2008). The IAF ceased its operations in Brazil from 1978 to 1983, but later negotiated an agreement with the Foreign Affairs Ministry to have a review of all projects funded in the country. The 1977 civil-society grant nonetheless served as a basis for activism for many Afro-Brazilians (Lennox 2009 and Johnson 2007). The Inter-American Foundation continues to fund Afro-Latin American civil-society organizations largely through a travel-grants program that sponsors the participation of leaders in international conferences, events, and meetings.

The legislative branch of the United States, specifically the U.S. Congress, through the Congressional Black Caucus (CBC), has also participated in regional and transnational efforts to address racism and racial inequality in Latin America. Between 2002 and 2006, the staff of the IAC Secretariat often acted as a liaison between the Congressional Black Congress and black activists and legislators in Latin America. This included speaking at events organized on Capitol Hill, consulting congressional staffers on issues facing black activists, facilitating and translating for meetings between leaders in Latin America and CBC members, and writing language that would be included in legislation on Afro-Latin Americans proposed by CBC members (Inter-American Dialogue 2004). During this time, CBC members were invited to the Conference of Black Legislators and were often called on by Afro-Latin Americans to discuss issues facing the region. A number of House resolutions have also been proposed by members of the CBC, including the 2003 recognition of the contributions of Afro-Latin Americans to the Americas. On July 18, 2005, the House passed H. Con. Res. 175, recognizing the injustices suffered by African descendants of the transatlantic slave trade in all of the Americas, and recommending that the United States and the international community work to improve the situation of Afro-Latino communities (Ribando Seelke 2008). While these resolutions are largely symbolic, they are important in raising visibility about the issues facing Afro-Latin Americans.[32]

The human-rights crisis affecting Afro-Colombians has been the most salient Afro-Latin American issue engaged in by the CBC for two major reasons. First, the Afro-Colombian Working Group has served as an effective advocacy group in lobbying the CBC, largely because of the diverse and credible members, which include Afro-Colombian grassroots organizations, human-rights NGOs such as Global Rights, the Washington Office on Latin America, Washington Office on Colombia, TransAfrica Forum, church associations, humanitarian organizations, academics, environmentalists, and other peace advocates. Second, Colombia is the third largest recipient of U.S. foreign aid, and the issues facing Afro-Colombians also represent the clearest case where the CBC can actually intervene without overstepping the sovereignty of Latin American governments. Therefore, some of the specific demands that Afro-Colombian organizations and their allies in the United States have made to the U.S. Congress include the earmarking of funds within Plan Colombia (the U.S. foreign-policy plan for Colombia and the war against drugs) to social programs for Afro-Colombians, the protection of leaders that have been threatened, and the consideration of human-rights violations against Afro-Colombian communities in the U.S.-Colombia free-trade negotiations.

In part because of pressure from Afro-Colombian activists and their allies, the Congressional Research Service was commissioned to write a report on African-descendant issues in 2004, which was followed by an updated report in 2006 on "Afro-Latinos in Latin America and Considerations for U.S. Policy." This report highlighted the work on Afro-Colombians in the region. The report outlines a number of actions made by the U.S. Congress and other government agencies, including various resolutions related to Afro-Colombians.

The U.S. Congress has manifested renewed interest in working with Latin American governments to address issues affecting the region's black population. In March 2008, then U.S. secretary of state Condoleezza Rice and then SEPPIR minister Edson Santos signed an agreement to eliminate racial and ethnic discrimination and promote equality of opportunity: the Joint Action Plan to Eliminate Racial Discrimination, or JAPER. The plan was publicly acknowledged through an official launch on October 31, 2008, with former assistant secretary of state and current U.S. ambassador to Brazil Thomas Shannon. Subsequent meetings have taken place in Brasilia, Salvador,

Washington, and Atlanta. This agreement is significant because it represents one of the first efforts to specifically address issues of racial equality in the region through a bilateral agreement with high-level participation from governments. Further, the initiative encourages sharing information on best practices, and has acted as a stimulus to give greater visibility to African-descendant leaders, and a motivating factor to develop mechanisms to better coordinate financing efforts.[33] A similar agreement to eliminate ethnic and racial discrimination was signed by U.S. deputy secretary of state James Steinberg and Colombian foreign minister Jaime Bermudez in 2010.

International Organizations Post-Durban

While many international foundations and multilateral institutions took an interest in addressing issues related to Afro-descendants in Latin America in the late 1990s and early 2000s, a number of factors contributed to a declining interest in this area. First, while the Durban conference was important, serving as a catalyst for the adoption of targeted policies for black populations in some countries, within the international community, and even within the UN itself—the conference was still marred with much controversy. While talking about race in Latin America should not be synonymous with the Durban conference, it became difficult for many in policy circles to separate the Durban conference from the need to address deep-seated racial inequities through regional and national policies.

The "Santiago +5" meeting, which took place in Brasilia and largely focused on Brazilian national issues of inclusion, was an attempt to distinguish the gains of Afro-Latin Americans from the controversy of Durban itself. Indeed, the discussions of broader issues of marginalization and discrimination brought in the participation of Brazilian feminist and gay-rights movements. Another follow-up meeting took place in Santiago a year after the Brasilia meeting, but without the same high-level participation as the first meeting. The United Nations was swift to qualify their support for the process due to concerns from the earlier WCAR process. A follow-up meeting to the Durban conference took place in Geneva in 2009, and was widely rebuked by the international media due to inflammatory remarks that reignited concerns about anti-Semitism and led to the walkout of most of the European delegations during the opening session. The United States did not participate due to concerns about potential anti-Semitism in the policy statements. The portrayal of the Durban process and related follow-up activities in the United States is an important issue because U.S.-based institutions have been a major supporter of international civil-society advocacy on issues of African descendants.

As a result, most U.S. donors have not supported African-descendant work related to these specific UN processes; therefore support has to come from domestic Latin American sources or from Europe. In addition, it is important to recognize that the World Trade Center attack in 2001 resulted in a re-prioritizing among U.S. government funders. Further, there was a trend to move funding away from regions like Latin America toward more impoverished regions such as Africa, or regions of strategic importance such as the Middle East. Finally, many of the actions undertaken specifically on behalf of Afro-descendants within the World Bank, the Inter-American Development Bank, Inter-American Dialogue, and other institutions, are best understood as the efforts of a handful of dedicated professionals within these institutions who believed in these issues, rather than institutional priorities. In 2006, the Inter-Agency Consultation on Race in Latin America (IAC), a program of the Inter-American Dialogue, facing financial difficulties halted work, and therefore the Dialogue ceased to serve a leadership role on policy for African descendants.

A Bridge to Tomorrow

It is difficult to predict the future of regional dynamics or the direction of transnationalism over the next few decades, but the history of transnational collaboration among black activists in the Americas has changed significantly over the last several decades. The preparations for the Durban conference represent an important watershed that merits the scrutiny of future generations. International agencies have been critical to the advancement of transnational issues, as we have seen, and in some cases cross-border support and funding often facilitated the formation of Latin American consciousness through specific activities aimed at bettering the lives of black Latin Americans. Nonetheless, transnational encounters as well as institutional interest in black populations in Latin America certainly ebb and flow depending on global political and economic issues. Many transnational partnerships and advocacy groups that date to the 1970s, as well as those that emerged in the 1990s, such as the Red de Mujeres and AfroAmérica XXI, are still active, while others have disappeared or been transformed.

New regional networks have also emerged post-Durban, many focusing on Afro-Latin American youth—among them, La Red Iberoamericana de Juventud Indígena y Afrodescendientes, the Circulo de Juventud Afrodescendientes, and Red de Jóvenes Afrodescendientes.[34] Broadening the participation of Afro-descendant youth in regional processes has become a key issue of discussion in the Organization of American States (OAS) and Organization of Iberian States (OEI). The OAS has made special efforts to address issues related to Afro-descendant and indigenous youth, and the OEI has sponsored two regional seminars for youth Afro-descendant and indigenous leaders. Spanish agencies, such as Agencia Española de Cooperación Internacional para el Desarrollo (AECID), have also taken an interest in African-descendant issues since 2005, due in part to the active involvement of the Secretaría General Iberoamericana (SEGIB) president Enrique Iglesias, a former IDB president who was actively involved in discussions and policies regarding African descendants while he was at the IDB.

These activities of newer youth networks also reflect a more acute global consciousness, particularly since many young black activists look to international conferences as ends in themselves and not as means to strengthen local processes and struggles. This generation is also more computer-savvy and is becoming increasingly fluent in foreign languages, leading to improved communication among network members in different countries. Finally, academic interest in the United States, Europe, and in some Latin American countries has also increased substantially with the emergence of many international academic networks like AFRODESC, initiated by academics affiliated with the Institute for Research on Development (IRD) in France and some academics in Mexico. In the United States, a number of research groups have emerged to look specifically at the African Diaspora in Latin America—too many to mention here.[35]

CONCLUSION

While Afro-Latin Americans will continue to face economic, political, and cultural challenges in a region plagued by inequalities, they have made advances over the last several decades. We argue that this is in part because Afro-Latin Americans have constructed pan-African alliances and transnational collaborations that have played a significant role in raising global awareness and influencing national policies. By highlighting the gains and shortcomings of such alliances among black activists and academics in Latin America and the Caribbean, as well as recent efforts by international funding agencies, we suggest that transnational efforts to address the issues that affect Afro-Latin Americans today constitute part of a rich, complex, and often contentious continuum.

We have also tried to place these developments in their proper historical context, showing how activists began to create pan-African alliances in the Americas in the early twentieth century, and demonstrating how this developed into transnational Afro-Latin American collaborations, with high points in the late 1970s, 1990s, and leading up to the Durban conference. We hope that placing these recent movements in historical context allows us to highlight the many achievements of Afro-Latin Americans, as well as the continual challenges in the fight against racial marginalization and disenfranchisement.

Perhaps one of the most important lessons that history offers us is that efforts at building pan-African, transnational alliances must recognize the diversity of black people in the Americas on the one hand, and the complex power dynamics that emerge when black women and men convene from countries with vastly different resources, on the other. There is no one, unified Black Movement in Latin America, nor can we speak of national black movements without glossing over the diversity, political fragmentation, and contestation of space within these movements. We believe that such reflection will strengthen the work of the movements as a whole and promote collective processes that are democratic and socialized in black communities through organizations. It also means that efforts such as these have to recognize that black people in Latin America and the United States are likely to forge multiple alliances based on mutual interests and goals.

Another important lesson to be drawn from this history relates to the pivotal role of indefatigable activists who continue to fight for equality and justice in countries throughout Latin America. While actors and institutions outside of Latin America have been crucial to Afro-Latin American activists' struggles and triumphs, they have not been the leaders of these efforts. Organizations such as the World Bank, the Organization of American States, the Inter-American Development Bank, and the Inter-American Dialogue have played important roles in shaping this history. In the same vein, African Americans situated in a number of places have played an important role in promoting issues related to Afro-Latin Americans in the United States, evidenced in the OAA experience, the work of TransAfrica Forum, the involvement of members of the Congressional Black Caucus, and the initiatives of black academics. Nonetheless, Afro-Latin American leaders and activists are at the forefront of the movement to transform their own societies, even as they realize the limits and promises of transnational connections, particularly with organizations in the United States.

NOTES

1. See Helg 1995.
2. Estimates range from 100 million to as high as 250 million. See Inter-American Dialogue 2003.
3. See the Universal Declaration of Human Rights at http://www.un.org/en/documents/udhr/.

4. Marcus Garvey (1885–1940), Jamaican-born black pan-Africanist and black nationalist, established the Negro Improvement Association, which gained influence throughout the Americas. He is regarded as one of the principal black militant leaders in the post–World War II era. Although ironically, one of the last remaining UNIA chapters is in El Limón, Costa Rica, and this chapter periodically marches in community parades.

5. See Rist 2006, 48–80; Helg 2007.

6. See http://www.mujeresafro.org.

7. Among the many issues raised by black women were labor-market discrimination, health, violence against women, and the recognition that black women face both racism and sexism, resulting in double discrimination, and the lowest socioeconomic outcomes than any other group.

8. Afro-Argentine and Afro-Paraguayan counterparts joined the Afro-Uruguayans, although at the last minute, the Paraguayans sent word that financial restraints did not allow them to attend the meeting.

9. Founding members of the network (created in 1998) included: Mundo Afro—Uruguay; Geledés, Instituto da Mulher Negra—Brazil; Asociación de Mujeres Afrocolombianas—Colombia; Centro de Mujeres Afrocostarricenses—Costa Rica; Asociación de Mujeres Garifunas de Guatemala—Guatemala; Centro de Articulação das Populações Marginalizadas—Brazil; Organización Negra Centroamericana—Honduras; Centro de Desarrollo Étnico—Peru; Asonedh—Peru; Federación de Comunidades Negras—Ecuador; Proceso de Comunidades Negras—Colombia; Arte y Cultura por el Desarrollo—Costa Rica; Movimiento por la Identidad de Mujeres—República Dominicana; Escritorio Nacional Zumbi dos Palmares—Brazil; Unión de Mujeres Negras—Venezuela; Parlamento Andino—Venezuela; Red de Mujeres Afrocaribeñas y Afrolatinoamericanas; Red Continental de Organizaciones Afroamericanas; Organización Negra Centroamericana; Rede de Advogados de Operadores de Direito contra o Racismo—Brazil; Red Andina de Organizaciones Afro; Instituto Puertorriqueño de Estudios de Raza e Identidad—Puerto Rico.

10. The 2009 World Conference Against Racism was held in Geneva, Switzerland. Major countries such as Canada, Israel, the United States, New Zealand, Germany, Italy, Sweden, the Netherlands, Poland, and Australia did not participate, thus significantly weakening the conference's moral force.

11. Though the OAA would have little involvement with the IAC as it developed, early civil-society advisors were members of the Alianza network.

12. Statement of purpose that emerged out of the follow-up meeting in Washington, DC, in March 1997.

13. As is the case with many transnational organizations, language issues were also a major challenge for the OAA.

14. It is also important to emphasize that even the OAA's efforts were the culmination of other previous meetings of Afro-Latin Americans.

15. Interview with Jurema Werneck (2010); Interview with Dorys Garcia (2008)—both members of the Red de Mujeres. Three hundred women participated in the conference, representing thirty-two countries. See http://www.mujeresafro.org/. In anticipation of the UN International Conference on Population and Development to be held in 1994, civil-society organizations in Brazil, many of them feminist organizations, held a national conference, and the final document was called "Our Rights for Cairo." Many activists from black feminist organizations participated in that national conference. Afro-Brazilian women also participated in Beijing,

including Nilza Iraci and Sueli Carneiro of Geledés and Wânia Santanna, among others. In fact, the First Conference of Black Latin American and Caribbean Women held in Santo Domingo in 1992, where the Red de Mujeres Afrolatinoamericanas was founded, was originally proposed by a number of black feminists in Latin America who met each other at previous UN world conferences.

16. In Brazil, Luiza Bairros (later named minister for the Racial Inclusion Ministry—SEPPIR) worked at the United Nations, and a number of activists became involved—such as Edson Cardoso, then affiliated with the Movimento Negro Unificado, who learned about the conference in his capacity as a staffer for an Afro-Brazilian congress member. Afro-Brazilian activists from NGOs were also best poised to play a central role in regional processes because one of the regional UN offices was located in Brazil, and the Brazilian government had already stepped up to host the Regional Preparatory Conference.

17. Epsy Campbell became vice-presidential candidate in Costa Rica in 2006 and presidential candidate in 2010.

18. Representatives of GALCI were active in Durban preparations. Also, due to the personal and professional ties between Michael Turner, former Ford Foundation Program Officer in Brazil, and Afro-Panamanian activist Humberto Brown, GALCI was one of the only U.S.-based organizations that had fluid dialogues with Latin American activists from various countries and not just Brazil.

19. Later named Global Rights.

20. See UN Report A/CONF.189/PC.2/5, p. 5.

21. See http://www.un-documents.net/durban-p.htm for "The Durban Programme of Action."

22. Rodríguez 2004.

23. The word Afro-descendant is a useful political term and addresses some of the concerns raised in Santiago about the different, and even derogatory, use of the word *negro*. However, "Afro-descendant" often serves as a technical term used by development officials, savvy activists, and to a lesser extent, government officials in Latin American countries. In Colombia, for instance, there is an ongoing debate about the word, considering that *negro* and *comunidades negras* were the traditional language of vindication of the movement in Colombia, and the fact that the term *afrodescendientes* largely remains foreign to the many black people in the country.

24. The Santiago declaration has specific language condemning anti-Semitism, and the Latin American preparatory documents take a clear and consistent stance against anti-Semitism throughout. The Durban conference was also plagued by a series of controversies of global magnitude, among them the issue of Zionism, reparations for African nations as a remedy for colonization, and a proposal to classify slavery as a crime against humanity.

25. In the declaration titled "La Declaración Conjunta de Grulac y Las Organizaciones No Gubernamentales y representantes de pueblos, movimentos y procesos de América," forty-four organizations signed on, with all of the black representatives from organizations affiliated with the Red de Mujeres Afrolatinoamericanas y Caribeñas, Alianza, or both.

26. Throughout the process, there were key collaborations with individual black activists and other anti-racism advocates in the United States. However, regional networks responsible for mobilizing around Durban did not include organizations from the United States.

27. The entities included: Special Secretariat for the Promotion of Racial Equality (Brazil), the National Institute against Discrimination, Xenophobia and Racism (Argentina), the National Council for the Prevention of Discrimination (Mexico), and the National Commission on

Amazonic Peoples, Andean Peoples, and Afro-Peruvians (Peru). It is less clear the extent to which countries have implemented policies for black and indigenous populations within the framework of the Santiago and Durban conferences, or if it is even in the mandate of these entities to actually implement policies. See Inter-American Dialogue 2004.

28. The World Bank has traditionally had a poverty-alleviation focus, and there were concerns among some staff members that a targeted race approach might dilute general poverty-alleviation work. There were also specific discussions with countries regarding terminology—ultimately Afro-Latin Americans was used because it included the entire region. Kellogg Foundation participated in the initial meeting, but did not officially join the donor collaborative.

29. British funding resulted after an extensive study by Ernst Ligteringen (DFID consultant), "Inter-Agency Consultation on Race in Latin America: Propositions for a Strategic Framework" (November 2002).

30. Or "All Count" with the connotation that "all matter."

31. Kellogg has earmarked $25 million for the endowment and has committed to raising $25 million from other partners. In 2013, the endowment will become an independent operation with sustainable sources of funding, principally from Brazil.

32. House Resolution 47 was passed in February of 2004; however, little action was taken, largely because the legislation does not outline specific policies or programs or have a specific budget.

33. Some of the activities that JAPER has identified as priority areas include education, including equal access to quality education and the role of education in countering ethnic and racial discrimination; culture and communication; equal protection of the law and access to the legal system; labor and employment; health; housing and public accommodation; domestic enforcement of anti-discrimination laws and policy; sports and recreation; social, historical, and cultural considerations that may be related to racial or ethnic prejudice; and access to credit and opportunities for vocational training. These areas will be addressed through training, technical exchanges, scholarships, and fellowships.

34. The Red de Jóvenes was consolidated at the 2004 IAC meeting in Honduras, where 40 percent of the participants were youths. The Inter-American Foundation made a conscious decision to focus this meeting on emerging leadership, and as a result prioritized funding the participation of youths.

35. The Afro-Latino Working Group housed at the Center for Latin American studies at UC Berkeley held a graduate-student conference in February of 2007 called "Beyond Visibility." The conference, sponsored by the Inter-American Foundation and many centers and departments on Berkeley's campus, included black activists from Latin America and received over sixty abstracts from young scholars doing empirical research on Afro-Latin Americans.

REFERENCES

Anderson, Benedict. 1991. *Imagined Community: Reflections on the Origin or Spread of Nationalism.* New York: Verso.

Brisbane, H. Robert. 1949. "His Excellency: The Provincial President of Africa." *Phylon* 10 (3):261–262.

Congreso de Cultura Negra de las Américas. 1977. *Proceedings from Primer Congreso de la Cultura Negra de las Americas: Conclusiones, recomendaciones y proposiciones.* August 24–28.

————. 1989. "Segundo Congreso de Cultura Negra de Las Américas." *Cuadernos Negros Americanos* 1(1):11–54, 85–89.

Cronon, E. David. 1955. *Black Moses: The Story of Marcus Garvey and the United Negro Improvement Association.* Madison: University of Wisconsin Press.

Davis, Darién J. 1996. "PostScript." In *No Longer Invisible: Afro-Latin Americans Today*, 359–378. London: Minority Rights Group.

————. 1998. "Nationalism and Civil Rights in Cuba: A Comparative Perspective: 1930–1960," *The Journal of Negro History* (Fall): 35–51.

Davis, Darién J, and Judith Williams. 2006. "Pan-Africanism, Negritude and the Currency of Blackness." In *Beyond Slavery: The Multifaceted Legacy of Africans in Latin America and the Caribbean*, ed. Darién J. Davis. Denver: Rowman and Littlefield.

Edwards, H. Brent. 2003. *The Practice of Diaspora: Literature, Translation, and the Rise of Black Internationalism.* Cambridge, MA: Harvard University Press.

Hall, Stuart. 1990. "Cultural Identity and Diaspora." In *Identity: Community, Culture, Difference*, ed. Jonathan Rutherford. London: Lawrence & Wishart.

Helg, Aline. 1995. *Our Rightful Share: The Afro-Cuban Struggle for Equality, 1886–1912.* Chapel Hill: University of North Carolina Press.

————. 2007. "To Be Black and to Be Cuban: The Dilemma of Afro-Cubans in Post-independence Politics." In *Beyond Slavery: The Multifaceted Legacy of Africans in Latin America and the Caribbean*, ed. Darién J. Davis. Denver: Rowman and Littlefield.

Inter-Agency Consultation on Race in Latin America and the Caribbean. Available at www.iac.org.

Inter-American Dialogue. 2003. *Afro-Descendants in Latin America: How Many?* Available at http://www.thedialogue.org/reportsbooks.

————. 2004. *Race Report 2004: Constitutional Provisions and Legal Actions Related to Discrimination and Afro-Descendant Populations in Latin America.* Washington, DC.

Johnson, Ollie A. 2007. "Black Politics in Latin America: An Analysis of National and Transnational Politics." In *African American Perspectives on Political Science*, ed. Wilbur C. Rich. Philadelphia: Temple University Press.

Keck, Margaret, and Kathryn Sikkink. 1998. *Activists beyond Borders: Advocacy Networks in International Politics.* Ithaca, NY: Cornell University Press.

Lennox, Corinne. 2009. "Mobilizing for Group-Specific Norms: Reshaping the International Protection Regime for Minorities." Department of International Relations, London School of Economics.

Nascimento, Abdias do, and Elisa Larkin Nascimento. 2000. "Brazil: Dance of Deception: A Reading of Race Relations in Brazil." In *Beyond Racism: Embracing an Interdependent Future*, 7–32. Atlanta: Southern Education Foundation.

Pereira, A. Amilcar. 2008. The civil rights movement e o movimento negro contemporâneo no Brasil: Idas e vindas no "Atlântico negro." BRASA IX, Tulane University, New Orleans, LA, March 27–29, 2008.

Ribando Seelke, Clare. 2008. "Afro-Latinos in Latin America and Considerations for U.S. Policy." Update in CRS Report for Congress. Washington, DC.

Rist, Gilbert. 1996. *Le développement: Histoire d'une croyance occidentale.* Paris: Les Presses de Sciences Po.

Rodríguez, J. Romero. 2004. "Entramos Negros; salimos afrodescendientes: Breve evaluación de los resultados de la III Cumbre Mundial Contra Racismo." *CMCR en América del Sur* 5(2).

Rudwick, M. Elliott. 1959. "DuBois versus Garvey: Race Propagandists at War." *Journal of Negro Education* 28(4):428.

Telles, Edward. 2004. *Race in Another America: The Significance of Skin Color in Brazil.* Princeton, NJ: Princeton University Press.

Vieira, Rosângela Maria. 1995. "Brazil." In *No Longer Invisible: Afro-Latin Americans Today*, ed. Minority Rights Group. London: Minority Rights Group, 19–46.

Walters, W. Ronald. 1993. *Pan Africanism in the African Diaspora.* Detroit: Wayne State University Press.

PART 2

Double-Consciousness and Black Identity— Globalized

Haitians in the Dominican Republic:
Race, Politics, and Neoliberalism

Lauren Derby

Up until the earthquake in Haiti in January 2010, there had been a systematic pattern of human-rights violations towards poor Haitians in the Dominican Republic, which has had an enormously stigmatizing impact on the estimated one million Haitians living there. Anthropologists, literary critics, historians, legal scholars, and documentary filmmakers have established a pattern of egregious human-rights violations against Haitians, including deportations, violence, denial of citizenship, as well as mistreatment of Haitian women working in Dominican assembly plants hiring Haitian labor in the frontier.[1] Indeed, there has been both systematic violence against Haitians on the part of the Dominican state, and public acts of popular violence, peaking around 2005 after a period of deep financial collapse in the Dominican Republic when it was estimated that some 10,000 Haitians were deported, and civilian brutality went as far as Haitian victims even being beheaded and burned alive. The international community and courts must do its part to condemn these violations and pressure the Dominican state to stop these depredations and provide citizenship to the Haitian children born on Dominican soil, once and for all.

It is easy to consider this pattern of brutality as the result of longstanding anti-Haitian prejudice, which has not been confined to the Dominican Republic but rather has pan-Caribbean origins. Indeed, since the Haitian Revolution (1794–1804), Haiti has served as a symbol of black insurrection, one that became the focus of planter dread from Cuba to Trinidad. Rumors of black atrocities spread quickly across the islands, causing horror and panic among whites that resulted in slave lockdown, and repression against mulattos and freedmen who were inevitably presumed to be the masterminds of slave revolt (Gonzalez-Ripoll et al. 2004). Since the eighteenth century, Haiti has been a potent symbol of black desires for sovereignty, as well as white fears of "Africanization" (Palmié 2002). A genealogy of anti-Haitianism must commence with 1804 and the black martial profile cut by Toussaint Louverture, who was born a slave but rose to become a master military strategist who succeeded in defeating the French army and staving off incursions by the British and Spanish militaries. And in the Dominican Republic, Haiti staged several military interventions onto Dominican terrain, eventually occupying the country from 1822–1844 in an effort to protect the newly independent black republic from further military invasion and thus ensure the survival of the only free black republic in the Americas. For this reason, some scholars have naturalized anti-Haitian enmity as an ahistorical cross-class prejudice among Dominicans, which has been a constant in Dominican history.

Anti-Haitianism is often cast as an ideology that cuts across the Dominican social hierarchy, and that constitutes an ever-present murderous loathing waiting to erupt. Yet not only has anti-Haitianism ebbed and flowed over time, but its content and form have changed dramatically as well. It commenced as a fear of a far more cosmopolitan, capitalized, and militarily superior neighbor with imperialistic designs, since Haiti at independence had the largest standing army in Latin America; then it transformed into the twentieth-century dread of inundation by a black subproletariat driving contemporary prejudice.[2] The latter emerged in the early twentieth century with the rise of the sugar-plantation economy, as Haitians came to monopolize the occupational niche of cane cutters for U.S.-owned firms; as such, contemporary anti-Haitianism is essentially a class-based prejudice based on labor-market segmentation.[3]

A virulent style of anti-Haitianism emerged during the early twentieth century as Haitians came to be associated with cane cutting, a form of labor associated with slavery—their presence thrust upon the Dominican Republic by U.S.-owned companies. In the nineteenth century, Haiti had been seen as a far richer and more cosmopolitan nation with a superior military, and the Haitian occupation, of course, garnered support among former slaves who found freedom under Haitian rule when slavery was abolished. It was only in the period 1910–1920 that the stereotype of Haitians as indigent cane cutters became univocal and hegemonic, as Haitians in the Dominican Republic came to reside at the bottom of the new status hierarchy that emerged with the rise of sugar monoculture. Yet as Aviva Chomsky has discussed in the case of Cuba, anti-Haitianism was not mere racism; it combined with, and was augmented by, resentment towards the United States. As she states, critics "argued that the West Indians were undesirable because they were imported by foreign companies, and their presence facilitated foreign profits from Cuban resources"; thus twentieth-century anti-Haitianism has a strong component of anti-imperialism embedded within it. Chomsky continues that in times of crisis, immigrant scapegoating in Cuba was a "way of displacing critiques of power-holders, both native and foreign, onto the most powerless" (Chomsky 2000).

One must be angered at the ill-treatment of Haitians in the Dominican Republic, yet the issue of who is to blame is complex. Certainly the Dominican government is a large part of the problem, and the harsh system of repression on the *bateyes* of the sugar plantations, which includes army surveillance of the *bateyes* to keep the Haitians on site, and military involvement in recruiting and transporting workers from centers in Leogane to the plantations, is undeniable and unforgivable. Yet let us not forget that U.S. entrepreneurs devised the contemporary contract-labor system in the Caribbean at the turn of the twentieth century. By 1925, most Dominican sugar plantations belonged to foreign corporations, and 98 percent of exports were sold to the United States. First, British West Indians and later Haitians were imported directly by the sugar concerns as an indentured labor force at the turn of the twentieth century, since Dominicans had ample access to land and thus little incentive to engage in sugar harvesting for the low wages offered. This is why firms devised a scheme that took advantage of the relative labor surplus in the highly depressed post-abolition economies of the British West Indies, where slaves had formed a majority. Haitians eventually took over as the central labor stream at a time when conveniently both nations were under U.S. military occupation, and U.S. sugar conglomerates had restructured both economies as sugar monocultural producers with rapidly expanding sugar-cane production. Although to be fair, both nations' economies were locked in stiff competition with Cuba, which sold almost its entire sugar harvest to the United States, and through the reciprocity treaty had a highly protected and privileged relationship to the United States in relation to the neighboring islands. And the Cuban harvest was also staffed by Haitian *braceros* pushed out by demographic pressure at home.

Local governments became more directly involved with the *bracero* issue during the 1930s Depression, when sugar prices took a tumble and immigrant labor was scapegoated, leading to calls for labor nationalization in Cuba and the 1937 Haitian Massacre in the Dominican Republic (James 1992; Plant 1987). The contract-labor relationship between the Dominican and Haitian governments was formalized under the regimes of strongmen François Duvalier and Rafael Trujillo, the latter looking to secure a labor source for an industry in which he had come to have an important private interest, while for Duvalier it became part of a broader system of extortion from the national coffers that totaled some $10 million a year from the Haitian treasury (Plant 1987). The 1952 accord (drafted under Paul Magloire and Rafael Trujillo) that became the basis for subsequent bilateral contracts provided a kickback to the Haitian government, and supposedly guaranteed rights to workers such as salaries on a par with Dominican workers and paid return transport—but these have been false promises. The contracts themselves are actually quite generous; the problem has been one of compliance. Roger Plant reported that none of the Haitians he interviewed were aware of its provisions.[4] And the fact that Haitians are paid in piece work makes it nearly impossible to guarantee that they meet the Dominican minimum wage, which is hourly.

Another party that gets off scot-free in the literature is the Haitian government; yet in its investigation of the treatment of Haitian *braceros*, the International Labor Organization (ILO) railed against Haiti, heaping much of the blame for the horrendous conditions of migrants on Haitian governmental neglect. Indeed, the nonperson status of migrants was directly addressed in the convention, which stipulates that *bracero* travel documents were supposed to be left with the Haitian embassy, an institution that is actually charged with monitoring *batey* conditions (Plant 1987). The Haitian ambassador collects a share of wages that is supposed to be returned to the *braceros* at the end of the harvest, yet rarely reaches them (Lemoine 1985). Yet while profiting substantially from the *bracero* head tax—which was the chief source of internal revenue for some years—the Haitian government has patently failed at fulfilling its responsibilities to these workers (Moral 1978). Moreover, François Duvalier made off with a shocking two million dollars profit from *braceros* at a time when Haiti was in far better shape than it is today. Haitian government officials are complicit with the system of coercion since they also staff the border with auxiliary police who prohibit Haitians from returning to Haiti (Lemoine 1985).

As one strand of conservative nationalist thought, anti-Haitianism was codified and officialized during the Trujillo regime (1930–61) in state-sponsored history texts by Manuel Arturo Peña Battle and others, which were promoted and disseminated by the state as a means of justifying the 1937 Haitian Massacre after the fact. Books like Joaquín Balaguer's ([1947] 1984) *La isla al revés: Haití y el destino Dominicano* (Balaguer was undersecretary of foreign relations during the 1937 Haitian Massacre and was responsible for defending the act in the face of international criticism) took the idea of nineteenth-century Haitian imperial aggression and recast it in demographic terms as an impending, polluting poison seeping across the border and contaminating the Dominican nation.[5] In the political arena, anti-Haitianism is an ethnicized nationalist discourse frequently deployed as political currency to discredit political rivals, one that became disturbingly common under neoliberalism as the national economy came to be perceived as besieged by powerful U.S. financial interests.[6] Not surprisingly, Joaquín Balaguer's Reformista Party was frequently the one responsible for making political capital out of anti-Haitianism. The most striking case in point was the electoral campaign of José Francisco Peña Gomez, who was widely believed to have won the election in a landslide until the opposition party saturated the media with sensationalist images of Haitian *vodoun* (his birth parents were Haitian immigrants), landing Balaguer in the presidency for the third time in 1994 (Matibag 2003). Indeed, Balaguer played a singular role in keeping the anti-Haitian flame alive over the course of the twentieth century, even if this cannot entirely explain its popular support.

While anti-Haitianism has surfaced at particular times as a discourse of state, it certainly has not been a constant in Dominican popular political ideology. At various junctures, oppositional political projects have fostered cross-border organizing and alliances. For example, the Unión Patriotique brought Haitians and Dominicans together as allies against imperialism during the U.S. occupations of both nations (Haiti from 1915–34; Dominican Republic from 1916–24), and in the 1860s freemasons came together under the banner of the Confederación Antillana as Puerto Rican Ramón E. Betances, Haitian Antenor Firmin, Dominican Pedro F. Bonó, and Cuban José Martí developed a language of subaltern mulatto transnationalism and confraternity as a form of resistance to statist liberalism and conservative annexationist images of nationhood (Arroyo 2008). Nor was this merely vacuous discourse; transnational networks were forged as members traveled from island to island, even giving birth to subversive travel accounts such as José Martí's eloquent tribute to the Haitian-Dominican frontier, *Apuntes de un viaje*, which describes border towns such as Dajabón and Ouanaminthe in loving detail. Free border-crossing and Haitian-Dominican friendship was cast as a symbol of the kind of utopian transnational democracy Martí hoped to will into existence, a world before passports and border militia, where wild fruits abounded and peasants sang their morning greetings.[7] While generations of Dominicans learned in school in Trujillista-era history textbooks that Toussaint Louverture had vowed to take over the island under the motto "La isla es una e indivisible" the island one and indivisible—those words were ironically also uttered in the pro-Haitian unification conspiracy devised by the Dominican José Nuñez de Cáceres in 1822, which came to fruition when he turned the keys of Santo Domingo over to Jean-Pierre Boyer, president of Haiti, thus commencing the twenty-year Haitian occupation. While anti-Haitianism emerged as an important nationalist discourse among conservatives, there is plenty of evidence of Haitian-Dominican solidarity within and across civil society.

Indeed, the enmity driving the recent monstrous acts of violence against Haitians demands explanation precisely because they are unlike anything else in past Haitian-Dominican relations. The 1937 Haitian Massacre, in which some 20,000 Haitians were mercilessly slaughtered, was patently an act of state terror with no voluntary popular participation to speak of, except by anti-Haitian reactionaries in the capital city of Santo Domingo who were far from the actual events. Participating Dominican recruits were primarily military and former convicts who had had their prison sentences commuted by agreeing to help colonize the border, and who were given land by the Trujillo regime—groups that felt especially obligated due to state patronage.[8] While participants cloaked their participation in the robes of honor, that they did what they were told because they were *hombres de deber*, this language belies the generalized trepidation that was a constant under the predatory dictatorship of Rafael Trujillo (1930–61). Dominicans who assisted did so out of abject terror that they would be next—these fears, of course, themselves serving as evidence of the trust and codependence among the two populations, especially among the poor in the borderlands where the killings took place. Many Dominicans resisted, transporting their loved ones, family, and friends to safety in the sugar *bateyes* or across the border. In the aftermath, their horror and guilt lingered on in fear of the animals Haitians left behind when they fled—the pigs, chickens, and goats that were taken as malevolent shapeshifter *bacases*—demonic animals poised to exact vengeance on those who had engaged in such evil acts. It was said there would be an invasion of ambulant dead *zonbi* after the fact, stories that on the part of Haitians might suggest boasting about their superior occult powers, but on the part of Dominicans expressed fears of retribution—that they would be punished for this terrifying and unjustified holocaust.[9] Popular narratives of the massacre relate a wrenching tale of families separated, neighbors killed, and wives and children lost. Since Haitians and Dominicans had formed a common rural underclass in most regions of the border, the two populations fused through frequent unions. Haitian-Dominican difference was apparent to all, and was primarily marked by language, a holdover from the colonial period when Santo Domingo and Saint-Domingue were but a few letters apart, and popular relations were amicable. Official explanations that the massacre resulted from a skirmish over cattle theft were patently false and had no purchase in the borderlands. Cattle-raiding was a common practice along the frontier, but it was by no means divided along national lines; there were large ranchers on both sides of the border, and extensive grazing across the frontier was the norm until the U.S. military occupations when the border was closed and land rights were privatized. Moreover, let us not forget the important fact that most of the Haitians killed were not actually Haitian at all but rather Dominican, since the majority had been born on Dominican soil.[10]

The case of politician José Francisco Peña Gomez is often invoked to prove anti-Haitianism's central stranglehold on Dominican culture, when it could equally be argued that his frustrated political career demonstrates exactly the obverse. Peña Gomez was the wildly popular politician who was widely believed to have won the presidency in a landslide in 1994 only to have the election stolen by Joaquin Balaguer's Reformista Party. Orphaned in the 1937 massacre, his parents poor Haitian peasants from Mao, his narrative is a populist dream since he was raised by a Dominican family and ended up studying at the Sorbonne.[11] Yet his purported "Haitian" roots were never an issue until the *Reformistas* relentlessly worked this fact in the press to gain political capital. Still, the instrumental use of his ancestry in the political theater does not necessarily evidence popular sentiment. As any observer of U.S. elections should know, race in politics conforms to an instrumental, not expressive logic; this is a domain in which anything that can be used to counter an opponent will be. Nor should it be particularly surprising that adversary Balaguer would seek to drum up anti-Haitianism, since he himself was undersecretary of foreign relations during the 1937 massacre and thus was personally responsible for defending the slaughter in the face of international criticism; he then wrote a key anti-Haitian tract after the massacre so as to justify the brutal ethnicide, *La Isla al revés*. Balaguer has had a singular role in fanning the flames of anti-Haitianism in the political arena, but this by no means proves its existence at the popular level. Today the Partido Revolucionario Dominicano (PRD) is having a dramatic resurgence in rural areas as a party of opposition against current president Leonel Fernández and his perceived pandering to the urban middle class, and Peña Gomez's popularity is having a dramatic posthumous renaissance, especially in rural areas and among the urban informal sector. Were anti-Haitianism such a potent political ideology, this might not be the case.

Indeed, it is quite possible that the phantom of Balaguer may be behind part of the recent wave of anti-Haitianism. Current president Leonel Fernández came into office in a very curious and fragile intraparty alliance. In 1996, Leonel ran alongside Juan Bosch as vice-presidential candidate for the Partido de la Liberación Dominicana (PLD)—the other candidates being Balaguer's Partido Reformista and Peña Gomez. Leonel teamed up with Balaguer in order to secure a majority against the ever-popular Peña Gomez in what was popularly termed a "devil's pact"; this was a good bet since Balaguer had had three long runs in office, and his patronage machine had dominated Dominican politics since the 1965 U.S. intervention and civil war, and was rumored to control the ballot boxes. Leonel Fernandez thus came into office with a very split party base, with many *Reformistas* within the party rank and file despising him. Leonel has since secured his own solid foundation of support through urban patronage and craftily cultivating the Dominican-U.S. Diaspora as a political bloc, but some of the inconsistencies surrounding legal definitions of Haitian citizenship in Dominican courts may indeed be due to infighting among intrastate factions, as Leonel had to kowtow to some of the remaining old guard Balagueristas who helped him secure and maintain the presidency.[12] This could help explain the glaring inconsistency of his supporting the International Court regarding the citizenship of Haitian offspring, and then having this decision overturned in a lower court by a judge who most likely, given Balaguer's three terms in office, was a *Reformista* appointee. Thus, contemporary anti-Haitian state discourse may be the result of remnants from the Balaguer period; certainly it is no longer uncontested as it was during the Trujillo period.

As a form of racialized nationalism, anti-Haitianism provides a repertoire of stock "images of difference," which while providing a ready nationalist rhetoric, do not inevitably have an impact on social practice (Gilman 1985). Dominicans conform to a rather "profound duality" between private and public, which as Ann Twinam (1999, 5) has theorized elegantly has long been characteristic of Spanish America, a split-ting that Peter Wilson described in *Crab Antics* (1973) as a divide between reputation and respectability. Even as Dominicans frequently articulate the nationalist rhetoric of anti-Haitianism, their practice often belies this; they may have Haitian lovers, children, and wives, just as Dominican men claim to be *hombres serios* even when they keep informal unions of wedlock as "public secrets" — "that which is generally known, but cannot be articulated" — which women frequently are aware of even if they wish it were not so (Taussig 1999). As Carlos Esteban Deive reminds us, Dominican kinship systems simultaneously include the stable nuclear public family and private polygy-nous unions (Deive 2007).[13] Thus, like other identity markers, anti-Haitianism has a far more subtle and complex relationship to social practice than is often assumed.

Moreover, even as we certainly must call for full citizenship rights for Haitians and their offspring, let us not forget that poor black Dominicans have faced indiscriminate and unpredictable violence from the state as well. *Redadas* or police roundups of young men, especially in the *barrios marginados* such as Capotillo and Guachupita, have been an all too common feature of public life for the poor. During Balaguer's notorious "doce años," for example, on average a police victim was found dead on a Santo Domingo street every 36 hours, and between 1966 and 1971 there were more than a thousand political assassinations, most of the victims members of Balaguer rival Juan Bosch's PLD party.[14] Indeed, basic rights of citizenship are sorely lacking not only for Haitians in the Dominican Republic, but poor (and often black) Dominicans as well.[15] This history of state subjugation helps explain why official anti-Haitianism often lacks purchase for the poor.

Of course, the question remains how we explain the timing of the recent wave of atrocities against Haitians on Dominican soil. One answer may lie in the bottom-ing out of the Dominican economy as a result of neoliberalism, for which Haitians provide a ready and vulnerable scapegoat. If the United States helped give rise to the sugar monocrop economy that for so long defined the Caribbean, its free-trade poli-cies have rendered sugar superfluous. For one thing, U.S. farm subsidies have made high-fructose corn syrup the sweetener and preservative of choice in manufactured food products, drastically reducing the market for sugar and driving down world prices for sucrose. If corn was once the staple crop of southern U.S. slaves, since the 1950s it has become the success story of intensive capitalized agriculture, of which U.S. farms now produce 70 percent of global production. Between 2003 and 2005, American taxpayers spent 34.75 billion in crop-subsidy benefits to farmers to produce corn fit only for livestock feed and corn syrup, which has made processed foods such as soft drinks shrink in price since the mid-1980s (Woolf 2008). The rise of "king corn" has expanded American waistlines, accounting for much of the growth in obesity here, while the same period has seen sugar prices drop precipitously, thus causing food shortages in the Caribbean. Americans eat four times the amount of corn syrup they did in 1970, as well as a diet of grain-raised beef that is higher in saturated fats than cattle fed on grass. Our profligate consumption of corn byproducts has made sugar all but obsolete and brought the cane sugar industry to the point of near collapse. While many Caribbean islands such as St. Kitts have abandoned sugar altogether, others have sought solace in tourism, which offers very little if any significant job creation. And unlike Great Britain, whose sense of responsibility for its former colonies has ensured a steady market for British West Indian bananas in the European Economic Community, the United States has left its former colonies to free-fall on their own. Haiti has lost the U.S. sugar market, and tourism has not been a viable option given the successive waves of political instability since Jean-Claude Duvalier's departure in 1986, which has forced many to the Dominican Republic seeking work.

These larger structural constraints, combined with the fact that the Dominican Republic is the largest net recipient of Caribbean immigrants in the region, have caused immense pressure on the Dominican economy and given rise to a large and growing informal sector, a Dominican subproletariat that often lacks *papeles* (citizenship documents) and is itself subject to arrest alongside Haitian migrants.[16] Notwithstanding the fact that the Dominican Republic boasted high rates of economic growth in 2000, nearly a third of young people age fifteen to twenty-four are unemployed, and more than one-fifth of Dominicans live below the very low official poverty line of $2 per day (Marie 2001). The Dominican national debt had quadrupled by the 1980s, and while debt servicing locks the country into sugar exports, the collapse of sugar prices has made it even harder to pay off the interest, which consumed more than one-third of sugar earnings in the early 1980s (Plant 1987).

Indeed, the existing terms of trade place powerful constraints upon the Dominican government, a problem in which U.S. consumers are themselves complicit. The Dominican government had a point when it said, "One of the worst forms of slavery today is practiced by the developed countries when they keep down the prices of basic products by subsidizing and dumping products competing with those that are vital for the countries of the Third World" (Plant 1987, 139). And here the United States has played a significant role. In the 1970s the United States started flooding Haiti (via Haitian entrepreneur middlemen) with subsidized rice so cheap that it came to replace the locally grown tubers, rice, and corn that had been Haitian dietary staples, driving local farmers out of business and into the slums of Port-au-Prince and across the border seeking work (Williams 2008). Today "Miami rice" has become a dietary staple, and Haiti imports three-quarters of its demand, making Haiti the fourth most important market for exported U.S. rice. (Through provisioning wheat as food aid to the Dominican Republic and Haiti, the United States has fostered dependency there by establishing bread as a primary subsistence product.[17]) To make matters worse, the price of rice has doubled over the past couple of years, causing food riots in Port-au-Prince, largely due to soaring petroleum costs. Of course, the United States is not solely responsible here, and some protectionism on the part of host governments could have forestalled this dependency on an item now critical to the domestic subsistence economy; but the debt trap did not make this option easy.

Since the 1980s, the Dominican Republic has embarked upon a model of economic reform that has included International Monetary Fund (IMF) stabilization measures that have hit the poor very hard. And the U.S. decision to drastically cut sugar quotas for the Dominican Republic in the early 1980s made it even harder for the nation to conform to their marching orders to increase exports. A peso devaluation and a wage freeze were intended to make the country more appealing to foreign investment, but it did so at a great human cost, as wage levels sank to the lowest in the Caribbean (even lower than Haiti), and agricultural employment declined by over 50 percent (Martin, Migley, and Teitelbaum 2006).[18] Since the 1980s there has been a shift to tourism and free-trade assembly, but the fact that over 60 percent of those hired are women has caused social strain, since men are virtually excluded from job growth, and rising levels of 15 percent unemployment and 40 percent underemployment have increased that strain.[19] For those who do not find work in export free-trade zones, the only other growth sector is tourism, which has engendered a dramatic spur in prostitution as well as emigration. Indeed, the two are related, since Dominican women travel to Spain and Switzerland to work as domestic servants and cabaret dancers, often resorting to sex work due to its higher remuneration; also, Dominican prostitutes have long found ready work in Port-au-Prince.[20] To make matters worse, in 2003 a large bank failure and government bailout triggered a major financial crisis in the Dominican Republic involving skyrocketing inflation and peso devaluation that painfully squeezed the fragile middle sectors and Dominican underclass, as Steven Gregory documents in his deeply compassionate study (Gregory 2007). Given these conditions, it should not be a surprise that when the IMF froze a $657 million standby agreement, Dominicans took to the streets in a two-day general strike.[21]

Nor was this the first time that Dominicans had protested in response to crippling IMF austerity measures. In 1984, in response to low sugar prices and drastic reductions in the U.S. sugar quota, the government signed a restructuring agreement with the IMF, which forced a 200 percent price increase on imported goods, including medicines, and a rise in basic foodstuff prices. In response to these overnight price hikes, incensed mobs ransacked and looted stores, burned vehicles, and damaged buildings, engaging in pitched battles with the police in twenty Dominican cities, resulting in the closure of the national university, the public transport system, and a radio and TV station. All told, the cost of the violence was 100 dead, 3,300 arrested, and more than 1,000 people injured.[22] Then–Dominican president Jorge Blanco was forced to kowtow to popular demands in the face of what he termed a "grave economic crisis." These protests later spread to Caracas and elsewhere in Latin America as the debt crisis spread, forcing U.S. banks to cobble together a $500 million emergency loan package for Brazil, Mexico, and Argentina (Farnsworth 1984). Given longstanding associations between Haitians, sorcery, and illicit money-magic in the Dominican Republic, it should come as little surprise that in a period of market collapse, Haitians would be invoked as the bogeymen of choice.[23]

Yet the earthquake in Haiti in 2010 demonstrates clearly that this recent history of enmity need not be the inevitable trajectory of Haitian-Dominican relations on the ground. The Dominican government was the first one on the scene, evacuating victims to Dominican hospitals, including a border clinic set up for this purpose, which conducted sixty amputations a day during the first weeks in the capital and the border. Orders given to protect even Haitians illegally in the country abruptly suspended police harassment, which is frequently routine.[24] With this official example in place, Dominicans universally expressed empathy for the plight of their neighbors, recalling a ferocious earthquake in Santiago that swallowed an entire village. One Dominican woman, in a powerful act of solidarity, left her children behind to nurse orphaned Haitian babies in a Santo Domingo hospital.[25] And when a Dominican civilian bringing medical supplies across the border was killed by Haitian bandits, Dominicans proclaimed this was the result of the criminals unleashed by the destruction of the Port-au-Prince prison, not a reflection on national character. The cholera epidemic that closed the border and prohibited movement of people and goods after November 1910 created rage at authorities in frontier communities, such as Bánica, that rely upon Haitian commerce, and where illicit Haitian-Dominican night markets were set up in the cemetery to evade censure.[26] This truce could prove transitory if the Haitian community in the Dominican Republic is flooded by relatives turned refugees, of

Lauren Derby

course, and there is a high risk of this occurring; Haitian migration is a touchy subject in this context since 93 percent of rural day labor in the Dominican Republic is already conducted by Haitians (Liriano 2011). Yet Dominicans and Haitians today can and should find common ground since many of their problems actually result from the same set of structural conditions.

NOTES

Portions of this essay have appeared in *Caribbean Studies* 36(2)(2008):250–265, and appear here with permission.

Support for the research and writing of this essay came from the University of California, Los Angeles (UCLA) Institute of International Studies, and a UCLA COR Faculty Grant as well as a grant from the American Council of Learned Societies. Thanks to Kiran Jayaram and Martha Arguello for critical feedback. I originally started thinking about anti-Haitianism on a collaborative Fulbright grant with Richard Turits, with whom I developed many of the ideas presented here.

1. See the documentaries *Sugar Babies* (Siren Studios, 2007), *The Price of Sugar* (Uncommon Productions, 2007), and *Poto Mitan* (Tét Ansamn Productions, 2009).

2. I treat shifts in images of Haiti over time in my essay "National Identity and the Idea of Value in the Dominican Republic" (Derby 2003, 5–37). For more on Haitian-Dominican relations historically, see Matibag 2003; Cambeira 1997; and San Miguel 2005.

3. As in the plantation under slavery, see Mintz and Price 1992. This view contrasts with, for example, Fennema and Loewenthal 1987.

4. This should not come as a surprise, since the contracts have all been secret except during the PRD regime of Antonio Guzmán.

5. As Pedro San Miguel notes, however, the oppositional view of Haiti was shared even by progressive liberal thinkers such as Pedro Francisco Bonó (San Miguel 2005, 35–66).

6. See Ernesto Sagás (2000) for more on the use of anti-Haitianism as political currency; and for more on inflation and nationalist anxieties in the Dominican Republic, see Derby 1998, 451–493.

7. Martí 1992, 56. Steven Gregory explores other subversive travel accounts of Haiti in his "Voodoo, Ethnography, and the American Occupation of Haiti: William Seabrook's *The Magic Island*" (1992, 169–208). For more on nineteenth-century liberal thought and images of nationhood, see González et al. 1999.

8. Turits 2004.

9. These stories were collected in a series of visits to the frontier in 1989, made possible by a Fulbright grant, by myself, Richard Turits, Edouard Jean-Baptiste, and Ciprián Soler, with assistance from Jean Ghasmann.

10. Although they were considered ethnic Haitians, see Derby 1994, 488–526; and Richard Turits 2002, 589–635. We conducted oral histories with Haitian Massacre survivors in the border colonies formed by Stenio Vincent in 1988–89; research also funded by Fulbright. The closing of the frontier, however, actually commenced in 1907 when the U.S. took over customs houses, and was completed during the occupation.

11. See Matibag 2003.

12. For state factionalism and infighting theorized in another context, see Stanley 1996.

13. See Vega 2007 for a striking example from the colonial period—a prominent smuggler who was father-in-law to one of Christopher Columbus's children and yet whose primary consort was an attractive black woman with whom he sired many children, in addition to others with other slaves.

14. Amnesty International report cited in Taylor 2009, 213–214.

15. A chilling example from March 10, 2010, appears at http://www.soydominicano.net/video/ brutal-desalojo. Thanks to Roland Alum for sharing this reference with me.

16. Of course, NAFTA has served to augment the informal sector throughout Latin America, especially Mexico (see Salas 2006, 15; Lattimer 2003; Gregory 2007, 36–37).

17. Under the food aid program called Agricultural Trade (see Warman 2007, 204).

18. Comparative hourly wage levels in the Caribbean for the Dominican Republic were $0.55 and $0.58 for Haiti in 1988, a gap that widened 30 cents more by 1998 (Safa 1995; and the United Nations Development Programme Human Development Report 2003).

19. Morrison and Sinkin 1982, 819–836. I wish to thank Carel Alé, who collected some of the data presented here. Dominican firms stepped into the vacuum caused by capital flight by crossing the border and employing Haitian women sewers in Ouanaminthe; see Traub-Werner 2008, 205–230; and Werner, "Coloniality and the Contours of Global Production in the Dominican Republic and Haiti," *Antipode: A Radical Journal of Geography*, in press.

20. For more on the gendered implications of these trends, see *Feminization of Migration: Gender, Remittances and Development* 2007.

21. Gregory 2007, 236. There are some positive growth sectors, however, such as Dominican success at cornering the European organic banana market, but this is still a relatively small, boutique niche; see Raynolds 2008, 161–184.

22. "Four Killed in Protests in the Dominican Republic," *New York Times*, April 24, 1984, A5; "Dominican President Says Riots Have Ended," *New York Times*, April 26, 1984, A12; "Toll in Riots Rises to 11," *Los Angeles Times*, 24 April 1984, A1.

23. See my essay "Haitians, Magic, and Money" (Derby 1995); and Krohn-Hansen 1995, 129–146.

24. I personally experienced this in a trip to the border just after the earthquake in January 2010, and was thus able to compare Haitian treatment with visits over the course of the past year.

25. I heard this on Dominican radio days after the earthquake, and people applauded her generosity.

26. Abercio Alcántara, personal communication.

REFERENCES

Arroyo, Jossianna. 2008. "Technologies: Caribbean Knowledges, Imperial Critiques, 1860–1990s." Paper presented to the Tepoztlán Institute of Transnational History, July 2008.

Balaguer, Joaquín. 1983 [1947]. *La isla al revés: Haití y el destino dominicano*. Santo Domingo: Fundación José Antonio Caro.

Barry, David. 1997. *A Turbulent Time: The French Revolution and the Greater Caribbean*, ed. David Gaspar and David Patrick Geggus. Bloomington: Indiana University Press.

Bergen, Renée, and Mark Schuller. 2008. "The Organic Agro-Export Boom in the Dominican Republic: Maintaining Tradition or Fostering Transformation?" *Latin American Research Review* 43(1):161–184.

Cambeira, Alan. 1997. *Quisqueya la Bella: The Dominican Republic in Historical and Cultural Perspective.* London: M. E. Sharp.

Chomsky, Aviva. 2000. "Barbados or Canada? Race, Immigration and Nation in Early Twentieth Century Cuba." *Hispanic American Historical Review* 80(3): 415–462.

Curtiss, M. N., and Ali N. Curtiss. 2009. Personal communication, January.

Deive, E. Carlos. 2007. "The African Inheritance in Dominican Culture." In *Dominican Cultures: The Making of a Caribbean Society*, ed. Bernardo Vega, 87–130. Princeton, NJ: Marcus Weiner Publishers.

Derby, Lauren. 1994. "Haitians, Magic and Money: *Raza* and Society in the Haitian-Dominican Borderlands, 1900 to 1937." *Comparative Studies in Society and History* 36(3)(1994):488–526.

———. 1998. "Gringo Chickens with Worms: Food and Nationalism in the Dominican Republic." In *Close Encounters of Empire: Writing the Cultural History of U.S.–Latin American Relations*, ed. Gilbert M. Joseph, Catherine C. LeGrand, and Ricardo D. Salvatore, 451–493. Durham, NC: Duke University Press.

———. 2003. "National Identity and the Idea of Value in the Dominican Republic." In *Blacks and Coloureds in the Making of National Identity in Nineteenth-Century Latin America*, ed. Nancy Priscilla Naro, 5–37. London: Institute of Latin American Studies, University of London.

"Dominican President Says Riots Have Ended." 1984. *New York Times*, April 26, A12.

Farnsworth, Clyde H. 1984. "Third World Trade vs. Debt." *New York Times*, April 26, D1, D3.

Faux, Jeff, Carlos Salas, and Robert E. Scott. 2006. "Revisiting NAFTA: Still Not Working for North America's Workers." *Economic Policy Institute* 28, September, Part 2: Mexico.

Feminization of Migration: Gender, Remittances and Development. 2007. United Nations INSTRAW, Working Paper 1.

Fennema, Meindart, and Troetje Loewenthal. 1987. *Construcción de raza y nación en República Dominicana.* Santo Domingo: Editora Universitária.

"Four Killed in Protests in the Dominican Republic." 1984. *New York Times*, April 24, A5.

Gilman, Sander L. 1985. *Difference and Pathology: Stereotypes of Race, Sex and Madness.* Ithaca, NY: Cornell University Press.

González, Raymundo, et al., eds. 1999. *Política, identidad y pensamiento social en la República Dominicana (siglos XIX y XX).* Madrid: Dos Calles.

González-Ripoll, Dolores, Consuelo Naranjo, Ada Ferrer, Gloria García, and Josef Opatrny. 2004. *El rumor de Haití en Cuba: Temor, raza y rebeldía, 1789–1844.* Madrid: Consejo Superior de Investigaciones Científicas.

Gregory, Steven. 1992. "Voodoo, Ethnography, and the American Occupation of Haiti: William Seabrook's *The Magic Island.*" In *Dialectical Anthropology: Essays in Honor of Stanley Diamond.* Vol. 2, *The Politics of Culture and Creativity*, ed. Christine Ward Gailey, 169–208. Gainesville: University Press of Florida.

———. 2007. *The Devil behind the Mirror: Globalization and Politics in the Dominican Republic.* Berkeley:

University of California Press.

Haney, Bill. 2007. *The Price of Sugar*. Film. Uncommon Productions.

James Figarola, Joel, et al. 1992. *El vodú en Cuba*. Santo Domingo: Ediciones CEDEE.

Krohn-Hansen, Christian. 1995. "Magic, Money and Alterity among Dominicans." *Social Anthropology* 3:129–146.

Lattimer, Mark. 2003. Preface to *Migration in the Caribbean: Haiti, the Dominican Republic and Beyond*. London: Minority Rights Group International.

Lemoine, Maurice. 1985. *Bitter Sugar: Slaves Today in the Caribbean*. Chicago: Banner Press.

Liriano, Jhonatan. 2011. "Haitianos son el 93% de obreros del campo." *Listín Diario*, February 1.

Marie, Michael. 2001. "The Dominican Republic: Latin America's Latest Economic Miracle?" *Dollars and Sense* magazine, March/April.

Martí, José. 1992. *Apuntes de un viaje (mi estadia en Santo Domingo)*. Santo Domingo: UASD.

Martin, Philip, Elizabeth Migley, and Michael Teitelbaum. 2006. "Migration and Development: Whither the Dominican Republic and Haiti?" *International Migration Review* 36(2):570–592.

Matibag, Eugenio. 2003. *Haitian-Dominican Counterpoint: Nation, State, and Race on Hispaniola*. New York: Palgrave.

Mintz, Sidney, and Richard Price. 1992. *The Birth of African American Culture: An Anthropological Perspective*. Boston: Beacon Press.

Moral, Paul. 1978. *Le paysan Haitïen: Étude sur la vie rurale en Haiti*. Port-au-Prince: Ediciones Fardin.

Morrison, Thomas K., and Richard Sinkin. 1982. "International Migration in the Dominican Republic: Implications for Development Planning." *International Migration Review* 16(4):819–836.

Palmié, Stephan. 2002. *Wizards and Scientists: Explorations in Afro-Cuban Modernity and Tradition*. Durham, NC: Duke University Press.

Plant, Roger. 1987. *Sugar and Modern Slavery: A Tale of Two Countries*. London: Zed Books.

Poto Mitan. 2009. Film. Tét Ansamn Productions.

Safa, Helen. 1995. *The Myth of the Male Breadwinner: Women and Industrialization in the Caribbean*. Boulder, CO: Westview Press.

Sagás, Ernesto. 2000. *Race and Politics in the Dominican Republic*. Gainesville: University Press of Florida.

San Miguel, Pedro L. 2005. *The Imagined Island: History, Identity, and Utopia on Hispaniola*. Chapel Hill: University of North Carolina Press.

Serrano, Amy. 2007. *Sugar Babies*. Film. Siren Studios.

Stanley, William. 1996. *The Protection Racket State: Elite Politics, Military Extortion, and Civil War in El Salvador*. Philadelphia: Temple University Press.

Taussig, Michael. 1999. *Defacement: Public Secrecy and the Labor of the Negative*. Stanford, CA: Stanford University Press.

Taylor, B. Erin. 2009. "Modern *Dominicanidad:* Nation-Building and Politics of Exclusion since the 1880s." *Dialectical Anthropology* 33(2):209–217.

"Toll in Riots Rises to 11." 1984. *Los Angeles Times*, 24 April, A1.

Traub-Werner, Marion. 2008. "La globalización, el libre comercio, y la frontera haitiano-dominicano." In *Ciudades y Fronteras: Aproximaciones críticas a los complejos urbanos transfronterizos*, ed. H.

Dilla, 205–230. Santo Domingo: Manatí.

Turits, Richard. 2002. "A World Destroyed, A Nation Imposed: The 1937 Haitian Massacre in the Dominican Republic." *Hispanic American Historical Review* 82(3): 589–635.

———. 2004. *Foundations of Despotism: Peasants, the Trujillo Regime, and Modernity in Dominican History.* Stanford, CA: Stanford University Press.

Twinam, Ann. 1999. *Public Lives, Private Secrets: Gender, Honor, Sexuality, and Illegitimacy in Colonial Spanish America.* Stanford, CA: Stanford University Press.

United Nations Development Programme Human Development Report. 2003.

Vega, Bernardo, ed. 2007. *Dominican Cultures: The Making of a Caribbean Society*. Princeton, NJ: Marcus Weiner Publishers.

Warman, Arturo. 2007. *Corn and Capitalism: How a Botanical Bastard Grew to Global Dominance.* Chapel Hill: University of North Carolina Press.

Williams, Carol J. 2008. "Tracing the Roots of the Food Crisis in Haiti." *Los Angeles Times*, 13 May, A1, A5.

Wilson, J. Peter. 1973. *Crab Antics: The Social Anthropology of English-Speaking Negro Societies of the Caribbean.* New Haven: Yale University Press.

Woolf, Aaron. 2008. *King Corn*. Film. New Video Group.

Navigating the Racial Terrain: Blackness and Mixedness in the United States and the Dominican Republic

Kimberly Eison Simmons

In 1999, Anthony, an African American student studying in the Dominican Republic, was detained at the border overnight when he and some Haitian friends decided to visit Haiti for the weekend. Having accepted the invitation to visit his friends' families across the border from Dajabón, about two hours from Santiago where he was studying, Anthony and his friends had crossed the border into Haiti without incident; but a problem arose when they tried to return to the Dominican Republic on Sunday. The border was closed. With Haitian passports in hand, along with their Dominican visas, Anthony's friends were prepared to pay a nominal fee to enter the Dominican Republic. Unlike his friends, Anthony did not carry his passport with him and could not establish his citizenship at the border. Anthony was dark-skinned and thought to be Haitian, which made his situation even more difficult to resolve. In that moment, to the border officials, he became an undocumented Haitian trying to cross the border into the Dominican Republic. Because the officials did not believe that he was an American student studying in the Dominican Republic, he had to spend the night in a building on the border until the border officially opened the next day. Early Monday morning, Anthony contacted the Council on International Educational Exchange (CIEE) office in Santiago, and someone from the staff faxed a copy of his passport to border officials prompting his immediate release, and he traveled back to Santiago without further incident.

I heard this story for the first time when I became resident director of the CIEE

Study Center in Spanish Language and Caribbean Studies in Santiago in January of 2000. The previous director recounted the story and commented that since that incident, she was encouraging the African American students to carry copies of their passports with them as proof of U.S. citizenship. More to the point, she asked them to carry their passports to prove that they were not Haitian. I wondered what the students thought about this suggestion, especially in a country where many of them felt a connection to place, because the Dominican Republic is part of the African Diaspora (Simmons 2001a, 2006). CIEE had a general practice of faxing copies of all of the students' passports to the U.S. Embassy to register them as Americans in the country, not only in the Dominican Republic but worldwide. However, in the Dominican Republic, the African American students were the only ones encouraged to carry a copy of their passports with them at all times. White, Latino/a, and Asian American students were not told to carry a copy of their passports.

As director, I made the suggestion that *all* students carry a copy of their passports with them as another form of identification, in part so that the African American students would not be singled out in orientation. I was also careful not to predict their experiences by suggesting that Dominicans would think that they were Haitian because of their color, and in some cases, because of their natural or braided hair (Candelario 2000). There, braids are usually associated with Haitian women, and many of the African American women students wore braids, had short, natural hair-styles, or wore their hair in natural curly locks. Dominican women, on the other hand, tend to wear their hair in straight relaxed style (Candelario 2007). This practice is changing, however, especially among the younger generation with experience in the United States among African Americans and other people of African descent (Simmons 2009). Yet hair was still a marker of racial, and therefore national, identity for many people in the Dominican Republic, and as a result, African American students were sometimes harassed on this basis. Not all African American students were associated with Haitians, however. It bears mentioning that those African American students who were lighter in complexion, even those with natural hairstyles, were not thought of as Haitian. Only the darker-skinned students, with or without natural hairstyles, were so identified.

Beyond the kinds of racial identifications made on the basis of hairstyle in the Dominican Republic, there also is a practice of referring to people in public by using skin-color categories (such as *morena* or brown) to get their attention. This is usually the case when the person's name is not known. It is common to hear, for example, "Ven aquí morena" (Come here, brown girl) while walking down the street. Other terms such as *gringo/a* or *rubio/a* (blond) were used if the students were perceived by Dominicans to be American or had blond hair. As a result of these kinds of accumulated experiences over the course of the semester, students began to call their whiteness, blackness, Latino(a)ness, and Americanness into question as new ideas about the significance of these categories and identities arose in the Dominican Republic.

In this article, I draw on the experiences of the students as a way to situate the seemingly conflicting racial projects of the Dominican Republic and the United States to show that, for African Americans and Dominicans, the question of race is actually very similar when it becomes a question of color. I discuss blackness and mixedness as situated processes that encompass ideas of ancestry as well as phenotypic expression in both countries. I argue that racial discourses, and the politics surrounding race and color, for Dominicans in the United States, and African Americans in the Dominican Republic, are very similar because of historical processes of colorization—which I define as intragroup racial and color naming practices. Using notes from orientations, meetings, and focus groups with the students over the course of four-and-a-half years, as well as interviews and focus groups with Dominicans who have visited and/or lived in the United States, I suggest that while notions about race and color have emerged within particular national contexts and have been seen as bounded by those contexts, they can nonetheless be transformed on the basis of individuals' interactions with other racial systems that, though specific to one or another location, are based on common ideas about color. I suggest that growing interactions between African Americans and Afro-Dominicans, and a growing understanding of race and the racial systems in both the United States and the Dominican Republic, contribute to the reconstruction of identities among Dominicans who migrate to the United States, and among African American students studying in the Dominican Republic.[1] Thus, African Americans in the Dominican Republic and Dominicans in the United States encounter a racial dilemma—they must negotiate the new racial definitions that they encounter in different national contexts as they have been historically shaped by state policies and laws as well as informal ways of classifying people based on skin color.

PROGRAM IN SPANISH LANGUAGE AND CARIBBEAN STUDIES

Because of its location and programmatic theme, Spanish Language and Caribbean Studies, the study-abroad program in the Dominican Republic, attracts more students of color than most other CIEE programs (Simmons 2001a, 2006). Students from all over the United States—from liberal arts colleges, large state universities, predominantly white colleges and universities, to historically black colleges and universities—participate in the program. From 2000 to 2004, I reviewed students' application materials and personal statements, and it was clear that Latino/a students, especially Dominican American students, chose the program to learn more about their heritage, while African American students were interested in studying abroad in a place where there were other people of African descent. In general, students were interested in Dominican studies, the Hispanic Caribbean, women's studies, Dominican-Haitian relations, service learning, and Caribbean studies. Many students also expressed an interest in learning Spanish somewhere other than Spain, Mexico, or South America.

While all of the students in the program came to learn more about the history and culture of the Dominican Republic and the Caribbean in general, they learned even more as they were marked as Dominican, Haitian, American, Chinese, and Hindu (in the case of Indian American students). For those marked as Haitian, Dominican-Haitian relations became not only a course that students were interested in but also a lived experience, as the darker-skinned African American students were often considered by both Dominicans and Haitians to be Haitian or of Haitian descent. Lighter-skinned African American students were considered to be Dominican or of Dominican descent. So, members of the same larger community in the United States, the black community, had very different experiences in the Dominican Republic based on their skin color, and therefore on what nationality they were perceived to be.

Dominican American students were thought of as "Dominican" but not "Dominican Dominican," as "Dominican Dominican" referred to Dominicans living in the Dominican Republic, whereas "Dominican" meant having Dominican-born parents or Dominican ancestry. "Dominican" allowed for Dominicans to be Americanized (as expressed in language ability, style of dress, mannerisms, and hairstyle). Puerto Rican students were considered Puerto Rican, but Asian American students were all grouped under the category *chino/a* (Chinese). It did not matter if students were Japanese American, Filipino American, they were all called *chino* in public and described this way. Indian American students (from India) were called "Hindu" even if they were Muslim. White students often heard *gringo/a*, *Americano/a*, or *rubio/a* (blond) as descriptions of themselves (Simmons 2001b). So, students were marked in different ways and were thus reminded of their perceived "otherness" (or sameness) based on their skin color and hairstyle, how well they spoke Spanish, their mannerisms, and how they dressed.

Like other semester-long programs, the Fall program began in August, and the Spring program started in January. We began the semester with a week-long orientation where students learned more about the program and course offerings, and met their host families and the *estudiantes de apoyo* (support students) from the host university, La Pontificia Universidad Católica Madre y Maestra (PUCMM). PUCMM established this peer group to help facilitate American students' acclimation to Dominican culture and life. This involved social outings as well as English-Spanish conversation partners. During the middle of orientation week, I led a discussion about race and identity in the Dominican Republic while referring to my own research. I used the video *Mirrors of the Heart*, part of the *Americas* documentary series (1993), as a way to introduce the topic. Semester after semester, students made similar comments about what they had heard about the Dominican Republic before they arrived. African American students, in particular, spoke of Anti-Haitianism and said that Dominicans were "confused" about *who they were*. I always invited the *estudiantes de apoyo* to attend this meeting so that they could hear the comments and exchanges and also help to contextualize and explain Dominican identity with regard to ideas of blackness and mixedness.

I was always struck by the comment that "Dominicans are confused about who they are . . . they don't know that they are black." I tried to respond by asking the students to step back and consider the historical context and socialization practices (Simmons 2006). This line of argument—that Dominicans did not learn that they were black in the same way that Americans did—proved unsatisfying to the students because they could not understand how it was possible for people who *looked like them* not to see themselves as black (as they did). There is a segment in the *Mirrors of the Heart* video that discusses the politics of skin color, "good" and "bad" hair, and marrying up in the Dominican Republic. In this segment, a Dominican poet and proponent of Afro-Dominicanness states, "We haven't been able to grasp our negritude yet." Students tended to react strongly to the ideas expressed in the video. When I said, "This is similar to what happened in the United States among African Americans years ago," they looked at me in disbelief. For many of them, they were proud to be African American, of their history, and for what it meant to them to be black, but they did not think about the processes and movements that facilitated that kind of pride. I would tell them about the historical preference for lightness, about people who chose to define themselves as mulatto rather than as black, about skin-lightening creams in the United States, about "good" and "bad" hair, and about marrying up as a strategy to lighten the next generation. Many of the students could identify with, and had indeed experienced, the politics of skin color and colorization practices of naming—marking light to dark skin tones, as well as "good" and "bad" hair—but they were often surprised to learn about the other points of similarity.

After students had been in the country for one month, we had another meeting, similar to a retreat, to discuss the students' experiences overall and to learn about their classes and homestays. Some of the *estudiantes de apoyo* also attended this meeting.

Students were settled at this point and could reflect and speak openly about their experiences, any culture shock, and what they were learning. During this meeting, we allowed students to speak in English to fully express themselves (most other interactions between students and CIEE staff were in Spanish per the CIEE language policy). It was during this meeting that we learned more about their racialized experiences, perceptions of Dominican culture, and incorporation into Dominican life. Some of the female African American students commented that their host mothers invited them to go to the salon to get their hair "done," which for the Dominicans meant getting it straightened. While some of the students wore their hair straight and thus frequented Dominican salons, other students with braids and natural styles took the suggestion to mean that something was *wrong* with their hair, that it was not attractive, and that the style needed to change. For many of the host mothers, braids were associated with Haitian women (although this idea changed over time as more students with braids came to the Dominican Republic from the United States).

Dominican American students also experienced similar pressure when host mothers mentioned the salon. Again, while some of the Dominican American women students wore their hair in a straight style, others preferred to wear natural curly locks. They commented that this was how they *liked* their hair, and they resisted the social pressure to change it. To host mothers, students become the "host daughters," and since preteen and teenage girls often go to the salons with their mothers, this invitation by the host mothers could be interpreted as a familial gesture. Nevertheless, the students did not feel that way, because they had come to understand the politics of the salon. As sociologist Ginetta Candelario explains:

> The Dominican salon acts as a socializing agent. Hair care and salon use are rites of passage into Dominican women's community. At the salon, girls and women learn to transform their bodies—through hair care, waxing, manicuring, pedicuring, facials, and so forth—into socially valued, culturally specific, and race-determining displays of femininity. (2000, 135)

These students valued their hair the way it was, and the braids, dreadlocks, short naturals, and curly locks meant something to them culturally; their hair was a personal reflection of *who they were* (Craig 2002; Rooks 1996). As a result, many of them took the invitation to the salon as an affront.

Mestizaje and the "One-Drop Rule": Racial Ideologies in Latin America and the Hispanic Caribbean and the United States

As the "master symbol of the nation," *mestizaje* exhibits an "uneasiness about blackness" and indigenous ethnic-bloc formation. Despite the ambivalence toward Indianness, valorizations of "mixedness" privilege European-Indian heritage and marginalize—if not erase—blackness and Africanness from the national landscape. (Harrison 1995, 55)

The Americas have long been an arena for extraordinary mixtures of cultures and peoples born of diasporas from Africa, Asia, and Europe. These mixtures have given rise to different racial constructions, known in the Caribbean as creolization and in Latin America as *mestizaje*, that have been used to syncretize and refashion race and ethnic mixture into distinct forms of national identity. (Safa 1998, 3)

The literature surrounding race mixture in Latin America and the Hispanic Caribbean focuses largely on racial and cultural whitening processes, creolization, and racial and cultural newness (Wade 1993, 1997; Winn 1999; Wright 1990; Duany 1994, 1998, 2002; Safa 1998, 2005; Yelvington 2001; Rahier 2003). Howard (2001); Sagás (2000); Torres-Saillant (1995, 2000); Candelario (2001, 2007); Levitt (2001); and others examine the politics of race in the Dominican Republic and experiences in the Dominican Diaspora. Yet few have examined what happens to ideas about race, and specifically understandings of race in the Dominican Republic, as a direct result of Dominicans' experiences with race, racism, and racializing practices in the United States. What impact do U.S. racial ideologies have on Dominicans' sense of themselves, their history, and the categories they use to define themselves?

Ana Aparicio has suggested that the idea of blackness is changing for second-generation Dominicans in the United States:

The identity issue that most second-generation Dominicans engage with is "what kind" of Black identity they embody. That is . . . many people I worked with feel that others tried to pressure them to make a choice between being Dominican and Latino or being Black. They do not see the two as separate but feel that Black friends would often urge them to identify themselves as Black. . . . They acknowledge membership in the Black diaspora, but they infuse this with Latino or Dominican elements of identity. (Aparicio 2006, 138)

Ginetta Candelario, comparing the experiences of Dominicans in New York City and Washington, DC, with regard to blackness has noted the following:

These Dominicans [in Washington, DC] identify as black nearly twice as often as Dominicans in New York City precisely because the Dominican community in D.C. is small, has origins in West Indian and U.S. origin African-American communities in the Dominican Republic, took root in a segregated Southern city, and came of age in the midst of a large, economically and politically diverse African American community. (Candelario 2001, 69)

Both Aparicio and Candelario discuss Dominicans' experience with African Americans as friends and as being part of the same community. These relationships play an important role in Dominicans' navigating the racial terrain of the United States, where they are perceived to be black as well as Latino/a.

In the Dominican Republic, change is also taking place. Historically speaking, for much of the twentieth century, Dominicans constructed a racial identity without a positive historical reference to African ancestry. Instead of embracing ideas of African ancestry and blackness, Dominicans attributed these ideas to Haitians and other West Indians in the Caribbean. Dominicans were largely socialized to not think of themselves and their experience within the context of global blackness.[2] Because of the unique history of the Dominican Republic and Haiti—one that is intertwined due to colonization, unification of the island from 1822 to 1844, and subsequent waves of Haitian migration to the Dominican Republic—Dominicans constructed a relational sense of themselves vis-à-vis Haitians. This means that if Haitians were black, Dominicans were nonblack, and if Haitians were "African-like," Dominicans were not. This nonblack, non-"African-like" identity construction translates into how Dominicans see themselves, as well as how they explain their history, ancestry, and cultural practices.

This type of Dominican–Haitian positioning has roots in Dominicans' notions of themselves as being "a special breed of Spaniards" during the colonial period:

Consequently, skin color came to be of secondary importance for social differentiation, although not completely unimportant. At the end of the eighteenth century and in the early nineteenth century, Dominicans perceived themselves as a very special breed of Spaniards living in the tropics with dark skins, but, nevertheless, culturally white, Hispanic, and Catholic. (Moya Pons 1981, 24–25)

This suggests that before there was a "we-they" articulation of mixedness and black-ness, there was an articulation of Dominican whiteness as in *blancos de la tierra* or whites of the land (Moya Pons 1981, 25). Dominican elites, from the late 1880s to 1910–1920, were very instrumental in cementing ideas of Dominicanness in terms of race and nation (Martínez-Vergne 2006). Rafael Leonidas Trujillo, dictator of the Dominican Republic from 1930 to 1961, built on this early foundational idea within the context of *Hispanidad* (the appreciation of everything Spanish):

> Blackness is the fundamental characteristic of the Haitian Other and is situ-ated outside the ideological biology of national identity, which is conceived as a mixing of European, Indian ancestry (the Taínos), and eventually "African blood." This great anxiety of Dominican racial formation vis-à-vis blackness and African ancestry is at work, for example, when individuals who in other Latin American contexts might call themselves "mulatos" prefer to self-identify as "indios." (Rahier 2004, 288)

The African Diaspora Meets the One-Drop Rule and Mestizaje: Race and Nation

Because the Dominican Republic is part of a global African Diaspora, there are some shared characteristics and similarities based on slavery and its consequences, migra-tion, and other experiences. Dr. Ruth Simms Hamilton, the late pioneer of African Diaspora studies, and my professor and mentor, defined the African Diaspora in this way:

> The African diaspora is conceptualized as a global aggregate of actors and sub-populations, differentiated in social and geographical space, yet exhibiting a connectedness based on a shared history of common experiences, conditioned by and within a dynamic world ordering system. (Hamilton 2007, 10)

The points I want to emphasize here are "connectedness" and a sense of "a shared history of common experiences." It can be said that while there are differences in processes of racialization throughout the African Diaspora, in terms of categories that are used to define people, there are similarities when we consider slavery and racialist thinking as Europeans used early biological notions of race and the idea that Africans were inferior in order to justify slavery in the Americas. As Baker (1998), Harrison (1995), Smedley (1993), Blakey (1994), and others suggest, the idea of African inferiority was prevalent during slavery throughout the African Diaspora. This positionality links people of African descent historically and contemporaneously, mapping a shared historical experience of slavery, systems of inequality, and relationships where racialized identities were created and re-created. As Lee Baker states:

> English colonists developed a unique ideology about human differences as institutional and behavioral aspects of slavery solidified. These changes continued into the early eighteenth century. Slavery developed throughout the Americas as a system of bondage that was unique in human history. Its primary distinctiveness rested on the fact that this form of slavery was reserved exclusively for Black people and their children. (Baker 1998, 13)

Thus, race not only became a way of identifying others and maintaining relations of power but also established the foundation for racial attitudes and racist practices that exist today, as Faye Harrison suggests (Harrison 1995).

One distinguishing feature of racial ideology in the United States is the historic construction of the bipolar racial categorization of black and white (Davis 1991; Smedley 1993). This is the result of the linking of racial projects to historical events (e.g., slavery, segregation, Civil Rights Movement, etc.), and has created a particular relationship among power, resources, and specifically racialized populations. Because of this historic bipolar formation, and despite the presence and struggles of other groups in the United States, racial politics are still often painted in black and white, especially in the South. This is not the case in much of Latin America and the Caribbean.

Many Latin American and Caribbean countries created categories to describe the "newness" of its people as a result of mixture between European colonizers, enslaved Africans, and indigenous peoples (Safa 1998, 2005) among others. The idea of mixture as the defining process of peoplehood was nevertheless based on ideas of biological difference and social stratification that were also held in the United States. However, throughout Latin America, rather than pursuing projects of segregation and the social isolation of African-descended people, intermarriage was encouraged in order to "whiten" the population (Wade 1997). Ideas of race throughout much of Latin America and the Hispanic Caribbean, therefore, found expression in ideas about creolization and nationhood, yet a racial system that attached meaning and status to phenotypic differences was still prevalent. This suggests that the institution of slavery left an imprint on Latin America as it did in the United States (Rout 1976). It is for that reason that ideologies of nationhood are also articulations of racial understanding, as one's sense of belonging to the nation is conceptualized in racial terms (Brodkin 2000; Medina 1998; Anderson 1983). Place, therefore, is a marker for race and history. As anthropologist Laurie Medina has outlined, "The identity of people with territory is reinforced through constructions of history which account for and produce both people and place simultaneously, demonstrating that the history of 'a people' is the history of 'their place'" (Medina 1999, 136; see also Brodkin 2000). Thus, the history of the Dominican Republic is also the history of the people, and their understanding of that history, through socialization and experience, manifests itself in the oft-heard statement "We Dominicans are a mixed people." Mixedness is associated with the Dominican Republic, and therefore blackness is associated with Haiti—a different *place*.

Defining Race and Color in the United States and the Dominican Republic

The race system that evolved in the United States is distinctive in several ways. First, the dichotomous race categories of black and white are set and inflexible. Unlike in South Africa or Latin America, there is no legal or social recognition of a "racial" category in between ("mixed-race"); and one cannot belong to more than one race. Second, the category "black" or "African American" is defined by any known descent from a black ancestor, thus conflating and socially homogenizing individuals with a wide range of phenotypes into one racial category. Third, one cannot transcend or transform one's "race" status; in other words, no legal or social mechanism exists for changing one's race. (Smedley 1993, 9)

While there is no mechanism for changing one's race in the United States, there have been attempts to change one's color. Marrying up and lightening creams point to a preference for lightness, not only because of internalized ideas of beauty but also because of the upward social mobility that lightness afforded in terms of access to resources and social networks. For the current generation, light-skinned black people have been defined as black in the United States.[3] The "one-drop rule" makes the United States unique in its racialization process, naming practices, and black-community formation. All of the African American students in the program defined themselves as black and/or African American, commenting that this is what *they were*. Being black meant something specific to them in the United States, and this specificity was challenged by their experiences in the Dominican Republic. All of a sudden, they were struggling to figure out what it meant to be black. In the U.S. context, according to the U.S. Census, white and black are defined in the following way:[4]

> White—"A person having origins in any of the original peoples of Europe, the Middle East, or North Africa. It includes people who indicate their race as 'White' or report entries such as Irish, German, Italian, Lebanese, Near Easterner, Arab, or Polish."
>
> Black or African American—"A person having origins in any of the Black racial groups of Africa. It includes people who indicate their race as 'Black, African Am., or Negro,' or provide written entries such as African American, Afro-American, Kenyan, Nigerian, or Haitian."

These definitions suggest that this is how it *is*, that race is made by grouping "original peoples of Europe" together or by anyone "having origins in any of the Black racial groups." The words "original" and "origins" are not linked to the sociopolitical, historical, and cultural contexts and processes that contributed to these definitions. As defined, the Irish seem "naturally White" as African Americans seem "naturally Black." Whiteness scholars discuss the process of becoming white (see Frankenburg 1993; Roediger 2006; Brodkin 1998). Process is lost in these definitions. As official racial definitions in the United States, they are becoming increasingly more problematic due to increased transnational migration and the greater recognition of biraciality, which has challenged the fixedness of these definitions, a process that has resulted in the 2000 addition of a multiracial category on the census.

In the Dominican Republic, on the other hand, mixed categories have long been used on the census and the national identification card. While the United States emphasized the idea that blackness resulted from the presence of "any" African ancestry, the Dominican Republic focused on defining mixture. A former director of the Office of International Students once told me that "In the United States, if you have one drop of black blood, you are black. In the Dominican Republic, one drop of white blood makes you white, or at least, mixed." Throughout the twentieth century, the Dominican state accounted for mixture with notions of ancestry, and these notions were socialized into the population through various means. Angela, a college-educated Dominican woman with children, argued the following:

> There are two classifications of *indio, claro* (light) and *oscuro* (dark). Dominicans are *mesclados* (mixed). Unlike the United States, there are no racial divisions here. Race means color here, not nationality. *Blanco*/white and *negro*/black produce the rare color *indio*. We don't have any distinct groups here because we are a

mixture. *Indio* is a mixture of *blanco*/white and *negro*/black, more or less a *mulato*. The majority of Dominicans are *indio*.

Here, Angela makes the claim that to be Dominican is to be mixed, and her comment that the mixture is "more or less a *mulato*" suggests awareness on her part of what *mulato* is in terms of recognition of African ancestry. For that reason, preference is given to *indio*, a category representing *mezcla* and *liga* (mixture) without direct reference to Africanity or blackness. Terms such as *mezcla* and *liga* refer to the mixture associated with being Dominican and are commonly used when referring to race in the Dominican Republic. Dominican racialization highlights the idea that Dominicans are a "mixed race" people.

During the dictatorship of Rafael Leonidas Trujillo (1930–61), whitening practices were set into motion to increase immigration from Europe (to intermarry with Dominicans) and to decrease immigration from other Caribbean countries. Toward this end, Trujillo orchestrated a massacre of Haitians in the Dominican Republic to rid the country of Haitians in the border regions. This effort was known as *la dominicanización de la frontera*—"Dominicanization" of the border (Paulino 2005).

Promoting Mestizo-ness

Tourism, including sex tourism, has become a major industry in the Dominican Republic over the past several years (Brennan 2004; Gregory 2006). In the tourist magazine *Aquí*, the *mestizo* is promoted, and as the title suggests, the Dominican Republic is the land of *mestizos*. *Mestizo* was the racial category of choice on the census, while *indio* was used on the national identification card. *Mulato* was not used as an official color category until 1998 (Simmons 2001c, 2005). Unlike *mulato*, *mestizo* did not imply having African or black ancestry. According to the *Enciclopedia Dominicana* (the Dominican Encyclopedia), in 1976 and 1997, *mestizo* was defined in the following way:[5]

Mestizo—En general nombre dado a la persona nacida de padre y madre de diferentes castas. En América aplicábase a los hijos de los matrimonios mixtos españoles e indios. Durante la colonización, que duró desde el siglo XVI hasta mediados del XIX, el mestizaje o fusión de raza fue un fenómeno que acompañó todo el proceso.[6]

[Mestizo—In general it is a name given to the person born of a father and mother of different castes. In America it applies to the children of the mixed marriages between Spaniards and Indians. During colonization, the period that lasted from the sixteenth century until half of the nineteenth century, *mestizaje* or fusion of race was a phenomenon that accompanied the entire process.][7]

Here, the category *mestizo* is defined as children born to Spanish and Indian parents; this was used as the category of choice on the Dominican census. In the definition, there is reference to *mestizaje* as a "fusion of race" process that creates the *mestizo* category. It was *mestizo* that was the official "intermediate" racial category on the Dominican national census from the 1920s to the 1950s.[8] As a category, *mestizo* privileges two other ancestries over African ancestry, therefore, the articulation of a *mestizo* identity implies indigenous, and in this case, Taíno heritage.

Mulato was also defined in the Dominican Encyclopedia and suggests having African ancestry:

Mulatto—Name given in America to the children of Spaniards and blacks. The mulattos, many born in the Spanish colonies or those born in the city due to emigration, maintained their enslaved condition, although many ended up acquiring freedom. The mulattos ended up constituting an important ethnic category resulting from racial mixture.... Different types exist within the racial category of mulatto: (a) mulatto, or white mulatto, is the offspring of a European and a black; (b) Moorish mulatto, or simply Moorish, is the result of the mixture between a white man with a white mulatto woman; (c) blackish mulatto was the child of a black man and a brown mulatto woman. They tended to pass for black because of their dark color; (d) *pardos* or *zambos* resulted from the union of blacks with Indians. This mixture according to skin tone sustained a large subdivision. Many mulattos married whites and other mulattos.[9]

Even though *mulato* does not appear as an official state category until 1998 (on the national identification card), *indio* often mirrors *mulato* in its articulation. A white *mulato* could also be defined as *indio claro*, while a black *mulato* could be defined as *indio oscuro*. There are different shades of *indio* as there are types of *mulato* in the above definition.[10] *Mestizo* was preferred because it did not connote having African ancestry.

Like *mestizo*, *indio* represents a racial in-betweenness, and here again, there is no reference to African ancestry. In this way, *indio* becomes a way to talk about, describe, and label color variation among Dominicans. Some Dominican scholars, notably Carlos Andújar (Andújar 2004) have noted that *indio* is connected to the idea that the Taíno Indians, who were the original inhabitants of the island of Hispaniola before Columbus, had varying skin tones. Referring to the preference for *indio*, Andújar suggests there has been an "amnesia negra" or black amnesia (2004) with respect to the idea of African ancestry in the Dominican Republic. The Dominican Encyclopedia also had a definition of *negro*, or black, that referred to slavery and being a "native" of Africa:

> Blacks—Natives of Africa, brought to America as slave labor to work in the mines and in the large plantations. The sale of blacks constituted a lucrative business in America that was regulated by licenses granted by the Spanish Crown.[11]

In all of the above definitions, the categories refer to "America" in the larger sense, not the Dominican Republic per se. In this way, the encyclopedia provides a definition of *mestizo*, *mulato*, and *negro* within the context of the region and the Americas. The definition and meaning of *mestizo*, given in the *Enciclopedia Dominicana*, refers to a specific type of mixture: Spanish-Indian. This is how *mestizo* has been, and generally is, defined throughout Latin America. If we take the meaning literally, there is no reference to blacks or Africans in this mixture. This brings me back to my previous point about *mestizo*, and *mestizaje* in general; it is a term that is constructed in a bipolar European–indigenous way that excludes people of African descent. While other countries claimed *mestizo* identities (e.g., Mexico, Ecuador, etc.), they were descendants of Spaniards and indigenous people; but in the Dominican Republic, the term came to represent mixture in general, with a strong ancestral tie to the Taínos with or without actual ancestry. Interestingly, there was no definition for *indio* in the *Enciclopedia Dominicana*—the most common way of describing color and mixture in the Dominican Republic.

BLACKNESS AND THE PRIVILEGING OF LIGHTNESS AND NEAR-WHITENESS IN THE UNITED STATES AND THE DOMINICAN REPUBLIC

Throughout the United States (multi-racial societies emerged in Charleston and New Orleans, but only temporarily) the one-drop rule defined mixed bloods (even the lightest mulattos) as black. (Skidmore 2003, 1391)

In the United States, people who identify themselves as African-Americans range from fair-skinned, blond-haired, and blue-eyed individuals to those with dark brown skins and wooly hair. (Smedley 1993, 7)

The same light mulatto defined as black in the United States might be classified as "coloured" in Jamaica and white in Puerto Rico. Sixty percent of [or] more of the migrants from Puerto Rico are perceived in the United States as blacks, yet most of those 60 percent are racially mixed and were known on the island by one of the many color terms other than black, and many of them as white. (Davis 1991, 121)

Again, definitions of race in Latin America usually juxtapose *mestizaje* with the racial binarism of the United States and its black–white racial construct (often with reference to the "one-drop rule"). While African Americans do not often define themselves as mixed, having mixed heritage "somewhere in the family" is often acknowledged given the range of skin tones in the black community. Students often spoke of having mixed ancestry (European and Native American most often) in meetings and discussions. One way that this historic mixture, and resultant diversity in skin tone, is expressed is in the everyday usage of such terms as light-skinned, brown-skinned, dark-skinned, etc. These categories emphasize color within the group and represent a type of intragroup racialization—or what I prefer to call colorization—practice. In this way, black becomes the larger racial category while light to dark color categories address issues of phenotypic diversity within the group.

Lightness and the Politics of Colorization among Dominicans and African Americans

All of us aspired to be on the lighter side of the spectrum. Don't get me wrong. None of us wanted to be white-white like those pale, limp-haired gringos, whites who looked as if they'd been soaked in a bucket of bleach. The whiter ones of us sat out in the sun to get a little color indio, while others stayed indoors rubbing Nivea on their darker skin to lighten it up! (Alvarez 1993, 42)

In 1993, Dominican-born writer Julia Alvarez wrote about her personal experiences with skin color in the Dominican Republic in *Essence* magazine, a magazine with a predominantly African American women's audience. She talked about how blackness is something that Dominicans have hidden "behind the ear" (Candelario 2001, 2007), suggesting the concurrent presence and concealed nature of blackness. To relegate blackness behind the ear, in the oft-used refrain, is to make it invisible and insignificant. In order for something to be relegated to a place that is hidden presupposes that what became invisible was, at one time, visible. In others words, the act of placing black behind the ear is an act of disavowal. The "lighter side of the spectrum" that Alvarez talks about reflects the politics of skin color in the Dominican Republic, which has historically involved whitening practices such as skin-lightening creams and "marrying up"[12] with the hope of lightening the next generation. This was also the case historically among African Americans in the United States. In a country where mixedness is espoused and expressed in terms of being *mestizo*, *indio*, and more recently *mulato*, being lighter (*claro*) is preferred to being darker (*oscuro*). Arguably, this preference still exists for some African Americans (Simmons 2009; Russell et al. 1992; Hunter 2005; and in such films as *Black Is . . . Black Ain't* [Riggs 1995]; *A Question of Color* [Sandler 1993]; and *School Daze* [Lee 1988]).

Working with the students over time, and learning more about their experiences both in the United States and in the Dominican Republic, I realized that African Americans and Dominicans understand race and color from different vantage points, socialization, and experience. For example, despite mixture, African Americans, for the majority of the twentieth century, were defined, and have defined themselves as black[13] (Omi and Winant 1994; Davis 1991), while Dominicans were defined and defined themselves as nonblack with reference to being mixed; they defined Haitians, in relation to themselves, as black. However, like Dominicans, African Americans also use color categories among themselves—light- to dark-skinned—to describe skin color (Simmons 2001c, 2005; Russell, Wilson, and Hall 1992). Dominicans use *indio*[14] to represent light to dark color variation (Torres Salliant 2000; Candelario 2007; Howard 2001; Sagas 2000; Aparicio 2006).

The Dominican Republic encouraged and practiced ideas of mixture through miscegenation and whitening practices over time. While the United States practiced miscegenation during the colonial period, laws were later passed that made interracial marriages illegal (Brodkin 2000). This early miscegenation resulted in the formation of a diverse black community in terms of color, and represented a type of gray area in the early twentieth century as some mixed people defined themselves as mulatto in the United States (Simmons 2009). During the early 1900s, the message was clear: to be lighter was better or preferred. This is evident in popular children's rhyming games: "If you're light, you're right, if you're brown, stick around, if you're black, get back." It was also evident in the marketing of skin-lightening creams during the early 1900s.

I bought a poster entitled "Black is Black" in the early 1990s at an African American festival. The poster depicts three women with varying skin tones from light to dark, and represents the skin-color diversity in the black community. There is also a similar poster with three men with varying skin tones. Here, the politics of skin color and questions of authenticity are leveled as blackness becomes the overarching identity. That said, depending on how one looks at the poster, the lighter-skinned woman is in the foreground while the darker-skinned woman is in the background.

*Marketing Lightness and Near-Whiteness in the United States
and the Dominican Republic*

In both the United States and the Dominican Republic, African Americans and Dominicans internalized lightening or whitening ideals over time. Marrying up was
a practice in both the Dominican Republic and the United States among African
Americans. Both Dominican and African American women used skin-lightening
creams (some continue to do so). Advertisements in the early to mid-1900s contain
images of a brown-turned-light/white woman after applying a whitening cream.
These advertisements ran in Dominican and African American newspapers around
the same time (1930–1933) in both the Dominican Republic and the United States.
The idea was that lighter skin was more attractive and "better" than darker skin. These
creams are still sold in pharmacies and department stores in the Dominican Republic,
and I have seen similar products in beauty supply stores in South Carolina.

In October 2007, there was tremendous controversy surrounding a party that was
planned in Detroit, a predominantly black city, called "Light Skin Libra Birthday Bash."
I first heard about the party on a syndicated radio program, *The Michael Baisden Show*.
Black people were outraged because the party promoter planned this party privileging
light-skinned women (who, along with Libras, were to be admitted for free). A Web
article entitled "Jiggaboo's and Wannabe's Revisited: Light Skin Only" (2007) situ-
ates this party in the context of Spike Lee's *School Daze* (1988), with the Jiggaboos the
darker-skinned black women, and the Wannabes lighter-skinned black women who
want to be white. According to the author, Detroit DJ and party promoter Ulysses "DJ
Lish" Barnes said that this was the first party he was planning and that there would
also be "Sexy Chocolate" and "Sexy Caramel" parties at a later date. These parties
promoted sexualized images of black women as being dark- or brown-skinned and
"sexy." As a result of the controversy and boycotts, all of the parties were canceled.
Their conceptualization, however, speaks to the continued salience of color as a mode
of intraracial distinction in the United States.

WHEN BEING BLACK OR *INDIO/A* IS CALLED INTO QUESTION: NAVIGATING A NEW RACIAL SYSTEM[15]

If the Dominican Republic privileges mixture, and the United States classifies people
into "distinct" groups, then what happens when someone from the Dominican

Republic travels to the United States and encounters a new, and somewhat different, racial system, as is the case with the U.S. students in the Dominican Republic? What happens when racial categories, once understood, embodied, and accepted as fixed, are called into question? What happens when a self-defined black person from the United States travels to the Dominican Republic and is all of a sudden defined as *indio/a claro/a* or *oscuro/a*? In turn, what happens when a self-defined person with an *indio/a* identity travels to the United States and is all of a sudden defined as black? Encountering a new racial system means that people have to navigate and negotiate "who they are" within this new context. This often involves making sense of the categories, racial politics, and colorization in that new place. While U.S. students did not apply for identification cards where they would have been classified according to color, they were addressed by friends and strangers alike in color terms.

In the United States, Dominicans quickly learn how Americans define them given the historic black-white racial categorization practice. Chiqui Vicioso, famed Dominican writer, describes her own personal experience in the United States with race, encountering a new racial system, and reconstructing a "new" identity for herself. In 1960, when entering the U.S. Immigration area at JKF airport, Chiqui was asked about "india clara" on her passport. She said, "That is my color. In Santo Domingo we are classified by skin color. I am *india clara*, that means "light Indian" (Vicioso 2000, 1014). The U.S. Immigration official then made the comment that there were no "Indians" in the Dominican Republic. Her *india*-ness was called into question, and it was made even more complicated when she and her family moved to New York where there were "morenos (Black Americans) who looked like us girls" (Vicioso 2000, 1015) in her neighborhood. Chiqui's experience in New York, among African Americans, prompted her to reexamine her own racial identity.

This was also the case with a group of women who formed the organization known as Identidad de la Mujer Afro (Identity of the African-Descended Woman), founded in 1989 in Santo Domingo. As a result of their experiences abroad, these women questioned their *india* identities and later redefined themselves as *mulata*, Afro-Dominican, and/or black (Simmons 2001c). As a collective, they organized a women's movement and placed black women at the center of Identidad, referring to itself as a black feminist organization combating racism and sexism in Dominican society. I began working with Identidad in 1993 and followed their trajectory as they promoted Dominican blackness and worked to create alliances with Haitian women and other "Afro-American"[16] women throughout the region.

The Dominican Republic was undergoing a more general shift around the time Identidad began using and promoting *mulato* instead of *indio*. In 1988, when new identification cards were issued throughout the country, *mulato* was added as a category. According to state officials issuing the cards, *mulato* was supposed to replace *indio*, but that did not happen; *mulato* was an option as was *indio*. Before 1988, *indio* was the only category on the *cédula* representing mixture. *Mulato* not only emerges with members of Identidad Mulato, but also with the first term of Dominican President Leonel Fernandez in 1996, who defined himself as a *mulato*. During his campaign, there were heated debates about race and nationality (Howard 2001; Sagás 2000) involving him and his political opponent Francisco Peña Gomez, who was described in the Dominican media as "black" and of "Haitian descent." Fernandez, who had spent years in the United States, defined himself as mulatto, a mixture of black and white, and said that the Dominican Republic was comprised primarily of mulattos (Larry Rohter, *New York Times*, July 1, 1996, page A3). The usage of *mulato* on the *cédula* is just one example of how *mulato* has emerged as a new racial category in the Dominican Republic as a result of encountering a new racial system in the United States, a period of critical reflection, and interactions with other people of African descent.

CONCLUSION: PERCEIVED IDENTITIES, MULTIPLICITY, AND NAVIGATING THE TERRAIN

At the beginning of this article, I discussed Anthony's experience at the border when he was detained because Dominican immigration officials thought he was Haitian. In 1998, when I was completing my dissertation research, I made this same trip with close Dominican friends and my family, and my experience was quite different. We were invited to visit our friend's brother in Dajabón over the weekend and to go to Haiti for the day on Sunday, the day the border is officially closed. My husband (David), our oldest daughter (Asha), who was one year old at the time, and I are all light in complexion. Our friends said that we would cross the border as Dominicans and that there was no need to bring our passports; "Dominicans do not need them," he said. They also suggested that we not have conversations with people because our Spanish would make people wonder if we were "de allá" (the United States). If asked, they would say that we were their cousins visiting from the United States. This was our first trip to Haiti, and I was a bit nervous, given the situation of not having our passports and the border being closed.

As we approached the border, there was someone inside at a desk. One of our friends told the official that we wanted to visit Haiti for the day. The border official gave all us slips of paper and we were allowed entry into Haiti. As we crossed the bridge connecting the Dominican Republic and Haiti, the only marker delineating the two countries was a link chain from one side of the bridge to the other. There was no sign indicating that we were in Haiti, but as we stepped over the chain, I realized that we must have crossed the border. When we reached the other side of the bridge in Haiti, we were in Ouanaminthe and were met with a few transportation options. We got into a truck and traveled through the town. We later asked the driver if there was an art gallery where we could purchase Haitian art. After we left the art gallery, we returned to the border to cross back into the Dominican Republic.

Earlier in the day, we had crossed without incident, but now as we stepped back over the same chain, we were faced with a large cement structure ahead that read "República Dominicana" (Dominican Republic). I looked back toward the Haitian side and saw only people, trees, trucks, and motorcycles as we walked in the direction of an imposing border symbol. A Dominican man greeted us as we stepped back over the chain and began a conversation with me. I recalled what our friends had said about not talking (that my Spanish was not "Dominican Dominican"), but the man didn't say anything about my Spanish. He simply led us to the processing area where we returned our slips of paper, paid a nominal fee, and entered the Dominican Republic as Dominican.

Over time, in the Dominican Republic, I was defined as *india clara*, *mulata*, and Dominican. African American students had a shorter amount of time in the country, but were still faced with new definitions of themselves because of the Dominican racial system. They often had to come to terms with being "mixed," defined as *indio* or *india*, Dominican and/or Haitian, and importantly for some of them, not being defined as black. For the students who were defined as black, this often meant that they were perceived to be Haitian. One of the students said during the one-month meeting, "I don't mind being thought of as Haitian because I do look like them. It's just that it is not who I am." The students who were considered black were viewed outside of the cultural and historical context of the United States, albeit within the context of the African Diaspora. It was also difficult for many of the students who were not considered to be black, but rather mixed. This was traumatic for many students who had a firm sense of themselves, their racial identities, and their history in the United States.

Importantly, the idea that self-defined black students from the United States could be divided, due to Dominican notions of race, color, and ancestry, was unsettling. On the one hand, darker-skinned African American students were still defined as black, being considered to be of Haitian, or perhaps of Jamaican descent, in the Dominican Republic. Lighter-skinned African American students, on the other hand, were defined as Dominican and/or *indio/a* (Simmons 2006). In the United States, they were part of the same community and were defined as black (perhaps light-skinned and dark-skinned according to colorization naming practices), but in the Dominican

Republic, they were viewed differently based on color, hair type and style, and other physical characteristics. The discussion here shows that both African Americans and Dominicans tried to make sense of their own identities and sense of history within a new context where they were defined in new ways. African Americans came to understand "mixedness" and Dominican blackness, while Dominicans came to understand American blackness, creating an epistemological shift in both mixedness and blackness for both African Americans and Dominicans.

NOTES

Reprinted with permission. Originally published in *Transforming Anthropology* 16(2): 95–111, ISSN 1051-0559, electronic ISSN 1548-7466, and 2008 by the American Anthropological Association. All rights reserved. DOI: 10.1111/j.1548-7466.2008.00019.x. Minor edits and changes were made for this publication.

1. This is just one way the identities are being reconfigured in the Dominican Republic. Dominican scholars and activists are examining versions of history and concepts of identity as a way to rewrite and recast ideas of race and identity.

2. See Thomas 2004, 2007; Slocum and Thomas 2007; and Clarke and Thomas 2006 for discussions of blackness in a global context in relation to the Caribbean region.

3. There were always people who could, and did, pass for white. Some were classified and lived as white.

4. U.S. Census Bureau, 2000.

5. All of the translations are mine.

6. *Enciclopedia Dominicana* (Barcelona: Publicaciones Reunidas, 1976), 4: 240.

7. *Enciclopedia Dominicana* (Barcelona: Publicaciones Reunidas, 1976), 4: 240, translation by author.

8. In general, *mestizo* means "mixed," and for this reason, it was incorporated into state definitions and void of any reference to African ancestry.

9. *Enciclopedia Dominicana* (Barcelona: Publicaciones Reunidas, 1976), 5: 71–72, translation by author.

10. There was no definition of *indio* in the Dominican encyclopedia, although there were references to the Taínos and indigenous people.

11. *Enciclopedia Dominicana* (Barcelona: Publicaciones Reunidas, 1976), 5: 90, translation by author.

12. "Marrying up" refers to when a person chooses a spouse with a lighter skin tone with the hope of lightening the next generation.

13. Negro and colored have also been used as racial designators.

14. *Indio* literally means "Indian," but is not used in that way. It is often used instead of mulatto to represent being mixed and between black and white.

15. This is a new area of research. This builds on my current research in the Dominican Republic

and in the United States with Dominicans and African Americans.

16. Here, I am referring to Afro-Brazilian, Afro-Venezuelan, Afro-Colombian, Afro-Cuban, Afro–Puerto Rican women, etc.

REFERENCES

Alvarez, Julia. 1993. "Black Behind the Ears." *Essence* 23(10):42, 129, 132.

Anderson, Benedict. 1983. *Imagined Communities: Reflections on the Origin and Spread of Nationalism.* London: Verso.

Andujar, Carlos. 2004. *Identidad Cultural y Religiosidad Popular.* Santo Domingo: Editorial Letra Gráfica.

Aparicio, Ana. 2006. *Dominican-Americans and the Politics of Empowerment.* Gainesville: University Press of Florida.

Baker, Lee. 1998. *From Savage to Negro: Anthropology and the Construction of Race, 1896–1954.* Berkeley: University of California Press.

Black Is ... Black Ain't. 1995. Marlon Riggs, producer/director. California Newsreel.

Blakey, Michael L. 1994. "Passing the Buck: Naturalism and Individualism as Anthropological Expressions of Euro-American Denial." In *Race*, ed. Steven Gregory and Roger Sanjek, 270–284. New Brunswick, NJ: Rutgers University Press.

Brennan, Denise. 2004. *What's Love Got to Do with It? Transnational Desires and Sex Tourism in the Dominican Republic.* Durham, NC: Duke University Press.

Brodkin, Karen. 1998. *How Jews Became White Folks and What That Says about Race in America.* New Brunswick, NJ: Rutgers University Press.

———. 2000. "Global Capitalism: What's Race Got to Do with It?" 1998 AES Keynote Address. *American Ethnologist* 27(2):237–256.

Candelario, Ginetta E. B. 2000. "Hair Race-ing." *Meridians: Feminism, Race, Transnationalism* 1(1):128–156.

———. 2001. "'Black behind the Ears'—and Up Front Too? Dominicans in the Black Mosaic." *Public Historian* 23(4):55–73.

———. 2004. "Voices from Hispaniola: A Meridians Roundtable with Edwidge Danticat, Loida Maritza Pérez, Myriam J. A. Chancy, and Nelly Rosado." *Meridians: Feminism, Race, Transnationalism* 5(1):69–91. Interviews were conducted by Ginetta E. B. Candelario and further coordinated and assembled by the staff of the journal.

———. 2007. *Black behind the Ears: Dominican Racial Identity from Museums to Beauty Shops.* Durham, NC: Duke University Press.

Clarke, Kamari, and Deborah A. Thomas, eds. 2006. *Globalization and Race: Transformations in the Cultural Production of Blackness.* Durham, NC: Duke University Press.

Craig, Maxine Leeds. 2002. *Ain't I a Beauty Queen? Black Women, Beauty, and the Politics of Race.* New York: Oxford University Press.

Davis, F. James. 1991. *Who Is Black? One Nation's Definition.* University Park: Pennsylvania State University Press.

Domínguez, Virginia. 1994. *White by Definition: Social Classification in Creole Louisiana.* New Brunswick, NJ: Rutgers University Press.

Duany, Jorge. 1994. *Quisqueya on the Hudson: The Transnational Identity of Dominicans in Washington Heights.* Dominican Research Monographs, CUNY Dominican Studies Institute.

———. 1998. "Reconstructing Racial Identity: Ethnicity, Color, and Class among Dominicans in the United States and Puerto Rico." *Latin American Perspectives* 25(3):147–172.

———. 2002. *The Puerto Rican Nation on the Move: Identities on the Island and in the United States.* Chapel Hill: University of North Carolina Press.

Frankenburg, Ruth. 1993. *White Women, Race Matters: The Social Construction of Whiteness.* Minneapolis: University of Minnesota Press.

Gregory, Steven. 2006. *The Devil behind the Mirror: Globalization and Politics in the Dominican Republic.* Berkeley: University of California Press.

Hamilton, Ruth Simms, ed. 2007. *Routes of Passage: Rethinking the African Diaspora.* East Lansing: Michigan State University Press.

Haney Lopez, Ian. 1996. *White by Law: The Legal Construction of Race.* New York: New York University Press.

Harrison, Faye. 1995. "The Persistent Power of 'Race' in the Cultural and Political Economy of Racism." *Annual Review of Anthropology* 24:47–74.

Howard, David. 2001. *Coloring the Nation: Race and Ethnicity in the Dominican Republic.* Boulder, CO: Lynne Rienner Publishers.

Hunter, Margaret L. 2005. *Race, Gender, and the Politics of Skin Tone.* New York: Routledge.

Levitt, Peggy. 2001. *The Transnational Villagers.* Berkeley: University of California Press.

Martínez-Echazábal, Lourdes. 1998. "Mestizaje and the Discourse of National/Cultural Identity in Latin America, 1845–1959." *Latin American Perspectives: Race and National Identity in the Americas* 25(3):21–42.

Martínez-Vergne, Teresita. 2006. *Nation and Citizen in the Dominican Republic, 1880–1916.* Chapel Hill: University of North Carolina Press.

Medina, Laurie Kroshus. 1998. "History, Culture, and Place-Making: 'Native' Status and Maya Identity in Belize." *Journal of Latin American Anthropology* 4(1):134–165.

Mirrors of the Heart. Video no. 4 in *Americas* Series (1993). Annenberg/CPB Collection. P.O. box 2345, South Burlington, VT 05407-2345.

Moya Pons, Frank. 1981. "Dominican National Identity and Return Migration." In *Migration and Caribbean Cultural Identity*, paper no. 1, 23–33. Gainesville: Center for Latin American Studies, University of Florida.

———. 1995. *The Dominican Republic: A National History.* New Rochelle, NY: Hispaniola Books.

Omi, Michael, and Howard Winant. 1994. *Racial Formation in the United States from the 1960s to the 1990s.* 2nd ed. New York: Routledge.

Paulino, Edward. 2005. "Erasing the Kreyol from the Margins of the Dominican Republic: The Pre- and Post-Nationalist Project of the Border, 1930–1945." *Wadabagei* 8(2):35–71.

Question of Color, A. 1993. Kathe Sandler, executive producer. California Newsreel.

Rahier, Jean Muteba. 2003. "Introduction: Mestizaje, Mulataje, Mestiçagem in Latin American Ideologies of National Identities." *Journal of Latin American Anthropology* 8(1):40–50.

———. 2004. "The Study of Latin American 'Racial Formations': Different Approaches and Different Contexts." *Latin American Research Review* 39(3):282–293.

Roediger, David R. 2006. *Working toward Whiteness: How America's Immigrants Became White: The Strange Journey from Ellis Island to the Suburbs*. New York: Perseus Books Group.

Rooks, Noliwe M. 1996. *Hair Raising: Beauty, Culture, and African American Women*. New Brunswick, NJ: Rutgers University Press.

Rout, Leslie B., Jr. 1976. *The African Experience in Latin America*. Cambridge: Cambridge University Press.

Russell, Kathy, Midge Wilson, and Ronald Hall. 1992. *The Color Complex: The Politics of Skin Color among African Americans*. New York: Harcourt Brace Jovanovich.

Safa, Helen. 1998. "Introduction." *Latin American Perspectives: Race and National Identity in the Americas* 25(3):3–20.

———. 2005. "Challenging Mestizaje." *Critique of Anthropology* 25(3):307–330.

Sagás, Ernesto. 2000. *Race and Politics in the Dominican Republic*. Gainesville: University Press of Florida.

School Daze. 1988. Spike Lee, producer/director.

Simmons, Kimberly Eison. 2001a. "Black Students and Study Abroad." *Anthropology News* 42(3). *ABA Section News*. Arlington, VA: American Anthropological Association.

———. 2001b. "A Double-Edged Sword: White Privilege." *Anthropology News* 42(4). *ABA Section News*. Arlington, VA: American Anthropological Association.

———. 2001c. "A Passion for Sameness: Encountering a Black Feminist Self in Fieldwork in the Dominican Republic." In *Black Feminist Anthropology: Theory, Politics, Praxis, and Poetics*, ed. Irma McClaurin, 77–101. New Brunswick, NJ: Rutgers University Press.

———. 2005. "'Somos Una Liga': Afro-Dominicanidad and the Articulation of New Racial Identities in the Dominican Republic." *Wadabagei* 8(1):51–64.

———. 2006. "Racial Enculturation and Lived Experience: Reflections on Race at Home and Abroad." *Anthropology News* 47(2):10–11.

———. 2009. *Reconstructing Racial Identity and the African Past in the Dominican Republic*. Gainesville: University Press of Florida.

Skidmore, Thomas. 2003. "Racial Mixture and Affirmative Action: The Cases of Brazil and the United States." *American Historical Review* (December 2003):1391–1396.

Slocum, Karla, and Deborah Thomas. 2007. "Introduction: Locality in Today's Global Caribbean: Shifting Economies of Nation, Race, and Development." *Identities* 14(1/2):1–18.

Smedley, Audrey. 1993. *Race in North America: Origin and Evolution of a Worldview*. Boulder, CO: Westview Press.

Thomas, Deborah. 2004. *Modern Blackness: Nationalism, Globalization, and the Politics of Culture in Jamaica*. Durham, NC: Duke University Press.

———. 2007. "Blackness across Borders: Jamaican Diasporas and New Politics of Citizenship." *Identities* 14(1/2):111–133.

Torres-Saillant, Silvio. 1995. "The Dominican Republic." In *No Longer Invisible: Afro-Latin Americans Today*, ed. Minority Rights Groups, 109–138. London: Minority Rights Publications.

———. 2000. "The Tribulation of Blackness: Stages of Dominican Racial Identity." *Callaloo*

23(3):1086–1111.

Twine, France Winddance. *Racism in a Racial Democracy: The Maintenance of White Supremacy in Brazil.* New Brunswick, NJ: Rutgers University Press.

Vicioso, Sherezada. 2000. "Dominicanyorkness: A Metropolitan Discovery of the Triangle," trans. Daisy Cocco-DeFilippis. *Calaloo* (23)3:1013–1016.

Wade, Peter. 1993. *Blackness and Race Mixture: The Dynamics of Racial Identity in Colombia.* Baltimore: Johns Hopkins University Press.

———. 1997. *Race and Ethnicity in Latin America.* Chicago: Pluto Press.

Whitten, Norman E., and Arlene Torres. 1995. *Blackness in Latin America and the Caribbean.* Vols. 1 and 2. Bloomington: Indiana University Press.

Winn, Peter. 1999. "A Question of Color." In *Americas: The Changing Face of Latin America and the Caribbean,* 277–306. Berkeley: University of California Press.

Wright, Winthrop. 1990. *Café con Leche: Race, Class, and National Image in Venezuela.* Austin: University of Texas Press.

Yelvington, Kevin. 2001. "The Anthropology of Afro-Latin America and the Caribbean: Diasporic Dimensions." *Annual Review of Anthropology* 30:227–260.

Negotiating Blackness within the Multicultural State in Latin America: Creole Politics and Identity in Nicaragua

Juliet Hooker

This essay explores the ways that Afro-descendant Creoles are currently re-imagining their collective identities in Nicaragua, in the context of multi-cultural policies that guarantee collective rights to land and culture to both the indigenous and Afro-descendant inhabitants of the country's Atlantic Coast. It traces changes in the way English-speaking Creoles imagine and represent their identity within a Nicaraguan nation that is portrayed as overwhelmingly *mestizo* or Indo-Hispanic. The central aim is to analyze how and why a strong "black" racial group identity that is imagined in terms of transnational connections to the African Diaspora, including to an African past and Afro-Caribbean ancestry, is currently unfolding among many Creoles. In doing so, the essay traces shifting conceptions of Creole identity, focusing in particular on the connections between the current emphasis on blackness on the one hand, and changes to Nicaragua's model of multiculturalism that begin to recognize the existence of racial hierarchy (by implementing specific policies to combat racism and racial discrimination) on the other hand. In particular, I try to show both how multicultural policies impact the self-making strategies of Nicaraguan Creoles, and how such policies are shaped by the forms of activism that emerge from current imaginings of Creole collective identity.

My analysis of the way Afro-descendant Creoles in Nicaragua are currently imagining their collective identity and negotiating blackness in the context of official multiculturalism is framed by two seemingly unrelated events. The first was a special series about Afro-Latin Americans that ran in the *Miami Herald* during 2007, specifically an article focused on the "emergent black cultural and civil rights movement" among Creoles in Nicaragua. The article was notable both because the comments of those interviewed in the article showed how Creole racial identity is currently being imagined, and also because of the reactions it provoked among other sectors of the Creole community. Interestingly, what was most striking about the article was the quote and accompanying photograph of a contestant in a Miss Black Pride beauty pageant being held in the Creole community of Pearl Lagoon. When speaking about her dress to the reporter, the young Creole woman said: "It reminds me of Africa. I'm so proud of my heritage and my ancestry" (Burch 2007). This seemingly innocuous statement of pride in one's racial ancestry was noteworthy for a number of reasons. One of them was that (at least to this observer) there was nothing about the pink sequined dress pictured in the accompanying photograph that would immediately signal a connection to Africa. Another reason was because of the mere fact of the reference to Africa itself, given that it would seem to be more temporally and geographically feasible for Nicaraguan Creoles to establish a connection to people of African descent in the Diaspora.

The second event that frames my analysis of current formulations of Creole collective identity in the context of state multiculturalism in Nicaragua occurred at a conference on the black presence in Mesoamerica, where I presented a paper on Creole politics and history and the construction of Nicaraguan citizenship in the nineteenth and twentieth centuries. At the end of my presentation, a prominent historian of Africa asked, "Where is Africa?" In other words, he wanted to know what role a connection to an African past played in Creole self-making practices. When confronted with this question, I realized that it was not one I could readily answer, in large part because a connection to Africa seemed rather absent from Creole accounts of their historical development as a group, which tended to emphasize links to people of African descent in the Caribbean. This question, coupled with the young black beauty-pageant contestant's comment about Africa, led to another set of questions: What does it means to be Creole and/or black or Afro-descendant in Nicaragua today, in the context of a self-proclaimed multicultural state? What does it mean to be Creole and/or black in multicultural Nicaragua? How is blackness negotiated and lived today in a state where multiculturalism has become official state policy, but where historically, racial hierarchy and racism have not been recognized? How are these identities negotiated and remade in the context of struggles for justice and equality?

In order to examine these questions, it is necessary to understand the historical context in which these different self-conceptions of Creole identity are unfolding in Nicaragua. Creoles are not the only Afro-descendants in Nicaragua, but they are the group generally most associated with blackness. It is crucial to note that in Nicaragua there are two primary groups of people of African descent: the descendants of slaves brought by Spaniards during the colonial period, and descendants of free and enslaved blacks and mulattos who formed maroon communities on the Atlantic Coast. Creole and Garifuna populations on Nicaragua's Atlantic Coast are examples of the latter, while the remaining population of African descent in the rest of the country (which has not developed a separate group identity from the national *mestizo* majority) is an example of the former.

In Nicaragua as a whole, as in other Latin American countries, there is a close connection between skin color and social class. But the racialization of space (that is, the designation of some regions of the country as the only ones where racial "others" who were viewed as "inferior" and "savage" resided) has also served to legitimize internally colonizing state practices. Historically, the identification of the Atlantic Coast with blackness thus functioned to justify the political exclusion of *costeños* (as the region's inhabitants are known), especially Creoles (Hooker 2010).

The Afro-descendant population in Nicaragua is relatively small, and as a group they face difficult conditions. According to the latest census carried out in 2005, Nicaragua's total population is 5,142,098, of which only 19,890 persons, or less than 1 percent, self-identified as Creole. The vast majority of Creoles live on the Atlantic Coast, where they represent 5.4 percent of the region's total population of 620,640 inhabitants (INEC 2006, 15, 52, 54, 184, 188).[1] According to a 2006 report on racism and ethnic discrimination, "In Nicaragua, there exists an underlying racism, whose most evident expression is the unequal human development of the country. The majority of the territories occupied by Indigenous peoples [and Afro-descendants] are among the poorest with the least access to basic social services" (Cunningham Kain 2006, 35). The report identifies the variety of ways that racism manifests itself in Nicaragua today, including prejudice based on skin color in hiring, invisibility in daily public life, discrimination against use of non-Spanish mother tongues (such as Creole English), devaluation of local knowledge, discrimination in artistic production, and so forth. The disparities from which Afro-descendants (and Creoles in particular) suffer are evident when one compares socioeconomic, health, and literacy indicators for the Atlantic Coast with the rest of the country. For example, on the Atlantic Coast the levels of unemployment reach 90 percent. Of the 5,398 schools in the country, only 361 are found in the region, and the illiteracy rate exceeds 50 percent (Cunningham Kain 2006, 56). In the autonomous regions only 25–30 percent of the population has access to potable water compared to over 70 percent in the country as a whole. The maternal mortality rate on the Atlantic Coast is two to three times higher than the rate for the rest of the country, and the infant mortality rate is significantly higher in the region as well (PNUD 2005, 77, 80–81). Despite recent advances in collective rights for Creoles and other Afro-descendant *costeños*, these gains have not translated into concrete improvements in the general socio-economic conditions of or access to basic services for these populations.

The aim of this essay is to better understand and explain the interplay between state multicultural policy and the kinds of collective identities and types of rights demands being advanced by Nicaraguan Creoles and other Afro-descendant groups in Latin America. In order to do this, I first place the Nicaraguan case in comparative perspective, situating it against wider trends in the region around Afro-descendant political mobilization. I then discuss the evolution of racial politics in Nicaragua and the features of the model of multiculturalism that was adopted there in the 1980s. Finally, I analyze Creole self-making strategies in light of these transformations. This is a qualitative study that draws on a variety of sources, including archival materials, secondary historical works, government laws and reports, contemporary accounts of Creole identity in popular media (such as newspapers), official reports produced by *costeño* nongovernmental organizations, and ethnographic field research on the Atlantic Coast.

AFRO-DESCENDANT POLITICAL MOBILIZATION
AND THE LATIN AMERICAN STATE

In recent decades, Afro-descendant social movements in Latin America have waged increasingly visible and successful struggles for various kinds of collective rights to overcome the racial discrimination and social exclusion to which they have historically been subjected. In response, Latin American states and national publics have begun to acknowledge the persistence of racism in their respective societies, and Afro-descendants have won important collective rights from the state in many countries in the region.[2]

The collective rights won by Afro-descendants in Latin America can generally be classified within two broad frameworks: rights to enable the preservation of land and culture, and rights to remedy the effects of racial discrimination. These two broad rubrics correspond to the different kinds of normative justifications for collective rights for minority groups put forward by theorists of multiculturalism. Rights to land and culture are viewed as legitimate for minority cultures in multinational states because the languages, cultures, and identities of these groups in such states will always be unfairly disadvantaged compared to those of the majority group. As a result, justice requires the adoption of permanent collective rights that allow minorities to preserve their cultures—such as language rights, communal land rights, and self-government in the territories in which they live. Indigenous peoples in many Latin American countries and some Afro-descendants have gained these kinds of collective rights (as in Guatemala, Honduras, Nicaragua, Bolivia, Ecuador, etc.). Meanwhile, minority groups in states that have been structured on the basis of racial hierarchies that determined access to political power and educational and economic resources are viewed as entitled to positive rights to overcome racialized inequality. For example, these temporary collective rights include measures such as affirmative action in education and employment (Brazil), or rights to political representation (Colombia). These two broad rubrics of rights have combined in various ways to produce different regimes of multicultural recognition for Afro-descendants in Latin America.[3]

Based on different configurations of rights to land and culture, and positive anti-racial discrimination rights for Afro-descendants, we can identify three models of multiculturalism in Latin America. In the first model, Afro-descendants and indigenous peoples have achieved fairly similar levels of collective rights to the preservation of land and culture; in the second model, indigenous groups have gained collective rights to land and culture, but Afro-descendants have not; while in the third model, indigenous and Afro-descendant groups have gained different levels of collective rights to land and culture, but Afro-descendants have also won positive anti-racial-discrimination rights. In the first type of model of multiculturalism in Latin America, Afro-descendants and indigenous peoples have both gained the same kinds of collective rights to land and culture and have been included in the same legal categories. This is the model that has been implemented in much of Central America, particularly Guatemala, Honduras, and Nicaragua. In the second model, Afro-descendants have not been viewed as either cultural minorities or subordinated racial groups and have failed to gain any kind of collective rights. So far this has been the case in Mexico. Finally, in the region's third model of multiculturalism, Afro-descendants have been recognized as cultural groups entitled to certain—lower—levels of cultural accommodation than indigenous peoples. Additionally, this model includes positive rights to redress racial discrimination for Afro-descendants. This is the model of multiculturalism that has emerged in Brazil, Colombia, Ecuador, and Peru.

Some of the differences in the kinds of models of multiculturalism Latin American states have implemented can be attributed to the types of Afro-descendants present in each country. For analytical purposes it is thus possible to develop a typology of Latin American Afro-descendants—consisting of four principal types or groups—that can help us understand the kinds of organizations these groups have developed, and the types of collective rights they have struggled for. The first group is what we might call *Afro-mestizo* people, who are the descendants of slaves brought during the colonial period who over time integrated into the lower socioeconomic levels of colonial society, and later into the dominant *mestizo* cultures and national identities of most Latin American countries. While their phenotypical differences from the national population suggest that they are subject to racial discrimination (given the close association between social class and skin color in Latin America), in most cases they have not developed a separate racial/cultural group identity or made demands for collective rights. *Afro-mestizos* can be either urban or rural, and they probably represent the largest proportion of Afro-descendants in the region (we can find *Afro-mestizos* in practically every country in Latin America with an Afro-descendant population, but some notable cases would be Mexico, Brazil, Peru, and Panama). A second group of Afro-Latin Americans comprises the descendants of slaves brought during the colonial period who have developed a strong racial group identity and have struggled for collective rights against racial discrimination. They tend to be overwhelmingly in urban settings. The various urban black movements located in many of Brazil's major cities are an example of this type of group.

A third group of Afro-descendants in Latin America comprises the descendants of "maroon" communities whose ancestors managed to escape from (or otherwise avoid) slavery to establish communities outside colonial society. These Afro-descendant groups developed separate racial/cultural collective identities distinct from those of the dominant *mestizo* majority, and forged a relationship to land or territory in the colonial period before the establishment of state sovereignty over the areas they occupied. They have historically struggled for collective rights, in particular rights to communal lands or territory. Creoles in Nicaragua, and Garifuna in Honduras, Nicaragua, and Guatemala are examples of this type of Afro-descendant group. Finally, throughout Central America, we find a fourth group of Afro-Latin Americans who are the descendants of West Indian immigrants who arrived as laborers in the enclave economies that existed in the late nineteenth and twentieth centuries along the Caribbean coast of the isthmus. They have organized as a racial/cultural group and struggled for equal civil rights and positive anti-racial-discrimination rights. The black movements in Panama and Costa Rica are examples of this kind of Afro-descendant group. It is important to keep in mind, however, that these are broad conceptual categories intended to help us understand the kinds of social movements and forms of political organization developed by Afro-Latin Americans. In practice the boundaries between the different categories are quite fluid, and they may often overlap. In many countries, multiple types of these Afro-descendant groups live alongside one another—as in Colombia and Brazil, for example, where we find Afro-*mestizos*, urban black movements, and the descendants of maroon communities.

In general, Afro-descendants who have organized as racial groups have struggled for equal civil rights and anti-racial-discrimination rights, while those who have mobilized primarily in terms of an ethnic-group identity different from the majority *mestizo* national identity have sought collective rights to land and culture. There also seems to be a strong spatial logic—rural versus urban—which may determine the kinds of rights that Afro-descendants have struggled for (and the kinds of organizations they have formed). Rural Afro-descendants, for example, often conceive of their collective identities in ethnic terms and emphasize the need for collective rights to land and culture. Meanwhile urban Afro-descendants have generally organized in terms of a racial group identity and have focused more on struggles for equal rights and positive anti-racial-discrimination rights. As a result, in many countries in Latin America, the struggles of urban and rural Afro-descendants have been somewhat disconnected from each other. This is not always the case, however—as in Brazil, where urban black movements appear to have championed the struggles for communal land rights of rural Afro-Brazilians, particularly *quilombo* communities (see Linhares 2004). It is also true that in a number of countries, Latin American Afro-descendants (especially, it seems, those where maroon communities are present) have organized as both ethnic and racial groups and have formed organizations that struggle for both kinds of collective rights, although they may emphasize one kind of normative justification for collective rights more than the other. This, for example, is the case with the Garifuna in Honduras (see Anderson 2007).

For many Latin American Afro-descendants, the issue of how they fit into the dominant categories of minority group rights in models of multiculturalism in the region has thus been a pressing question. The different types of collective rights accorded to Afro-descendants, and the changing forms of Afro-descendant identity are in a dialectical relationship to each other.[4] Identities are not static, and in Nicaragua in particular, the relevant question is how to understand changes in Creole collective identity in light of the various features of the model of multiculturalism adopted in the country since the 1980s.

The model of multiculturalism adopted in Nicaragua has generally been much more successful in recognizing the collective rights to land and culture of Afro-descendant *costeños*, but has been far less successful in addressing continuing racialized inequalities and persistent racial hierarchies that reproduce the political and social exclusion and impoverishment that continue to make Afro-descendants one of the most marginalized and vulnerable sectors of the population. The absence of positive anti-racial-discrimination rights in Nicaragua's multicultural model is emblematic of the general absence of an approach to how to overcome racial hierarchies that deny Afro-descendants their fair share of political power and equal access to educational and economic empowerment. In Nicaragua, for example, while Afro-descendant *costeños* have gained some of the most extensive rights to the protection of land and culture in the region, including regional autonomy, communal land rights, and bilingual education, it is also the case that they continue to be marginalized in the political structures of the country, including regional governments, and that they continue to suffer from racial discrimination and racism. Moreover, as a result of the regionalization of collective rights, Afro-descendants outside the Atlantic Coast have until recently had access to neither of the two types of collective rights described here (other than general anti-discrimination guarantees in the constitution that apply to all citizens).

CREOLE IDENTITY AND RACIAL POLITICS IN NICARAGUA

Historically, the dominant way in which Creoles have understood or portrayed their group identity has not necessarily been in terms of blackness. While their self-representations have shifted over time, it is safe to say that although Creoles are the group most closely associated with African descent in Nicaragua, this is not the only or even the dominant way in which they have understood and described their own identity.

Creoles live on the Atlantic Coast of Nicaragua, where they are the largest Afro-descendant group. The Atlantic Coast is very different from the rest of Nicaragua, which is generally portrayed (in historiography and nationalist ideology) as a uniformly *mestizo* nation (Gould 1998). Yet this self-understanding bears little, if any, resemblance to the reality on the Atlantic Coast, a region that encompasses approximately 50 percent of the national territory and 10 percent of the country's population. The Mosquito Coast (as it was then known) did not officially become a part of the Nicaraguan republic until 1894; prior to that it was a British protectorate. Today the region is inhabited by six distinct ethno-racial groups, including three indigenous groups, the Miskitus, Mayangnas, and Ramas; two groups of African descent, Creoles and Garifuna; and *mestizos*, who began migrating to the region after 1894. The region was never fully integrated into Nicaraguan political, economic, or sociocultural life, and its indigenous and Afro-descendant inhabitants thus possess languages, cultures, and collective identities that are quite different from the dominant Indo-Hispanic culture and *mestizo* identity of the rest of Nicaragua.

Creoles (not to be confused with *criollos*, the term used to describe Spaniards born in the Americas during the colonial era) were a group of free people of color that emerged in the late eighteenth century on the southern Mosquito Coast. They were of mixed African, Amerindian, and European descent—predominantly mulattos descended from free and enslaved Africans who had arrived on the Mosquito Coast in the seventeenth century and formed maroon communities at Bluefields and what had been other British settler communities after the departure of the British at the end of the eighteenth century. They developed a creolized English language and hybrid culture. By the nineteenth century, Creoles were identified primarily as a group of African descent. Creoles became increasingly socially and politically dominant on the Mosquito Coast over the course of the nineteenth century, to the extent that by mid-century, they were vying for political power in the region with the Miskitu. By the end of the nineteenth century, Creoles played a central role in the politics and society of the Mosquito Coast. Beginning in the late nineteenth century, but particularly during the first half of the twentieth century, when banana companies and other North American business interests were dominant on the Atlantic Coast, the region had a high rate of immigration of West Indian (especially Jamaican) laborers, who came to work on banana plantations as well as for mining and logging companies. While some of these workers returned to their home countries, many stayed on the Atlantic Coast and were absorbed into the Creole group (Gordon 1998, 66–67).

According to Edmund T. Gordon, over time, Creoles developed multiple strands of what he calls "Creole common sense" to describe their collective identity, which they deployed at different times. These included a black racial identity conceived as linked to transnational African Diaspora communities elsewhere in the Americas, and an "ethnic" identity defined in terms of the group's cultural difference from Indo-Hispanic Nicaragua due to its links to Anglo-Saxon cultures and societies. Gordon argues that there was a shift in Creole political activism and sensibilities throughout the twentieth century, from an initial rejection of the Nicaraguan state in the period immediately following the annexation of the region to Nicaragua in 1894, to greater acceptance from the 1930s to the 1960s. In terms of racial politics, he argues that the 1920s saw heightened Creole activism associated with Garveyism, while in the 1960s, as the Civil Rights Movement was unfolding in the United States, Creoles developed a cultural movement that explicitly contested racial discrimination (Gordon 1998, 51–85). This movement dissipated with the triumph of the Sandinista revolution in 1979, but has arguably reemerged in recent years among Creoles, after the implementation of multicultural policies.

During the 1980s, Creoles were in open conflict with the Nicaraguan state. They, like most other *costeños*, had not been involved in the struggle of the FSLN (the Frente Sandinista de Liberación Nacional, or Sandinista National Liberation Front) to overthrow the authoritarian regime of the Somoza family, which had dominated Nicaraguan politics from the 1930s until 1979. By the early 1980s, *costeños* had become disenchanted with the Sandinista government.[5] Indeed, many *costeños*—including some Creoles, but especially the Miskitu—joined the *contras* (the counterrevolutionary guerrilla forces that were trying to overthrow the FSLN with the aid of the United States) at this time. In an attempt to resolve the armed conflict on the Atlantic Coast and mute international condemnation, the *Sandinistas* adopted a number of multicultural policies in 1986. As a consequence, the Nicaraguan state adopted constitutional language that enshrined a multiethnic, regional model of autonomy in which all *costeños* shared equally in self-government.

The Nicaraguan constitution approved in 1986 recognized the "multiethnic nature" of the Nicaraguan nation and enshrined the following collective rights for all the "communities of the Atlantic Coast": to preserve and develop their distinct cultures, languages, and religions; to establish their own forms of social organization and administer their local affairs according to their historical traditions; to have ownership of their communal lands; to use and benefit from the region's natural resources; and to enjoy regional autonomy (Constitución Política 1987). Additionally, the Autonomy Law approved the same year establishes an autonomy regime for the Atlantic Coast, within which "the members of the communities of the Atlantic Coast" are guaranteed "absolute equality of rights and responsibilities, regardless of population size and level of development" (Estatuto de Autonomía 1987). Creoles thus have the same rights as other *costeños* in Nicaragua's model of multiculturalism, which grants the same levels of rights to Afro-descendants and indigenous peoples on the Atlantic Coast.

In Nicaragua's model of multiculturalism, heterogeneous multiracial and multiethnic regions for the exercise of self-government were created. The Autonomy Law divides the Atlantic Coast into two administrative units: the Northern Autonomous Region of the Atlantic Coast (RAAN) and the Southern Autonomous Region of the Atlantic Coast (RAAS). Two indigenous groups (Miskitus and Mayangnas), one Afro-descendant group (Creoles), and *mestizos* inhabit the Northern Autonomous Region, or RAAN. Three indigenous groups (Miskitu, Mayangna, and Ramas), two Afro-descendant groups (Creoles and Garifunas), and *mestizos* inhabit the Southern Autonomous Region, or RAAS. Currently, *mestizos* are estimated to constitute a demographic majority in both regions. The Miskitus are the second-largest group in the RAAN, where they are concentrated, followed by the Mayangnas and small numbers of Creoles. In the RAAS, where they have historically settled, Creoles are the second-largest group, followed by small numbers of Miskitus, Mayangnas, Ramas, and Garifunas.

Because of the decision to create heterogeneous regions for the exercise of autonomy, rather than spatially segregated units controlled by each group, Creoles did not gain a national homeland over which they could exercise exclusive control with the adoption of multicultural policies in the 1980s. The multicultural policies adopted in Nicaragua in the 1980s instead set up a context in which Creoles find themselves sometimes collaborating, but also sometimes competing, with two other powerful groups on the Atlantic Coast: *mestizos* on the one hand, who have continued to play an important role in the region's politics since the adoption of regional autonomy, and indigenous *costeños* on the other hand—who have often been allies in struggles for justice and equality, but have also historically been rivals for power.

Demographic changes on the Atlantic Coast have played an important role in shaping the shifting context of Creole politics and identity today. For example, while the Atlantic Coast continues to be identified with its original Afro-descendant and indigenous inhabitants who controlled the region before the arrival of *mestizos*, as a result of intensifying migration, *mestizos* are now the majority of the population in the region.[6] This shift has taken place against the backdrop of existing rivalries between Afro-descendant and indigenous *costeños*. As the two dominant groups on the Atlantic Coast before it became a part of Nicaragua, Creoles and Miskitus have traditionally seen each other as rivals for political power, and tensions between them can be traced back to the colonial period. Since the adoption of multicultural rights in the 1980s, indigenous political movements have been much more visible and powerful than Afro-descendant ones on the Atlantic Coast. It is against this backdrop that current shifts in Creole identity and political mobilization are taking place.

CREOLE POLITICS AND IDENTITY IN THE MULTICULTURAL STATE

Creole politics and identity have not remained static since the adoption of multi-cultural rights in Nicaragua. Instead, there have been important shifts in the way Afro-descendant Creoles are currently imagining the collective identities on the basis of which they are mobilizing politically. Indeed, it is in the context of official multicul-turalism that the current emphasis on a black racial group identity among Creoles is taking place. This shift in Creole identity can be seen in the changing terms or labels by which the group itself is being described by its own members. For example, recently it has become more common for younger Creole intellectuals to make a distinction between "black" and "white" Creoles when referring to darker- and lighter-skinned members of the group, a distinction that often, though not always, corresponds to social-class position, with the former being less well educated and wealthier than the latter. The use of the "black" and "white" Creole labels suggests that currently, certain Creoles see themselves as a cultural group of which those who identify with a black racial group identity are a subset. In this sense, the use of the terms black and white is not simply descriptive of skin color or phenotype, it is also indicative of patterns of self-identification with blackness among Creoles, and of political mobilization on the basis of a black racial group identity as well.[7]

The emphasis on, or reassertion of, a black identity conceived in terms of trans-national connections to the African Diaspora among Nicaraguan Creoles in recent years has manifested itself in various forms. In what remains of this essay, I am going to focus on three areas where this shift can be observed: (1) political mobilization, including the creation of Creole political parties that emphasize a black racial group identity; (2) struggles for communal land rights; and (3) civil society activism around racism and in favor of positive anti-racial-discrimination rights.

Since the 1990s, there have been tangible changes in Creole political activism, from the creation of and participation in what were generally conceived as multiethnic political parties, to the rise of a political party called Coast Power (also known as the Coast People Political Movement) founded in 2005 by prominent Creole political leaders, whose aim is to achieve greater Creole/black representation in the regional governments on the Atlantic Coast. Publicly, Coast Power's stated goal is the promo-tion of *Costeñismo* (a concept it defines rather vaguely), but it is widely perceived as a Creole political movement that emphasizes a strong black racial group identity among Creoles. For the 2006 regional elections in the RAAS, for example, Coast Power en-tered into an electoral alliance with YATAMA—*Yapti Tasba Masraka Nani* or descendants of mother earth in Miskitu, the main indigenous political organization in Nicaragua, which is an almost exclusively Miskitu party in its leadership, membership, and vot-ing base. This led to 40 percent of YATAMA/Coast Power candidates to the RAAS Regional Council being Creole, the largest percentage ever put forward by a regional or national political party.[8] Similarly, in the Miskitu-dominated RAAN, where Creoles are feeling a growing sense of social and political marginalization—particularly in the capital city of Bilwi, where a thriving Creole community used to exist—the past couple of years have seen the emergence of a small but vocal black movement (see Rigby 2007). Creoles' feeling of marginalization in Bilwi and the RAAN is aggravated by the view of some Miskitus that land rights are "indigenous rights" and therefore do not apply to Creoles, because Afro-descendants do not have the same spiritual connection to the land as indigenous peoples.

The struggle for the demarcation and titling of communal lands is also an area where we can observe shifts in Creole self-making strategies and their political activism. As noted above, struggles for communal land rights pose important chal-lenges for Afro-descendants because they have generally been seen as indigenous rights par excellence. For Nicaraguan Creoles, this has been a complicated arena as well. On the one hand, the legal categories adopted in Nicaragua with regard to communal land rights were inclusive of Afro-descendant *costeños*, yet they nevertheless seemed to privilege static understandings of collective identity that weakened the legitimacy of Creole land claims (see Goett 2007). In the 1990s, this political-institutional context appears to have led communities with mixed ancestry engaged in struggles for communal lands to privilege indigenous rather than Afro-descendant identifications (see Hale, Gurdian, and Gordon 2003). On the other hand, there have also been instances of collaboration between indigenous peoples and Afro-descendant communities making joint land claims on the Atlantic Coast, as in the case of the Rama-Creole Territory in the RAAS, which encompasses both indigenous Rama and Afro-descendant Garifuna-Creole communities. In fact, in recent years, organizing around struggles for communal land rights appears to have been a site for the strengthening of Creole identity.

It is thus possible to observe the emergence of a strong discourse of a black racial group identity conceived in terms of transnational links to other people of African descent in the Diaspora among some Creoles involved in communal land demarcation processes. For urban Afro-descendant Creole communities in the RAAS, for example, the adoption of a new Communal Property Law in 2002, which established the mechanisms for the demarcation and titling of *costeño* communal lands, was a galvanizing moment that led them to organize and elect communal boards to carry out land claims. The requirements of Law 445 (as it is known) call for detailed ethnohistorical mapping, including (1) an account of the community's historical antecedents; (2) its demographic, social, economic, and cultural characteristics; (3) the traditional forms of land and resource use practiced in the community; (4) an account of overlapping claims and conflicts over boundaries with other communities or *terceros* (third parties) and of communities, entities, or persons occupying adjacent lands to those being claimed (Ley del Régimen de Propiedad, 2003: articulo 46). Creole mobilization in Bluefields to fulfill these requirements and to constitute the communal authorities recognized by Law 445 seems to have spurred political organizing in terms explicitly linked to a black racial group identity and to the idea of regaining Creole communal lands. In a call for Creoles to attend a meeting to elect representatives to the communal boards in 2003, for example, a prominent longtime Creole politician, Pentecostal church leader, and past president of the RAAS Regional Council exhorted listeners of his popular radio show to attend in order to decide "who is going to represent you as *black*, [who] is going to represent you before the central government and the region" (Rayfield Hodgson, cited in Goett 2007, 367).

Another area in which these shifts in Creole identity and politics can be observed is in the increasing activism around racism and in favor of positive anti-racial-discrimination rights by Creole civil society organizations. In recent years, Afro-descendant *costeños* for the first time formed a National Commission of Afro-descendant Peoples, composed of Garífuna and (mostly) Creole civil society organizations. In 2009, among other resolutions, the commission "demanded the visibilization of the Kriol[9] and Garífuna populations as *'Afro descendant Peoples'* in national legislation, public policy and any other national documentation regarding these historically invisibilized peoples, deprived of their political, economic and social rights and excluded from the processes of decision-making and communal, regional and national development" (Comisión Nacional de Pueblos Afro-descendientes 2009 [emphasis in the original]). As a result of their mobilization, Creole NGOs were able to successfully persuade the National Assembly to declare the International Day Against Racism a national holiday, and to formulate and include penalties for crimes of racial discrimination in the penal code for the first time in Nicaragua's history.

Creole NGOs and civil society organizations have also forcefully protested examples of racist treatment of Afro-descendants in national life. The shadow report to the Committee on the Elimination of Racial Discrimination (CERD) produced by Creole civil society organizations, for example, noted the routine racist depictions of the Atlantic Coast—and particularly its Afro-descendant inhabitants—that continue to appear in the national media in Nicaragua, particularly the two largest newspapers in the country, *La Prensa* and *El Nuevo Diario.* This despite the fact that, as a result of pressure from *costeño* civil society organizations, these news outlets have been forced to apologize in the past for their racist depictions of the region and of black people. According to the report, "The media tend to ridicule the cultural celebrations of indigenous and Afro-descendant peoples, making them appear degenerate or perverted . . . they promote the use of racist popular sayings [*refranes*], as well as the caricaturing of indigenous [people] and Afro-descendants in the national newspapers" (JEHN-CEDEHCA 2008, 17). The report also noted the virtual absence of Afro-descendants in national government posts during the two center-right administrations of Arnoldo Alemán (1997–2001) and Enrique Bolaños (2002–2006), a situation that has changed dramatically since the FSLN's victory in the presidential elections of 2006, as the FSLN has appointed a number of Afro-descendant (and indigenous) *costeños* to prominent government posts as a result of its electoral alliance with YATAMA (for a list of these posts, see JEHN-CEDEHCAA 2008, 24).

One of the most visible examples of this upsurge in Creole civil society activism around racism and its effect in spurring national discussions about racial discrimination in Nicaragua has been the so-called Chamán case, in which a Creole legislator before the Central American Parliament (PARLACEN), Brigette Budier, was denied entrance to a popular nightclub in Managua. As the lead paragraph of an article about the case, entitled "Disco's Door Policy Sparks Race Debate," explains: "It's happened countless times before, in establishments all across the country: a black person denied entrance because of racial discrimination" (Rogers 2009). Budier brought her case before the national media and the Human Rights Ombudsman's office and filed a legal complaint, which led government prosecutors to open the first-ever racial-discrimination investigation in Nicaragua's history, under the new penalties for racist conduct that Creole activists succeeded in inserting in the penal code. The investigation of the admission policies of various upscale nightclubs in Managua garnered significant attention from the public, and led to a heated debate about whether the investigation had been politically motivated, as some argued, or if this had indeed been an instance of racism. As the same article explains, the Chamán case "has forced the country to confront its long-ignored culture of racism" in a very public way. The current emphasis on asserting a black racial group identity among Creoles, and the consequent focus on political activism around racial discrimination, is thus forcing the Nicaraguan state to begin to recognize the persistence of racial hierarchy in the country despite the existence of official multiculturalism, and to implement specific policies to combat racism and racial discrimination.

It is important to understand why Creoles have begun to emphasize a black racial-group identity understood in transnational terms as part of an international network of people of African descent in the Diaspora. I would suggest that for Creoles, who as a group have long been culturally distinct from the rest of Nicaragua, this shift has enabled them to find a language with which to describe the kinds of racialized oppression to which they are subject and which cannot be encompassed solely by the language of cultural difference. In trying to make visible the continued operation of racism in Nicaragua despite the existence of official multiculturalism, they seem to be drawing on links to other people of African descent whose struggles can serve as models for their own.

The implication of this analysis of Creole politics for studies of Afro-Latin American political mobilization more broadly is that such shifts in the way Afro-descendants conceive and represent their collective identities should not be seen as either foreign, imperial impositions or as inauthentic, cynical attempts to gain rights from the state, but rather as creative, organic responses to changing circumstances. In other words, they should be viewed as *self-generated* strategies for negotiating official multicultural models whose categories do not always readily recognize Afro-descendants, and which might nevertheless continue to conceal persistent racial hierarchies. As scholars of the African Diaspora have noted, the identities of black diasporic subjects are always constituted on multiple levels; what is necessary is to pay close attention to the specific ways in which Afro-descendant identities in Latin America are being re-imagined by different discursive means to meet the different political contexts in which their struggles for justice and equality are taking place.

In conclusion, multicultural policies have both had an impact on the self-making strategies of Nicaraguan Creoles, and have in turn been shaped by the forms of activism that are emerging from current imaginings of Creole identity. Such shifts are not always welcome, and may sometimes be viewed as threatening. For instance, in a recent discussion on *costeño* communal land rights and political empowerment, a long-standing Miskitu political leader observed that the younger generation of Creole leaders (those who are now in their thirties and forties) are much more confrontational and difficult to deal with than the older generation (those in their sixties and seventies). Setting aside questions of personal relationships and generational divides, it seems clear that this perception is related to the ways in which Creoles are currently conceiving and representing their collective identity, and the kinds of political mobilization they are undertaking as a result. In Nicaragua today, Creoles are finding new ways to struggle for justice and equality in a changing political-institutional context. Shifts in Creole self-representation correspond to the salience and relevance of particular forms of identity in different circumstances—in this case, a strong racial-group identity articulated in terms of blackness that seems to better meet the terrain of struggle in which they find themselves, one in which an official multiculturalism that recognizes cultural or "ethnic" identity exists, but racism has still not been fully grappled with. Moreover, it is also important to note that the assertion of a strong black racial group identity among Creoles has not precluded their collaboration and alliance with indigenous *costeños*. What we may be seeing in Nicaragua is thus the emergence of a strong black racial group identity among Creoles that parallels the existing strength of indigenous, and particularly Miskitu, collective identity and political activism. Most centrally, this shift in Creole identity and politics is beginning to force the Nicaraguan state and public to grapple with the continued existence of racial hierarchy in the country, a persistent feature of national life that has not been fully recognized despite the adoption of multicultural rights more than two decades ago.

NOTES

This essay is reprinted courtesy of the University Press of Florida. It originally appeared in 2012 in *Comparative Perspectives on Afro-Latin America*, eds. Kwame Dixon and John Burdick (Gainesville, FL: The University Press of Florida).

1. The population of the Atlantic Coast as a whole is the sum of the 306,510 inhabitants of the South Atlantic Autonomous Region (RAAS), where most Creoles live, and the 314,130 inhabitants of the North Atlantic Autonomous Region (RAAN). According to the census there are also 3,271 self-identified Garifuna in the country as a whole (INEC, 2006, 52, 54, 184). The 2005 census did not include categories for non-Creole or non-Garifuna Afro-descen-

dants. The figures for the total Creole population provided by the 2005 census are quite low, significantly lower than previous estimates of the size of this group. This may be due to high levels of migration outside the country, particularly to the United States and Caribbean countries such as the Cayman Islands, that began in the 1970s as the Sandinista struggles against the Somoza regime intensified. This out-migration has continued in recent decades with the phenomenon of "ship-out" (by which Creoles, especially men, leave to perform relatively well-paid menial labor on cruise ships) or other forms of temporary labor migration.

2. This discussion of the kinds of collective rights gained by Latin American Afro-descendants and their relationship to the kinds of collective identities they have formulated, and forms of political organization they have developed, is a further refined version of a discussion that originally appeared in Hooker 2008.

3. For an elaboration of the normative justifications of different types of minority group rights, see Kymlicka 1995. For a critique of this bifurcation in conceptions of collective rights for minority groups in theories of multiculturalism, and a discussion of how this fails to address the complex situation of Latin American Afro-descendants in particular, see Hooker 2009.

4. For instance, according to Eduardo Restrepo, following constitutional changes in Colombia in the 1990s, there was a shift in Afro-Colombian identity from an emphasis on a racial group identity focused on struggles against racial discrimination, to an identity that is understood in explicitly ethnic terms and that privileges cultural and ethnic difference as the basis of black political projects (Restrepo 1997).

5. The conflict stemmed from the Sandinista government's initial hostility to demands for self-government by Creoles and other *costeños*. Creoles initially welcomed the Sandinista triumph, because they believed it would allow them to realize their demands for self-government, but these goals were not easily reconciled with the FSLN's brand of *mestizo* nationalism. As a result, their initial support for the revolution turned into active resistance by 1981. By 1984 the Atlantic Coast was a war zone, and the FSLN's international image had been damaged by accusations that it had committed human rights violations against indigenous groups.

6. The growing size of the *mestizo* population in the region has had serious consequences for the distribution of political power on the Atlantic Coast, particularly the composition of the regional governments. The net effect has been *mestizo* preponderance in both regional councils. Between 1990 and 2010, for example, 52 percent of regional-council members in the RAAS have been *mestizos*, while only 25 percent have been Creole (see González Pérez 2008, 226–228).

7. The case of the Garifuna in Nicaragua appears to be different, as they have always emphasized their black identity and participated in transnational Garifuna associations and networks of black organizations, such as ONECA (Organización Negra Centroamericana).

8. The regional councils are the legislative bodies of the autonomous regions. Together with the regional coordinator or governor (who is elected from the ranks of the council, is the region's top executive, and may also serve as the representative of the central government in the region), they form the regional government for each autonomous region. The members of the regional council are elected in regional elections in which only inhabitants of the Atlantic Coast or their descendants are allowed to vote and run for office. Each regional council has forty-five members.

9. Due to its phonetic spelling in Spanish, *Creole* and *Kriol* are used interchangeably or jointly in Nicaragua. The census category, for example, is "Creole (Kriol)."

REFERENCES

Anderson, Mark. 2007. "When Afro Becomes (Like) Indigenous: Garifuna and Afro-Indigenous Politics in Honduras." *Journal of Latin American and Caribbean Anthropology* 12(2) (November):384–413.

Burch, Audra S. 2007. "Afro-Latin Americans, A Rising Voice: Nicaragua." *Miami Herald*, 10 June.

Comisión Nacional de Pueblos Afro-descendientes. 2009. "Resolución 21 de Marzo: Día Internacional para la Eliminación de la Discriminación Racial." Nicaragua.

Cunningham Kain, Myrna. 2006. "Racism and Ethnic Discrimination in Nicaragua." Nicaragua: Centro para la Autonomía y Desarrollo de los Pueblos Indígenas.

Goett, Jennifer. 2007. "Diasporic Identities, Autochthonous Rights: Race, Gender, and the Cultural Politics of Creole Land Rights in Nicaragua." PhD dissertation, University of Texas-Austin.

González Pérez, Miguel. 2008. "Governing Multi-Ethnic Societies in Latin America: Regional Autonomy, Democracy, and the State in Nicaragua, 1987–2007." PhD dissertation, York University.

Gordon, Edmund T. 1998. *Disparate Diasporas: Identity and Politics in an African Nicaraguan Community.* 1st ed. Austin: University of Texas Press.

Gould, Jeffrey L. 1998. *To Die in This Way: Nicaraguan Indians and the Myth of Mestizaje, 1880–1965.* Durham, NC: Duke University Press.

Hale, Charles R., Galio C. Gurdian, and Edmund T. Gordon. 2003. "Rights, Resources and the Social Memory of Struggle: Reflections on a Study of Indigenous and Black Community Land Rights on Nicaragua's Atlantic Coast." *Human Organization* 62(4):369–381.

Hooker, Juliet. 2008. "Afro-Descendant Struggles for Collective Rights in Latin America." *Souls: A Critical Journal of Black Politics, Culture and Society* 10(3):279–291.

———. 2009. *Race and the Politics of Solidarity.* New York: Oxford University Press.

———. 2010. "Race and the Space of Citizenship: The Mosquito Coast and the Place of Blackness and Indigeneity in Nicaragua." In *Blacks and Blackness in Central America: Between Race and Place,* ed. Lowell Gudmundson and Justin Wolfe, 246–277. Durham, NC: Duke University Press.

INEC. 2006. *VIII Censo de Población y IV de Vivienda: Población, Características Educativas.* Vol. 2. Managua, Nicaragua: Instituto Nacional de Estadísticas y Censos, November.

JEHN-CEDEHCA. 2008. "Informe Alternativo: Implementación de la Convención Internacional Para la Eliminación de la Discriminación Racial (CEDR)." Regiones Autónomas de la Costa Caribe: Centro de Derechos Humanos, Ciudadanos y Autónomicos y el Movimiento Jóvenes Estableciendo Nuevos Horizontes.

Kymlicka, Will. 1995. *Multicultural Citizenship: A Liberal Theory of Minority Rights.* Oxford: Oxford University Press.

Linhares, Luiz Fernando do Rosário. 2004. "Kilombos of Brazil: Identity and Land Entitlement." *Journal of Black Studies* 34(6):817–837.

Nicaragua, Asamblea Nacional de. 1987. *Constitución Política de Nicaragua.* Managua, Nicaragua: Editorial el Amanecer.

———. 1987. *Estatuto de Autonomía de las Regiones de la Costa Atlántica de Nicaragua.* Managua, Nicaragua: Editorial Jurídica.

————. 2003. *Ley del Régimen de Propiedad Comunal de los Pueblos Indígenas y Comunidades Étnicas de las Regiones Autonómas de la Costa Atlántica de Nicaragua y de los Ríos Bocay, Coco, Indio y Maíz*. Managua, Nicaragua: Editorial Jurídica.

PNUD. 2005. *Informe de Desarollo Humano 2005. Las regiones autonómas de la Costa Caribe: Nicaragua asume su diversidad?* Managua, Nicaragua: Programa de Naciones Unidas para el Desarollo.

Restrepo, Eduardo. 1997. "Afro-Colombianos, antropología y proyecto de modernidad en Colombia." In *Antropología en la modernidad: Identidades, etnicidades y movimientos sociales en Colombia*, ed. María Victoria Uribe and Eduardo Restrepo, 279–319. Bogotá: Instituto Colombiano de Antropología.

Rigby, Betty. 2007. "Vida sociocultural de los Creoles de Bilwi." Master's thesis, URACCAN.

Rogers, Tim. 2009. "Disco's Door Policy Sparks Race Debate: Brigette Budier Has Become the Nicaraguan Rosa Parks." *Nica Times*, February 27–March 5.

Ethnic Identity and Political Mobilization: The Afro-Colombian Case

Leonardo Reales Jiménez

In 1995 I was the student with the darkest skin color at the University of the Andes, one of the most influential academic institutions in Colombia. I was the only Afro-indigenous person out of more than ten thousand students. Some colleagues called me "the Negro of the university" and made jokes about my indigenous background. I did not know how to respond to their racist verbal attacks. My ethnic identity did not exist at that time, and for many reasons I was confused about my weak racial ("skin-color") identity.

In the late 1990s I joined the Afro-Colombian National Movement CIMAR-RON. While volunteering at CIMARRON, my Afro-Colombian (ethnic) identity grew significantly stronger. In 2001, after supporting local and national campaigns promoting affirmative-action policies for Afro-Colombians, I became the teacher of the "identity and political participation" workshop at the Afro-Colombian National School 'Nelson Mandela,' a training program on Afro-Colombian leadership, human rights, and social development. My shift from a weak "racial" identity to a strong ethnic identity was evident, and it did not take much time for me to be engaged in supporting the creation of a sociopolitical movement based on the Afro-Colombian ethnic identity discourse.

Many Afro-Colombian leaders have gone through similar (personal) experiences while acquiring and defending the so-called Afro-Colombian ethnic identity. Understanding how those leaders got involved in different Afro-Colombian struggles and identity discourses helps comprehend their contemporary political goals. The purpose of this text is twofold: (1) to explain why some Afro-Colombians' ethnic identity has been (is) weak, whereas others have historically maintained a strong one; and (2) to study in detail the main outcomes and current challenges of the Afro-Colombian communities' political mobilization produced as a result of their ethnic-identity-building process.

This chapter is divided into six parts: First, an introduction, in which an overview of the Afro-Colombian ethnic-identity discourse and its direct relationship to the "state ideology" is presented; second, prior relevant research and a theoretical framework regarding the study of Afro-Colombians and their ethnic identity are underlined; third, crucial aspects of Afro-Colombian history are studied; fourth, the institutionalization of the Afro-Colombians' ethnic identity is explained; fifth, the political mobilization and current agenda of Afro-Colombians are highlighted; and six, a conclusion, in which the main political challenges of the Afro-Colombian communities are underscored.

This chapter also describes the weak institutional change regarding the elimination of racist practices against Afro-Colombians. It should be pointed out that it took almost two hundred years of republican history to recognize the Afro-Colombian contribution to the nation. Not until 1991, through the (new) constitution, did the state (and the political elites) recognize, for the first time in national history, the existence of Afro-Colombians as a distinct ethnic group. Yet today, neither the Colombian state nor the national political elites have publicly recognized that racism and racial discrimination against Afro-Colombians have historically been definitive factors of national life.

After winning the war for independence in the nineteenth century, the state officially imposed the idea that Colombia was meant to be a Roman Catholic and homogenous (ethnic) nation despite its "racial" differences. Many Afro-Colombians believed that their "whitening" was an effective strategy to succeed socioeconomically and politically. Others did not follow the state ideology and defended their identity as a distinct group. The latter, however, did not construct an Afro-Colombian identity discourse (at the national level) that could have helped achieve their communities' cultural, political, or socioeconomic goals.

Some social researchers have underlined that this (political) discourse was created in the 1970s (Mosquera 2000), when Afro-Colombian organizations realized that it could be utilized as a decisive tool to politically mobilize the group, which was characterized by its weak social cohesion. Other academics indicate that the Afro-Colombian identity discourse should not and cannot be explained without taking into account the role of Afro-descendants during the colonial era and the war for independence. Both researchers and academics, however, fully agree that the challenges of the identity-building process of Afro-Colombians and their political mobilization as a group currently face the most complicated limitations that have ever existed in the country. This chapter explores those limitations while providing a broad explanation of Afro-Colombians' struggles throughout national contemporary history.

PREVIOUS RESEARCH AND THEORETICAL FRAMEWORK

Although there is still much research to be performed in order to explain the crucial contribution of Afro-descendants to Colombian politics, some authors have provided detailed analyses of historical (contemporary) experiences of Afro-Colombians. The following well-documented texts are critical sources for the study of the identity-building process of Afro-descendants in the country. The first one, *Racismo y discriminación racial en Colombia*, was written by Juan Mosquera (2000). His text is known as an extensively researched work that explores the goals of Afro-Colombian organizations and community leaders in the 1980s and 1990s. The second one, *Gente negra en Colombia: Dinámicas socio-políticas en Cali y el Pacífico*, is a recent book edited by Olivier Barbary and Fernando Urrea (2004). This text describes how political struggles in the Pacific region provided some political activists with an unprecedented opportunity to voice their thoughts while promoting an identity discourse. The third one, *Racismo y exclusión socio-racial en Colombia*, was written by the author in 2005. This text explains how both official and nonofficial racist practices have affected society throughout Colombian history. The fourth one, "La construcción del discurso étnico en la movilización política afrocolombiana (1970–2003)," is an undergraduate thesis that was written by Juan Estupiñán (2004), who studied in depth the characteristics of the Afro-Colombian identity discourse in the last three decades.

Agudelo (2002), Hoffmann (2002), Oslender (2002), Pardo (2002), Cunin (2003), and Restrepo (2004) have also written academic articles that explore or criticize the construction of such a political discourse and its unsuccessful effect on Afro-Colombian mobilization and political participation at the national level.

Other texts explain the socioeconomic and political context that characterizes the Afro-Colombian population as an ethnic group. It should be underscored that there are several authors who study racial exclusion in Colombia (Mosquera 2000; Sánchez and Bryan 2003; and Reales 2005). They focus on how Afro-Colombians were excluded from the political and higher-education systems until the 1990s. Their works are utilized to explain how the (unofficially recognized) racist practices have affected many Afro-Colombians' identity.

There is also a national human-rights framework that protects Afro-Colombians.

It is based on laws created to support minority (ethnic) populations. Documents and reports from the movement CIMARRON (2004) and the United Nations Mission to Colombia (2002) were analyzed in order to have a human-rights approach in this chapter.

I have made a great effort to examine the existing body of literature in Spanish and English (published in the United States and Colombia) in order to assemble the broadest array of relevant materials related to the text. Throughout the research process, I analyzed the key contribution made by Afro-Colombian organizations in both the academic sphere and political discourses in Colombia, which warrants further examination and represents a critical supplement to research works of this kind.[1]

Afro-Colombian (ethnic) identity has been a very complex term for academics to define. The self-identification issue, as a matter of fact, complicated the implementation of Law 70 (Law of Black Communities), as some public institutions (or even Afro-Colombian organizations) did not accept that certain people should identify themselves as Afro-descendant. Some Afro-Colombians still believe that in order to exercise Law 70's special rights, the beneficiary has to be Afro-Colombian in skin color (meaning a black person), while others defend people's ancestry as the main label of Afro-Colombian identity.

The above controversy about who belongs to the Afro-Colombian communities and who does not, and how one might define Afro-Colombian identity, resulted in the creation of two theoretical discourses that still lead the study of Afro-Colombians as an ethnic group: the so-called Creole-genetic discourse and the Afro-genetic one (Restrepo 2003). Both discourses are known for leading the study of Afro-descendants in the country. Both discourses also focus on the continuities and breakups of African ethnic groups' legacies in the Americas, as well as the contribution of their descendants to society (Estupiñán 2004). These discourses, however, define Afro-Colombian identity from different perspectives, as will be argued below.

Creole-genetic researchers, represented in the work of Wade (1997), Escobar (1997), Pardo (2000), and Hoffmann (2001), understand Afro-Colombian identity as a result of the group's collective memory. This memory is related to the way leaders and activists assess distinct historical events that influence or feed the sense of belonging to Afro-Colombian communities as an ethnic group. From this perspective, Afro-Colombian leaders and political activists seek to strengthen such a sense of ethnic belonging and/or consciousness to make it easier to negotiate claims with the state (Estupiñán 2004).

Creole-genetic authors argue that most Afro-descendants lost their link to Africa once they arrived in the Americas. These authors note that ancestral knowledge disappeared as a result of slave trade–related issues. They tend to point out that the reconstruction of Afro-Colombian identity should be based only on the historical facts that occurred in the Americas, including the social interaction of Afro-Colombians with "whites," mestizos, and indigenous persons (Estupiñán 2004). For these authors, Afro-Colombian leaders and political activists should stop thinking of Africa as a reference for their identity-building process.

The Afro-genetic perspective, which is represented in the work of Escalante (1964), De Friedemann (1993), Romero (1998), Maya (1998), Oslender (2002), and Arocha (2004), portrays Afro-Colombian ethnic identity as a direct product of the African groups' legacy and heritage throughout Colombia. Afro-genetic authors argue that some Afro-Colombian communities survived and defended a strong (and diverse) identity based on their ancestral sociocultural expressions and religious practices (Oslender 2002; Reales 2005). Most of these expressions come from West Africa, the region of origin of the vast majority of Afro-descendants in Latin America (Maya 1998; and Estupiñán 2004).

Afro-genetic authors ensure that Afro-Colombian ethnic identity may be seen as the product of the communities' resistance to colonial and republican (institutionalized) racist practices and ethnic homogenization projects. Afro-genetic authors emphasize that the only way to comprehend the ethnic identity of many Afro-Colombians is through the analysis of their African roots, and the way these roots were "easily reproduced" in regions such as the coastal areas, where Afro-Colombians settled and have lived since colonial times.

It should be pointed out that both Creole-genetic and Afro-genetic authors defend the human-rights treaties and national laws that protect Afro-Colombians as a group. They also generally agree with the definition of low political mobilization of Afro-Colombians as this group's attempt to influence the existing distribution of power (Mosquera 2000).

Terms such as Afro-descendants, people of African descent, or Afro-Colombians were not used in the nineteenth century. Those concepts were recently created to sociopolitically mobilize Afro-descendants in several places. The Europeans (and their "white" and "mestizo" descendants) called the people of African descent *negros*, *pardos*, *morochos*, *morenos*, *mulatos*, and *zambos* (Reales 2001). These racist terms persisted in most Latin American countries in spite of the abolition of slavery and the approval of equity laws. These terms come from the socio-racial structure inherited from the colonial era. As Anthony Marx (1998) would say, the Colombian state created "race" while imposing the idea of the pursuit of a national homogenization. This is why "whitening" practices like the ones inscribed in the Brazilian social order, were (are) present throughout Colombia. However, one cannot make generalizations about this aspect, given the ethnic self-awareness of some Afro-Colombians. Who then are they, and why is it common to find different reactions to state discourses among

Afro-descendant people? The author intends to answer these questions in the following pages.

WHO ARE THE AFRO-COLOMBIANS?

The experiences of Afro-descendants across Colombia are complex and diverse, even when most of them have historically remained (equally) ignored by the Colombian state. The Afro-Colombian population ranges from a large numerical majority in coastal regions or other territories they have settled in since escaping slavery, to a small numerical minority in other zones. There are variations in tradition (and even in language), and they descend from different tribal groups across Africa (Minority Rights Group International 1995). Some Afro-Colombian leaders think, however, that they have been, and are being, successful in forging a common identity under the rubric of all being Afro-descendants, bearing the same negative legacy of slavery and racism that their ancestors began fighting centuries ago.

It should be underlined how important self-identification can be for Afro-Colombians as an ethnic group. Constitutionally, belonging to an ethnic group means being able to make particular rights claims upon the state. This is one of the main reasons why defining the Afro-Colombian population is relevant at both human-rights and political levels.

According to the Afro-Colombian Plan of Development (1999), which is considered by many Afro-Colombians as the most important "ethnic development" official report ever in the country, the term *Afro-Colombian population* refers not only to the people physically identified as "black," but also to those persons whose African background is "evident" as regards their cultural expressions. This report states that the terms *ethnic* and *cultural* may be used interchangeably when defining Afro-Colombian communities and other minority groups. The same document establishes that both the phenotype and cultural characteristics should *always* be taken into account when locating, counting, and evaluating the Afro-Colombian population as an ethnic group.[2]

In order to make it easier to identify Afro-Colombians based on their appearance, Mosquera (2000) suggests dividing them into three groups: Afro-Creoles, Afro-mestizos and Afro-indigenous. Afro-Creoles are those who keep a similar phenotype as black Africans. These Afro-Colombians were (are) called "Negros" by "whites" and "mestizos." Most Afro-Creoles live in the coastal regions as well as in highly populated cities.

Afro-mestizos are "mixed people" of (white) European and (black) African origin. In the colonial era they were called "mulattos," an offensive term that is still used by some Colombians. Most Afro-mestizos live in the Caribbean region, even though many of them are settled in big cities. Afro-indigenous people have African and indigenous backgrounds. They live in the valleys of the Caribbean region. It should be noted, however, that most of these people neither identify themselves as Afro-Colombian nor as indigenous, mainly due to internalized racism practices that affect Colombian society.

Two Afro-Creole communities are always the subject of special attention when defining Afro-Colombians as an ethnic group: the *raizales* and the *palenqueros*. As the Colombian Ministry of Interior (1998) underscored, the Afro-Colombian *raizales* (on San Andrés Island) are a "unique" ethnic community in the country. The *raizales* speak both *bandé* (a language of African origin) and English and have religious traditions that are not practiced anywhere else in the country. Despite the state recognition of the *raizales*, their people are permanent victims of racist practices that have produced internalized racism problems among them. Some *raizales* do not even speak Spanish, but they still hear from intellectuals that their nation's motherland is Spain, which tends to negatively affect their heritage as an ethnic community (Mitchell 2002).

The heritage and history of the *palenqueros* has also been ignored, even when the UN Educational, Scientific and Cultural Organization (UNESCO) declared this Afro-Colombian community as a patrimony of humanity. The *palenqueros* live in Palenque de San Basilio, a small town founded by escaped slaves four centuries ago that is well known for being the *first free town in the Americas*. Central for this community is the language of *Palenquero*, the only Creole language in the Americas comprising a Spanish basis with some characteristics of Bantu languages (De Friedemann 1993). The *palenqueros'* language constitutes a vital factor reinforcing ethnic and sociopolitical cohesion among community members.

The *palenqueros* are not only threatened by the market transformation, which shrinks local production modes, but also because the Colombian internal armed conflict is affecting their surroundings. Outside their small town, the *palenqueros* are commonly subjected to racial discrimination and ethnic stereotyping, leading to a denial of their cultural values. As UNESCO (2005) underlines, the increasing influence of commercial media and unsuitable basic education and high school curricula are rapidly eroding the community's heritage, which leads to cultural homogenization.

In short, Afro-Colombians are a diverse ethnic group. Their ancestors were (black) African slaves from several ethnic groups in Africa, who were brutally brought to the country against their will. As a result of racist practices and other human-rights violations against them, many Afro-Colombians have been affected by self-esteem problems. However, and despite the above threats, other Afro-Colombians have resisted the state ethnic projects and maintained their ethnic identity as a valuable cultural and political tool.

It should be mentioned that Colombian legislation establishes that individuals have the right to not identify as an ethnic minority. Some Afro-Colombians still do that. Denying the African or indigenous (ethnic) background is a common occurrence in certain parts, since some people believe that they are more likely to succeed socio-economically and politically if they deny their ethnic origins. This is why empowering Afro-Colombians based on their identity is not an easy task. Despite these historical obstacles, the Afro-Colombian identity-building process is slowly growing stronger throughout the country.

What Is Afro-Colombian Identity?

Individuals and groups create identities to live with their "own" personality. People, in fact, have the opportunity to know and interact with other identities (Ramos 2003). This is why there is a vast diversity of identities, and it is not surprising to find cases of multiple identities at different levels. Taylor (1994) suggests that a person's own identity is negotiated through dialogue—partly overt, partly internal—with others. Taylor's idea seems to be accurate, since identity-building processes depend on dialogical relations with others.

The fact that a person has two or three (ethnic) identities should not be surprising. This is a common occurrence among Afro-mestizos and Afro-indigenous activists whose self-awareness of their two or three ethnic backgrounds is strong. In Colombia, however, most people tend to exalt their European origin and avoid or deny their African and/or indigenous roots. In any case, there are no "natural" identities (Bayart 1996). All identities, including the ethnic ones, are created and subjected to permanent transformation.

The Afro-Colombian case is a good example of Bayart's idea. One cannot assume that Afro-Colombians have a "natural" ethnic identity. Some community leaders settled in the so-called Afro-Colombian ancestral territories argue that their traditions have been "naturally" transmitted for decades, suggesting the existence of a fixed identity. Although their intention is to reinforce cohesion among Afro-Colombians (particularly Afro-Creoles), the truth is that "Afro-centric" ideas have made those persons who have ambiguous feelings regarding their ethnic origin move away from the Afro-Colombian identity-building process.

A complete definition of Afro-Colombian identity may include elements from the two theoretical discourses studied in this text. This is why Afro-Colombian identity can be assessed as a response to both the negative legacy of slavery that Afro-Colombians' ancestors faced, and recent racist practices against them. As evidenced above, the diversity among Afro-Colombian communities is obvious, but their history of marginalization has been notoriously similar. This history is related to racist practices and constitutes the basis of their claims as an ethnic group.

The African-American identity discourse and other human-rights struggles have also had a decisive influence on the Afro-Colombian identity-building process. Behind the Afro-Colombian identity discourse is a political strategy that looks for the end of racist practices and other human-rights violations against people of African descent. This particular strategy is fed by collective memories that make it easier to promote and reinforce the social cohesion among Afro-Colombian communities.

Sánchez (1999) suggests that collective memories have been transmitted through many cultural traditions and sociopolitical mechanisms that inevitably influence Afro-Colombians' claims. These traditions and mechanisms should not be seen as "natural" issues. They may be (and are) transformed when circumstances affect, negatively or positively, the communities' lives. Collective memories include historical facts that have characterized the Afro-Colombian struggle for the respect of their rights. Those memories also serve as key references for the Afro-Colombian ethnic-identity-building process. This process should not be classified only as a political issue or just as a matter of cultural reference. As Ramos (2003) points out, a one-dimensional approach to the study of identities of diverse (ethnic) communities may be problematic, as occurs in the Afro-Colombian case.

In summary, Afro-Colombian identity, which is still under construction, may be defined as the self-awareness that many Afro-Colombians have with regard to their "belonging" to the diverse "Afro-descendant" group. This self-awareness is linked to memories that make it possible to classify them as an ethnic minority. It is correct to use the term *Afro-Colombian ethnic identity*, while understanding not only the political strategy that exists behind it but also its social goals. Among these goals, exalting Afro-Colombian history and promoting the elimination of racism and other human-rights violations remain as priorities.

AFRO-COLOMBIAN POLITICAL HISTORY

The Afro-Colombian ethnic-identity-building process and mobilization began to grow stronger in the late 1970s. That is why some authors tend to focus their research on this period when explaining the Afro-Colombian political situation and ethnic identity. I am skeptical about explaining these aspects without taking into account the historical legacy of Afro-Colombian communities. Pedro Ferrín, an Afro-Colombian leader and former congressman, asserts that "one cannot grasp the Afro-Colombians' political struggles without studying their history and contribution to the country."[3]

The history of Afro-Colombians is a critical reference of their ethnic-identity-building process and political mobilization. This history has been ignored by the Colombian state. As Mosquera (2000) would say, Afro-Colombians "shine for their invisibility" in the stories that most Colombian intellectuals usually tell about their nation. De Friedemann (1993) points out that the "invisibility" that has affected Afro-Colombian communities can be defined as the permanent negation of their African past, and the elites' idea that Afro-Colombians were (are) incapable of contributing to the country culturally, economically, or sociopolitically. This is why the Afro-Colombian legacy has remained "invisible" in school books for two hundred years of republican ("democratic") history.

Although Afro-Colombian communities have, for decades, experienced cultural imperialism,[4] some of them have consciously decided to exclude themselves from state policies and discourses as a strategy of resistance. They have historically settled in regions where the Colombian state has had limited presence or no presence at all. This helps explain why the elites were not fully successful in whitening and culturally dominating all Afro-Colombians. In any case, those Afro-Colombians who adopted the self-exclusion resistance struggle as a strategy to survive, and defend their ethnic "authenticity," have not succeeded politically or economically. In fact, most of them have continued living in marginalization and poverty, as if almost nothing has changed since slavery times.

Teaching Afro-Colombian history is paramount for many Afro-Colombian leaders. As will be argued in the last section of this chapter, Afro-Colombians have used "new" information (recent research) on historical events as a political tool to enforce the Afro-Colombian ethnic-identity discourse. It is important to emphasize that this discourse has not been (is not) fixed. Its supporters constantly bring it "up to date" in order to include not only the diversity among Afro-Colombian communities but also their "new" political challenges. This discourse is still under both construction and transformation, and it has been notoriously fed by local and foreign ethnic struggles, which have also relied on historical realities.

Afro-genetic authors have underscored how the strong political relationship between the Roman Catholic Church and the Spanish elites (and their descendants) made it possible to maintain the so-called African slavery in Latin America for more than three centuries. These elites dehumanized those who were enslaved in Africa to be brought to the Americas against their will. Juan Mosquera, an Afro-Colombian political leader, illustrates this fact as follows: "The elites supported the 'new' category, *the Negroes*, to dehumanize Afro-descendants, and spread their racist ideas through the education system. Some Afro-Colombians followed their rules, but others resisted and maintained a strong identity and legacy despite their exclusion."[5]

In the period 1810–1820, when the war for independence in Colombia began, society was divided by statute and custom into socio-racial castes (*sociedad de castas*), which comprised, broadly speaking, Euro-mestizos, free people of African descent (Afro-mestizos and Afro-indigenous persons), indigenous people, and (black) slaves. The castes were ruled by white people (both Europeans and Creoles). Free Afro-descendants were not permitted to become professionals or to enter the various civil or military bureaucracies. When the militia was created, free Afro-descendants were permitted to serve, but only in segregated units (Kinsbruner 1994).

The term *casta* was a pejorative reference to those of mixed blood, before and during the independence process. Mellafe (1984) points out that the preference was to be considered Euro-mestizo just to be close, socio-racially speaking, to the rulers. Some Afro-mestizos and Afro-indigenous purchased a "pure-blood certificate" from authorities. This operation, known as *gracias al sacar*, was utilized not only to gain social respect but also to have access to state benefits. Many Afro-mestizos and Afro-indigenous then perceived *el blanqueamiento* (whitening) as the best strategy to ascend in the so-called socio-racial pyramid (structure) inherited from the colonial era.

It is hard to tell how many Afro-descendants bought those certificates, since selling operations were usually hidden. Most historians suggest that the numbers of certificates sold was likely low due to lack of economic resources among Afro-descendants (Reales 2001). The situation of slaves was obviously worse. Although sometimes owners were "respectful" to their slaves and manumitted them after years or decades of work, most slaves were treated as wild beasts. This is one of the reasons why, from the first days of Spanish American slave society, running away, or *el cimarronaje*,[6] was a common occurrence.

Revolts, rebellions, protest movements, and other forms of mobilization were notorious manifestations of the hostility expressed by slaves for their condition. Theft and destruction of property were constantly recorded and had to do not only with their material condition and poverty, especially in the cities, but also with their general situation as victims of oppression (Klein 1986). The Spanish Empire took advantage of their situation to offer slaves freedom if they joined the Royalist Army. This provided Afro-descendant slaves and people of African descent in general an unparalleled opportunity to improve their social status.

The Spanish Crown also opened the doors to several professions and education by selling "certificates of whiteness," while the Creole elites, temporarily in power, intended to keep the same people under strict control, as well as the institution of slavery. Thus, many Afro-descendants, both slaves and free people, remained strong supporters of the monarchy and rapidly constituted a serious military threat to the new regime (Rodríguez 1998). They demonstrated excellent fighting qualities and defeated republican armies in different places.

Thousands of people of African descent perceived the Crown as a protector, while the Creole elites still oppressed them. Domínguez (1980) suggests that these events made Simón Bolívar, the would-be Creole liberator of Venezuela, Colombia, Panama, Ecuador, Peru, and Bolivia, realize that the balance of forces to win the war rested on the political ability to mobilize Afro-descendants on one side or another. Bolívar then had no choice but to also offer them freedom and military rank if they joined the patriot armies.

Some Afro-Colombians do not know much about the contribution of their ancestors to independence, in particular, and the nation, in general. "Afro-Colombians tend to 're-invent' their ethnic consciousness when understanding the importance of such contribution."[7] Further, Afro-Colombians are not told, in the education system, that the Creole elites were afraid to release Afro-descendants into Bolivarian society.

Bolívar believed that sooner or later, *la pardocracia* (Afro-mestizos' rule) would govern the liberated countries if he did not limit the aspirations of Afro-descendants. He realized that it was impossible to return to prewar conditions, that it would no longer be a question of resisting (free and enslaved) Afro-descendants' expectations, but of controlling them. In 1819, when he was reinforcing the army, Bolívar recruited five thousand slaves (Lynch 2006). Invoking Montesquieu's philosophy on political and civil liberties, Bolívar argued that left in a free society without freedom for Afro-descendants, they would be prone to rebellion:

It is a political maxim drawn from history that any free government that commits the absurdity of maintaining slavery is punished by rebellion and in some cases by extermination, as in Haiti: What is more appropriate or just in the acquisition of liberty than to fight for it? Is it right that only free men should die for the emancipation of slaves? Is it not expedient that the slaves should acquire their right on the battlefield, and that their dangerous numbers should be reduced by a process that is both effective and legitimate? In Venezuela we have seen free populations die and the slaves survive. I do not know whether this is politic, but I do know that unless we recruit more slaves in Colombia the same thing will happen again.[8]

Women of African descent also challenged the socio-racial system that characterized the "Bolivarian world," before, during, and after the independence process. These women were known for defending their individual rights in the courts. Permanent demands for freedom and equality would be heard until the institution of slavery was abolished some thirty years after the war for independence was won. Blanchard (2002) points out that the independence struggles gave both women and men of African descent the perfect opportunity to voice their thoughts. The elites, however, strongly refused to have a society in which Afro-descendants could enjoy the same rights and liberties. The executions of General Manuel Piar and Admiral José Padilla were a clear indication of this racist behavior.

Some Afro-mestizos achieved high military rank as a result of their evident success on the battlefield. General Piar and Admiral Padilla undoubtedly were the most famous cases. They obtained the highest rank and became indispensable officers in winning battles during the first years of the war for independence. Nonetheless, Bolívar and his supporters, fearing the triumph of *la pardocracia*, ordered the executions of both officers. He knew that he had to manage the patriot army carefully—to include Afro-mestizos, but only as subordinate partners. Autonomous (Afro-descendant) leaders were not allowed at all. Therefore, Piar and Padilla became a challenge to the ideals of Bolivarian society. According to a royalist chronicler, "Piar was one of the most terrible enemies and had great influence among the *castes*, to whom he belonged. He was thus one of the few leaders who could inspire the population."[9]

Padilla, hero of the Battle of Maracaibo in 1823, was the founder of the Colombian navy and the patriot officer who won the naval war against the Crown. After liberating the "Bolivarian seas," Bolívar stated that Padilla was the most important man in Colombia (Torres 1990). However, Bolívar had serious reservations about Padilla's sociopolitical ambitions, as shown in one of his letters:

> Padilla will be able to do whatever he wants if he keeps leading his people. Equality before the law is not enough for the pardos in their present mood. They want absolute equality as a social and public right. They will demand "la pardocracia," that they, the pardos, should rule. This is a very natural inclination which will ultimately lead to the extermination of the privileged class.[10]

In 1828, General Francisco Santander and Admiral Padilla were accused of leading a conspiracy against Bolívar. Bolívar gave Padilla's execution order without hesitation, whereas Santander was condemned to banishment. Padilla faced the firing squad shouting, "Cobardes" (cowards) and refusing a blindfold (Lynch 2006). Admiral Padilla, who thought that it was better to die free than to live as a slave, was executed for challenging a society in which Afro-descendants were not allowed to succeed in politics (Reales 2001).

The executions of Piar and Padilla clearly indicate that the Creoles wanted to maintain the socio-racial structure inherited from colonial times. Santander, who would become ruler of Colombia in the 1830s, agreed with the reproduction of such structure. As Lynch (2006) would say, the Creole elites, far from facing extermination, were more capable of preserving power for themselves, as they proved in the course of the nineteenth century and beyond.

In 1830 the Creole elites did not want to follow Bolívar's rules anymore. His dream of uniting the six nations that he had liberated with the key support of Afro-descendant soldiers was not achieved. What then was the fate of these soldiers? Many of them escaped to live in maroon towns where they defended their ethnic identity and African traditions; others either continued serving "their" nations or were re-enslaved by their former owners.

British pressure to eliminate slavery made the Colombian state end that institution,[11] without affecting the interests of the Creole elites. The state approved significant reparations for slave owners. It allowed them to offer the same nonqualified "jobs" to former slaves, and it supported the elites perpetuating the socio-racial structure and racist practices against Afro-descendants that had existed before the independence wars (Reales 2001). In the midst of the abolition process, the most prestigious Colombian newspaper, El Neogranadino, summarized the last provision as follows: "The African race is destroying the civilized races. As Spanish Americans, we need to encourage the immigration of white Europeans to improve our blood and behavior. We need to make effective this immigration before liberating the Negroes."[12]

In the 1850s, more than three decades after the elites' promise of ending slavery in the freed nations, the abolition process came to an end. Despite the key contribution of thousands of soldiers and women of African descent to independence and the abolition of slavery, most Afro-descendants neither were included in society as equal citizens, nor were they given real opportunities to enjoy their rights. As Sharp (1968) would say, Afro-descendants had become free before the law, but their skin color continued to be the sign of their inferior status. The Colombian elites had no political will to incorporate Afro-descendants into decision-making spaces (Hebe 1974).

Afro-Colombians continued to be dehumanized despite the advent of the "republican world." Those who survived the war for independence did not substantially improve their political situation or living conditions, not even when freedom and civil and political rights were legally granted. Two centuries later, Afro-Colombians, who are still marginalized as an ethnic group, have found in the reconstruction of this (their own) political history a valuable tool to feed and empower their identity-building process.

INSTITUTIONALIZATION OF AFRO-COLOMBIAN ETHNIC IDENTITY

Afro-Colombian history remains invisible in school books in spite of the domestic human-rights laws that mandate the integration of Afro-Colombian studies in the curricula for basic and secondary education. That history is still being reconstructed to reinforce the Afro-Colombian identity discourse. This "reconstruction" process began in the late 1960s, when an emerging Afro-Colombian movement intended to mobilize people against racism (Estupiñán 2004). This mobilization, however, only influenced a few human-rights activists and academics who were interested in exploring the Afro-Colombian situation.

In the 1970s, some Afro-Colombian students took advantage of identity discourses and human-rights struggles that were taking place in South Africa and the United States to rethink and propose an Afro-Colombian identity discourse. These students deeply admired the Afro-American consciousness,[13] and the struggle of Nelson Mandela. Juan Mosquera, who is one of the founders of the Afro-Colombian National Movement CIMARRON, illustrates this crucial moment for the identity-building process as follows:

> There is no doubt that we were impressed with Mandela's dream and other struggles in Africa but we took the civil rights movement as our main source of inspiration. We decided to analyze in depth Martin Luther King's thoughts and Malcolm X's political ideas. We also studied the struggle of the black communists and the Black Panthers' movement. We did it by relying on the few books on this topic that had been translated into Spanish. Our contacts in Spain sent us the books. Such texts were not sold in Colombia for obvious reasons.[14]

After exploring in detail distinct analytical approaches to the study of oppression that affected ethnic groups at both national and international levels, Mosquera and other students within the emerging Afro-Colombian movement proposed *el cimarronismo contemporáneo* (contemporary maroonage) as a political (ethnic) ideology. They picked this term to seek recognition for the long history of resistance of many of their ancestors to racist practices and state (ethnic) homogenization discourses.

"Afro-Colombian contemporary maroonage" became the main ideological reference for Afro-Colombians in the early 1980s. Their ethnic-identity-building process was reinforced, and for the first time in history, the *raizales*, the *palenqueros*, and Afro-Colombians from the coastal areas and most populated cities in the country united their political efforts around an ideology. They decided to follow the same path, not only to "improve" their identity discourse at the national level but also to become a substantive political force (Smith 1986).

Afro-Colombians have not fully achieved the above (main) goals of contemporary maroonage. "Many Afro-Colombians, especially some Afro-indigenous people, are reluctant to support this ideology due to internalized racism-related problems and/ or skepticism about succeeding as an ethnic group in a racist country."[15] In any case, contemporary maroonage is seen as the keystone of the identity-building process and political mobilization of the Afro-Colombian communities. It is important to underscore that this ideology has never focused on racial or "blackness" issues.[16] "The Afro-Colombians' diverse background is what essentially helps mobilize the so-called 'contemporary maroons' and their supporters in the country."[17]

In the 1980s, anthropologists and historians used their research findings to support the Afro-Colombian ethnic-identity-building process led by contemporary maroons. There were two forces that made it possible for academics to engage with the Afro-Colombian ethnic-identity-building process: first, they thought their research would reach further if they took their findings out from academic spaces and shared them with Afro-Colombian community leaders; and second, they became aware of the noxious impact of the armed conflict on small towns where several Afro-Colombian and indigenous communities were settled. As a result of this impact, Afro-Colombian activists and indigenous leaders joined their political endeavors to create a "bi-ethnical alliance" during the Constitutional Assembly that produced the (new) Constitution in 1991.

The state recognized in 1991, through the new Political Constitution, that Colombia was (is) a multiethnic and pluricultural nation. The Constitution also included article 55, an affirmative-action law for Afro-Colombians. That article was ruled through Law 70 of 1993, known as the "Law of the Afro-Colombian Communities." Law 70 promotes the respect for economic, social, and cultural rights of Afro-Colombians as an ethnic group.

The new national legislation made it easier to enhance the relationship between Afro-Colombian organizations and the state. For most Afro-Colombian leaders, the ethnic-identity discourse that had been previously influenced by the contemporary maroonage ideology was officially institutionalized when all state institutions recognized that Afro-Colombians could negotiate their claims as an ethnic group. The official recognition of their ethnic identity as a distinct minority group gave the Afro-Colombian advocates an unparalleled opportunity to spread their ethnic discourse at both national and international levels.

The Afro-Colombian communities in the Pacific coastal areas undoubtedly became the main beneficiaries of institutional changes promoted by Law 70 (Roldán and Sánchez 2002). This law established that the members of these communities had the right to own collective lands. The state, however, did not provide the same right to other Afro-Colombian "ancestral" communities such as the *palenqueros* or the *raizales*. This is one of the reasons why some Afro-Colombian leaders are skeptical about the impact of those institutional changes brought about by Law 70. In any case, many Afro-Colombians in the Pacific region have not even had the chance to fulfill the right to own collective lands, as their lands are affected by the internal armed conflict and drug-trafficking activities.

The legal recognition of Afro-Colombians as an ethnic group has been understood as a political result of the mobilization of contemporary maroons and their supporters. It should be pointed out, however, that those activists constructed their identity based on the struggles of Afro-descendants throughout Colombian history. As Ingrid Bolívar (1998) would say, the emerging Afro-Colombian ethnic identity is a sociopolitical construction that was based on the legacy of the Afro-Colombian communities. This construction is not fixed (Hurtado 2001). It is still under a process of constant transformation in which academics, Afro-Colombian activists, and the state itself are, and will continue to be, involved.

The Afro-Colombian ethnic-identity-building process has faced several limitations in the last decade. Neither the state nor the political elites have recognized the existence of racist practices as a structural problem. Although Law 70 exalted the Afro-Colombian contribution to the nation, it did not include specific mechanisms to eliminate racist practices. Law 70, nonetheless, made it possible to approve other laws to enhance the Afro-Colombian ethnic identity and mobilization. One of these "ethnic" statutes (Law 649 of 2000) established, for instance, that Afro-Colombians would always have the right to elect two congressmen as an ethnic group. Law 649 was approved after four years of controversial congressional debates. Some congressmen, in fact, came to say that approving an affirmative-action law of this kind would create enormous racial divisions among Colombians (Reales 2005). The way political elites intended to weaken the Afro-Colombian identity and political-mobilization processes was perfectly clear in those debates. Pablo Victoria, former leader of the Conservative Party, summarized most of his colleagues' point of view as follows:

> I am confused about the privileges for ethnic minorities that we are discussing here. I want somebody to answer me what is the real ethnic minority of Colombia . . . because if we analyzed the nation in detail, we would discover that whites are that minority. . . . Besides, they call themselves Afro-Colombians, indicating that the word "Afro" is more important for them than their actual nationality. In

other words, they suddenly started feeling that they were from Africa. . . . That
is why I think they should go there, where they could be fairly elected along with
other Negroes. . . . A law like this would damage our democracy and values.[18]

Despite their limitations, Afro-Colombians continued to negotiate with the state
as an ethnic group, and the impact of their mobilization made possible the approval of
Law 649. Their identity and mobilization, nevertheless, still face complex problems,
as argued below.

AFRO-COLOMBIANS: POLITICAL MOBILIZATION AND CURRENT CHALLENGES

The Colombian state "protects" the Afro-Colombian identity through different laws.
It has also recognized how important the Afro-Colombian contribution to the nation
has been. However, the truth is that the Afro-Colombian communities continue to be
victims of racist practices and other human-rights violations at both public and private
levels (Reales 2009). Most contemporary maroons suggest that the Afro-Colombians'
paradoxical situation is due to unrecognized racist practices. "Both private and state
institutions have shown us an obvious lack of knowledge about our struggles as if we
were in the nineteenth century. They do not really want to make effective certain laws
that would enhance our ethnic discourse and political mobilization."[19]

One of the most recent examples of the lack of political will to protect, in practice,
the Afro-Colombian identity occurred in late 2005, when the Colombian National
Institute of Statistics (DANE) developed the National Census.[20] The DANE had previously come to an agreement with Afro-Colombian organizations and activists, who
were successfully mobilized at the national level, regarding the so-called "ethnic identity question." The agreement basically established that all respondents (Colombian
parents) would be asked to indicate their opinion on the following question: "Based
on your cultural characteristics and/or physical appearance, do you identify yourself
as: (1) Indigenous; (2) Roma; (3) Raizal; (4) Palenquero; (5) Black; (6) Moreno; (7)
Afro-Colombian or Afro-descendant; (8) None of them."[21]

It is important to underline that the term *moreno* (brown) refers to mixed persons of
(black) African, indigenous, and (white) European descent. This term characterizes the
ambiguous zone in which many dark Afro-Colombians are located. With the inclusion of
this term in the "ethnic question," most Afro-Colombian leaders agreed that the census
would give them a portrayal of the actual number of Afro-Colombians living in the

country. In Colombia, as happens in other Latin American nations, hearing the expression "I'm a Moreno. My grandparents were the blacks . . ." is still a common occurrence.

The DANE never honored the above agreement. A few weeks before conducting the census, this state institution changed the "ethnic question" without explaining its reasons. According to Igor Correa, "The current administration cheated on the Afro-Colombian communities because it did not want to give them more tools to strengthen their identity, or recognize that Afro-Colombians comprise some 30 percent of the total population."[22] It should be underscored that the government designed its last Plan of Development and public policies in accordance with the statistics provided by the census.

In late 2005, respondents were asked to indicate their opinion on the following (new) ethnic question: "Based on your cultural characteristics and/or physical appearance, do you identify yourself as: (1) Indigenous; (2) Roma; (3) Raizal; (4) Palenquero; (5) Black, Afro-Colombian, Mulatto or Afro-descendant; (6) None of them."[23]

As can be seen, the term *moreno* was not included in the (new) question. Moreover, the DANE found it appropriate to lump the terms "Black," "Afro-Colombian," "Mulatto," and "Afro-descendant" all together. Juan Mosquera summarizes what the DANE did to Afro-Colombians as an ethnic group during the 2005 Census as follows:

> The DANE manipulated the ethnic question to hide the actual statistics regarding the Afro-Colombian population. On one hand, the current administration perfectly knew that despite the advances in the Afro-Colombian ethnic identity-building process and the communities' political mobilization, there are still thousands (probably millions) who have African background but still identify themselves just as "Morenos." The term "Moreno" was eliminated on purpose. It was very likely that many people rejected the option (5) in the question, since it was (is) still problematic for many Afro-Colombians. Using a racial term (black) and ethnic terms (Afro-Colombian and Afro-descendant), as if they were equal, can be confusing in those areas where racism and internalized racism practices still affect people of African descent.[24]

As expected, most people on San Andrés Island and Palenque de San Basilio identified themselves as members from their ("ancestral") communities. In spite of external threats and inevitable self-esteem problems caused by the Eurocentric and stereotyping education system, these two Afro-Colombian communities have maintained a strong ethnic identity. It is important to note that both the *raizales* and the *palenqueros* have agreed to be considered part of the Afro-Colombian population as a "diverse" ethnic group. They decided to use a distinct (own) category in the National

Census not only to exalt their ethnic self-awareness but also to have more options of receiving specific benefits when implementing public policies. "Both communities are small (in numerical terms) and can only legally demand *small scale* ethnic-oriented policies. This is probably why the current administration, through the DANE, had no objection to including their categories in the ethnic question."[25]

What has happened to the self-identification of the vast majority of Afro-Colombians? Has the Afro-Colombian political mobilization been successful in seeking self-identification among communities? How many Afro-Colombians are in the country? These questions are still subject to discussion at both academic and Afro-Colombian NGO levels.

According to the census, the Afro-Colombian population constitutes 10 percent of the total population, that is, some 4 million people. This official figure was not accepted by most Afro-Colombian leaders, who argue that Afro-Colombians make up at least 30 percent of the total population. They use this higher percentage based on the findings of the national survey that was conducted by community leaders during the implementation of the Afro-Colombian Plan of Development in 1999. This plan found that Afro-Colombians made up 30 percent of the total population. Curiously, the plan was supported by the state, through the Department of National Planning (DNP). This institution recognized that the Afro-Colombian population was formed by some 12 million people (30 percent of Colombians).

This percentage was also accepted by the Inter-American Development Bank (IADB) and other international financial institutions that supported the 2005 Census. Consultants from the IADB, who had met with Afro-Colombian leaders, also considered that Afro-Colombians represented more than 30 percent of the total population based on their field research in populated areas (CIMARRON 2005). The Afro-Colombian mobilization made it possible to include the ethnic question in the 2005 Census with the support of IADB, which served as a mediator of the "political agreement" mentioned above. The agreement was not fulfilled, affecting both the Afro-Colombians' identity-building process and their mobilization in many regions.

It should be emphasized that Afro-Colombian activists have been partially successful in terms of mobilizing and encouraging ethnic self-identification of Afro-descendants. As has been argued above, some Afro-Colombians' ethnic self-awareness is still strong, due to their historical struggle of resistance to state homogenization discourses, while other people of African descent have a weak ethnic identity, due not only to the same discourses but also to (unrecognized) racist practices and internalized racism problems. Such complex practices and problems were seen in both the 1993 and 2005 national censuses.

In 1993, for the first time in national history, the state included an ethnic question in its census. The only reference to the Afro-Colombian population was the term "black." As most Afro-Colombian activists expected, not many Afro-Colombians self-identified with that "racial" category. According to the 1993 Census, Afro-Colombians made up 1.6 percent of the population (DANE 2006). To sum up, in only twelve years the state figures regarding Afro-Colombians have significantly changed. In 1993, Afro-Colombians "represented" 1.6 percent of the population. But six years later, in 1999, the state recognized that they "represented" 30 percent of the total population; but six years later, soon after the 2005 Census, the state "confirmed" that Afro-Colombians constituted 10 percent of Colombians. The significant variations in these figures indicate that the above practices and problems are still decisive factors in national life.

Colombia is the only Latin American country that has had such substantive variations regarding data on Afro-descendants in such a short period of time. Pedro Ferrín, an Afro-Colombian leader and former congressman, asserts that "the lack of political will to properly count the Afro-Colombian communities is undeniable. This is why little has been done to address Afro-Colombian issues."[26] Most activists agree with Ferrín on this topic. As a matter of fact, some of them have proposed to conduct local and national surveys in order to count the communities, while empowering their identity-building process and political mobilization.

Having accurate statistics is paramount for the Afro-Colombian population. Data are used as a political tool when demanding special policies and seeking support of international financial institutions and development agencies. The so-called affirmative-action policies and programs are, for instance, key for most Afro-Colombian activists and organizations.

Despite the (negative) impact of the 2005 Census on the identity-building process and human-rights struggle of Afro-Colombians, leaders and advocates continue to mobilize their communities to promote quotas, especially for university admissions. As Telles (2004) would say, quotas are clearly the most efficient method for guaranteeing greater representation of people of African descent, but they also face the greatest opposition among various types of affirmative action, because they are thought to violate principles of meritocracy and fairness.

Telles's statement can be applied to Colombia, where most elites oppose affirmative-action laws and plans. Such strong opposition is one of the challenges that Afro-Colombians face. Most Afro-Colombian advocates point out that it will be hard to end racist practices and empower a discourse without preparing Afro-Colombian youth for higher education and government positions. As Juan Mosquera notes, "Mobilizing people around affirmative-action policies is crucial for their identity-building process. The percentage of Afro-Colombians in the good universities should not and cannot continue to be .01 percent (or less) of all students."[27]

I support affirmative-action policies and programs for Afro-Colombians as an ethnic group, but I think they are not sufficient to overcome Afro-Colombians' "identity problems" and racism in the country. I believe that mixing such special policies and universal policies may embody the "ideal" solution to the complex Afro-Colombian disadvantageous situation. The advantages of this mixture have been seen in the outcomes of national training programs on social development and leadership, such as the Afro-Colombian National School 'Nelson Mandela.'

Programs of this kind produce a fundamental shift in the language of most attendants. After knowing more about the actual contribution of their ancestors to the nation, trainees undergo a change in consciousness, from "racialized" and internalized self-doubt to "ethnic pride" and self-respect. With new ethnic self-awareness, alumni in general return to their communities to secure public resources and promote Afro-Colombian political mobilization campaigns, while supporting the implementation of universal policies.

In summary, the so-called Afro-Colombian political agenda is focused on empowering the ethnic-identity discourse and politically mobilizing people around the need of overcoming socioeconomic problems, racist practices, and other human-rights violations.[28] Fulfilling this agenda, nevertheless, will not be an easy task for Afro-Colombians, due to another complex matter, the impact of the internal armed conflict and drug-trafficking-related activities.

This problem has disproportionately affected the Afro-Colombian communities as an ethnic group (Reales 2009) and has weakened the identity-building process and mobilization, especially in the ancestral lands of the Pacific region (Conferencia Nacional Afrocolombiana 2002). In spite of this disadvantageous situation, Afro-Colombian activists continue to work on identity consolidation based on the historical legacy of their ancestors.

CONCLUSION

The lack of well-documented studies explaining the origin, outcomes, and challenges of the ethnic-identity-building process of Afro-Colombians and their political mobilization as an ethnic group continues to be evident. This chapter indicates that the Afro-Colombian ethnic identity–building struggle and the political strategy behind its social goals have been partially successful in mobilizing Afro-Colombians throughout the country.

Afro-Colombians have used this recent discourse to politically mobilize an ethnic group historically characterized by its "weak" national (social) cohesion. This ethnic identity discourse is fed by memories and research findings regarding the key role played by Afro-descendants in the war for independence, and their contribution to the nation throughout history. Their legacy is permanently used by many Afro-Colombian activists when educating community leaders on ethnic self-awareness and Afro-Colombian leadership. In other words, the hallmark of the still weak political mobilization of Afro-Colombians as an ethnic group is found in their identity-building process.

Some Afro-Colombians' identity, ethnic pride, and self-respect are strong, while others' are weak. The latter followed the state ethnic homogenization projects and/or were (are) still affected by internalized racism-related problems. The first maintained their strong identity as a result of their historical resistance to institutionalized racist practices and the above projects. The obvious diversity among Afro-Colombian communities is also used to strengthen the ethnic-identity discourse at the national level, as they are all victims of similar racist practices and human-rights violations. To sum up, Afro-Colombians' efforts have not been sufficient to overcome their problems, due to the weak cohesion among many of their communities and the lack of political will to make effective human-rights laws. Despite such limitations and the noxious impact of the conflict on most of them, Afro-Colombians continue to be optimistic as regards their ethnic-identity discourse and political mobilization for the long term.

NOTES

I would like to thank Ronald Michael, Professor Emeritus, California University, for his valuable insights on this chapter.

1. I wish to thank Tonya Williams, an African American colleague, for bringing this issue to my attention.

2. According to the state, the percentage of Afro-Colombians has significantly changed in the last fifteen years. The percentage has tremendously varied due to problems related to the absence of ethnic consciousness that have affected Colombian society for decades.

3. Pedro Ferrín, Afro-Colombian leader and former congressman, interview with the author, 11 April 2007.

4. Young (1990) states that experiencing cultural imperialism means to experience how the dominant meanings of a society render the particular perspective of one's own group invisible at the same time as they stereotype one's group and mark it out as the "other."

5. Juan Mosquera, Afro-Colombian political leader, interview with the author, 23 April 2007.

6. The Spaniards initially used the word *cimarrones* for the animals (bulls, horses, etc.) that escaped from their stables.

7. Igor Correa, Afro-Colombian activist and social researcher, interview with the author, 24 April 2007.

8. Bolívar a Santander, Cañafistola, 20 de Mayo de 1819, *Cartas Santander-Bolívar*, 1:92. In Lynch 2006.

9. Díaz, *Recuerdos sobre la Rebelión de Caracas*, in Lynch 2006, 336.

10. Bolívar a Santander, Lima, 7 April 1825, *Cartas Santander-Bolívar*, 4:344. In Lynch 2006.

11. Blackburn (1988) describes how substantive were the triumphs of British antislavery policies. Note: It should be recalled that the British Empire was the most important commercial partner of the Bolivarian nations.

12. "Raza Hispano-Americana." *El Neogranadino*, Bogotá, 30 August 1850. Note: The translation is mine. For a discussion on this provision, see Reales (2001).

13. Gotanda (1995) points out that African American consciousness refers to black-nationalist and other traditions of self-awareness among African Americans.

14. Juan Mosquera, Afro-Colombian political leader, interview with the author, 23 April 2007.

15. Igor Correa, Afro-Colombian activist and social researcher, interview with the author, 24 April 2007.

16. It should be recalled that in most Latin American nations, "race" basically refers to skin color differences.

17. Juan Mosquera, Afro-Colombian political leader, interview with the author, 23 April 2007.

18. Pablo Victoria, *Gaceta del Congreso de Colombia*, no. 564 (Bogotá 1997). Note: The translation is mine. For discussion on these congressional debates, see Reales 2005.

19. Juan Mosquera, Afro-Colombian political leader, interview with the author, 23 April 2007.

20. Igor Correa, Afro-Colombian activist and social researcher, interview with the author, 24 April 2007.

21. For more information on this question, see CIMARRON, *Boletín Institucional*, Bogotá, August 2005. Note: The translation is mine.

22. Igor Correa, Afro-Colombian activist and social researcher, interview with the author, 24 April 2007.

23. The DANE (2006) defends itself by saying that the (new) ethnic question made it possible to properly count Afro-Colombians throughout the country. Note: The translation is mine.

24. Juan Mosquera, Afro-Colombian political leader, interview with the author, 23 April 2007.

25. Igor Correa, Afro-Colombian activist and social researcher, interview with the author, 24 April 2007.

26. Pedro Ferrín, Afro-Colombian leader and former congressman, interview with the author, 11 April 2007.

27. Juan Mosquera, Afro-Colombian political leader, interview with the author, 23 April 2007.

28. As happens in other Latin American nations, Afro-descendant women and children (particularly those who are dark-skinned) are the main victims of human-rights violations in Colombia.

REFERENCES

Afro-Colombian National Movement CIMARRON. 2004. *Report on the Human Rights Situation of Afro-Colombians (1994–2004)*. Bogotá: CIMARRON.

———. 2005. *Boletín Institucional.* Bogotá: CIMARRON

Agudelo, Carlos. 2002. "Etnicidad negra y elecciones en Colombia." *Journal of Latin American Anthropology* 7(2):168–197.

Arocha, Jaime. 2004. *Utopía para los excluidos: El multiculturalismo en África y América Latina.* Bogotá: Universidad Nacional de Colombia.

Barbary, Olivier, and Fernando Urrea. 2004. *Gente negra en Colombia: Dinámicas socio-políticas en Cali y el Pacífico.* Cali: Cidse-Ird-Colciencias.

Bayart, Jean-François. 1996. *L'illusion identitaire.* Paris: Librairie Arthème Fayard.

Bello, Alvaro. 2002. *La equidad y exclusión de los pueblos indígenas y afrodescendientes en América Latina y el Caribe.* Santiago, Chile: ECLAC.

Blackburn, Robin. 1988. *The Overthrow of Colonial Slavery, 1776–1848.* London: Verso.

Blanchard, Peter. 2002. "The Language of Liberation: Slave Voices in the Wars of Independence." *Hispanic American Historical Review* 82(3):449–553.

Bolívar, Ingrid. 1998. "Identidades: Dejarse engañar o perecer." *Revista Colombiana de Antropología y Arqueología* 10(2):141–155.

Conferencia Nacional Afrocolombiana. 2002. *Desplazamiento Afrocolombiano: Texto de la Conferencia Nacional Afrocolombiana.* Bogotá: Proceso de Comunidades Negras.

Constitución Política de Colombia. 1991. Bogotá: Presidencia de la República.

Cunin, Elizabeth. 2003. "La política étnica entre alteridad y estereotipo: Reflexiones sobre las elecciones de marzo de 2002 en Colombia." *Análisis Político* 48:77–93.

De Friedemann, Nina. 1993. *La saga del negro: Presencia africana en Colombia.* Bogotá: Pontificia Universidad Javeriana.

Departamento Nacional de Estadísticas (DANE). 2006. *Colombia: Una nación multicultural: Su diversidad étnica.* Bogotá: DANE.

Departamento Nacional de Planeación. 1999. *Plan Nacional de Desarrollo Afrocolombiano (1998–2002).* Bogotá: Departamento Nacional de Planeación.

Diène, Doudou. 2004. *Informe sobre la Misión del Relator contra el Racismo a Colombia llevada a cabo en 2003.* Geneva: UNOHCHR.

Domínguez, Jorge. 1980. *Insurrection or Loyalty: The Breakdown of the Spanish American Empire.* Cambridge, MA: Harvard University Press.

Escalante, Aquiles. 1964. *El negro en Colombia.* Bogotá: Universidad Nacional de Colombia.

Escobar, Arturo. 1997. "Política cultural y biodiversidad: Estado, capital y movimientos sociales en el Pacífico colombiano." In *Antropología de la modernidad,* ed. María Uribe and Eduardo Restrepo. Bogotá: Instituto Colombiano de Antropología.

Estupiñán, Juan. 2004. *La construcción del discurso étnico en la movilización política afrocolombiana (1970–2003).* Monografía. Bogotá: Universidad de los Andes.

González, Felipe, and Jorge Contesse. 2004. *Informe: Sistema judicial y racismo contra afrodescendientes.*

Santiago, Chile: CEJA.

Gotanda, Neil. 1995. "A Critique of Our Constitution Is Color-Blind." In *Critical Race Theory: The Key Writings That Formed the Movement*, ed. Kimberley Crenshaw, Neil Gotanda, Gary Peller, and Kendall Thomas. New York: The New Press.

Hebe, Clementi. 1974. *La abolición de la esclavitud en América Latina*. Buenos Aires: Editorial la Pléyade.

Hoffmann, Odile. 2001. *Conflictos territoriales y territorialidad negra*. Bogotá: Biblioteca Nacional Luis Ángel Arango.

———. 2002. "Collective Memory and Ethnic Identities in the Colombian Pacific." *Journal of Latin American Anthropology* 7(2):118–139.

Hopenhayn, Martín. 2001. *Discriminación étnico-racial y xenofobia en América Latina y el Caribe*. Santiago, Chile: ECLAC.

Hurtado, Mary. 2001. "La diversidad como eje de un proyecto educativo del Pacífico colombiano." In *La educación en el museo*. Bogotá: Museo Nacional.

Kinsbruner, Jay. 1994. *Independence in Spanish America: Civil Wars, Revolutions, and Underdevelopment*. Albuquerque: University of New Mexico Press.

Klein, Herbert. 1986. *African Slavery in Latin America and the Caribbean*. Oxford: Oxford University Press.

Lynch, John. 2006. *Simón Bolívar: A Life*. New Haven: Yale University Press.

Martín-Barbero, Jesús. 1999. "El futuro que habita la memoria." In *Museo, memoria y nación*, ed. Gonzalo Sánchez and Maria Emma Wills. Bogotá: Museo Nacional.

Marx, Anthony. 1998. *Making Race and Nation: A Comparison of South Africa, the United States, and Brazil*. New York: Cambridge University Press.

Maya, Adriana, ed. 1998. *Geografía humana de Colombia*. Vol. 6, *Los afrocolombianos*. Bogotá: Instituto Colombiano de Cultura Hispánica.

Mellafe, Rolando. 1984. *La esclavitud en Hispanoamérica*. Buenos Aires: Editorial Universitaria de Buenos Aires.

Ministerio del Interior de Colombia. 1998. *Las comunidades negras: Nuevos espacios para la democracia participativa*. Bogotá: Presidencia de la República.

Minority Rights Group International. 1995. *No Longer Invisible: Afro-Latin Americans Today*. London: Minority Rights Group International.

Mitchell, Dulph. 2002. "Una mirada cultural a la historia social y lingüística del Archipiélago de San Andrés, Providencia y Santa Catalina." In *Encuentros en la diversidad*, vol. 2. Bogotá: Ministerio de Cultura de Colombia.

Mosquera, Juan de Dios. 2000. *Racismo y discriminación racial en Colombia*. Bogotá: Movimiento Nacional Cimarrón.

Oslender, Ulrich. 2002. "The Logic of the River: A Spatial Approach to Ethnic-Territorial Mobilization in the Colombian Pacific Region." *Journal of Latin American Anthropology* 7(2):86–117.

Pardo, Mauricio. 2000. *Acción colectiva: Estado y etnicidad en el Pacífico colombiano*. Bogotá: Instituto Colombiano de Antropología e Historia.

———. 2002. "Entre la autonomía y la institucionalización: Dilemas del movimiento negro colombiano." *Journal of Latin American Anthropology* 7(2):60–85.

Ramos, Víctor. 2003. "¿Existe una identidad latinoamericana?" *Revista Utopía y Praxis Latinoameri-*

cana 21. Maracaibo: Universidad de Zulia.

Reales, Leonardo. 2001. "Prensa, abolición y racismo hacia los Afrocolombianos, 1810–1851." *Tesis de Pregrado en Historia.* Bogotá: Universidad de los Andes.

———. 2005. "Racismo y exclusión socio-racial en Colombia." *Tesis de Maestría en Análisis de Problemas Políticos, Económicos e Internacionales Contemporáneos.* Bogotá: Universidad Externado de Colombia/IAED.

———. 2009. "La población afrocolombiana y el Plan Nacional de Desarrollo 2006–2010." In *Reflexión para la planeación: Balance general del Plan Nacional de Desarrollo.* Bogotá: Departamento Nacional de Planeación.

Restrepo, Eduardo. 2003. "Entre arácnidas deidades y leones africanos: Contribución al debate de un enfoque afroamericanista en Colombia." *Tabula Rasa* 1. Bogotá: Tabula Rasa.

———. 2004. "Ethnicization of Blackness in Colombia." *Cultural Studies* 18(5) (September):698–715.

Rodríguez, Jaime. 1998. *The Independence of Spanish America.* Cambridge: Cambridge University Press.

Roldán, Roque, and Enrique Sánchez. 2002. *Titulación de los territorios comunales afrocolombianos e indígenas en la Costa Pacífica de Colombia.* Washington, DC: Banco Mundial/Ministerio del Medio Ambiente de Colombia.

Romero, Mario. 1998. "Familia afrocolombiana y construcción territorial en el Pacífico Sur." In *Geografía humana de Colombia.* Vol. 6, *Los afrocolombianos,* ed. Adriana Maya. Bogotá: Instituto Colombiano de Cultura Hispánica.

Sánchez, Gonzalo. 1999. *Museo, memoria y nación.* Bogotá: Ministerio de Cultura/Instituto Colombiano de Antropología e Historia.

Sánchez, Margarita, and Maurice Bryan. 2003. *Report: Afro-descendants, Discrimination and Economic Exclusion in Latin America.* London: MRGI.

Sharp, William. 1968. "El negro en Colombia: Manumisión y posición social." *Razón y Fábula* 5. Bogotá: Universidad de los Andes.

Smith, Amir. 1986. "Visión socio cultural del negro en Colombia." Bogotá: Centro de Investigaciones de la Cultura Negra en Colombia/Editorial PRAG.

Sojo, Carlos. 2001. "Social Exclusion and Poverty Reduction in Latin America and the Caribbean." Washington, DC: The World Bank.

Taylor, Charles. 1994. "The Politics of Recognition." In *Multiculturalism: Examining the Politics of Recognition,* ed. Amy Gutmann. Princeton, NJ: Princeton University Press.

Telles, Edward. 2004. *Race in Another America: The Significance of Skin Color in Brazil.* Princeton, NJ: Princeton University Press.

Torres, Jesús. 1990. *El Almirante José Prudencio Padilla.* Bogotá: Imprenta y Publicaciones de las Fuerzas Militares de Colombia.

United Nations Educational, Scientific and Cultural Organization (UNESCO). 2005. *The Cultural Space of Palenque de San Basilio.* Paris: UNESCO.

Wade, Peter. 1997. *Gente negra, nación mestiza: Dinámicas de las identidades raciales en Colombia.* Bogotá: Instituto Colombiano de Antropología/Ediciones Uniandes.

Young, Iris Marion. 1990. *Justice and the Politics of Difference.* Princeton, NJ: Princeton University Press.

The Grammar of Color Identity in Brazil

Seth Racusen

What logic does a social structure impose upon public policy? Could an identity structure be too complex or diffuse to implement categorical public policy such as affirmative action? Conversely, what impact does categorical public policy have upon an identity structure? Must categorical policy impose its own categories of identity on its public? This chapter examines the nature of the Brazilian social structure, which I characterize as a grammar of color identity, and its interaction with categorical public policy such as affirmative action in higher education. Opponents of affirmative action have claimed that Brazilian identity is too diffuse and subjective to be able to implement affirmative action: that it would be impossible to define or verify beneficiaries for the purposes of affirmative action. In their view, categorical policy cannot be implemented in a country without clearly delineated categories, and instead would racialize Brazil. The Black Movement rejoined that clear categories exist in many contexts, such as the official deployment of lethal violence, and that Brazil is therefore already racialized. This chapter explores the contours of Brazilian identity and the implications of a nuanced identity structure for affirmative action.

I theorize that the Brazilian structure of identity is constituted through a highly colorized and nuanced "grammar" of identity that expresses the relationality and positionality of individuals in each context. Under this nuanced grammar, appearance, mediated and re-inscribed by social class and performance, has tremendous consequences for life outcomes. Social scientists have repeatedly found a significant gap between whites and others in life outcomes such as education, socioeconomic status, health indicators, and mortality studies. Thus, the color of poverty is widely recognized. The controversy is whether the color of poverty in Brazil is better remedied through race-based or class-based policies, or a combination. I argue for the combination of policies and defend affirmative action as a positive good that provides opportunities to those previously excluded, and also incentives that counterbalance Brazil's assimilationist tendencies.

At the heart of the current debate over affirmative action is an idea that state preferences in higher education will overwhelm popular identity, similar to the hypothesized effect of casinos on indigenous identity in the United States. I argue that this constitutes a simplistic view of the relationship of incentives and actors, as well as the relationship of public and private power. I argue that in Brazil, the state "made race" in the way that states shape markets. No state official could have anticipated the plethora of categories that Brazilians, especially darker Brazilians, would use to describe themselves and each other. Nor did the state assign Brazilians those identities. Further, although I argue that the Brazilian state shaped identity, the state did not create the identities it specified in censuses (Nobles 2000). Why have the overwhelming majority of Afro-Brazilians historically identified as *moreno* rather than *pardo* or *preto*, the census categories? A full answer, beyond the scope of this chapter, requires an examination of state policy, including immigration policy, cultural and information policy under Vargas, educational curricula, as well as symbolic and other state action.[1] The sociologist Clovis Moura and others have suggested that the term *moreno* offered Brazilians a way to lighten themselves and to soften the significance of the distinctions (Moura 1988). Thus, the Brazilian "identity market" has been shaped by the whitening preference, as well as heralding the browning of Brazil. I claim that a fluid, interactive relationship developed historically between state action and societal identity.

Scholars have identified multiple systems of deploying identity within Brazil.[2] Of those multiple systems, I distinguish two, for the purpose of simplicity: (1) state identity, generally expressed in the five terms used by the census bureau, and (2) societal identity, which draws upon a wide vocabulary of terms, including *moreno* and its many variants. It is the second system, societal identity, where many of the controversies about categories and state policy reside. Although Brazilians do not use societal identity to apply for affirmative action, many of the salient characteristics of Brazilian identity also apply to the use of state identity.

By "grammar," I refer to ordered rules for the representation of identity, and additional rules about how to invoke those representations. Thus, I claim that Brazilian identity is not fixed but representational, and negotiated through the grammar, which expresses status positions and overall relations of power within a given context—all of which are dynamic elements. These identity terms possess a relational aspect, expressing relations of power between the identifier, the identified, and the relevant audience. It is not a "calculus" of identity,[3] but a grammar of color identity in the sense that grammatical rules inform the usage of terms.

In my account, the Brazilian grammar of identity contains two key features: a ranking grammar, and a grammar of deracialization. In the first, the grammar of ranking, virtually all Brazilians learn by adolescence to make nuanced evaluations of each other's physical appearance, modifiable by considerations of social context. The primary but not sole physical evaluation is skin color. The primary consideration of social context is social class. Finally, this ranking is fully evident in social life—particularly within an informal but observable color hierarchy within the service sector, in which positions of greater customer contact are reserved for whites and lighter Brazilians.

The second claim about the "grammar" of Brazilian color identity pertains to deracialization. Unlike most structures in which the dominant group deracializes itself and thereby makes itself synonymous with the nation and racializes others, in Brazil subordinated individuals also assert some racelessness. The most popular identity for the Brazilian "brown" is *moreno*, an identity that emphasizes racelessness and Brazilianness and deemphasizes a particular location within the color hierarchy.

I argue that these two grammars interact to produce the Brazilian structure of identity. One might view the two grammars as counterbalancing: that the ranking grammar would either undermine, or be subsumed by, the grammar of deracialization. However, both grammars locate the *moreno* in second place and enable the dominant societal position of whites. The deracialization grammar provides a "face saving" for the *moreno*, while the ranking grammar reaffirms the societal position of whites. Thus, the two grammars increase the discursive flexibility of the Brazilian color hierarchy.

Although I defend affirmative action, I concede a tension between affirmative action and the nuanced grammar of identity. This tension emanates in part from the Brazilian reliance upon the nuances of appearance in drawing distinctions. Although appearance is mutually constituted with descent, social class, performance, association, and other factors, physical appearance has been the primary aspect in Brazilian distinctions. There can be considerable variance between how some Brazilians view themselves and how they are viewed by others. Thus, a candidate for affirmative action may claim an identity that others may not perceive, creating a problem in the perceived legitimacy of affirmative action. Second, Brazilian identity has been historically animated by a steep whitening preference, in which darker Brazilians have been socialized to marry white and "improve" their child's race. This creates an additional tension in the gap between self-identity and other assignment. Finally, affirmative action arguably provides the first material incentive to claim a darker identity: either brown or black. How might Brazilian universities define eligibility for affirmative action given the grammar of identity?

In this chapter, I explore this theory of the grammar of identity in three sections. The next section reviews the understanding of categories in Brazil in previous anthropological and survey work and suggests that Brazilian identity is best understood as a relational color hierarchy. The second and third sections analyze a recent national study, the 2002 PESB, to illustrate the grammar of color evident in contemporary identity. The last section explores how this grammar interacts with the implementation of affirmative action.

LITERATURE ON RACIAL CLASSIFICATION IN BRAZIL

The study of race and racial classification in Brazil has been dominated by a northern-centric understanding of race that presumed U.S. race relations as the norm. Both the idea of Brazilians collectively as a race, and the differentiation among Brazilians were understood through this northern prism. The national narrative mutually constituted Brazilians as a race and the racial identity of individual Brazilians. According to this narrative, Brazilians represented a meta-race of people who do not make meaningful distinctions about their identities.

Seminal studies showed that Brazil did not have U.S-style racial dynamics, which said little analytically about Brazilian dynamics.[4] The anthropologist Marvin Harris sought to unearth an underlying logic to Brazilian identity based upon assumptions drawn from the mapping of identity in the United States. Although Harris acknowledged that the usage of terms "*varies with individuals* in keeping with varying personal relations" (Harris 1964, 27), and also that the "noise" and "ambiguity" of Brazilian identity could be functional to the maintenance of the social structure (Harris 1970, 12), he did not theorize those insights, treating variation as noise, rather than information about the relations between persons. He concluded that there was so much noise and ambiguity about the classification of Brazilians that he could not find a "general cognitive formula" for identity claims (Harris 1964, 23).

Both in natural experiments that evaluate the identity of drawings,[5] and also in social surveys that elicit open-ended self-identification, several studies have reported that Brazilians use one hundred identity terms.[6] This plethora of responses generated several analytic moves. Several prominent anthropologists sought to identify the most widely used terms and found between eight and sixteen prominent categories.[7] Because terms were used in multiple combinations, they sought to identify which terms were most salient (Sanjek 1971, 1130). Of the eighteen terms identified in these works, twelve terms were reported in two or more of the studies. Approximately half of the twelve terms have been found statistically salient in social surveys (Telles 2004).

The first wave of anthropologists recognized that few Brazilians actually fit designated "types," and acknowledged that the actual use of terms did not correspond to a physical mapping (Hutchinson 1957). Harris found some regularity in the use of terms at the end of the continuum, such as *claro* (light), *branco* (white), *alvo* (very white), and *negro* (black), and several in-between terms, such as *sarará* (lighter brown person with reddish hair),[8] and *cabo verde* (darker brown with African and perhaps also indigenous origins)—but not for the popular term *moreno* (brown, to be discussed later) and its many derivatives. In concluding that he could not find a "calculus" of identity, Harris emphasized the differences attributed by Brazilians in the meaning and usage of these terms and, thus, the absence of a clear mapping between category and appearance. These differences reflect ambivalence in responding (Teixeira 1986; Blanco 1978), the subjective desire to whiten, the "conflicting" characteristics possessed by some Brazilians in intermediate categories (Blanco 1978), and the "linguistic ambiguity" of identities (Teixeira 1986). This "linguistic ambiguity" included the use of a modifying term, references to other characteristics, and comparisons to other persons.

A more contemporary wave of anthropologists moved beyond the preoccupation with the mapping of terms and physical appearance. Merida Blanco uncovered the social and relational context that eluded Marvin Harris. From Blanco, one could surmise that the "noise" Harris perceived in the logic of identity actually represented individuals positioning themselves in relationship to each other—such as "I am darker than you," or "He is lighter than me"—rather than claiming precise positions (Blanco 1978). Sansone has suggested that Brazilians demonstrate a "pragmatic relativism" about identity that depends "on the way they wanted to be seen by the interviewer, and on the most socially convenient answer at a particular time" (Sansone 2003, 50–51). Thus, Sansone emphasizes relationality and context:

> The same person can use different terms during the same interview, manipulating different codes to emphasize, in relation to the researcher or eventual listeners, deference or submission, authority, equality, friendship, sexual interest in the interviewer, membership in a status group or professional category . . . , or the consciousness of their own black identity. (Sansone 2003, 46)

In this section, I review literature influential for a theory of a grammar of color identity, which emanates from several sources. The first is the increasing recognition of the considerable ambiguity in identity (Telles 2004, Teixeira 1986), which was uncovered and misunderstood by Harris. Relational identity was not part of his theoretical model, nor would his research project allow him to conceptualize the relationality of identity. The second source was Anani Dzidzienyo's highly influential article "The Position of the Black in Brazil," which emphasized performance: a "racial etiquette" in speech and conduct in which all Brazilians, especially blacks, "know their place" (Dzidzienyo 1971). Merida Blanco described a systematic "color etiquette" between Brazilians in their language of identity claims (Blanco 1978). Finally, Livio Sansone's recent work strongly points towards a grammar of color identity. Both Blanco and Sansone studied identity in social contexts, which reveal the social aspect of identity: that it communicates relationships between parties in a given context, and that, in so doing, identities are not fixed, but representations.

WHAT IS A GRAMMAR OF COLOR IDENTITY?

To begin, what is a grammar of color identity? I use the term "grammar" in several senses: the observable rules in the use of language to communicate identity, and the deeper structures that give meaning to those rules.

First, I use the term "grammar" in the structural sense that a grammar arranges relations between parts: in this case between actors that speak and receive. Bauman and Gingrich suggest three grammars that structure a social order: (1) an orientalized grammar of self and other—"what is good in us is lacking in them" (such as the binary distinctions made under British colonialism and under Jim Crow in the United States); (2) a segmented grammar that permits sliding scales of self and other (such as the caste system of India); and (3) a grammar of encompassment that includes some but not all, and minimizes the otherness of those included (such as the assimilationist policies of Portuguese colonialism) (Bauman and Gingrich 2004). Within each of these grammars, the dominant actor expects the other to "recognize themselves" within the structure, which makes it a structure. How do the three grammars conceptualize the ambiguities of intermediate categories? When ambiguities are located within "special" classificatory slots, such as under apartheid, the rules of the special categories reveal the logic of the structure. However, Bauman and Gingrich view projects of *métissage* as combining the grammars of orientalization and self-encompassment by viewing self and other as amalgamated representations of the "best of both ... worlds" (Bauman and Gingrich 2004, ix–xi). Antonio Sérgio Guimarães has discussed this phenomenon in the Brazilian context:

[The] discursive slippage between Europeanness, Brazilianness, and mestiçagem clearly reveals the "European" character of this imagined nationhood, operating through the Creolization of Europeanness by the whitening of mestiçagem.[9]

The structural grammar locates Brazilians within a complex structure that differentiates Brazilians and also dissolves the differentiations. Second, a grammar possesses and conveys ordered rules and relationships of communication. Although the Brazilian grammar is highly sophisticated, Brazilian children learn it at an early age. Children can perceive the white/black dichotomy by age ten, and most of the many nuances between white and black by age fifteen (Blanco 1978; Sanjek 1971). Despite the ambiguity in Brazilian identity, I claim that a common evaluative schema lies beneath the multiple possible characterizations of self and other. It is a nuanced schema that signifies selected physical characteristics: skin color, hair texture, and facial features. These characteristics are often described in terms of "good" and "bad," referring to characteristics perceived as European and African, respectively. In addition to physical appearance, performance and social class also influence positionality in the structure. This is a grammar of color ranking.

This grammar of color ranking is learned by the contrasts within a family (Blanco 1978) and is continually reinforced by the most private and public interactions. For example, marriage constitutes an institution of status that draws upon and reinforces the grammar (Teixeira 1986). Spouses should be, at most, only a few shades apart (Hutchinson 1957; Dzidzienyo 1971). Those further apart are called a "mosca no leite" (fly in the milk) (Hutchinson 1957, 120), which clearly conveys the lack of belonging.

Anthropologists recognize a white/black dynamic within this grammar of color ranking. Blanco saw the white/black dynamic as the conceptual anchor of the ranking system, which draws distinctions of lighter and darker rather than white and black (Blanco 1978; Teixeira 1986). In Robin Sheriff's view, the white/black polarity constitutes one of several "registers" of racial discourse (Sheriff 2001; Sansone 2003; Telles 2004), and therefore also represents a conception of self.

The language of navigating on a daily basis constitutes a second set of rules: a grammar of deracialization. Brazilians deploy terms to soften distinctions and convey ambiguity (Sheriff 2001; Blanco 1978). *Moreno* is the most important and ambiguous term, which suggests many physical locations from brunettes, to browns, to blacks (Telles 2004, 83). In his *Dictionary of Latin American Racial and Ethnic Terminology*, Stephens cites seven definitions of *moreno* and thirty-eight lexical derivatives of *moreno* (1989, 319–325). Some definitions suggest specific locations within the color hierarchy, while other definitions allow for considerable ambiguity. Here are selected definitions and illustrative subdefinitions:

1b. "person with brown skin color";
2. person of color, generally light-skinned, but often without regard to true skin color";
3a. "racially mixed person who is considered white socially; social white";
4a. "white person with brunet hair";
4d. "person who is not all white, but whose skin color is fair, whose hair is brunet, long, and not curly, and whose features are less black than white";
4e. "dark-skinned person who generally has brunet hair, generally describing the average Brazilian in a non-racial way";
5a. "black person";
6. "mulatto";
7. "Gaucho woman, woman of the countryside, young girl." (Stephens 1989, 320)

Three definitions suggest greater specificity within the color hierarchy: (4a) "white person with brunet hair," (1b) "person with brown skin color," and (5a) "black person." Two locations are very specific: (6) "mulatto" and (7) "Gaucho woman, woman of the countryside, young girl." Two other definitions indicate locations with greater nuance: (3a) "racially mixed person who is considered white socially; social white," (4d) "person who is not all white, but whose skin color is fair, whose hair is brunet, long, and not curly, and whose features are less black than white." Finally, two definitions most suggest the ambiguity of *moreno*: (2) "person of color, generally light-skinned, but often without regard to true skin color," and (4e) "dark-skinned person who generally has brunet hair, generally describing the average Brazilian in a non-racial way." Thus, the term *moreno* can stretch to cover a wide spectrum of persons.

Stephens's thirty-eight lexical derivatives of *moreno* also illustrate the complex framing of *moreno*. These derivates include (1) fourteen combined terms that describe skin color,[10] (2) seven terms that refer to other physical features (especially hair texture but also eye color),[11] (3) eight terms that combine "types,"[12] and (4) four terms that evaluate positionality.[13] Of these thirty-eight variants of *moreno*, I briefly discuss five illustrative terms. *Moreno claro* ("person whose skin color and/or hair are light brown") and *moreno escuro* ("person with dark skin color and perhaps brunet hair") are fairly popular and are reported in some social surveys. Thus, *moreno* can certainly indicate a position within the color hierarchy. Several uses indicate that physical appearance is not solely about skin color, but also highly evaluative of other characteristics: *moreno de cabelo bom* ("brown or brunet with *good* [straight] hair") and *moreno de cabelo ruim* ("brown or brunet with *bad* [kinky] hair"). The terms that modify "type" indicate the overlapping of *moreno* and other terms. For example, compare these two: *moreno mestiço* ("person with mestizo brown skin color") and *moreno mulato* ("person whose skin color is of one who is not a pure *mulato*"), to *mulato mestiço* ("*mulato* with mestizo-like features").[14] Finally, consider the uses of *moreno* that also characterize social positionality: *moreno fino* ("fine brown," "dark-skinned person with features considered good, generally those of a white"), *moreno bem suspecito* ("very suspicious brown or brunet," "person of the upper class, considered white, but often with some black ancestry") (Stephens 1989, 319–325). Thus, *moreno* represents a variable color location in-between white and black that is mutually constituted with whiteness and blackness. In Brazil, mixedness is mutually constituted with whiteness and blackness.

In his highly influential account, Gilberto Freyre viewed the *moreno* as the quintessential Brazilian, who claims to be Brazilian rather than to locate himself in a specified position:

In Brazil, the new very supple or elastic use of the word moreno has become one of the most expressive semantic-sociological happenings that has ever characterized the development of Portuguese America as a society whose multiracial composition is increasingly becoming what an inventor of new words would perhaps be so bold as to describe as metaracial. That is, a society where instead of sociological preoccupation with minute characterizations of multiracial intermediates or nuance types, between white and black, white and red, white and yellow, the tendency is, or begins to be, for those not absolutely white, or absolutely black, or absolutely red-skinned, or absolutely yellow members of the Brazilian society or community to be described, and to consider themselves almost without discrimination, as morenos. (Freyre 1966, 113–114)

There are several tensions within Freyre's claim. First, the metaracial claim rests upon the idea that at some previous moment there were discrete races that mixed. In his seminal work *The Masters and the Slaves*, Freyre claimed that Brazilian mixing was possible because of the "miscibility" of the Portuguese, who had previously mixed with the Moors (Freyre 1986). However, if Brazilian "metaracialness" was predetermined by Portuguese "metaracialness," the other "races" have been erased as historical actors. Finally, despite Freyre's claim, this chapter illustrates the popular "sociological preoccupation with minute characterizations of multiracial intermediates or nuance types."

Moreno might be best viewed as a term conveying ambiguity rather than lexical precision. In Teixeira's view, "*Moreno* is a category used, in our understanding, precisely for its imprecision and ambiguity, and ability to be used for practically all individuals in different locations." Thus, Brazilians use the term *moreno* to create a "positive ambiguity" about someone, drawing attention to someone's proximity to whiteness (Teixeira 1986, 31). Some usages suggest nuance, and other usages seek to create ambiguity, especially by those not fully white who seek to claim identities that deemphasize a particular location within the color hierarchy.

CONJUGATED IDENTITY

The idea of conjugated identities distinguishes terminology used in the first, second, and third person and to indicate the relationship of speaker, audience, and the "object" of commentary. First-person identity refers to self-identity, second-person identity is your characterization of me to my face, and third-person identity is the characterization of someone not present.

Although the first wave of anthropologists viewed Brazilian identity as a single identity system, contemporary anthropologists have conceptualized multiple "maps" or "registers" within the overall identity structure. Blanco discerned five "maps" used by her informants in discussing identity. Blanco's informants used multiple "maps" depending on whether an identity was (1) what the person considered himself (first person); (2) what she called him (second person), or (3) what she really considered him (third person); (4) what others collectively viewed him as (the third-person plural or community assessment); and (5) how I rank him in relationship to me (another third-person tense that emphasizes explicit ranking of self and other).[15] Blanco's five "maps" reflect how context informed her informants' speech about themselves and others. According to Sheriff, individuals could view her question about identity:

> Was I asking them to classify themselves in racial terms, to describe their color in relative terms, or to tell me how they would typically be referred to in polite everyday conversation? (Sheriff 2001, 34)

Sheriff identifies three "registers." The first, already discussed, was a white/black polarity, which Telles discussed as the "Black Movement system of racial classification" (Telles 2004, 85). She saw two additional "registers": a "descriptive discourse" used to "describe rather than classify" self and others, and a "pragmatic discourse," which reflected how people treated each other. Sheriff's "pragmatic discourse" corresponds to Blanco's second map—which I refer to as second-person conjugation. Her descriptive discourse collapses what I differentiate as first- and third-person identity.

Anthropological research has illustrated the usage of conjugated identities. In general, terms that seek to soften distinctions are used in the first and second person, and sharper terms are used in the third person. Brazilians generally use derogatory terms in the third person: to describe someone who is not present. Third-person usage is less likely to reflect polite deracialized terminology: "more precision may be used when the subject is not present" (Teixeira 1986, 29). Similarly, the color of infants, a second-person conjugation that resembles a third-person conjugation, is more readily discussed than the color of adults (Sheriff 2001, 35). The use of derogatory terms in the second person is well known to be an insult. These terms include *branco da terra* ("earthy" white),[16] *negro*,[17] *crioulo*,[18] *preto*, and *mulato*, especially referring to men (Teixeira, 1986, 31). Sansone has also distinguished second- and third-person usage (Sansone 2003, 45).

Multiple conjugations can be expressed within a conversation. One of Teixeira's respondents referred to herself twice in the same conversation. Interestingly, she referred to herself in the first person as *escura* and in the third person as *preta* (Teixeira 1986, 28). Thus, she followed the general rules of usage, in which *escura*, a softer term for being black, would be used in the first or second person, and *preta*, a direct term, would generally be used in the third person. Although this dichotomy is overly simplified, I suggest that third-person usage generally reflects the ranking grammar, and that first- and second-person usage generally reflects the deracialization grammar.

RELATIONALITY

The first wave of anthropologists, highly influenced by Harris, recognized that the use of terms expressed the "relation of the referent to the speaker," and also considered "the presence of other actors and their relations to the speaker and the referent" (Sanjek 1971), but without theorization. Hutchinson noted that one individual liked by everyone and who appeared to be *escuro* was called *moreno*, with the qualification that he had *cabelo ruim* (bad hair) (Hutchinson 1957, 120). One of Sanjek's informants identified himself as *alvo* (yellowish skin and wavy hair). Sanjek reports, "When he said he was *alvo*, the other people standing around us began laughing and told him, and me, that he was not *alvo*" (Sanjek 1971, 1131). These researchers viewed the relational context as noise.

The grammar is relational in several senses. First, the terms are relational:
Branco and Preto are absolute terms, defined through opposition, compared to claro and escuro, which are relative categories open to conflict because they can be manipulated and ambiguous. What is claro in relation to one person could be more escuro in relation to another. (Teixeira 1986, 30)

In addition to the usage of terms such as *escuro* (dark) or *claro* (light), *escuro* and *claro* are used to modify other identities, such as *moreno escuro* or *moreno claro*, thereby increasing the relativity of those terms. Second, individuals frequently assess themselves and others in comparative references, such as "mais clarinha que voce" (lighter than you), "mais escura que não sei quem" (darker than who knows), or even "da cor de fulano" (comparing to the color of someone) (Teixeira 1986, 26).

POSITIONALITY

The terms also acknowledge the power relations between speaker, audience, and the person being described, the "object" of the articulation. The relative status of each matters. Sansone reports that it is customary in Bahia to grant a few "somatic points" to someone liked (Sansone 2003, 45). Blanco noted that it mattered who was in the room:

> It became clear that in the process of labeling photographs, an informant was consciously or unconsciously taking into account the points of view of the other participants in the conversation. (Blanco 1978, 74)

Communication about Brazilian identity reflects and reproduces understandings about the relative status and power of all participants in each context. This includes the speaker, the audience, and the persons to whom they refer, whether or not present. Brazilians express their perceptions of their relative standing in terms of color, status, and power through their communication about their respective identities. Sheriff claimed that this was evident in the deployment of diminutives and labels like *moreno*:

> When they are employed in the pragmatic register, such diminutives, as well as words like Moreno, refer less to a person's real color than to the relationship between speakers. (Sheriff 2001, 51)

Although they vary in their usage of terms describing others, Brazilians commonly perceive the relative positionality of others. Blanco reported that informants used different terms to describe each other, but commonly ranked the relative color positionality of either community members or of photographs (Blanco 1978).

In Blanco's view, individuals conceptualized color categories just below their self-placement, so as to include themselves in the lightest category possible, which she termed egocentric identity (Blanco 1978, 133). Accordingly, individuals stretched the boundaries of *moreno* toward their own self-identity: "The lightest informants restricted its (*moreno*) use to the light half of the spectrum, while the darkest informants extended toward their own territory. Middle informants did the same" (Blanco 1978, 127). Thus, the use of *moreno* varied with the color of the speaker. The classification of others could also indicate self-placement. Blanco reported that the physical characteristics respondents emphasized in characterizing others often reflected someone's self-placement (Blanco 1978). In this sense, self-placement could express self-interest in elevating one's identity.

Finally, the anticipated perspective of the lightest person present establishes the framework for conversation (Blanco 1978). In the presence of a white, the labeling of others was consistent with the presumed white perspective (Blanco 1978; Sansone 2003). A white generally did not wish to embarrass his darker colleagues to their faces and would either avoid the use of any term or use the lightest possible term, such as *escuro* or *escurinho* rather than *preto* or *negro*, the actual terms for black. For example, a white academic told a light brown colleague in my presence that he did not even know that this colleague was black until informed by him. He intended that as a compliment, illustrative of the grammar of deracialization.

Contexts

The context of the communication also matters. Sansone (2003) distinguishes between "hard" and "soft" social spaces. In "hard" social spaces, including work, marriage, dating, and interaction with the police, being black is a disadvantage. In "soft" social spaces, which are "implicitly" black, being black is not necessarily a hindrance and sometimes conveys prestige. Sansone identifies leisure as a "soft" social space and includes beach soccer, bars, encountering neighbors on street corners, and samba parties. He also suggests that there are "explicitly" black spaces, where being black is an advantage, such as *capoeira* (African-derived martial art), *Candomblé* (Afro-Brazilian religion), *batucada* (African percussion at a samba), or a *bloc-afro* (Afro-Brazilian dance group) (Sansone 2003, 52–53).

Sansone and Blanco have persuasively argued for context, that identity is communicated in social settings. Since many racial discrimination complaints, which entail racial insults and extremely derogatory language and behavior, have been manifest in the so-called "soft" and "implicitly" black settings,[19] a "soft" setting is only relatively "softer." Further, the disproportionate presence of Afro-Brazilians in riskier occupations and in more vulnerable societal locations is widely acknowledged. That is, Afro-Brazilians can be vulnerable within both the "soft" and "hard" settings.

FINDING THE GRAMMAR OF IDENTITY IN A SURVEY

Having suggested a theory of the grammar of color identity, this chapter next draws upon secondary analysis of a social survey to illustrate the theory. Since I claim identity to be relational, social, and contextual—best illustrated by ethnographic fieldwork—I must acknowledge the limits of an interview as a research strategy to study the grammar of color identity. The relationship between an interviewer and respondent in a quantitative survey is markedly different from that which an anthropologist might develop over time with her "informants." The survey interviewer remains a stranger, who has developed limited rapport before asking sensitive questions. Further, the anthropologist can also draw upon ethnographic data gathered through participant observation of interactions between her "informants" and their friends and associates, which would best enable the testing of the theory.

I have identified two kinds of grammar in Brazil—a ranking grammar and a deracialization grammar—and claimed that the grammars possess the following characteristics: (1) a conjugation, (2) relationality, (3) positionality, and (4) context. Of the four characteristics of a grammar, this section primarily explores the relationality of identity illustrated both in the ranking grammar and the deracialization grammar. The other aspects of the grammar are not so readily apparent from a survey.

This section examines a national survey conducted by the Federal Fluminense University of Rio de Janeiro in 2002: the Pesquisa Nacional Brasileira (PESB) or National Brazilian Social Survey, influenced by the U.S. General Social Survey and the work of Brazilian anthropologist Roberto da Matta. The PESB included a battery of questions on racial identity, racial attitudes, and other political and social attitudes, with a national sample of 2,364 adults.[20] This section analyzes several of the racial-identity items.

PESB respondents were asked for their color in an open-ended question, a subsequent question using the five census categories: *preto* (black), *pardo* (brown or "tan"), *branco* (white), *amarelo* (Asian or "yellow"), and *indío* (indigenous or "Indian"), and a third item that offered a choice between *branco* (white) and *preto* (black). The interviewer also noted her impression of the respondent's color. This section will primarily analyze respondent self-reported open-ended identity.

In open-ended identity, reported in table 1, Brazilians identified in many

TABLE 1. OPEN-ENDED IDENTITY RECODED

	FREQUENCY	%	CUMULATIVE %
Branca (census category for white)	920	38.9	38.9
*Morena**	627	26.7	65.6
Parda (census category for brown)	325	13.7	79.3
Negra (of the black race)	160	6.8	85.9
Morena clara (light *morena*)	77	3.3	89.2
Preta (census category for black)	74	3.1	92.3
Amarela (census category for Asian)	35	1.5	93.8
Other[†]	121	5.1	98.9
Don't Know	25	1.1	100.0
TOTAL	2,364	100	

Morena includes variations of *morena* (27) other than *morena clara*.
[†]Other includes: *Clara* (light, 18), other variations of *Branca* (17), *Mulata* (17), *Misturada* (mixed, 13), other variations of *Parda* (13), no response (12), and other smaller categories.

SOURCE: Secondary analysis of the 2002 PESB by author.

(sixty-six) open-ended categories, a finding consistent with previous research. A relatively small number of those categories are statistically significant, also consistent with previous research (Telles 2004). In the PESB, seven categories were claimed by at least thirty persons, which account for 92 percent of all respondents.

Of the seven categories, three, *branca, parda,* and *preta,* are census categories. Over half (56 percent) of the respondents use these categories, a figure slightly lower than previous findings. Only 17 percent of respondents identified as either *parda* or *preta,* a figure also lower than previous findings (Brandão and de Marins 2007). For darker Brazilians, the preferred term remains *moreno,* and nearly 30 percent of respondents identified as *moreno, morena clara,* or another variant of *moreno* (coded as *morena outra*). As indicated by the previous discussion of the term *moreno,* I claim that the popularity of these terms demonstrate the grammars of both ranking and deracialization.

Many identified in categories that modified and/or combined terms. Some categories modified the predominant terms, such as *meio moreno* ("kind of" *moreno*). Other variations on *moreno* included "*meia morenaça*" (a "kind of" stunning, attractive female *morena*), "*morena fechada*" (very dark *morena*), "*morena achocolatada*" ("chocolate-colored" *moreno*), and "*morena tropical*" (tropical *morena*). A "*morena tropical*" links her identity to the country, characterized as a tropical country. Other combinations included *branca clara* (light *branca*), *morena parda* (*parda*-like or tan *morena*), *parda clara* (light *parda*),

TABLE 2. COMPARISON OF THE OVERALL AND "NARRATIVE" SAMPLES OF THE PESB 2002

		OVERALL	"NARRATIVE"
AGE	18–24	18.0%	11.6%
	25–34	22.2%	18.3%
	35+	59.8%	70.1%
SEX	Feminino	52.9%	59.8%
EDUCATION	Até 8a série	56.8%	63.3%
	Ensino médio	31.1%	28.7%
	Superior	12.1%	8.0%
	Não Capital	76.1%	76.6%
REGION	Norte	4.8%	1.6%
	Cento-oeste	6.5%	14.3%
	Nordeste	27.9%	31.5%
	Sudeste	45.2%	30.7%
	Sul	15.6%	21.9%
ATTRIBUTED	*Preto*	11.1%	7.2%
	Pardo	42.6%	52.2%
	Branco	45.0%	39.4%
OPEN-ENDED	*Branca*	38.9%	34.9%
	Morena	29.8%	27.8%
	Negra	6.8%	3.6%
	Outra	5.1%	20.6%
	Parda	13.7%	11.1%
	Preta	3.1%	1.6%
	Renda	551	627
	N	2,364	252

SOURCE: Secondary analysis of the 2002 PESB by author.

mulato médio (medium *mulato*), and *meia parda* ("kind of" *parda*). The relative positioning was also demonstrated through negative self-references to darkness, such as "*meio encardida morena clara*" (a "kind of" very dirty *morena clara*.) This last identity is extremely self-deprecating and reveals the strong presence of Fanonian self-hatred within the grammar of color identity (Winant 1994).

This section examines one set of respondents to the open-ended identity question. About 11 percent of the respondents did not simply use a category or a combined term, such as *moreno claro*, but a phrase or narrative. The chapter uses content analysis to analyze that phrase or narrative for evidence of the grammars, and refers to these respondents as the "narrative" sample.

Table 2 compares the "narrative" sample to overall respondents. The "narrative" sample is older and slightly more likely to be female and slightly less likely to be educated than the overall sample. There is no difference in the urbanization of the samples. The "narrative" sample is more likely to reside in the central west and less likely to reside in the southeast. Perhaps most significantly, the "narrative" sample is more likely to identify as *pardo* in census categories and as "other" (a coded category) in open-ended identity, and less likely to identify as *"negra"* or *"preta."* Finally, the "narrative" sample is more likely than the overall sample to self-lighten. Some 8.4 percent of the overall sample viewed themselves as *branco* but were viewed as *pardo* or *preto* by the interviewer. In the "narrative" sample, that figure nearly doubled: 14.7 percent of respondents viewed themselves as *branco* and were classified *pardo* or *preto* by the interviewer.

Table 3 summarizes my coding of the "narrative" sample. Please note that responses could receive more than one code: expressions of ambivalence overlap with

TABLE 3. SUMMARY OF CODING OF "NARRATIVE" SAMPLE

ANALYTIC CATEGORY	CODED ARTICULATION	COUNT
AMBIVALENCE AND DESIRE (N = 119)	Doubt	111
	Document	8
RANKING (N = 74)	Other comparators	34
	Modifications	14
	Lighter than *Preta*	13
	Not *Preta* not *Branca*	11
	"Burned from the sun"	3
DERACIALIZATION (N = 72)	Mixed	43
	Brazilian	14
	"Do not have race" or "race does not exist"	9
	Brazilian and Mixed	3
	"Not racist"	2
	Other comments about race	1
ETHNICITY (N = 38)	National Origin	38
BLACKNESS (N = 18)	*Negra* or *Preta*	18

SOURCE: Content analysis of the 2002 PESB by author.

expressions of both grammars. In all, I coded five larger categories in the "narrative" sample: (1) the language of ambivalence and desire, (2) the grammar of deracialization, (3) the grammar of ranking, (4) articulations of ethnic identity, and (5) articulations of blackness. Each will be treated briefly in the succeeding sections.

LANGUAGE OF AMBIVALENCE AND DESIRE

The largest articulation in the "narrative" sample was the ambivalence and desire about identity expressed by about 5 percent of the overall respondents (111). This subgroup generally resembled the overall "narrative" sample in being viewed as slightly more *parda* than the overall sample. The prominent response of this category was "Acho que sou *branca*" (I think that I am white). The verb *achar* connotes to believe, to suppose, to sense, to discover, or to consider, and thereby expresses desire and doubt.[21] In the context of the dynamics discussed previously, "acho que sou *branca*" can represent a claim to be white that might be negotiated in conversation. Through ambivalence, a shallower emotion, one might cautiously express more deeply held desires. In the context of the Brazilian color hierarchy, identity ambivalence often expresses the desire to whiten (Moura 1988). In total, 38 respondents used the verb *achar*.

Another articulation in this category, "*Morena, parda*, né!?," expresses ambivalence between two intermediate locations on the color hierarchy and could also indicate a desire to lighten toward *morena*. Another articulation, "Eu pra mim é *morena*" (To me, I am *morena*) represents an affirmation within a broader context of ambiguity that also allows that others might think differently. Another respondent articulated: "Dizem que é *parda*, e eu também acho, porque o *preto* é mais queimado" (They say that I am *parda*, and I also think so because *preto* is darker), expressing considerable ambivalence both by referring to herself in the third person and by couching her claim behind the view of others, all to support a claim to not be *preta*. However, the interviewer viewed her as *preta*.

Some respondents drew upon their formal identification rather than the view of others to support their claims. The most prevalent example was: "No meu documento está *parda*/sou *morena*" (In my document, my color is *parda*, I am *morena*). The speaker shows greater affinity for self-identity, referring to herself in the first person (sou *morena*), than for her documentation, a third-person reference, apparently seeking to be lighter than her document. Generally, the document was referred to in the third person: "No meu documento tem escrito: *moreno claro*." (Light *moreno* is written on my document.) One respondent seemed equally invested in both identities: "Eu sou brasileira e no meu registro sou *branca*, mas eu acho que sou *morena*" (I am Brazilian and I am white in my document, but I think I am *morena*). In this instance, the document indicated a white identity, which may explain the first-person reference.

GRAMMAR OF RANKING

This section analyzes the responses coded within the ranking grammar, which conveys many distinctions and nuances. Certain identity claims emphasize elements to communicate an upward posture within the overall color continuum. Some respondents voiced a cautious claim, perhaps to avoid embarrassment with the interviewer. In all, 30 respondents in the "narrative" sample responded with a negative reference, stipulating a color or identity they were not. Sometimes that was their only claim; more often, they also articulated a positive identity. Finally, nearly half of the respondents in this category (44 percent) identified as *moreno*, nearly double the rate in the overall PESB sample. This group was also more likely to be viewed as *pardo* by the interviewer (64 percent) than the overall sample. Thus, the grammar of ranking is not exclusively the province of *morenos*, but disproportionately articulated by those identifying as *moreno*.

Some respondents in this category expressed ambivalence about multiple identities, which made their identity explicitly comparative to other identities. A typical articulation is: "Acho que sou *parda* ou sou *preta*, sei lá" (I think that I am *parda* or *preta*, whatever), an expression of indifference about the identities. Most respondents who voiced multiple identities presented a more complex comparative positionality. One claimed to be "mais *moreno* do que *branco*" (more *moreno* than *branco*), which places the respondent somewhere on a scale between white and *moreno*, and claims a position closer to *moreno*. However, the mention of white in the expression also articulates a claim to be lighter than *moreno*. Many responses in this broader category might be best understood as ways to lighten, such as the respondent who emphasized being "*clarinho* uma coisinha*" (a little bit *clarinho*).

The relative positioning also included expressed mixedness: "Rapaz, eu sou *mestiço*, minha família é misturada, *branco* eu não sou." (Fella', I am *mestiço*, my family is mixed. I am NOT *branco*.) The term *rapaz* is an informal colloquialism or a preface to a story, and this respondent thought that his identity needed a preface. Another identified as "cor *negra*, filho de gente bem queimado" (color *negra*, son of those very burned, i.e., dark). This articulation indicated ambivalence about being too dark.

The negative reference predominated in this category, especially the insistence on not being "*preta*" or "muita *preta*." Thirteen respondents voiced being "lighter than black." One respondent declared, "Não me acho muito *preta* não" (I don't see myself as very black), identifying simply through negation of the "other." Another respondent stated, "Eu nem sou *preta* nem sou *morena*" (I am neither *preta* nor *morena*). This identity represented a double negation, indicating the mutual constitution of whiteness, blackness, and mixedness (*morenidade*), and a positioning relative to all three. In a country in which at least 38 percent of whites acknowledge African descent (Telles 2004, 92–93), this respondent wished to indicate that his whiteness was not also black or mixed.

Some respondents offered sharp, absolute negations, in contrast to the overall relationality of the terms. One respondent identified as "bem *morena*, porque o *preto* é *preto* e *morena* é *morena*" (bem *morena* [very *morena* or brownish], because *preto* is *preto* and *morena* is *morena*), drawing a sharp line between *preto* and *morena*. Another respondent exhibited ambiguity about her identity in general, and clarity about not being *preta*: "Minha cor é *morena* ou *parda*, não sei, não chega a ser *preta*" (My color is *morena* or *pardo*, I don't know. But it is not *preta*!) Another respondent also showed ambiguity about her identity and stated sharply that she was not black and that blackness belonged to others: "*Branca—morena—*mas não tem essa raça" (*Branca, morena,* but my color does not have THAT race!) Similarly, another respondent distinguished his entire clan from darker Brazilians: "A minha roça é toda *moreninha*, não tem nenhum *pretão*, não" (My family or home turf is all *moreninha* and does not have any real blacks). Finally, one respondent allowed that while she might be "a little darker than *parda*," she was certainly NOT *preta*: "*Parda*, assim um pouco mais escura, mas não sou *preta*" (*Parda*, perhaps even a little darker, but I am not *preta*!). These respondents making sharp distinctions from being black were perceived as *parda* by the interviewer.

Several respondents who sharply differentiated themselves from being black were actually seen as *preto* by the interviewer. One said, "Dizem que é *parda*, e eu também acho, porque o *preto* é mais queimado" (They say my color is *parda*, I also think so, because *preto* is burnt more [darker]). In this instance, the strongest source is the opinion of others, upon which the desire to lighten (*achar*) rests. This claim is voiced in a way to minimize the possibility of being called *preto* (Blanco 1978). Another respondent simply stated, "*Preta* não! *Morena*."

Another principal negative reference was the claim to be "nem *preta* nem *branca*" (neither *preta* nor *branca*), which constitutes mixedness as a negation. This identity was generally voiced in the third person, most simply: "Não é *branca*, nem *preta*" (My color is neither *branca* nor *preta*). A negative reference voiced in the third person makes this a highly impersonal claim. Others claimed a location: "Nem *negra*, nem *branca*, é uma mistura" (It is neither *preta* nor *branca*, but a mixture), also a third-person identity claim. Other respondents voiced more complex articulations. Some located themselves more precisely, such as "Nem é *preta*, nem é *branca*. Sou mais *preto* que *branco* (My color is neither *branca* nor *preta*. I am more *preto* than *branco*). The first phrase places the respondent in the general location, and the second phrase indicates a greater proximity to blackness, which is still bounded by the initial negation of being black. One respondent's claim was recorded by the interviewer in the third person: "Não é *branca* e muito menos *negra*. Na sua opinião sua cor é *clara*." (The color is not *branca* and much less *negra*. In her opinion her color is *clara*.) Perhaps the interviewer, who saw the respondent as *parda*, distanced herself from the self-assessment. Of the respondents who claimed to be neither *branca* nor *negra*, the interviewer perceived most as *pardo* and several as white.

Several respondents claimed to be "burned from the sun," an expression of ranking and deracialization. These respondents reluctantly admitted to not being white, but invoked nature to override their appearance. One respondent claimed to be "born white" but sunburned: "Nasci *branco* mas agora estou cheio de mancha por causa do sol" (I was born *branco* but now am full of marks[22] from the sun). Another respondent claimed, "Eu acho que sou *branco*, meio queimado de sol" (I think that I am white, partially sunburned). Here, the verb *achar* may again reveal the desire to whiten, because the interviewer perceived this respondent as *pardo*.

The grammar of ranking could be voiced cautiously. One respondent sought to whiten her identity while allowing the possibility that she might be seen as darker: "Acho que sou *branca*, mas meu pai tinha traços de *negro*" (I think that I am *branca*, but my father had *negro* traces). This response projected her desire to whiten over an acknowledgement of her father's appearance. However, the interviewer viewed her as *parda*.

Finally, self-hatred could emerge openly as the anchor of identity. One individual referred to himself in an openly derogatory fashion: "*parda*, raça ruim" (*parda*, awful race). This formulation echoes the view of Brazilian elites at the turn of the twentieth century who accepted the prevalent European racism that nothing would come from a country of degenerate mulattos (Skidmore 1993).

GRAMMAR OF DERACIALIZATION

The most prevalent expressions of the deracialized grammar were claims to be mixed, to be Brazilian, to "not have race," or that "race does not exist." These expressions broadly correspond to the ideology of racial democracy, and its claims that Brazilians do not make racial distinctions or are so mixed so as to render such distinctions relatively meaningless. Some claims placed the respondent in a more specific location within the broader category of mixedness, such as *mestiço* or mulatto, while others were claims to be mixed in a general sense, or to be Brazilian, or to be of indeterminate identity.

In general, the claims to be mixed arose from persons identifying as *pardo* in the census question. The most prominent voicing of being mixed was to claim to be *mista* or *misturado*, generally meaning mixed in a broader sense. These claims are distinct from "mestiça," which connotes a mix including indigenous ancestry, and from *mulato*, the most precise of the terms that connote the mixing of a black and a white. Often, the claim to be *mista* was a claim to be lighter brown: "Sou *mista—moreninha clara*" (I am mixed, a light *morena*). Another respondent claimed to be mixed and white: "É uma mistura, sou *branca*" (It's a mixture, I am white.) A different respondent viewed her mixedness as placing her outside of whiteness: "Não sei! *Branca* totalmente eu não sou pq [porque] tem mistura de raça na família" (I don't know! I am not totally white because my family has a racial mix). Sometimes the claim to be *mista* acknowledged blackness: "Ela acha que é uma mistura do *negro* com o *branco*, pois seu avô era *negro* e a avó era *branca*, então saiu uma *mulata*." (She thinks that she is a mixture of the *negro* and the *branco*, because her grandfather was *negro* and her grandmother was *branco*, therefore she was *mulato*"). The interviewer, who viewed the respondent as white, recorded her notes in the third person, which probably indicated a distancing from the respondent's claim to be mixed.

Mestiço often refers to indigenous ancestry but can also connote a broader sense of mixture. This respondent had difficulty claiming an identity: "Nem sei / é tudo *mestiço* / porque meu pai era *caboclo* / meu bisavo era de cor / e agora eu não sei explicar / é uma mistura né / minha vó era portuguesa / não sei como definir" (I don't know. My identity is all *mestiço* because my father was *caboclo*, my great-grandfather was of color, and now I don't know how to explain, it's a mixture, no. My grandfather was Portuguese. I don't know how to define.) In this instance, the claim to be *mestiço* was closely linked to not really knowing one's identity. The term *caboclo* refers to someone with indigenous ancestry, with connotations of being acculturated or westernized, perhaps through mixing with blacks or even whites. The term also connotes lower-class background, someone rural, and/or a copperish skin tone (Stephens 1989, 278–279). In general, the response "não sei" (I don't know) tended to be from respondents of lower socioeconomic class. Other responses included *todas* (all) and *indefinido* (indefinite), each representing a somewhat deracialized, ambiguous placement within the broader intermediate space.

Some claiming to be *mestiço* sought to locate themselves more specifically within the broader intermediate space: "*Parda*, eu sou *mestiço meio moreno, meio branco, meio preto*" (*Parda*, I am *mestiço*, half *moreno*, half *branco*, half *preto*"). Thus, this respondent viewed her multiple identities as locating her as something definite: a *parda*.

Mulato represents a derogatory biological reference to someone of white and black ancestry. One respondent simply declared: "*Mulato*, meu avo africano minha avö italiana" (Mulatto, my African grandfather, my Italian grandmother). However, another respondent wished to be lighter than *mulato*: "Sou *mulata*, filha de *negro* com *branco*, sou *morena*." (I am mulatto, daughter of a *negro* with *branco*, I am *morena*.) This usage of *morena*, a term of greater flexibility than *mulato*, suggests a positioning of being lighter than *mulato*. The grammars of deracialization and ranking were often combined in the specific identities.

The claims to be Brazilian were generally voiced by persons viewed as white by the interviewer. Thus, prominent among these claims are "cor brasileira, *branca*" (Brazilian color, white), and "cor *branca*, raça brasileira" (white color, Brazilian race). These claims suggest a broader location as a Brazilian and a claim to be a "Brazilian white," which acknowledges some relativity. Some claimed to be *morena*: "cor brasileira, *morena*" (Brazilian color, *morena*) or "Brasileira, *morena clara*" (Brazilian, light *morena*). The first respondent declared *morena* to be the "Brazilian color." In general, these identities acknowledged some mixedness and also being lighter.

Some claimed not to have race. For one respondent, human beings do not have race but views: "O ser humano não tem cor e nem raça tem atitudes" (Human beings do not have color and race but have attitudes). Another respondent attributed the absence of race to God: "Não tenho cor nem raça, tenho um deus que ama todas as raças" (I do not have color or race, I have a God who loves all the races). Among several implications from this characterization is that only others "have race": this racelessness races others. Another respondent declared racelessness as personal: "Eu não defino uma pessoa por cor para mim todos são ser humano" (I don't define a person for his color because to me everyone is a human being). For another respondent, racelessness is particularly Brazilian: "O brasileiro não tem cor ou raça porque é misturado" (The Brazilian does not have color or race because he is mixed). This most closely approximates the racial-democracy thesis that racelessness has especially developed in Brazil.

Some respondents questioned the meaning of race itself. One respondent opined, "Eu sou *parda*. E raça, raça é o quê? Não sei o que significa raça." (I am *parda*. Race, what is THAT? I don't know what race means.) Thus, she claimed a Brazilian location, *parda*, while also questioning the concept of race.

In another voicing of deracialization, some declared that it is "all the same." One white said, "Pra mim tanto faz, eu sou *branca*" (To me, it's all the same, I'm white). This could be read from the vantage of white privilege: for a white, race does not matter because whites are raceless. One black claimed, "Pra mim são iguais, *negro*." (To me, all are equal. *Negro*.) This articulation, which strongly resembles the first, that all races are equal, also shifts by positively affirming the equality of all races. These variants affirm the view that there are multiple ways to articulate and interpret racial democracy (Radcliffe and Westwood 1996).

CLAIMS OF ETHNIC IDENTITY

Mostly *brancos* and several *pardos* emphasized their claimed ethnic origin in their identities. The predominant claim was *"branca* italiana" (Italian white) or *"branca—* alemã e italiana" (white—German and Italian). No Brazilian reference was contained: European and whiteness carry enough prestige. Further, in Brazil, that claim could also suggest a whiter Brazilian rather than a relatively whiter Brazilian. *Pardos* also claimed their ethnic origin: "Não sou *branco* nem sou *preto*, minha mãe é descendente de polonês, e meu pai de *negro*" (I am neither *branco* nor *preto*. My mother is of Polish descent and my father is of black descent.) Although this ethnic option resembles the "flexible, symbolic and voluntary" options of whites in the United States (Waters 1998; Omi 1997), the positionality of European immigrants in Brazil is different than in the United States. In Brazil, European ethnicity can be a claim to be a whiter white, an option that does not generally exist in the United States (Omi 1997).

CLAIMS OF BLACKNESS

Brazilians have increasingly claimed to be black since the 1991 census campaign, evident in the overall survey. Eight respondents claimed to be *"negra"* or of the *"raça negra"* (the black race). Some of those who identified as *negra* also voiced ambivalence: "Eu me considero *negra"* (I consider myself *negra*). Another respondent articulated the ambiguity between identifying as *negra* and the color identities: *"Negra,* eu me acho *negra,* embora as pessoas digam que sou *mulata* ou *parda,* mas eu me acho *negra"* (*Negra,* I think that I am *negra,* but others say that I am *mulata* or *parda,* but I think I am *negra"*). This ambivalence does not seem in service of the ranking grammar but a reflection of the ambiguity between the ranking grammar and the newer grammar of the Black Movement. Three respondents who identified with the black race (*raça negra*) exhibited less ambivalence. One simply identified as *raça negra,* while two others also claimed a color identity, one claiming to be *branca* and the other *parda.* The interviewer disagreed with the former, and thought that the *"raça negra—branca"* respondent was *parda.* Indeed, persons identifying as *negra* can be of any shade, ironically paralleling the category *moreno* in that one aspect. *Raça negra* is an ideological category within a broader continuum of color-oriented differences. This articulation does not observe either of the hypothesized grammars—neither seeking to be ranked on the overall color continuum, nor seeking to be racialized, but indeed constructing a new conjugation for the first-person plural: "we."

RECONSIDERATION OF THE FINDINGS
AND THE GRAMMAR OF COLOR IDENTITY

The data presented in the previous section illustrates the highly colorized and nuanced grammar of identity prevalent in Brazil. Brazilians convey their identities through nuanced discursive strategies that seek to emphasize positions of advantage and deemphasize less favorable positions in the overall color hierarchy. These findings from the "narrative" sample illustrate the hypothesized elements of the grammar of color identity, other elements consistent with the grammar theory, and other elements that point toward a reformulation of the theory.

First, the "narrative" sample and the overall sample illustrate the relationality of color terminology within the ranking grammar and the deracialization grammar. The many variations of *morena* illustrate ranking and deracialization, especially terms such as *morena fechada*, *parda clara*, and *meia parda*. Terms such as *meio encardida morena clara* and *parda—raça ruim* indicate that Fanonian self-hatred animate many discursive choices. Thirty respondents defined their identity as a negative reference to another identity, sometimes without adding a positive reference. And as we saw, the two grammars, while heuristically distinct, are often jointly voiced.

Second, the ambivalence highly evident in the "narrative" sample was expressive of both grammars. The most prevalent expression of ambivalence was "acho que sou *branco*," which can indicate a desire to be seen as white and an acknowledgement that others might view me darker, and therefore can convey both grammars. Other expressions of ambivalence include referencing the point of view of others, an identification card, or other source that could allow someone to claim to be lighter. Blanco reported that her respondents would emphasize the physical characteristic (such as fingernail color) that would allow for the lightest claim (Blanco 1978). PESB respondents positioned themselves between multiple locations supported by the external reference that allowed the lightest interpretation.

Third, the ethnic identities articulated within the "narrative" sample can also be viewed as a ranking grammar. Some whites use their Europeanness to distinguish themselves from the mixedness of other Brazilian whites. Other whites and some *pardos* emphasized their Europeanness as a mixed Brazilian. Thus, Europeanness within Brazil can be a claim to be a whiter white or to be relatively lighter on the overall color hierarchy.

Finally, the articulations of blackness in the overall sample and "narrative" sample reflect the newer subjectivity that the Black Movement has promoted since the census campaign of 1991 (Nobles 2000). *Negra* identity represents a diverse identity in the Brazilian color hierarchy, because it seeks to unite Brazilians who might identify from near white to black (Brandão and de Marins 2007). Thus, it represents a marked shift from the hypothesized grammars of identity and would best be conceptualized as a third grammar, an attempt to establish a first-person plural. That conceptualization would resonate with the perspectives of Sheriff and Telles. Additional work is needed to explore the contours of this third grammar and how it interacts with the other grammars.

What should be evident from this data is that the assertion that race does not matter rests upon a particular interpretation of these identity claims. In that view, either the sheer number or complexity of the claims, or the strength of the idea of mixing yields a country of mixed persons. However, an attentive reading of the complex identities reveals that they are fully racialized and nuanced positions within the overall structure of identity (Moura 1988; Caldwell 2006). Despite Freyre's claim, Brazilians are preoccupied with "minute characterizations of multiracial intermediates or nuance types" (Freyre 1966, 113–114).

The survey offers limited evidence about the significance of context, another hypothesized element of the grammar of color identity. In one version of the survey, respondents were informed about the provision of affirmative action on the grounds of race at the beginning of the survey. In the other version, there was no such stimulus. This experiment was constructed to test the possible impact of affirmative action on identity. Despite Bailey's claims (Bailey 2009), the difference between the two surveys was slight. There was no difference in the census identity of the two samples (Almeida 2007, 265). In open-ended identity, there was a slight difference. Respondents identified as *negra* at a higher rate in the experimental sample (8.8 percent) compared to the nonexperimental sample (4.8 percent) (Bailey 2009). However, there were no other increases in brown or black identities (Almeida 2007), surprising since the controversies in affirmative action have pertained to individuals allegedly claiming to be *pardo* for the purpose of affirmative action. The fact that only *negras* and neither *pardas* nor *morenas* identified at a higher rate within the experimental sample warrants further study. Consistent with the thesis of the significance of context for the grammar

TABLE 4. CONCORDANCE BETWEEN SELF-PLACEMENT AND INTERVIEWER ASSESSMENT

	NARRATIVE	OVERALL
Branco	66%	81%
Pardo	71%	75%
Preto	35%	46%
N	249	2,365

SOURCE: Secondary Analysis of the 2002 PESB by author.

of identity, this finding suggests that only a small group of more ideologically oriented Afro-Brazilians responded to the stimulus. Thus, affirmative action might be viewed as a needed counterbalance to the tendency to self-lighten, a counterbalance that has only reached a smaller population of Afro-Brazilians.

Most of the analysis of the PESB has pertained to open-ended societal identity. Brazilian affirmative action requires candidates to use census categories. Two findings from the PESB about census categories warrant comment. First, respondents, in both the narrative and overall samples, were overwhelmingly able to identify within census categories (Almeida 2007, 232). I argue that that dynamic is consistent with the grammar of identity, because identity claims are articulated to concrete audiences within specific contexts. All but 52 (22 percent) respondents in the overall sample were able to claim a census identity. Of these 52, 42 were viewed by the interviewer as *pardo* or *preto*. Therefore, these individuals would not be materially harmed if they sought affirmative-action benefits. Thus, a very small number of Brazilians (10 or 0.4 percent of the total) did not claim a census category and might not have been eligible for affirmative action if their identity was verified by a college.

Second, the concordance between self-identity and interviewer assessment was lower for the "narrative" sample than the overall sample, as shown in table 4. For both samples, the concordance was lowest for *pretos* and much higher for *brancos* and *pardos*. The difference between the samples was greatest for *brancos* and *pretos*, who would be viewed as self-lightening and self-darkening, respectively, from the perspective of the interviewer.[23] Moreover, one in seven (14.1 percent) of the *pardo* respondents in the overall sample were viewed as *branco* by the interviewer. This discordance is of particular significance for affirmative action. The next and concluding section considers the interaction of the grammar of color identity and the implementation of affirmative action in higher education.

CONCLUSION: AFFIRMATIVE ACTION
AND THE GRAMMAR OF COLOR IDENTITY

How might the grammar of color identity impact the implementation of affirmative action? Most of the ninety-four Brazilian colleges and universities that have adopted affirmative action (Carvalho 2009) have adopted policies that effectively limit the potential complications of color identity. First, Brazilian affirmative-action universities admit more class-based than race-based candidates. Of the seventy public universities with affirmative action, virtually all (sixty-one or 87 percent) admit students from public schools compared to about half (forty or 57 percent) that admit Afro-Brazilians (Feres et al. 2010). Second, race-based affirmative action has been almost always combined with class-based affirmative action. Almost all (90 percent) of the forty universities that admit Afro-Brazilians also require a class-based criterion, usually public school attendance (Feres et al. 2010). Third, universities do not solicit open-ended identity, but census identity. These measures effectively curb the influence of the ambiguities of identity.

Given that universities have adopted such measures, how much does the grammar of color identity matter for the implementation of affirmative action? The ambiguities of Brazilian identity, mutually constituted in the daily processes of differentiation and discrimination, need to be understood to develop viable affirmative-action policies:

> If the Brazilian way of classifying is so ambiguous as to allow an individual to be classified differently from the way he classifies himself, to implement affirmative action requires some rather specific knowledge of our complex logic of classifications. In other words, it requires us to understand the objective and subjective elements used to connect an individual to a color or race group, making him the target of discriminations which interfere with the course of his social life. (Brandão and de Marins 2007, 39)

Thus, identity is not simply declared on a single day, but constructed through many iterative social interactions.

The grammar of identity, especially as expressed in the discordance between self-identity and interviewer assessment, has implications for the implementation of affirmative action in Brazilian higher education, both for the definition and verification of beneficiaries. The strategic use of identity has certainly been reported at the State University of Rio de Janeiro (UERJ) and the Federal University of Brasilia (UNB). One candidate for admissions at UNB, a blond female, stated, "If others are benefiting, why shouldn't I?" (Racusen 2009, 30). I argue that this constitutes a problem of legitimacy and not fraud because of the weight of that perception on the calculations of all candidates. Further, as mentioned earlier, one out of seven self-identified *pardos* on the PESB were viewed as *branco* by the interviewer, which poses problems for the coherence and even legitimacy of affirmative action. Indeed, the universities that verify the racial identity of candidates have rejected between 5 percent and 35 percent of the candidates (Racusen 2009, 35), which could indicate candidates' strategic use of identity and/or the discordance between self-identity and the view of others. Thus, I claim an underlying tension between identity and affirmative action that Brazilian universities have generally sought to limit.

The predominant approach of Brazilian universities has been to reserve approximately half of their admissions for public school students,[24] including a proportionate share of Afro-Brazilians within that half set according to state census data. This approach effectively represents class-based affirmative action that seeks to assure racial balance among public school entrants. Under this approach, some universities confirm the identity of their applicants by requiring proof of public school attendance, a less sensitive task than verifying racial identity. Thus, a white who might claim to be *pardo* for the purpose of affirmative action for these universities also merits affirmative action because of attending public school.

In addition to asking students for their census identity, many universities include a second identity question intended to curb the vagaries of *pardo* identity (Rabelo 2004). According to one study, 20 percent of public universities also require candidates to declare themselves to be *negro* (Feres et al. 2010). Universities use three different supra-identities: *negro, Afro-descendente,* or *Afro-Brasilero* (Afro-Brazilian) to define their beneficiaries (Feres et al. 2010). Of the three terms, the use of *negro* would narrow the beneficiary class, and the use of *Afro-descendente* would expand the beneficiary class. In one study, 49 percent of self-identified *pardos* and 91 percent of self-identified *pretos* also identified as *negro* (Brandão and de Marins 2007, 36). By contrast, 82 percent of *pardos*, 95 percent of *pretos*, and even the majority of self-identified whites (57 percent) also identified as *Afro-descendente* (Brandão and de Marins 2007, 35). Thus, the term *Afro-descendente* is overinclusive, and the term *negro* is underinclusive in the current moment. I question using the term *negro* for university admissions, not because I oppose black consciousness in Brazil, but because I argue that black consciousness should not be a requirement for university admission.[25]

The primary controversy pertaining to identity has arisen from the method an individual candidate must use to present her identity. Most of the universities (85 percent) accept candidate self-declaration alone to establish candidate identity. Six (15 percent) universities also require photos and/or interviews, which might also be subjected to university verification (Feres et al. 2010). This latter approach has mostly been adopted by universities, especially several highly competitive public universities, admitting private school Afro-Brazilians. Including private school students has opened Pandora's box, because private-school students of any color might claim to be *pardo* (brown) to gain admission.

The verification of the racial identity of these candidates has generated the greatest notoriety. Some affirmative-action supporters argue that the principle of the social constructedness of identity means that the subjective identity claims should be used without verification for the purposes of admissions to an affirmative-action program. This view concedes the complexity of identity and argues that, either for reasons of pragmatism and/or the recognition of the primacy of socially constructed identities, identity claims should be accepted without verification. In this view, the experience of being admitted as an affirmative-action student would serve as a moral sanction upon candidates, and would hypothetically inhibit such claims (Carvalho 2005). I argue that identity in Brazil is relational—and that as such, claims are made predicated upon their reception. Knowing that any claim would automatically be accepted would encourage Brazilians to darken for the purpose of affirmative action.

Although I share some of the concerns about the processes of verification, I defend the use of verification for high-demand opportunities. To democratize medical schools, engineering and law departments, and other high-demand courses, colleges may elect to include Afro-Brazilians from private schools as eligible for affirmative action. If so, some whites will also seek those seats, coached perhaps by their preparatory programs or parents, and advance a strategic claim to be *pardo*. The ensuing trouble is not that a few may deceive the system, but rather that all white applicants in those programs would be tempted to advance such a claim unless it is known that identity will be verified.

In those instances in which colleges do verify identity, I argue that verification can and should be conducted according to the principles of the social construction of identity. Candidate declaration of self-identity and submission of photographs, required initially at three universities (Racusen 2009), was problematic. Candidates denied admission based upon their appearance did not get to speak until appealing their denial. Although physical appearance matters, a myriad of other factors, especially family background (Brandão and de Marins 2007), matter as well. Most candidates who appealed on the basis of their family background were subsequently admitted (Racusen 2009). Most of the universities that verify have switched to an interview process that is vastly superior to the use of photographs. Colleges might also consider having applicants bring supporting materials, such as photos of their parents, and submit an essay about their family and identity to grant applicants an increased voice in the process. Further, selection committees might undergo training to assess identity. UNB initially expected its verification commission to reflect the popular social view, which may not be sufficient to ensure the legitimacy of the process. Thus I claim that the social construction of identity does not necessarily obligate colleges to accept self-asserted identity. Instead, the full acknowledgment of social constructed-ness—recognizing context, relationality, and positionality—places self-assertions in dialogue with the perceptions of others.

Finally, how might affirmative-action policy influence the grammar of identity? Brazilian identity has been shifting since 1990. In numerous surveys of open-ended identity over the past twenty years, Brazilians have become less likely to claim to be *moreno* and other traditional terms and more likely to identity as *parda*, *preta*, or *negra*. It is still unclear how much affirmative action will accelerate this broader secular trend. Most likely, it will contribute to this shift, but for reasons very different from the claim of opponents that affirmative action "imposes" the categories it prefers. Identity change does not necessarily come about for strategic advantage on a single day. One might be a *pardo* for the purpose of university admission without changing her identity. However, the experience of higher education has had an impact on Afro-Brazilian identity prior to affirmative action, and undoubtedly that impact will grow with the greater representation of Afro-Brazilians in the university.

NOTES

1. By "identity market," I refer to the fact that social contexts shape demand and also supply for particular identities. Thus, for example, the Brazilian taboo on being black created disincentives to identify as black, and effectively lowered the demand for blacks and increased the demand for browns. The theory of identity markets suggests that these shifts in demand produce shifts in the supply of identity. See Cunningham 2002.

2. Sheriff distinguishes three "discourses" or "registers" of identity: (1) a "descriptive discourse" used to describe rather than classify others, (2) a "pragmatic discourse" used to "treat" others in daily life, and (3) a bipolar "discourse on race" that distinguishes white and black and anchors the three discourses. Although Sheriff acknowledges the role of relationality and positionality within the labeling processes, her account does not theorize how relationality and positionality inform the use of the three "registers." Telles distinguishes three systems: the popular system, the IBGE, and the "Black Movement" system, a bipolar system of *branco/negro* (Telles 2004).

3. Reference to Harris's calculus of identity.

4. For example, Gilberto Freyre showed that Brazil did not resemble the post–World War I United

States that he observed. His work was rich descriptively but did not advance systemic claims about Brazilian practices. See Skidmore 2002.

5. In methodology that highly influenced a first wave of anthropologists, Harris constructed a series of drawings that combined diverse physical features, including skin tone, hair texture, lips, and noses, and asked his respondents to evaluate the drawings. In response to the 72 drawings, most respondents used nine categories, and each drawing received at least "20 different lexical combinations" (Harris 1964, 2–3).

6. Sanjek (1971) reported 116 categories, Harris (1964) reported 344 categories, and the 1976 National Census Household Survey (the Pesquisa Nacional por Amostra de Domicílios, or PNAD) reported 136 categories (Moura 1988).

7. These prominent anthropologists include Hutchinson, who found ten overall terms, but that few people fit into these "types" (Hutchinson 1957, 120). Harris found twelve common terms used in 31 combinations, but could not find the logic to the use of the terms (Harris 1970). Sanjek reported 116 terms in total, of which between ten and sixteen were widely used, and also studied combinations (Sanjek, 1971). Kottak received over forty responses which he organized into five groups (Kottak 1967). Sheriff reported approximately twelve terms (Sheriff 2001, 34), and Teixeira reported ten terms (Teixeira 1986, 28–35). Blanco found nine main terms. Telles identified six or seven terms that accounted for 95 percent of the responses (Telles 2004, 82).

8. Blanco (1978) found *sarará* to be inconsistently used because it represents contrasting characteristics.

9. Guimarães 1995, 221, cited by Caldwell 2006, 33.

10. The terms that describe skin color include: *moreno* alvo, *moreno* bem chegado, *moreno* bem *claro*, *moreno* bem escuro, *moreno claro*, *moreno* escuro, *moreno* escuro *claro*, *moreno* laranjado, *moreno* prata, *moreno preto*, *moreno* roxo, *moreno* ruivo, *moreno* trigueiro, *moreno* canelado, and *moreno* cor de canela.

11. The terms that refer to other features (especially hair texture) include: *moreno* cabelo sarara, *moreno* de cabelo bom, *moreno* de cabelo cacheado, *moreno* de cabelo escuhido, *moreno* de cabelo liso, *moreno* de cabelo ruim, and *moreno* de olhos verdes.

12. The terms that combine "types" include: *moreno* castanho, *moreno* cabo verde, *moreno* cabocolo, *moreno claro* caboclado, *moreno* mestico, *moreno* mulato, *moreno* sarara, and *moreno* preto.

13. The terms that characterize position include: *moreno* fechado, *moreno* fino, *moreno* bem suspecito, and *moreno* bronzeado.

14. Marvin Harris sought to differentiate these combinations.

15. Here also consider that Brazilian Portuguese reflects the perceived relationship of speaker and audience, such as the differentiation of *você* (you) and *o senhor* (a more polite "you" that acknowledges someone older and/or of higher social standing). See Blanco 1978, 77.

16. Hutchinson 1957, 118.

17. Twine 1998; Teixeira 1986.

18. Twine 1998, 46–52.

19. In my previous work, I found that 28 percent of the complaints in Sao Paulo occurred between neighbors, and another 2 percent occurred in other private settings. See Racusen 2002, 229.

20. See Almeida 2007 for a comprehensive discussion of the entire survey. See also Bailey 2009

for a thorough discussion of racial classification from a neo-Freyrian perspective of this and several other surveys.

21. Holanda Ferreira 1986, 29.

22. This can refer to freckles or other kinds of marks.

23. Others have shown that Brazilians of lower education and socioeconomic status are more likely to self-lighten (Telles 2004; Miranda-Ribeiro and Caetano 2005, 12).

24. According to one study, this figure might be closer to 40 percent. See Feres et al. 2010.

25. Frei David Raimundo dos Santos, a highly influential black Brazilian activist, agrees that black consciousness should not be a requirement to enter under affirmative action. As he recognizes, black consciousness in Brazil needs to be constructed and may occur in higher education or beyond (Raimundo 2009).

REFERENCES

Almeida, Alberto Carlos. 2007. *A Cabeça do Brasileiro*. Rio de Janeiro: Record.

Bailey, Stanley R. 2009. *Legacies of Race: Identities, Attitudes, and Politics in Brazil*. Stanford, CA: Stanford University Press.

Bauman, Gerd, and Andre Gingrich. 2004. *Grammars of Identity/Alterity: A Structural Approach*. Oxford: Berghahn Books.

Blanco, Merida. 1978. "Race and Face among the Poor: The Language of Color in a Brazilian Bairro." PhD dissertation, Stanford University.

Brandão, André Augusto, and Mani Tebet A. de Marins. 2007. "Quotas for Blacks in Higher Education and Forms of Racial Classification." *Educação e Pesquisa, Sao Paulo* 33(1):27–45.

Caldwell, Kia. 2006. *Negras in Brazil: Re-Envisioning Black Women, Citizenship, and the Politics of Identity*. New Brunswick, NJ: Rutgers University Press.

Carvalho, José Jorge de. 2005. "Usos e abusos da antropologia em contexto de tensão racial: O caso das cotas para negros na UNB." *Horizontes Antropológicos* 11:237.

———. 2009. "Cotas: Uma nova consciência acadêmica." *Folha de São Paulo* 20 (September).

Cunningham, E. Christi. 2002. "Identity Markets." *Howard Law Journal* 45:491–497.

Dzidzienyo, Anani. 1971. "The Position of Blacks in Brazilian Society." London: Minority Rights Group.

Feres Júnior, João, Verônica Toste Daflon, and Luiz Augusto Campos. 2010. "Ação afirmativa no ensino superior brasileiro hoje: Análise institucional." Report of the Grupo de Estudos Multidisciplinares da Ação Afirmativa. Rio de Janeiro: Instituto de Estudos Sociais e Políticos, Universidade Estadual do Rio de Janeiro.

Freyre, Gilberto. 1966. *The Racial Factor in Contemporary Politics*. London: MacGibbon and Kee.

———. 1986. *The Masters and the Slaves: A Study in the Development of Brazilian Civilization*. 2nd English language ed. Berkeley: University of California Press.

Galanter, Marc. 1984. *Competing Equalities, Law and the Backward Classes in India*. Oxford: Oxford University Press.

Guimarães, Antonio Sérgio Alfredo. 1995. "Racismo e anti-racismo no Brasil." *Novos Estudos* 43 (November):26.

Harris, Marvin. 1964. "Racial Identity in Brazil." *Luso-brazilian Review* 1.

———. 1970. "Referential Ambiguity in the Calculus of Brazilian Racial Identity." *Southwestern Journal of Anthropology* 26(1):2.

Holanda Ferreira, Aurélio Buarque de. 1986. *Novo dicionário da lingua portuguesa.* 2nd ed. Editora Nova Fronteira.

Hutchinson, Harry W. 1957. *Village and Plantation Life in Northeastern Brazil.* Seattle: University of Washington Press.

Jenkins, Laura Dudley. 2004. "Race, Caste, and Justice: Social Science Categories and Antidiscrimination Policies in India and the United States." *Conn. L. Rev.* 36:747.

Kottak, Conrad P. 1967. "Race Relations in a Bahia Fishing Village." *Luso-Brazilian Review* 4(2):35.

Miranda-Ribeiro, Paula, and André Junqueira Caetano. 2005. "Como eu me vejo e como ela me vê: Um estudo esploratório sobre a consistência das declarações de raça/cor entre as mulheres de 15 a 59 anos no recife, 2002." CEDEPLAR/Universidade Federal de Minas Gerais. Texto para discussão no. 250 (February).

Moura, Clovis. 1988. *Sociologia do Negro Brasileiro.* São Paulo: Atica.

Nobles, Melissa. 2000. *Shades of Citizenship: Race and the Census in Modern Politics.* Stanford, CA: Stanford University Press.

Omi, Michael. 1997. "SYMPOSIUM: Our Private Obsession, Our Public Sin: Racial Identity and the State: The Dilemmas of Classification." *Law & Inequality Journal* 15 (Winter):7.

Rabelo, Mauro. 2004. Interview. August 17.

Racusen, Seth. 2002. "'A *Mulato* Cannot Be Prejudiced': The Legal Construction of Racial Discrimination in Contemporary Brazil." PhD dissertation, Massachusetts Institute of Technology.

———. 2009. "Affirmative Action and Identity." In *Brazil's New Racial Politics*, ed. Bernd Reiter and Gladys L. Mitchell. Boulder, CO: Lynne Rienner Publishers.

Radcliffe, Sarah, and Sallie Westwood. 1996. *Remaking the Nation: Place, Identity, and Politics in Latin America.* London: Routledge.

Raimundo dos Santos, Frei David. 2009. Interview. Brasilia, 27 June.

Sanjek, Roger. 1971. "Brazilian Racial Terms: Some Aspects of Meaning and Learning." *American Anthropologist* 73:1126.

Sansone, Livio. 2003. *Blackness without Ethnicity: Constructing Race in Brazil.* New York: Palgrave Macmillan.

Sheriff, Robin E. 2001. *Dreaming Equality, Color, Race, and Racism in Urban Brazil.* New Brunswick, NJ: Rutgers University Press.

Skidmore, Thomas. 1993. *Black into White: Race and Nationality in Brazilian Thought.* Durham, NC: Duke University Press.

———. 2002. "Raízes de Gilberto Freyre." *Journal of Latin American Studies* 34:1.

Stephens, Thomas M. 1989. *Dictionary of Latin American Racial and Ethnic Terminology.* Gainesville: University of Florida Press.

Teixeira, Moema de Poli. 1986. *Família e identidade racial: Os limites da cornas relações e representações de um grupo de baixa renda.* Master's thesis, Rio de Janeiro, Museu Nacional, Programa de Pós-Graduação em Antropologia Social da UFRJ.

Telles, Edward E. 2004. *Race in Another America.* Princeton, NJ: Princeton University Press.

Twine, France Winddance. 1998. *Racism in a Racial Democracy: The Maintenance of White Supremacy in Brazil.* New Brunswick, NJ: Rutgers University Press.

Waters, Mary. 1998. "Multiple Ethnic Identity Choices." In *Beyond Pluralism: The Conception of Groups and Group Identities in America,* ed. Wendy F. Katkin, Ned Landsman, and Andrea Tyree. Urbana: University of Illinois Press.

Winant, Howard H. 1994. *Racial Conditions: Politics, Theory, Comparisons.* Minneapolis: University of Minnesota Press.

PART 3

Racism in "Raceless" Societies and the State: The Difficulties of Addressing What Ought Not Exist

Afro-Colombian Welfare: An Application of Amartya Sen's Capability Approach Using Multiple Indicators Multiple Causes Modeling (MIMIC)

Paula A. Lezama

martya Sen's Capability Approach has emerged as an alternative framework to long-established economical approaches that seek to analyze
individual welfare, poverty and human development from narrow monetary perspectives (Kuklys 2005; Clark 2005). The Capability Approach identifies
three elements—*functionings*, *capabilities*, and *agency*—to analyze individual welfare.
Functionings represent the achieved welfare of an individual: what a person manages to be or do in the different dimensions of human life. These "beings" and
"doings" vary in a wide range of aspects, from being adequately nourished and in
good health to more complex achievements like having self-confidence or walking
without shame. Capabilities express the set of available functionings an individual
has to choose from. They are the set of choices people have, or the freedom to
choose the life they want (Sen 1985b, 1999). In turn, agency is the human capacity
to determine one's life. It is by the free exercise of individual agency that people
achieve valuable capabilities (welfare). In this context, development policy must
be aimed to (re)create the institutional and social arrangements to guarantee
this free exercise. By using Sen's approach, I thus accept the conceptual premise
that human welfare is more about substantive freedoms enjoyed across multiple
dimensions (valuable capabilities), and less about how much income a person has.
Furthermore, I support the argument that cumulative development can best be
achieved by expanding the range of individual freedoms, as they have instrumental

value to achieving economic development, but most importantly, these freedoms have an intrinsic value in fostering human well-being.

From this standpoint, this research conceptualizes human welfare as the achievement of valuable capabilities, and it seeks to analyze it in comparative perspective. Specifically, it seeks to understand welfare differences between Afro-Colombians and non-Afro-Colombians in two dimensions, namely "knowledge" and "shelter" capabilities. Its aim is to understand how ethnic and racial characteristics affect the achievement of welfare for individual members of the Afro-Colombian population vis-à-vis non-Afro-Colombians in the analyzed dimensions, beyond income levels or consumption patterns. The two dimensions of human welfare analyzed here were chosen for both their intrinsic and instrumental relevance. The "knowledge capability," which represents the individual possibility to choose the level of knowledge and education a person wants and has reason to value, is translated into the functioning space (realized welfare) as years of education and training activities. In turn, these are closely linked to processes of social mobility, human capital accumulation, and economic growth. On the other hand, "being properly sheltered," people's opportunity to chose their preferred shelter conditions, is an intrinsic aspect of human development that translates into the functioning space as having enough space, access to drinking water, and public-services infrastructure. These are also instrumental factors contributing to health and educational outcomes. Living in an overcrowded environment, a lack of drinking water, and unsafe construction materials are factors highly correlated with a number of health deficiencies and low academic performance.[1]

This paper also seeks to contribute to the ongoing discussion about quantitative methods in the social sciences suitable to operationalize Amartya Sen's Capability Approach. By implementing a Multiple Indicators Multiple Causes (MIMIC) model to assess capabilities in two dimensions of human welfare, "knowledge" and "being adequately sheltered," as latent constructs (Jöreskog and Goldberger 1975), this research seeks to develop a quantitative application of the Capability Approach. The aim of MIMIC is to capture how a set of exogenous variables (e.g., ethnicity, gender, or being poor) expand or contract a given capability dimension (e.g., "knowledge"), which is assessed as an unobserved variable. In turn, that given capability determines specific outcomes or individual functioning achievements (e.g., achieved years of education). These individual functioning achievements are the set of indicators of the given latent construct. Although this technique does not allow the quantification of a capability dimension as such, it does allow the determination of what and how they are influenced, and in turn, which level of individual welfare a person is able to secure given the freedom or capability he or she enjoyed when choosing. Accordingly, lower-functioning achievement is associated with lower capability or less freedom, which in turn is caused by the interaction of factors such as age, gender, race, and location. The contrary also holds true. This methodology thus allows the identification of the impact of those factors over the knowledge and shelter capabilities, and in turn, how these impacts are translated into achieved welfare of an individual in the specific dimension. The study uses the 2003 Quality of Life Survey (ECV 2003 in Spanish)[2] implemented by the National Department of Statistics in Colombia. The QLS 2003 was a survey designed to assess the socioeconomic conditions of the Colombian population with a sample of 24,090 households and 85,145 individuals, representative at the national level. Calculations were performed using the Statistical Analysis System (SAS), and its procedure Covariance Analysis of Linear Structural Equation (CALIS).

Historically, Afro-Colombians have been marginalized from the benefits of modernity and democracy. Socially excluded, they have the worst living conditions in comparative terms to the rest of the population (Arocha 1998; Urrea et al. 2005; Escobar 2003). They have the highest illiteracy rates in the country, 15.2 percent against 8.1 percent of non-Afro-Colombians, and health and housing indicators follow the same trend (Urrea et al. 2005). Under standard welfare analysis of group disparities, the deprived conditions of Afro-Colombians have been considered as the accumulated result of low income and class disparities. However, the persistence and magnitude of the racial gaps in the country suggest that practices of racial discrimination are limiting Afro-Colombians' individual agency. Moreover, the results obtained from the statistical application in this paper further support this argument (see tables 2 and 4).[3] Consequently, it can be argued that systematic lower capability and functioning achievement for Afro-Colombians in relation to non-Afro-Colombians is to a large extent due to unyielding social practices of racial discrimination, and not only to class differences as has been traditionally argued. In this context, public policy must go beyond affirmative-action policies aimed at improving access to education, health, and housing. It is imperative to develop public policy toward increasing direct political participation, and to effectively enforce the rule of law, specifically the laws and treaties established to promote Afro-descendants' ethnic rights and to prevent discrimination against them. It is only by a successful combination of affirmative-action policies and the enforcement of the rule of law that Afro-Colombians could see their capabilities expanded.

AFRO-COLOMBIANS' CONDITIONS

Colombia, in the wider context of Latin America and the Caribbean, has been one of the nations living under the so-called myth of racial democracy. This myth is based on the belief that Latin American societies are the product of a harmonious coexistence and mixing of the different racial groups, and that these societies are free from racial tensions (Miller 2004; Skidmore 1993; Reiter and Mitchell 2009). The ideal of societies free from racial divisions emerged as a counter-discourse against colonial powers in Latin American in the late 1800s. Latin American elites saw in the development of an all-inclusive national discourse the power to create compliant societies to forge modern nations while resisting international exclusion by the "white power" nations of North America and Europe. Colombia was not a stranger to these processes of national and racial identity formation. Given the geographical segregation of blacks and indigenous communities in the country after the wars of independence, national elites sought to forge a national identity according to the "cult of the mestizo nation" or the cult of mixed race (Lasso 2007). According to Arocha (1998), the ideal behind the national constitution of 1886 can be summed up in a national motto: "One God, One Race, and [One] Tongue" (71). Although in 1890 indigenous communities were allowed to retain a separate identity within the utopia of the new republic, which was a concession that took place in the hope that Catholic missionaries would be able to eventually integrate them into the new Christian nation, Afro-descendants remained for the most part invisible to the national reality and identity formation of the country. Thus, the cult of the mestizo nation led to development of a national discourse based on the denial of racial categories in an attempt to avoid social conflict. Public discussions of the topic of race and racial discrimination were forbidden, and any mention of it was considered unpatriotic. As the nation was consolidating itself as a modern democratic society, the denial of race became increasingly part of a broadly supported mainstream. Nowadays, the myth of racial democracy survives, and Colombian society is still living to a great extent in a state of racial denial (Wade 1995). Although some progress has been achieved in terms of racial equality by the enactment of the 1991 national constitution, which recognizes the country's cultural and ethnic diversity, a meaningful recognition of the existence and importance of ethnic minorities has not been achieved yet, and the existence and pervasiveness of racial-discrimination patterns in Colombian society are still effectively denied by the state and broad parts of the predominantly white and mestizo society.

In the midst of this denial, Afro-descendants and ethnic minorities in general are the poorest of the poor. Although there are several possible causes for these disparities, such as a cumulative result of lower income and educational attainment, as argued by traditional analysis of class disparities, the persistence and magnitude of these inequalities suggest that racial discrimination is an important factor disadvantaging these subgroups of the Colombian population.

A first indication hinting at the troubled situation of Afro-descendants is provided by the fact that official statistical data collected in the country have systematically neglected ethnic and racial minorities, including the Afro-Colombian population. According to 1993 census data, the Afro-Colombian population was around 1.5 percent of the total population. Later on, according to the 2000 National Household Survey, this population increased to around 17.9 percent of the total population. In 2005 the National Census estimated the Afro-Colombian population to be 10.3 percent of the total population, which is not consistent with the previous number given for 2000 based on the National Household Survey. More recently, Urrea argued that Afro-Colombians represent between 20 percent and 22 percent of the national population: between 8.6 and 9.5 million people (2006). In this regard, this author explains how different methodologies and survey questionnaires lead to different numbers. Accordingly, variations in data, instead of reflecting real demographic changes, must rather be attributed to unreliable and changing census tools, as well as to widespread tendencies to "whiten" census participants and thus contribute to their invisibility. This invisibility then reinforces the marginalization and exclusion of the Afro-Colombian population (Nobles 2000).

Traditional poverty and inequality indicators show huge gaps between the Afro-descendant and non-Afro-descendant populations. This is aggravated by the spatial distribution of the Afro-population, which is mainly located in isolated zones of the Pacific and Atlantic coasts of the country. The Pacific and the Atlantic coasts are not only the regions with the largest population of African descent; they also are the least developed regions of the country. These areas are completely vulnerable not only for their lack of infrastructure, but also for the negative impact generated by the presence of illegally armed groups. Moreover, recent waves of migration to cities like Cali, Medellín, and Bogotá are the result of forced displacement and extreme conditions of poverty. According to the Consultation on Human Rights and Displacement (CODHES 2008), a Colombian nonprofit organization, Afro-Colombians represent about 22.5 percent of the total displaced population in the country. Thus, for Afro-Colombians, displacement is directly affecting not only their livelihoods but also their ethnic and cultural survival.[4] The next table presents the percentage of population under the poverty line based on the 2003 Quality of Life Survey. It uses a poverty level of two dollars per capita per day, and an indigent level of one dollar per capita per day, which are the thresholds internationally defined by the World Bank.

It is possible to observe that Afro-descendants and indigenous communities are always at the bottom, with significant difference between urban and rural settings. In terms of health and education, the numbers are no more encouraging. According to the 2005 census, the infant mortality rate among Afro-descendants is nearly twice as high as that of the rest of the population: 48.1 percent and 26.9 percent per 1,000

TABLE 1. PERCENTAGES OF POOR AND INDIGENT POPULATIONS
FOR 2003, BY URBAN-RURAL AREAS

NATIONAL POPULATION	POPULATION UNDER PL		POPULATION UNDER IL	
	URBAN	RURAL	URBAN	RURAL
Afro-Colombians	43.0%	76.8%	16.7%	46.9%
Indigenous/Gypsies	52.6%	81.0%	22.0%	44.2%
Mestizos/Whites	36.6%	72.6%	13.6%	39.2%
National Total	37.3%	73.2%	13.9%	40.1%

SOURCE: Urrea and Viafara 2007, 60, based on 2003 QLS.

live births, respectively. In addition, the infant mortality rate increases up to 77.5 percent in the department of Chocó, which is the home of about 44.1 percent of the total Afro-Colombian population of the country (National Department of Planning 2007),[5] and where Afro-Colombians make up 89 percent of the population. The infant mortality rate in Chocó is comparable to that of the Republic of the Congo, Ethiopia, and Mauritania in Africa, with about 79 percent, 75 percent, and 75 percent, respectively. Life expectancy for Afro-Colombians is about 66.4 years, while for the rest of the population it is around 72.8 years. It also worthy to note that life expectancy is even lower for the Afro-descendants living in the Chocó region, which has consistently lower standards in comparative terms, not only with the rest of the population, but also with the Afro-Colombian population located in different regions of the country (Observatory on Racial Discrimination 2008).

In addition, according to the 2005 census data, 11 percent of Afro-Colombian children did not attend elementary school, while for high school education the rate went up to 27 percent. The reasons for school absenteeism range from the lack of money to cover the cost of tuition and materials, to the lack of infrastructure, and to the availability of teachers. These problems persist despite the state's obligation to provide free elementary education up to the fifth grade to the entire population. The inability of the Colombian state to guarantee basic rights to its ethnic minorities contrasts sharply with the country's laws and human-rights protocols signed at the international level. In 1991, Colombia promulgated a new national constitution,[6] in which ethnic groups and minorities were granted special rights not only as compensation for a history of marginalization, but also as a means of preserving ethnic communities within their own cultural, social, and economic structures. In addition to the constitutional articles, there are three additional laws and legal norms directed towards fighting discrimination, yet the judicial system lacks effective guidelines to comply with these laws.[7] As a result, racial discriminators are not prosecuted, nor are victims compensated. Finally, there are no preventive measures to avert future episodes of racial discrimination (Observatory on Racial Discrimination 2008). Moreover, neither the adoption of the International Labor Organization (ILO) convention about indigenous and tribal communities,[8] nor the signing of the UN International Convention on the Elimination of All Forms of Racial Discrimination[9] have led to any major improvement in the living conditions of the Afro-Colombian population, which points to a weak state, unable or unwilling to protect all of its citizens and extend citizenship rights to them. Afro-Colombians' vulnerability is endemic to all aspects of human life since they are socially, economically, politically, and culturally excluded from Colombian society; they live as second-class citizens.

Nowadays, more than 150 years after the abolition of slavery, 18 years after the enactment of the 1991 national constitution and the signing of several international treaties and protocols, Afro-Colombians are still persistently marginalized, and legal recognition of Afro-Colombian rights has not translated into effective enforcement mechanisms and public policies to address their marginalization. This lack of a political and judicial mechanism to guarantee basic human and constitutional rights for Afro-Colombians, in conjunction with the harsh reality of their exclusion, points toward the proposition that their marginalization is less the result of low income and more the result of racial discrimination, and that racial discrimination is one important underlying cause of these precarious conditions.

AMARTYA SEN'S CAPABILITY APPROACH

Amartya Sen's Capability Approach (CA) is centered on the enhancement of individual freedoms as both the end and means of development. Sen's CA states that social arrangements and development policy should aim to expand people's capabilities, that is, "the substantive freedom he or she enjoys to lead the kind of life he or she values and has reasons to value" (Alkire 2005a, 1). According to the author, any welfare assessment must account for the factors expanding or constraining people's freedoms, which implies going beyond income levels. The author criticizes standard welfare economic approaches that concentrate their analyses in terms of wealth (opulence, income, and/or expenditure) or utility (happiness or human-fulfillment achieved outcomes mostly measured in terms of expanded choices of consumption). He argues that the analysis in terms of opulence assumes that income is an end in itself; consequently, it does not account for individual differences when converting income into valuable achievements (Sen 1985a, 1985b, 1999). Furthermore, the relation between low income and poverty is instrumental and variable—instrumental in the sense that there are other factors that influence poverty, and that income is just one means among others to reduce it. The ability to convert income into better living standards varies greatly among communities and individuals. In addition, as was noted also by Rawls (1971), the analysis of individual welfare in terms of utility does not set apart different sources of satisfaction and distaste, and cannot reflect the intrinsic value of aspects such as human rights. Besides, these traditional frameworks assume that individual rationality is based on self-interest, an assumption that has been widely criticized as people often consider wider concerns when deciding among a set of alternatives (Sen 1985b, 1990, 1999). Sen states that neither utility nor income allow us to evaluate comprehensibly individual welfare and social development.

To fill these theoretical gaps, Sen developed the Capability Approach, which assesses individual well-being by considering realized welfare and the freedom to choose among different options in order to reach one's fulfillment by the exercise of one's agency. It identifies three elements: *functionings*, *capabilities*, and *agency*. Accordingly, functionings express the realized welfare of an individual in each dimension of human well-being. In other words, a functioning is what a person has been able to achieve and secure; it is what he or she actually achieved (for example, finished years of education is a functioning indicator in the knowledge dimension of human welfare). Capabilities, in turn, represent the set of options available to the individual to achieve his/her desired level of well-being (Alkire 2005b, Saith 2001). A capability maps the actual possibilities laid out for an individual to reach his/her fulfillment. Thus, the knowledge capability would comprise the combination of different knowledge functionings from which the individual can choose the specific option he or she prefers (e.g., to go to a public or private school). Finally, Sen defines individual agency as "what the person is free to do and achieve in pursuit of whatever goals or values he or she regards as important" (Sen 1985a, 203); and in his book *Development as Freedom*, he argues that the aim of development must be the expansion of individual freedoms (Sen 1999). In this context, capabilities are determined by the extent to which an individual can exercise his/her agency, and the aim of development is to expand and guarantee the exercise of said agency. Sen's CA argues that individuals must be agents of their own development as they are the ones who must reason and decide what constitutes a valuable end in their lives.

Historically, the Western construction of race has imposed a social handicap on peoples of "color" across the globe. Thus, their real possibilities or capabilities are restricted by the status quo of social arrangements that limit their individual freedoms, as they are subjects not just of racial discrimination, but of other kinds of discrimination as well. Given that the impact of discrimination limits the exercise of individual agency, it negatively affects people's welfare across multiple dimensions. This negative impact takes place even when people are not considered poor by standard measures; but since these people are not considered "poor" by standard measures, and the fight against racial discrimination is not a top priority in public policy, their achievement of welfare has been, is, and will be limited until traditional paradigms of human welfare based on income stop being the drivers of public policy.[10] Hence, the importance of going beyond income levels when analyzing individual welfare of Afro-descendants and ethnic minorities. Furthermore, this supports the suitability of Amartya Sen's Capability Approach as the appropriate framework to analyze racial inequalities and Afro-Colombians' welfare, as it allows the consideration of the role that racial discrimination plays in limiting the exercise of individual freedom for members of ethnic and racial minorities as an explicit category of analysis.

USING MULTIPLE INDICATORS MULTIPLE CAUSES (MIMIC) MODELING TO APPLY AMARTYA SEN'S CAPABILITY APPROACH

Since a capability set is determined by the interaction of a wide range of aspects, and modeling such complexity requires a sophisticated methodology, "Latent Variable Modeling," of which Multiple Indicators Multiple Causes (MIMIC) modeling is a part, has proven to be a useful tool in this matter (Kuklys 2005; Di Tommaso 2007; Krishnakumar 2007). Specifically, the use of MIMIC modeling to estimate the "shelter" and "knowledge" capabilities is justified because capabilities are the set of choices from which an individual selects what he or she wants to achieve in a given point in time. What a person manages to "be" or "do" at that point is a functioning or achieved welfare (e.g., elementary school); but that level of achieved welfare is not saying much about the freedom that person enjoyed—the choices he or she had in the capability set—when achieving a specific level of welfare in the given dimension. Given the multidimensional character of capabilities as comprising the set of choices an individual has, it is very difficult to measure them directly; thus, we have to rely on a set of observed *functionings* (achieved welfare variables) to infer the behavior of individual capabilities (latent variable). A latent variable represents a complex conceptual construct that cannot be measured directly and has to be inferred or approached through a set of observed variables called indicators. By modeling capabilities as unobserved constructs in a MIMIC model, it is possible to account for both the factors

Paula A. Lezama

TABLE 2. VARIABLE DESCRIPTION AND MEASUREMENT

LATENT VARIABLES OR CAPABILITIES	FUNCTIONINGS OR ACHIEVED WELL-BEING (OBSERVED INDICATORS)	VARIABLE MEASUREMENT	INDIVIDUAL CHARACTERISTICS (EXOGENOUS CAUSES OF CAPABILITIES)
SHELTER	Dwelling conditions of the household	Categorical Variable (–1=low/0=middle/ 1=high quality)	Age
	Basic services conditions (electricity, water, waste management, and sanitary infrastructure)	Categorical Variable (–1=low/0=middle/ 1=high quality)	Gender
	Overcrowding (> 3 persons/room)	Dichotomous (1=yes/0=no)	Female head of household
KNOWLEDGE	Illiteracy	Dichotomous (1=yes/0=no)	Ethnicity
			Civil status
	Finished years of education	Ordinal	Being poor (LP)
	Technical education for work	Dichotomous (1=yes/0=no)	Working status

determining the set of choices or the freedoms a person enjoys, and the functioning achievement that they attained given that capability set. Although we cannot assign a specific number to the capability set since it is an unobserved variable, that does not diminish the importance of the exercise, as it allows us to determine the factors affecting it and how those impacts are translated into actual achievements or functionings. In other words, it is not possible to say that person A has x amount of capability in relation to person B who has y amount of capability. What we can say is that person A has a higher capability than person B, which factors are determining that, and how that difference in capabilities is translated into actual welfare for those individuals.

MIMIC models were developed by Jöreskog and Goldberger (1975), and they are part of a much larger family of statistical techniques called "latent variable methods,"

188

VARIABLE MEASUREMENT	HOUSEHOLD CHARACTERISTICS (EXOGENOUS CAUSES OF CAPABILITIES)	VARIABLE MEASUREMENT
Discrete	Risk (household located in a risk zone: flooding, landslides, overflow, geological faults, etc.)	Dichotomous (1=yes/0=no)
Dichotomous (1=male/0=female)	Area	Dichotomous (1=rural/0=urban)
Dichotomous (1=yes/0=no)	Famishing (not having at least one out of three meals a day given monetary constraints)	Dichotomous (1=yes/0=no)
Categorical (1=Non/2=Afro/ 3=Indigenous)	Crime victim (last 12 months)	Dichotomous (1=yes/0=no)
1=married/ 2=widowed/ 3=divorced/ 4=single	Income decile	1 to 10
Dichotomous (1=yes/0=no)	Disaster (household victim of natural disasters)	Dichotomous (1=yes/0=no)
Dichotomous (1=yes/0=no)	Property of the house (own, rent)	Dichotomous (1=yes/0=no)

which combine path analysis and confirmatory factor analysis techniques. As mentioned above, the aim of MIMIC modeling is to estimate the relationship between one or more exogenous, unobserved variables called "latent," and one or more indicators. This is accomplished by the analysis of covariance structures between the different endogenous and exogenous variables, and the latent construct. Thus, it is clear that there is need for a high correlation between the variables, although not as high as to not allow the estimation of parameters.[11]

On the basis of a conceptual construction of welfare as the achievement of valuable capabilities (functionings) through the free exercise of individual agency, the general aim of this exercise is to determine which factors affect individual capabilities either positively or negatively. Specifically, the aim is to determine which factors affect the knowledge and shelter capabilities, or the real possibilities to be knowledgeable and adequately sheltered, and how these impacts vary when you are an Afro-descendant in Colombia. These impacts are assessed through each capability indicator or functioning. Thus, higher capabilities are associated with higher functionings and vice versa.

Table 2 shows the different variables and dimensions applied here. It identifies the set of endogenous indicators and exogenous causes linked to the latent constructs. The set of exogenous causes influence the knowledge capability or the freedom a person enjoys when deciding the level of knowledge he/she wants. In turn, the latent capability is inferred by a set of indicator variables such as achieved years of education, which would reflect changes in the capability dimension. Thus, when there is a factor constraining the freedom to choose the knowledge level an individual wants to achieve, this would be reflected in lower outcomes in the given dimension. It is logical, then, to expect that in a given dimension of human welfare, lower outcomes are associated with lower levels of freedom or less options to choose the life one wants.

The estimation of a MIMIC model is made up of two parts: first, the measurement model, which links each "capability" (e.g., "knowledge") to its corresponding set of indicators or observed variables (e.g., years of education). This relationship is explained by factor loadings or validity coefficients that tell the extent to which a given indicator is able to measure the corresponding latent variable. Factor loadings have a similar interpretation to that of a beta weight in regression analysis;[12] thus, a standardized factor loading would tell us how much an indicator would change, given a one-unit change in the latent construct. In addition, each indicator includes a measurement error that explains the portion of the indicator that is measuring something else, other than what the latent variable is supposed to measure. Second, the structural part of the model represents the relationships between the latent construct and the exogenous causes. Such relationships are also explained by factor loadings, which illustrate the change in the particular "capability" given a unit change in a specific exogenous cause (e.g., race), holding the rest of the variables constant. In the structural part of the model, the exogenous variables are assumed to be free from measurement error, but each latent capability has an associated disturbance term, which is supposed to measure the unexplained variance of the latent variable due to omitted causes (Bollen and Davis 2009; Schumaker and Lomax 2004).

Following Bollen and Davis's (2009) mathematical notation, the MIMIC model for both the "knowledge" and "shelter" capabilities is formally represented as follows:

$$\eta = \Gamma x + \zeta \tag{1}$$
$$y = \Lambda_y \eta + \varepsilon \tag{2}$$

Where equation 1 represents the structural part of the model that depicts the relationships between each latent capability η (knowledge and shelter) and the exogenous variables (e.g., race, age, marital status), Γ is the matrix of factor loadings (beta weights) and ζ is the vector of disturbances. This equation measures the impact exogenous variables such as gender or race have on each capability dimension, while the disturbance term captures the portion of the capability that is not being explained by those variables. Equation 2 is the measurement part of the model that depicts the relationships between the latent variable η and each of its corresponding indicators' y's. These relationships are explained by the corresponding matrix of factor loadings Λ_y that give the expected change in the indicator, given a unit change in the latent variable.[13] Finally, ε gives the measurement-error term for each indicator variable, which accounts for the portion of the indicators that are measuring something other than the latent construct.

The measurement part of the model (equation 2) takes into account the different indicator metrics. As there is a combination of continuous, categorical, and dichotomous variables, there is a need to specify nonlinear relationships when either a categorical or dichotomous variable is presented. Hence, if an indicator y_j is measured as a continuous variable, equation 2 directly represents the relationship with the latent construct. On the other hand, following Muthén (1983, 45) and Krishnakumar and Ballon (2008, 996), the relationship in the measurement model (equation 2) with dichotomous or categorical indicators is best expressed as follows:

- y_{ij} represents a dichotomous variable in the indicators vector; for instance, living in an overcrowded household or not, where i identifies the individual and j the indicator. The correspondence between the indicator and the latent variable introduces a latent response variable $\tilde{y}_{ij}$ such that:

$$\tilde{y}_{ij} = \lambda_j y_i + b_j x_{ij} + \varepsilon_i \tag{3}$$

Where $$\tilde{y}_{ij} = \begin{cases} 0 \\ 1 \end{cases}$$

This means that if y_i in equation 3 in this case represents the latent capability dimension for *shelter* increases, and an individual located in an overcrowded household could move to a non-overcrowded household as a result of the increase in the capability dimension, such change is measured as going from $\tilde{y}_{ij} = 1$ to $\tilde{y}_{ij} = 0$, in which case the factor loading λ_j (beta weight) would present a negative sign.

- In the case of an ordered categorical indicator y_j with c categories, which will vary from 0, 1, to $c-1$—for instance, years of education, which in our case goes from 0 to 21—we have the next expression:

$$\tilde{y}_{ij} = \lambda_j y_i + b_j x_{ij} + \varepsilon_i \tag{4}$$

Where $\quad y_{ij} = c$ for $\tau_{cj} < \tilde{y}_{ij} \le \tau_{c-1j}$ and $c = 0, 1, 2 \ldots c-1$
$$\tau_{0j} = -\infty \text{ and } \tau_{c-1j} = \infty$$

This means that if y_i in equation 3 is changed to represent the latent capability dimension for *knowledge* increases, an individual with say $c = 5$ (five years of education) could increase to $c = 6$ or more as the result of the increase in the capability dimension. Such change is measured as going from $\tilde{y}_{ij} = 5$ to $\tilde{y}_{ij} = 6$, in which case the factor loading (beta weight) would present a positive sign depicting the positive relationship between the capability dimension and the corresponding indicator.

Latent class involves the analysis of variance/covariance structures.[14] This means that although latent modeling can analyze means structures in specific models, its primary aim is to assess the strength of the relationship between a given set of variables, and to explain as much as possible their variability (Kline 2005). This analysis is accomplished through the estimation of the model implied variance/covariance structure (Σ) composed in our case of three covariance structures, and which is later compared to the sample covariance structure (S) to determine how well the model explains the variability patterns of the data. If the difference between these two structures, the sample and the model implied variance/covariance terms, is small enough, then the model is said to be a reasonable depiction of the phenomenon analyzed, and inference would be reliable.

The first two variance/covariance terms we need to define are: one for the exogenous variables, denoted as Φ, and one for the disturbance terms, denoted as Ψ, as follows:

$$\Gamma \Phi \Gamma' + \Psi \tag{5}$$

This expression represents a matrix array of variance/covariance terms that measure the strength of the relationship between the set of exogenous variables (e.g., gender, race, marital status, and region) plus the variance of the disturbance term, which as mentioned above is the portion of variance of the latent construct that is not explained by the set of exogenous variables. Second, from the measurement model we have the variance/covariance term of the measurement errors, denoted as Θ. These are the terms that designate the portion of the indicator variables that are measuring something else other than the associated latent capability, and this matrix represents the covariance among them.

Finally, with the above two expressions it is possible to construct the overall covariance structure of the specified model (Σ):

$$\Sigma = \Lambda_y(\Gamma\Phi\Gamma' + \Psi)\Lambda_y' + \Theta_\varepsilon \tag{6}$$

This structure is the general expression of the variance/covariance term for the MIMIC model of latent capabilities. After this structure has been estimated, it is compared to the variance/covariance structure of the sample, and if the difference is close to zero, the model presents a good fit, and allows one to make reasonable inference from the phenomenon at hand.

In addition, the following stochastic assumptions must be met in order to estimate the model:

$E(\zeta) = 0$, expected value of disturbance must be zero

$E(\varepsilon) = 0$, expected value of measurement error must be zero

$Var(\varepsilon) = \Theta$, variance of ε must be Θ

$Var(\zeta) = \Psi$, variance of ζ must be Ψ

Path Diagram for MIMIC Model of Latent Capabilities

Latent variable models are usually expressed graphically using path diagrams. Their general aim is to show graphically the causal relationships between the variables in a given model. Path diagrams have several rules or customary representations: Firstly, latent variables are represented with circles or ellipses; secondly, exogenous causes and observed variables are represented as squares; thirdly, disturbances from the latent constructs and errors from the observed variables are drawn as small circles; and finally, arrows depict causal relationships. A one-headed arrow expresses a one-way causal relationship, and a two-headed arrow expresses a reciprocal relationship between any pair of variables.

FIGURE 1: PATH DIAGRAM FOR A GENERAL MIMIC MODEL

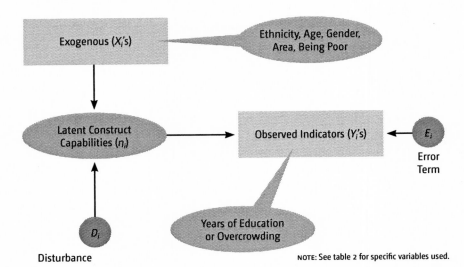

NOTE: See table 2 for specific variables used.

RESULTS

Integrating the theoretical approach and the statistical method, one can now present the estimated results and their corresponding analysis. The next chart shows estimated results for the factor loadings of the structural model for the knowledge capability. These factor loadings composed the matrix B in equation 1, and estimate the influence that personal and household characteristics have over the freedom a person enjoys in achieving the level of knowledge he or she wants. In addition, it is important to note that the sample size for this analysis is reduced from 85,145 individuals to 77,369 individuals, given that there is not information on education for children under five years old. Also, as was mentioned above, for practical reasons just the significant parameters at the 0.01 and 0.05 critical level are presented.

Table 3 presents the standardized coefficient and the unstandardized coefficient with its corresponding standard errors (standardized coefficients do not have standard errors). For comparison purposes, the standardized coefficients are commonly used. Thus, all other things being equal, a statistically significant negative coefficient on a dichotomous indicator implies a lower mean value of the knowledge capability for the groups identified by the exogenous indicator (Harrington 2008). These results show that the variables with higher explanatory power are: being poor, area, and working

TABLE 3. MIMIC MODEL OF KNOWLEDGE CAPABILITY ACHIEVEMENT: FACTOR LOADINGS OF THE STRUCTURAL MODEL

EXOGENOUS CAUSES	CAPABILITY DIMENSION KNOWLEDGE STANDARDIZED C.	U. COEFFICIENT	S. ERROR
Gender	−0.0853	−0.083	0.00315
Ethnic	−0.0368	−0.358	0.00276
Poor	−0.2721	−0.2648	0.00305
Urban/Rural	−0.2432	−0.2367	0.00272
Working	0.3232	0.3145	0.0303
Famishing	−0.0327	−0.0318	0.00282

status, with factor loadings of −0.2721, −0.2432, and 0.3232 respectively. Here, a factor loading of −0.2721 indicates that a one-unit change, which means going from non-poor to poor, produces −0.2721 standard units of change from its mean in the latent factor, keeping the rest of the explanatory variables constant. Thus, being poor and being in rural areas reduce significantly the capability or the freedom a person enjoys when choosing the level of knowledge he or she wants to attain; while working status has the contrary effect.

The factor loading for ethnic membership, although it is low, is statistically significant at the 0.05 alpha level, and implies that when holding all other variables constant, Afro-Colombian (and indigenous) people would have a lower freedom for achieving the knowledge they want in relation to the reference group: non-Afro-descendants. This can be expressed by saying that being black or indigenous is an individual characteristic that by itself reduces the capability of being educated. Furthermore, if the negative impact of being located in rural areas is summed up to indicate negative influence of ethnic background, it is possible to observe that the vulnerability of peoples of African descent is endemic. In addition, it is important to highlight the negative impact that gender has on the knowledge capability. From table 2, we know that gender is measured as a dichotomous variable, with 1 being male and 0 being female, thus, the negative coefficient implies that males have lower capability achievement than females. This could be explained by the fact that in Colombia school-enrollment rates for girls are higher than those of boys, which could be due to the nature and magnitude of child labor in the country. Boys are usually sent into the labor market at an earlier stage of life than girls. However, gender bias is still strong, but is more easily detected in the intra-household distribution of chores, and labor-market studies where income gaps persist between males and females.

TABLE 4. MIMIC MODEL OF KNOWLEDGE CAPABILITY ACHIEVEMENT:
FACTOR LOADINGS FOR THE MEASUREMENT MODEL

KNOWLEDGE CAPABILITY	STANDARDIZED C.	COEFFICIENT	S. ERROR
Years of education	0.9658	1.0	
Illiteracy rates	−0.4109	−0.4222	0.0059
Technical education for work	0.3685	0.3787	0.00529
R^2	0.3184		

Subsequently, table 4 illustrates the relationship between the latent knowledge capability and its functioning indicators assessed by the corresponding factor loadings (measurement part of the model, equation 2).

In this case, what these loadings tell us is the standard unit change of the indicator variable from its mean for each unit change of the latent construct. Thus, when there is an increase in the knowledge capability by finding a job or moving to urban areas—as the results explained before show—the achieved years of education would increase in 0.95 standard units from its mean. However, the contrary holds true also; if being a member of an ethnic minority decreases the freedom a person enjoys in attaining certain levels of knowledge, achieved years of education would be consistently lower in this segment of the population, as has been the case historically for Afro-Colombians. Given the observed indicators in the case of the illiteracy rates, the sign of the coefficient is consistent with the metric of the variable as this measures illiteracy as 1 and literacy as 0. Thus, an increase in the knowledge capability would decrease illiteracy by 0.4109 standard deviations from its mean, all other variables being constant. In this case, these results show that the freedom Afro-descendants enjoy in choosing their knowledge level has been historically lower than that of mestizos and whites—not just for the fact of being poor, as has been traditionally argued, but also for the fact of being black. They have been unable to attain higher levels of education as the result of cumulative effects of poverty and racial discrimination.

When fitting a statistical model to a data set, it is important to analyze how appropriate the fit statistics are, which tells the degree to which the model specified by the researcher is representing the given data properly (Schumacker and Lomax 2004). For this model, fit indices appear well behaved, with the exception of the X^2 index, which is too large. However, many authors have pointed out that a combination of reasonable indices by other measures allow one to pass over this chi square as it is very sensitive to large sample sizes, which is the case with this example. The rest of the indices perform reasonably well, which means that they are within the limits defined by the literature on this type of model.[15] In sum, the usefulness of fit statistics illustrates that the MIMIC model for the knowledge capability is appropriate for the data, and allows one to ensure that the inference made regarding the impact that the set of exogenous variables has on the knowledge capability is reliable enough—including the analysis made on the basis of the negative impact that ethnicity membership has over the given capability.

Continuing, the results of the structural part of the MIMIC model for the housing capability are presented. The next table shows the factor loadings of the structural model or the relationships between the latent construct and its causal factors.

Similarly to the results on the knowledge capability, all the coefficients are significant at 0.01 alpha level, but the coefficient for the "poor" variable becomes significant at the 0.05 alpha level. All coefficients have significant impact over the latent capability, and the variable that has the higher explanatory power is the variable "area," which is measured as 0 for urban and 1 for rural areas (see table 2). Area has a standardized factor loading of −0.5658, which means that, when holding all other variables constant, going from urban to rural changes the housing capability negatively: −0.5658 standard units from its mean. This is not surprising, since our indicators are mainly ones that refer to infrastructure—not only private infrastructure, but also public—and rural areas have a significant backwardness in relation to urban areas in terms of infrastructure. The second explanatory variable with high factor loading is income deciles. This is also not surprising, since this capability is highly correlated with the availability of economic resources—the higher the decile, the better the infrastructure available. The coefficient for the variable "risk," which expresses the location of a household in a geographical area vulnerable to natural disasters, presents a logical result, as being located in a risk zone decreases the housing capability by 0.127 standard units from its mean, when holding all the other variables constant.

TABLE 5. MIMIC MODEL OF HOUSING CAPABILITY ACHIEVEMENT: FACTOR LOADINGS OF THE STRUCTURAL MODEL

EXOGENOUS CAUSES	CAPABILITY DIMENSION HOUSING STANDARDIZED C.	COEFFICIENT	S. ERROR
Ethnic	−0.1696	−0.1561	0.00307
Poor	−0.0398	−0.0367	0.00441
Deciles	0.259	0.2716	0.00512
Area	−0.5658	−0.5209	0.00478
Risk	−0.127	−0.1169	0.0029

Paula A. Lezama

TABLE 6. MIMIC MODEL FOR SHELTER CAPABILITY ACHIEVEMENT:
FACTOR LOADINGS FOR THE MEASUREMENT MODEL

HOUSING CAPABILITY	STANDARDIZED C.	COEFFICIENT	S. ERROR
Basic services	0.8425	0.9150	0.00693
Dwelling	0.7188	0.7807	0.7807
Overcrowdinhg	−0.4604	−0.5	0.00529
R^2	0.7249		

However, what is more important is the size, sign, and significance of the coefficient for ethnic background, which implies that when holding all other variables constant, going from non-Afro-descendant to Afro-descendant decreases the housing capability in −0.1696 standard units from its mean. These results suggest that after weighting the impact that being poor (having lower income) and being located in rural areas have over the freedom a person enjoyed in achieving his or her valued level of knowledge and shelter, there is still a persistent negative impact associated with the ethnic background of the individual. Afro-descendants have consistently lower freedom in choosing the levels of welfare they want and have reason to value in both the housing and knowledge dimensions—not only because of their condition of poverty and their mainly rural location, but also because they are black.

Table 6 shows the results for the measurement model part of MIMIC for shelter capability.

The factor loadings for the measurement part of the MIMIC model for the housing capability show that an increase of one standard unit in the housing capability would increase the availability of basic services by 0.8425 standard units from its mean. Thus, if an individual moves from rural to urban areas, or from risk zones to zones free from risk of natural disasters, his or her capability or freedom to attain higher levels of welfare in the housing dimension increases. Whereas the loading for overcrowding depicts the opposite relationship: that an increase in the housing capability by one standard unit would have a decrease in the overcrowding variable of −0.4604 standard deviations from its mean. Hence, having more space or less people living in the same household would determine higher levels of achieved welfare in the shelter dimension. Finally, as the R^2 for this model is higher, showing a highly explanatory power, one has the result that the fit indexes reflect such power. The RMSEA is equal to 0.01008 < 0.06; CFI equal to 0.9921 > 0.95; NFI equal to 0.9920. McDonald's (1989) is equal to 0.9504, and NFI equal to 0.9920.

To summarize, it is possible to observe that after controlling for relevant individual, household, and external factors such as location, the coefficient for ethnic membership is significant and negative. This implies that at any average level of the knowledge and shelter capability dimensions, Afro-descendants in Colombia enjoy less freedom in achieving a desired quality of life. Also, it is important to highlight that, after having included outcome variables from a social-mobility perspective, such as working status and being poor as exogenous causes of capabilities, ethnic background continues to be significant. This suggests that in fact there is a component in welfare analysis of racial gaps in Colombia that cannot be assessed by focusing on class disparity alone and its specific concentration on income-based measures. This is paramount to saying that from a Capability Approach perspective, individual freedoms of Afro-Colombians are constrained by race-based discrimination. Consequently, it is their freedom and agency that must be enhanced, and not merely the access to resources that they have. This is not to deny the importance and instrumentality that the command over resources has in supporting the achievement of welfare. What is really important, however, is that these findings support the argument that there are other aspects of welfare that cannot be accounted for solely by income and resource access measures (Robeyns 2003). Finally, although one cannot identify the specific causal mechanisms by which race-based discrimination is taking place, these results also support the argument that more reliable and systematic collection of data of ethnic and racial minorities across dimensions is needed.

CONCLUSION

For Sen (1999), poverty can be a trap in which those who do not have access to education, health, and adequate food are unable to overcome their precarious circumstances. Also, Duncan (1969) argues that poverty is not a phenomenon that affects different social groups alike; on the contrary, historically marginalized social groups are affected in greater proportion by lack of access to resources such as education, health, and employment opportunities. Specifically, Duncan argues that "Negroes are poor mainly because they are 'Negroes' and are defined and treated as such by our society and their poverty stems largely not from the legacy of poverty but from the legacy of race" (87). Consequently, Afro-Colombians have fewer possibilities to prevail over conditions of poverty and exclusion, because social practices of racial discrimination persist and are rooted in everyday social interaction. Furthermore, racial discrimination prevents the achievement of welfare not only by those below poverty lines, but also by those who are not considered poor by income poverty measures.

From this perspective, the descriptive analysis of this study in conjunction with the results of the empirical application of the Capability Approach suggest that racial discrimination plays an important role in limiting Afro-descendants' capabilities or individual freedom. Although cumulative effects of class disparities play a major role in determining their lower outcomes, as the loadings for the poor and the income decile variable shows, cumulative effects of racial discrimination are taking place as well, as suggested by the factor loading of the ethnic variable. Besides, the analysis of group disparities based merely on social-stratification theories that use income-base measures as their main explanatory variable is hindering the political debate regarding the impact that racial discrimination has on individual welfare. Furthermore, this analysis is also misguiding the design and implementation of public policy toward mere increases of resource access. Wider considerations regarding human flourishing are not considered. For instance, political participation on an equal basis, the importance of commanding social respect on the basis of one's citizenship, and the possibility to claim justice when one's rights are violated are important missing aspects of the evaluation of Afro-descendants' welfare. These missing aspects cannot be properly accounted for by standard analysis of welfare measured as income levels, because what matters is not how much money people have, but what this money allows them to do.

As a consequence, the multidimensional nature of the Capability Approach calls for the recognition and analysis of racial discrimination as a separate dimension when assessing human welfare of individual members of ethnic and racial minorities, in this case Afro-Colombians. This inclusion would result in more accurate design of public policy toward the expansion of freedoms, and not just resource access. From this perspective, the social and political denial of the very existence of the phenomenon is limiting the collection of relevant data and the design of relevant public policy directed to address it. Thus, a good starting point toward the expansion of Afro-descendants' freedom in Colombia would be the end of the state of denial in which the society has lived regarding the existence of racial discrimination and the major role that it has played in the marginalization of this group. In addition, and on an urgent basis, more emphasis must be placed on the judicial and legal enforcement mechanisms to prevent and punish racial-discrimination practices. Without them, the guarantee of basic and constitutional rights for Afro-Colombians is an unreachable goal, and they will continue living as an underclass in the midst of modernity.

Finally, this paper also supports what other authors recently have pointed out regarding the appropriateness of "latent variable" methods, and specifically of MIMIC modeling to operationalize the Capability Approach. In doing so, it also shows that assessing people's welfare implies much more than measuring income levels, and that a reliable assessment of such complex and notoriously difficult-to-measure categories as "individual freedoms" is thus a highly relevant endeavor—and that this type of modeling offers important steps toward a more relevant economic science.

NOTES

1. Furthermore, there is a high correlation between each dimension and other dimensions of human welfare not analyzed, as each capability is analyzed separately. However, given the exploratory character of this study, and the lack of pertinent data, these interactions are not analyzed here. This exercise constitutes a much larger and complex future study. In addition, it is necessary to clarify that given the lack of adequate data, other dimensions of human welfare cannot be analyzed.

2. For practical purposes, from now on the survey will be referred to as QLS 2003 (its acronym in English).

3. Ethnic membership appears to have a consistently negative impact on individual capabilities, which means that being of African descent has in itself a negative impact on the set of choices an individual has to attain his/her desired level of welfare in a given dimension.

4. Forced displacement in the country is generating a spatial redistribution of poverty, as already vulnerable farmers are being violently separated from their traditional livelihoods and must migrate to the urban centers, enlarging previously existent urban peripheries of exclusion and misery.

5. "Long Term Plan for the Black Population, Afro-Colombians, Palenque y Raizal: Proposal y Process 2005–2007," National Department of Planning, 2007.

6. Afro-Colombians were granted collective property rights, community-oriented development and prior consultation rights, and the right to be free of discrimination, in the transitory article 55, later developed into Law 70, 1993. Comisión Consultiva de Alto Nivel para las Comunidades Negras Subcomisión de Planeación y Desarrollo Ley 70 de 1993—Decreto 2248 de 1995.

7. Article 13 of the national constitution, articles 58 and 147 of the penal code, article 48 of the disciplinary code for official functionaries, and article 33 of Law 70 of 1993 were introduced into the judicial system to punish acts of discrimination based on race or ethnicity. However, as argued by the Observatory on Racial Discrimination (2008, 60), none of them are effectively enforced.

8. It was integrated into the national legislation by Law 21 of 1991 (Ley 70 de 1993—Decreto 2248 de 1995).

9. New York, March 7, 1966, and ratified in 2004.

10. There has been plenty of research showing gaps between peoples of African descent and whites in the labor, health, and housing markets. These gaps persist across income levels, affecting not only the poor, but people whose incomes place them over the poverty line.

11. There is no clarity regarding the impact that the lack of independence between explanatory variables, that is multicollinearity, would have in the estimation of structural equation models. Some authors have argued this is a robust approach in the presence of such, yet research on this area is still very incipient (Grewal et al. 2004).

12. In regression analysis, beta weights are the regression coefficients estimated from the standardized data, and are used to compare the relative importance of the different explanatory variables. A beta weight expresses the average change in the dependent variable when the independent variable changes one standard deviation from its mean, holding all other independent variables constant or at their means (Garson 2008).

13. For instance, if the knowledge capability is contracted given a unit change in one of the external causes, the indicator variables (such as years of education) would be reduced so as to reflect such a contraction in the latent construct.

14. It is possible to have an intuitive meaning of *analysis of covariance structures* if we remember the relations behind the *squared multiple correlation coefficient*, R^2, in multiple regression analysis. The R^2 tells how much variance in Y is explained, predicted, and accounted for by the set of explanatory variables X_1 and X_2. For instance, for one dependent variable and two predictors, the R^2 is:

$$R^2 = \beta_1 r_{y1} + \beta_2 r_{y2}$$

Where β are the beta weights and their formal representation is as follows:

$$\beta_1 = (r_{y1} - r_{y2} r_{12})/(1 - r_{12}^2)$$

and

$$\beta_2 = (r_{y2} - r_{y1} r_{12})/(1 - r_{12}^2),$$

and r_{y1}, r_{y2}, and r_{12} are the bivariate correlations among the explanatory and criterion variables. From here, it is possible to understand that regression analysis estimates a set of parameters (beta weights) from the correlations among the variables, which in turn serve to construct the *squared multiple correlation coefficient* to explain as much variance as possible on Y given the correlation of the set of predictors X. Latent variable models develop this same type of analysis but for latent and intervening variables (combination of path and factor analysis).

15. For instance, the Root Mean Square Error of Approximation (RMSEA) is 0.0443 (RMSEA < 0.06); Confidence limits for RMSEA are 0.0410–0.0443. The Comparative Fit Index (CFI) is 0.9819 (CFI > 0.95); McDonald's (1989) measure of centrality is a fit index t-scaled to call between 0 and 1 (the closer to 1 the better fit the model has), and in our case is 0.9882. The Normed Fit Index (NFI) is 0.9818 (NFI > 0.95).

REFERENCES

Alkire, S. 2005a. "Capability and Functionings: Definition and Justification." *Briefing Notes.* Human Development and Capability Association (http://www.capabilityapproach.com/index.php).

———. 2005b. *Valuing Freedoms: Sen's Capability Approach and Poverty Reduction.* New York: Oxford University Press.

Anand, S., and A. K. Sen. 1994. *Human Development Index: Methodology and Measurement.* New York: United Nations Development Programme (UNDP).

Andrews, George Reid. 2004. *Afro-Latin America, 1800–2000.* New York: Oxford University Press.

Arocha, J. 1998. Inclusion of Afro-Colombians: Unreachable National Goal? *Latin American Perspectives* 25(3):70–89.

Ballet, J., J. L. Dubois, and F. Mahieu. 2007. "Responsibility for Each Other's Freedom: Agency as the Source of Collective Capability." *Journal of Human Development-Basingstoke* 8(2):185.

Barbary, O., H. F. Ramirez, and F. Urrea. 2002. "Identidad y ciudadanía afrocolombiana en la Región Pacífica y Cali: Elementos estadísticos y sociológicos para el debate de la 'cuestión negra' en Colombia." *Estudos Afro-Asiáticos* 24(3).

Bello, Á., and M. Rangel. 2002. "La equidad y la exclusión de los pueblos indígenas y Afro-descendientes en América Latina y el Caribe." *Revista de la CEPAL* 76:39–54.

Bharadwaj, A. S., V. Sambamurthy, and R. W. Zmud. 1999. "IT Capabilities: Theoretical Perspectives and Empirical Operationalization." *Proceedings of the 20th International Conference on Information Systems*, Charlotte NC, December 1999, 378–385.

Bollen, K. A., and W. R. Davis. 2009. "Causal Indicator Models: Identification, Estimation, and Testing." *Structural Equation Modeling: A Multidisciplinary Journal* 16(3):498–522.

Clark, D. A. 2005. "The Capability Approach: Its Development, Critiques and Recent Advances." Oxford: Global Poverty Research Group Working Paper 32. Available at http://www.gprg.org/pubs/workingpapers/pdfs/gprg-wps-032.pdf

Cohen, G. A. 1993. "Amartya Sen's Unequal World." *Economic and Political Weekly* 28(40) (October 2):2156–2160.

Comim, F. 2001. "Operationalizing Amartya Sen's Capability Approach." Paper presented at the Conference on Justice and Poverty: Examining Amartya Sen's Capability Approach, Cambridge, UK, 57 June.

CONPES. 2004. *3310 de 2004—Política de acción afirmativa para la población negra o afro-Colombiana*. Bogota, Colombia: National Department of Planning (DNP).

Consultoria para los Derechos y el Desplazamiento (CODHES). 2008. Afrocolombianos desplazados: Un drama sin tregua. Available at http://www.afrodes.org/afrodes/Idioma.html.

Grueso, Libia. 2007. *Documento propuesta para la formulación del Plan Integral de Largo Plazo Población Negra/Afro-Colombiana, Palenquera y Raizal 2007–2019*. Bogota, Colombia: National Department of Planning (DNP).

Deneulin, Séverine. 2006. *The Capability Approach and the Praxis of Development*. Basingstoke, UK: Palgrave Macmillan.

Deneulin, Séverine, Mathias Nebel, and Nicholas Sagovsky. 2006. *Transforming Unjust Structures*. Dordrecht: Springer, July 19.

Di Tommaso, M. L. 2007. "Children Capabilities: A Structural Equation Model for India." *Journal of Socio-Economics* 36(3):436–450.

Duncan, D. O. 1696. "Inheritance of Poverty or Inheritance of Race?" In *On Understanding Poverty: Perspectives from the Social Sciences*, ed. D. P. Moynihan and C. S. Schelling. New York: Basic Books.

Escobar, A. 2003. "Displacement, Development, and Modernity in the Colombian Pacific." *International Social Science Journal* 55(175):157–167.

Evans, P. 2002. "Collective Capabilities, Culture, and Amartya Sen's Development as Freedom." *Studies in Comparative International Development (SCID)* 37(2):54–60.

Garson, David. 2008. "Path Analysis." From *Statnotes: Topics in Multivariate Analysis*. http://faculty.chass.ncsu.edu/garson/PA765/path.htm (accessed 25 March 2009).

Gasper, D. 2004. *The Ethics of Development*. Edinburgh: Edinburgh University Press.

Gerring, John. 2001. *Social Science Methodology*. Cambridge: Cambridge University Press.

———. 2007. *Case Study Research*. Cambridge: Cambridge University Press.

Grewal, Rajdeep, Joseph A. Cote, and Hans Baumgartner. 2004. "Multicollinearity and Measurement Error in Structural Equation Models: Implications for Theory Testing." *Marketing Science* 23(4):519–529.

Harrington, D. 2008. *Confirmatory Factor Analysis.* Oxford: Oxford University Press.

Hicks, D. A. 2002. "Gender, Discrimination, and Capability: Insights from Amartya Sen." *Journal of Religious Ethics* 30(1):137–154.

Hogan, D. P, and D. L. Featherman. 1977. "Racial Stratification and Socioeconomic Change in the American North and South." *American Journal of Sociology* 83(1):100.

Jöreskog, K. G., E. B. Andersen, P. Laake, D. R. Cox, and T. Schweder. 1981. "Analysis of Covariance Structures [with Discussion and Reply]." *Scandinavian Journal of Statistics* 8(2):65–92.

Jöreskog, K. G., and A. S. Goldberger. 1975. "Estimation of a Model with Multiple Indicators and Multiple Causes of a Single Latent Variable." *Journal of the American Statistical Association* 70(351):631–639.

Kakwani, N., and J. Silber. 2008. "Introduction: Multidimensional Poverty Analysis: Conceptual Issues, Empirical Illustrations and Policy Implications." *World Development* 36(6): 987–991.

Kline, Rex B. 2005. *Principles and Practice of Structural Equation Modeling.* 2nd ed. New York: Guilford Press.

Krishnakumar, J. 2007. "Going beyond Functionings to Capabilities: An Econometric Model to Explain and Estimate Capabilities." *Journal of Human Development* 8(1):39–63.

Krishnakumar, J., and A. L. Nagar. 2008. "On Exact Statistical Properties of Multidimensional Indices Based on Principal Components, Factor Analysis, MIMIC, and Structural Equation Models." *Social Indicators Research* 86(3):481–496.

Krishnakumar, Jaya, and Paola Ballon. 2008. "Estimating Basic Capabilities: A Structural Equation Model Applied to Bolivia." *World Development* 36(6) (June):992–1010.

Kuklys, W. 2005. *Amartya Sen's Capability Approach: Theoretical Insights and Empirical Applications.* Dordrecht: Springer Verlag.

Lasso, Marixa. 2007. *Myths of Harmony: Race and Republicanism during the Age of Revolution, Colombia, 1795–1831.* Pittsburgh, PA: University of Pittsburgh Press.

Majumdar, M., and S. Subramanian. 2001. "Capability Failure and Group Disparities: Some Evidence from India for the 1980s." *Journal of Development Studies* 37(5):104–140.

Marasinghe, M. G., and W. J. Kennedy. 2008. *SAS for Data Analysis: Intermediate Statistical Methods.* Dordrecht: Springer Verlag.

Martinetti, E. C. 2000. "A Multidimensional Assessment of Well-Being Based on Sen's Functioning Approach." *Rivista Internazionale di Scienze Sociali* 2:207–239.

Medina, C. A. 2002. "Oferta laboral en Colombia de acuerdo al color de la piel." Bogotá: Cede, Facultad de Economía, Universidad de los Andes.

Miller, Grace M. 2004. *The Rise and Fall of the Cosmic Race: The Cult of Mestizaje in Latin America.* Austin: University of Texas Press.

Moynihan, D. P., and C. S. Schelling, eds. 1969. *On Understanding Poverty: Perspectives from the Social Sciences.* New York: Basic Books.

Muthén, B. 1983. "Latent Variable Structural Equation Modeling with Categorical Data." *Journal of Econometrics* 22(1).

National Department of Planning. 2007. "Long Term Plan for the Black Population, Afro-Colombians, Palenque and Raizal: Proposal and Process 2005–2007."

National Research Council of the National Academies. 2004. *Measuring Racial Discrimination*. Washington, DC: National Academies Press.

Nef, Jorge, and International Development Research Centre (Canada). 1999. *Human Security and Mutual Vulnerability*. Ottawa: IDRC.

Nelson, E. 2008. "From Primary Goods to Capabilities: Distributive Justice and the Problem of Neutrality." *Political Theory* 36(1):93.

Nobles, Melissa. 2000. *Shades of Citizenship: Race and Census in Modern Politics*. Stanford, CA: Stanford University Press.

Nussbaum, Martha C. 2000. *Women and Human Development: The Capabilities Approach*. Cambridge: Cambridge University Press.

Nussbaum, M. C. 2003. "Capabilities as Fundamental Entitlement: Sen and Social Justice." *Feminist Economics* 9(2–3), 33–59.

Nussbaum, M. C., and A. K. Sen. 1993. *The Quality of Life*. New York: Oxford University Press.

Oaxaca, R. L., and M. R. Ransom. 1999. "Identification in Detailed Wage Decompositions." *Review of Economics and Statistics* 81(1):154–157.

Observatory on Racial Discrimination. 2008. *Racial Discrimination and Human Rights in Colombia: A Report on the Situation of the Rights of Afro-Colombians*. Bogotá: Ediciones Uniandes.

Portilla, D. A. 2003. "Mercado laboral y discriminacion racial: Una aproximación para Cali." Bogotá: Documento CEDE, Universidad de los Andes.

Quinonez, S. A. 2007. Los Afrocolombianos: Entre la retórica del multiculturalismo y el fuego cruzado del destierro. *Journal of Latin American and Caribbean Anthropology* 12(1):213–222.

Rawls, J. 1971. *A Theory of Justice*. Cambridge, MA., Belknap Press/Harvard University Press.

Reiter, Bernd, and Gladys Mitchell, eds. 2009. *Brazil's New Racial Politics*. Boulder, CO: Lynne Rienner Publishers.

Rivas, N. Y., T. H. Saa, and C. E. Agudelo. 2000. "Impactos de la Ley 70 y dinámicas políticas locales de las poblaciones afrocolombianas: Estudios de caso." *Documento de Trabajo 50*. Cali, Colombia: Universidad del Valle: Facultad de Ciencias Sociales y Económicas.

Rivera, F. 2001. "Migrantes y racismo en América Latina: Dimensiones ocultas de realidades complejas." Versión final de investigación encomendada por el Instituto Interamericano de Derechos Humanos y el BID. Quito: Universidad Andina Simón Bolívar.

Robeyns, I. 2003. "Sen's Capability Approach and Gender Inequality: Selecting Relevant Capabilities." *Feminist Economics* 9(2):61–92.

Roche, J. M. 2008. "Monitoring Inequality among Social Groups: A Methodology Combining Fuzzy Set Theory and Principal Component Analysis." *Journal of Human Development* 9(3):427–452.

Saith, R. 2001. "Capabilities: The Concept and Its Operationalisation." QEH Working Paper Series 66. Oxford: Queen Elizabeth House, University of Oxford.

Schiller, B. R. 1970. "Stratified Opportunities: The Essence of the 'Vicious Circle.'" *American Journal of Sociology* 76(3):426–442.

———. 1971. "Class Discrimination vs. Racial Discrimination." *Review of Economics and Statistics* 53(3):263–269.

Schumacker, Randall E., and Richard G. Lomax. 2004. *A Beginner's Guide to Structural Equation Modeling.* 2nd ed. Mahwah, NJ: Lawrence Erlbaum Associates.

Sen, Amartya K. 1976. Poverty: An Ordinal Approach to Measurement. *Econometrica: Journal of the Econometric Society* 44(2):219–231.

———. 1979. "Equality of What?" The Tanner Lecture on Human Values, Stanford University, 22 May.

———. 1985a. "Well-Being, Agency and Freedom: The Dewey Lectures 1984." *Journal of Philosophy* 82(4):169–221.

———. 1985b. *Commodities and Capabilities.* Amsterdam: North-Holland.

———. 1990. "Development as Capability Expansion." In *Human Development and the International Development Strategy for the 1990s,* ed. Keith Griffin and John Knight, 41–58. London: Macmillan.

———. 1999. *Development as Freedom.* 1st ed. New York: Knopf.

Sen, A. K., and J. E. Foster. 1973. *On Economic Inequality.* New York: Oxford University Press.

Seth, S. 2009. "Collecting Capability Data on the Basis of Existing Surveys: The Case of India." Maitreyee. Human Development and Capability Association (http://www.capabilityapproach.com/index.php).

Skidmore, Thomas E. 1993. *Black into White: Race and Nationality in Brazilian Thought.* Durham, NC: Duke University Press.

Telles, E. E. 2007. "Incorporating Race and Ethnicity into the UN Millennium Development Goals." Available at http://www.thedialogue.org/PublicationFiles/telles.pdf.

Urrea, F. 2006. "La población afrodescendiente en Colombia." *Los pueblos indígenas y afrodescendientes en América Latina y el Caribe.* Santiago de Chile: CEPAL.

Urrea, F., and C. Viáfara. 2006. "Efectos de la raza y el género en logro educativo y status socioocupacional para tres ciudades de Colombianas." *Revista Desarrollo y Sociedad* (segundo semestre 2006):115–163.

Urrea, F., C. Viáfara, H. F Ramírez, E. Gómez, S. Vélez and F. Ruiz. 2005. "Pobreza y grupos étnicos en Colombia: Análisis de sus factores determinantes y lineamientos de política para su reducción." Informe final presentado al Departamento Nacional de Planeación. Bogota, Colombia: National Department of Planning (DNP).

Wade, P. 1995. "The Cultural Politics of Blackness in Colombia." *American Ethnologist* 22:341–357.

———. 2002. "Introduction: The Colombian Pacific in Perspective." *Journal of Latin American Anthropology* 7(2):2–33.

Wainryb, Cecilia, Judith G. Smetana, and Elliot Turiel. 2008. *Social Development, Social Inequalities, and Social Justice.* CRC Press.

Racism in a Racialized Democracy and Support for Affirmative Action Policy in Salvador and São Paulo, Brazil

Gladys Mitchell-Walthour

University affirmative-action policies in Brazil have come under attack from a number of scholars who believe the program is inappropriate for Brazil's multiracial population. Peter Fry et al.'s *Dangerous Divisions: Racial Politics in Contemporary Brazil* (2007) includes a number of opinion pieces by both scholars and activists against university affirmative action. On the other hand, sociologists such as Antonio Guimarães (2001) and Sales Augusto dos Santos (2006) support the programs. North American scholar Seth Racusen (2010) proposes a novel approach with a schema that would consider both class and race in university affirmative action. Much of the debate focuses on Brazilian racial identity and why the policy is inappropriate. There is also a focus on class, and the fact that Brazil's primary and secondary public schools are inadequate, and most of those attending these schools are Afro-Brazilian. For this reason, opponents of affirmative action believe resources should be allocated to improving public schools rather than supporting university affirmative action.

What is lost in most scholarship concerned with affirmative action is an examination of political opinions of those who would potentially benefit from such policies. This chapter examines determinants of Afro-Brazilian support of affirmative action. I focus on respondents in Salvador and São Paulo. My hypothesis is that Afro-Brazilians who believe blacks (*negros*) face difficulties in society due to racism and discrimination claim a black identification, and the highly educated are more likely to support affirmative-action policy than those who do not acknowledge racism as a major problem for blacks, who claim nonblack identifications, and are less educated. Previous research has shown that Afro-Brazilians who claim a black identification are more likely to vote for black candidates (G. Mitchell 2010a), and that those who identify as a black racial group tend to vote for black candidates (G. Mitchell 2009). Because Black Movement activists tend to be middle-class (Hanchard 1994; Burdick 1998), I believe those with higher education will support the policy more than those with lower education. The alternative hypothesis is that Afro-Brazilians with higher levels of education are more likely not to support affirmative-action policies than those with lower levels of education. Perhaps people with higher education believe they were successful based on merit, and that merit only should be considered for university admission rather than one's racial background. In fact, Stanley R. Bailey and Edward E. Telles (2006) find that among *negros* (*pretos* and *pardos*) and *brancos* there is less support for quotas in employment and in universities as education increases. Those with higher education are less likely to support affirmative action than those with lower education. Bailey and Telles use large-scale survey data collected in 2000 in the state of Rio de Janeiro.

Gislene Aparecida dos Santos's (2008) interviews reveal that Afro-Brazilian high school students are less supportive of affirmative-action programs for Afro-Brazilians, and most prefer that the policy be class-based. However, she also finds that Afro-Brazilian university students, through outreach, encourage Afro-Brazilian high school students to consider university admission under affirmative-action programs because it is a right granted to them as citizens. These students oftentimes begin to claim a black identification after attending university. Andrew Francis and Turrini-Pinto (2009) find that at the University of Brasilia, candidates for admission misrepresent their color to be considered for university affirmative action. However, using a survey, Bailey (2008) finds that nearly half of racially mixed Brazilians would choose white over black racial classifications if forced to choose one. He also finds that using photographs where respondents can determine if an individual is eligible for quotas for blacks (*negros*), most respondents do not believe those of lighter and medium skin tones deserve inclusion in the quotas. In fact, for the photographs of individuals with medium skin tone, 60 percent of mulattos do not find them deserving of quota inclusion. Nonetheless, Bailey also finds that in an experiment, simply mentioning a racial policy for *negros* increases the percentage of those identifying as such. These findings appear counterintuitive, but I believe that as in the University of Brasília case, when faced with the real-life choice of benefiting from affirmative action, some candidates for university admission will in fact change or misrepresent their identification to benefit from the program. I do not intend to contribute to the literature on changing racial identification to benefit from affirmative action. Rather,

I am interested in the determinants of support for affirmative action among Afro-Brazilians, and hope to contribute to social-science literature on political opinion and behavior of Afro-Brazilians.

This chapter focuses on Afro-Brazilians in Salvador and São Paulo, Brazil, exclusively. I examine whether support of affirmative-action policy is related to sociodemographic factors such as Afro-Brazilians' educational level, age, gender, income, color identification, and opinions about the major problems blacks (*negros*) face in Brazil. Presumably, respondents attributing blacks' problems to racism and discrimination might support racial policies aimed at reducing discrimination. Juliet Hooker, in *Race and the Politics of Solidarity* (2009), notes that political solidarity is racialized and shaped by race despite the fact that scholars of multicultural theories often do not discuss racialized solidarity. In the case of the United States, there are huge disparities between whites' and blacks' political opinions regarding racial injustice and racial inequality, Hooker posits that there are also differences in support for racial policies because of differential sympathy. She states, "As a result of racialization, the pain and suffering of nonwhites are either rendered invisible or, when visible, are seen as less deserving of empathy and redress than those of whites (2009, 40). While Hooker's work is largely theoretical and focuses on Afro-descended and indigenous communities in Nicaragua, her point regarding empathy and solidarity is well taken. This chapter only focuses on Afro-descendants and does not presume solidarity. On the contrary, I assume differences exist among Afro-Brazilians in terms of racial identification and political opinion. Examining responses about the major problem of blacks allows me to analyze differential sympathy, especially when noted by acknowledging difficulties blacks face because of race rather than simply class. More importantly, I will examine how a respondent's opinion about the major problem of blacks and sociodemographic factors impact their support for affirmative action. Throughout this chapter Afro-Brazilians are synonymous with Afro-descendants. All survey respondents identify as Afro-descendants, although they self-identify as belonging to various color or racial categories.

RACE, RACISM, AND RACIAL POLITICS IN BRAZIL

In the past, Brazilians viewed their country as distinct from the United States because of conceptions of race and racism. American racism is viewed as explicit, whereas Brazilian racism and discrimination are characterized as hidden and less clear because of class inequality and a racially mixed population. Social relations in

Brazil appear to be fairly integrated and racially harmonious among racial groups (Telles 2004). Edward Telles (2004) notes in his explanation of vertical and horizontal relations that there are huge gaps in educational attainment, income, and mortality rates between white Brazilians and nonwhite Brazilians; yet social relations appear to be racially integrated or less rigid in terms of intermarriage and residential segregation than in the United States and South Africa. Brazilian racism has been documented by various scholars, such as Florestan Fernandes's (1965) UNESCO-sponsored research documenting racial inequality in the 1950s; Carlos Hasenbalg's (1978) research showing differences in social mobility by race in the late 1970s; France Winddance Twine's (1998) anthropological research on racism in the 1990s; and Michael Mitchell and Charles Wood's (1998) work on police abuse of browns and blacks. Such research, along with Black Movement activists who have long acknowledged racism in Brazilian society, proves that Brazil has not been immune to racism in its society.

Traditionally, white Brazilian political elites promoted the idea that Brazil was a racial democracy where racism did not exist, because of its mixed-race citizenry; however, today the idea of racial democracy is often referred to as a myth among scholars and activists. Brazilian racial politics have changed dramatically. Affirmative-action policies in universities were first implemented in 2001. Federal Law 10.639/03, passed in 2003, requires public schools to teach African and Afro-Brazilian history. Black Movement activists supported and pushed for such policies, while at the same time encouraging Afro-Brazilians to embrace blackness. In addition, Black Movement activism has expanded the traditional boundaries of volunteer organizations and are now formal nongovernmental and nonprofit organizations (S. Santos 2010), nontraditional routes of activism are present in hip-hop organizations and activity (Reiter and Mitchell 2010; S. Santos 2010; Pardue 2004), "prevestibular" courses also serve as avenues for disseminating racial consciousness (S. Santos 2010), and political campaigns serve as a means of mobilization and teaching racial consciousness (G. Mitchell 2009). Given that much of the work of Black Movement activism continues to push for affirmative-action policies and encourage Afro-Brazilians to embrace blackness and contemporary activism, and is disseminated in these nontraditional ways, one must ask, how do Afro-Brazilians perceive such programs? Do they embrace a black identification, and does this impact their support for affirmative action? Does acknowledging racism as a problem blacks face, as opposed to simply a class problem, result in differential support for affirmative-action policies? This chapter seeks to answer these questions. Before my analysis, I briefly review the literature on Brazilian racial politics. Second, I define key terms such as racism, and racial and color identification. Lastly, I follow with analyses of my quantitative study.

CURRENT LITERATURE

The goal of this chapter is not to outline the specifics of affirmative-action policies throughout Brazil, nor do I seek to give a thorough review of scholarship on affirmative action. Rather, I situate my work in research on Brazilian politics and political behavior, and research on racial attitudes and racial politics. On the one hand, scholars do not consider race as significant to Brazilian politics (von Metteinheim 1986; Hagopian 1996; Mainwaring et al. 2000). On the other hand, racial politics and the role of race in Brazilian politics have been studied since the 1970s (de Souza 1971; M. Mitchell 1977, 2007; Pereira 1982; Soares and Silva 1987; Valente 1986; Câstro 1993; Hanchard 1994; Prandi 1996; Oliviera 1997, 2007; Johnson 1998, 2006; Nobles 2000; S. Santos 2000; Guimarães 2001; Telles 2004; Bailey 2009). My research contributes to this body of work with the hope of broadening knowledge on political opinion, racial identification, and racial attitudes of Afro-Brazilians.

Ethnographic and sociological scholarship differs in findings concerning black group identity. Robin Sheriff (2001), in her ethnographic work in a slum community in Rio de Janeiro, finds that Afro-Brazilians essentially have a bipolar view of race as white and black, but use various color gradations to soften the effect of color. In an effort to be polite, color gradations are used to describe a person, rather than the term "black." Stanley Bailey (2009) claims that racial group identity does not exist among Afro-Brazilians. Citing the 2002 PESP survey in which only 7 percent of respondents chose to self-classify as *negro*, Bailey concludes that "Brazil clearly lacks the sense of black racial group membership and many of the types of participation in antiracism found in the U.S. context (2009, 121)." Drawing from a 2000 racial-attitudes study conducted in the state of Rio de Janeiro, Bailey finds little difference in color categories between whites and Afro-Brazilians who agree that the *negro* movement is right, and that prejudice must be the object of a struggle to overcome it (126). He finds that *pretos* are most willing to participate in antiracism activities (127), and that *morenos* and whites differ significantly from browns, *pretos*, *negros*, and all others in the choice of "a lot" over "no" in willingness to become a member of an antiracism organization (131). Bailey notes this difference, and posits that differences between *moreno* attitudes and other Afro-Brazilian attitudes toward the *negro* movement may serve as a barrier for mobilization. Because the focus of these findings is to show that white and "nonwhite" Brazilian racial attitudes are not distinctly different, in contrast to clear differences between whites and blacks in the United States, there is no exclusive focus on Afro-Brazilians. I hope to contribute to the growing body of work on racial attitudes by exclusively focusing on Afro-Brazilians and trends within cities, using city surveys rather than state and national surveys. These trends may not be revealed in state and national surveys.

KEY TERMS

"Color" and "racial identification" refer to the color or racial group a respondent self-identifies as. Brubaker and Cooper (2000) note the processual nature of identification, making this term preferable to identity. In this article, *preto* and *negro* are considered separate categories. *Preto* is considered a color category, while *negro* is considered a politically charged racial category. Because *negro* was and continues to be promoted by the Black Movement, it is politically charged. Mainstream media use the term *negro* as the sum of *pardos* and *pretos*; however, I consider it a racialized identification because of its historical usage.

As Melissa Nobles (2000) demonstrates, during specific time periods political elites, academics, and census officials were motivated to use the census to further their political agendas, and at other times they were not. The addition of more mixed-race categories helped political elites empirically show that Brazil was becoming less black and more white. This was important as Brazil searched for a national identity in the early twentieth century. In contrast, political activists involved in the Black Movement pushed for a change of the color categories for the 2000 census. They were concerned with the use of the term *pardo*. They preferred that *moreno* be used in place of *pardo*. *Moreno* is used more in social settings than *pardo*, so members of the Black Movement believed more people would choose this term. The Brazilian Institute of Geography and Statistics (IBGE) did not replace *pardo* with *moreno*. In the most recent (2000) census, categories include white, black (*preto*), brown (*pardo*), yellow, and indigenous. In sum, it is important to note that categorization depends on political agendas and *who* categorizes. At different historical periods, white political elites categorized and constructed race to further their political and social agendas (Nobles 2000). On the other hand, Afro-Brazilian activists also had political agendas and wanted to identify people of African descent in ways that were politically beneficial to their agenda. My study relies on self-identification in an open-ended question that can be especially revealing considering the Black Movement's goals.

Racism and *racial discrimination* throughout the article are synonymous terms. Racism is negative differential treatment or perceptions of people based on one's perceived color or racial categorization of that individual. Telles (2004) documents racial inequality in occupational mobility, income, and educational attainment due to racial discrimination. He also discusses how discrimination operates as negative stereotypes in the Brazilian context. Negative stereotypes of blacks are often disseminated as humor through jokes in daily life (154), and in the media, blacks and browns are virtually nonexistent. When they do appear, they are portrayed with certain behaviors while whites are seen as beautiful, happy, and middle-class (155). In schools, teachers give more preference to lighter children and invest more in them (158).

Statistical comparisons of infant mortality show that in 2005, infant mortality was higher for blacks and browns than whites: 24.4 percent for *pretas* and *pardas*, and 23.7 percent for *brancas* (Paixão and Carvano 2008, 38). In 2006 the number of whites attending university was over four times the number of blacks and browns attending university (81). Despite inequalities in health and education, some argue that these are class inequalities. This is often the argument made in debates about university affirmative action. Those against affirmative action believe that public school education should be improved because poorer children attend such schools. Yet, Paixão and Carvano (2008) show that *pretos* and *pardos* who have finished college are 1.2 times more likely to be unemployed compared to whites with the same schooling. This difference can be attributed to racial discrimination.

Racism is explicitly practiced as police brutality—a problem Afro-Brazilians face. Michael Mitchell and Charles H. Wood (1998) find that the likelihood of assault by police officers on men increases depending on skin color and age. Younger black and brown men are more likely to be assaulted by the police than whites. Although income and education decrease one's chance of assault, it is important to note color differences. The darker one's skin color, the higher likelihood of assault by police officers. In my study, I am concerned with whether or not respondents cite discrimination as a hindrance in blacks' lives rather than simply acknowledging class barriers.

METHODOLOGY

I rely on an original survey carried out in Salvador and São Paulo, Brazil, in 2006. The survey has 674 respondents. Salvador is located in the northeast, a poor region, and is known as the "mecca" of Afro-Brazilian culture. It is nearly 70 percent African-descendant. São Paulo is in the south, a wealthier region of Brazil. Its population is nearly 30 percent African-descendant. According to the 2000 census, 20 percent of Salvador's population considered themselves *preto*. In São Paulo, 5 percent considered themselves *preto*. Black Movement activity has occurred in São Paulo since the 1930s (Hanchard 1994; Covin 2006), making it an interesting site of comparison. São Paulo is also home to the first university specifically for African descendants in Latin America.

In consultation with experts in survey methods from the Federal University of Bahia (UFBA), I chose the Salvador neighborhoods Federação, Peri peri, and Itapoãn. Federação is socioeconomically heterogeneous.[1] Part of the campus of UFBA, a prestigious public university, is located in Federação, which includes middle-class households. There are also very low-income households. Itapoãn is also socioeconomically diverse, but has a large proportion of low-income households. Peri peri is located in the suburbs. It is a low-income neighborhood. It is relatively easy to find African descendants in these neighborhoods. A total of 346 interviews were conducted in Salvador. Brazilian undergraduate students conducted interviews. They were trained in interviewing methods. Interviewers in São Paulo were affiliated with a student group that focuses on racial issues. All interviewers in São Paulo self-identify as *negro/a*. In Salvador, one interviewer self-identifies as white, one as *parda*, and the others identify as *negra*. Interviewers told potential interviewees that the study was with Afro-descendants and asked if any lived in the household. The respondent ultimately determined their selection to participate in the study. The survey does not include respondents who are self-identified whites *and* who were identified as white by interviewers. Thus when reporting results, white Afro-descendants are those who self-identified as white but were not identified as such by interviewers. Unlike large-scale Brazilian national surveys that include whites, *pretos*, and *pardos*, this survey is restricted to Afro-descendants in select neighborhoods.

In São Paulo, along with experts of research on race in Brazil, I identified neighborhoods with high populations of Afro-descendants, but that were also socioeconomically diverse. Neighborhoods chosen were Cidade Tiradentes, Casa Verde, Brasilândia, Campo Limpo, and Capão Redondo. Cidade Tiradentes is a low-income neighborhood located in the far east of São Paulo. Casa Verde is mostly middle-class in the northeast of São Paulo. Campo Limpo is located in the southwest and is known for its large social divisions. Capâo Redondo is located on the periphery in the south. I obtained neighborhood maps from the Institute of Brazilian Geography and Statistics (IBGE) in São Paulo, and randomization was introduced by randomly selecting streets where students conducted face-to-face interviews, and through interviewer selection. A total of 328 interviews were conducted.

Students were assigned to at least two neighborhoods. Randomization was also introduced as interviewers used a skip-number method and conducted interviews at every fifth house, or third house if the street did not contain many houses. Respondents were of voting age. Voting is mandatory for those who are 18 to 70 years old. However, citizens can begin voting at the age of 16. A total of 674 interviews were conducted in Salvador and São Paulo.

SELECTION BIAS

Since 2007, blacks and browns have outnumbered whites, and this was due to an increase in Afro-Brazilians identifying as black (*preto*). Nonetheless, nationally most Afro-Brazilians identify as brown (*pardo*). In the 2000 census, 45 percent of the population identified as white, 39 percent as brown, 6 percent as black, and less than 1 percent as yellow or indigenous. In Salvador, in the census, 66 percent of the population consider themselves black or brown. In São Paulo, 30 percent of the population consider themselves black (*preto*) and brown (*pardo*). In both cities, most Afro-Brazilians consider themselves brown. It is impossible to know how many Afro-Brazilians self-identify as white. My Salvador and São Paulo samples are biased because of the large number of respondents identifying as black (*preto* or *negro*).

These biases are accounted for because my sample includes a significant percentage of young people. Livio Sansone (2004) finds that younger people self-identify more as black. Stanley R. Bailey and Edward E. Telles (2006) find that younger and educated people are more likely to choose the *negro* category than older people. People with higher education are more likely to choose the *negro* category rather than the *moreno* category (Bailey and Telles 2006). They claim that for younger people, *negro* is associated with a modern identity that is influenced by black American culture dispersed by music. They also concur that educated Afro-Brazilians claiming the *negro* identity are more exposed to black activists' rhetoric than those who are less educated. This rhetoric encourages a collective black identity. Although my sample is biased, the study is especially useful as respondents were able to freely choose a color or racial identification without being restricted to census categories. This survey is not generalizable to the country of Brazil, because it is restricted to neighborhoods in the cities of Salvador and São Paulo. The survey is intended to add to existing literature restricted to other states or local communities.

Telles (2004) finds that the black and brown isolation index from whites in neighborhoods in Salvador is 82, which is close to Chicago's index of 83—Chicago being the most segregated city in the United States. An index of 100 indicates full isolation from whites. However, in the Salvador case, this is due to the large population of blacks rather than housing discrimination as present in the United States. This result is telling because it highlights the fact that neighborhoods in my Salvador sample are quite representative of Afro-descendant neighborhoods, considering that most black and brown neighborhoods are isolated from white neighborhoods. The segregation index for São Paulo is only 37, and the population percentage of blacks and browns is 25 percent (Telles 2004, 203). However, it must be again noted that isolation indexes are affected by the population percentage. Telles also shows that, with the exception of five districts, the districts in the center of São Paulo city are mostly white, and almost all of them are less than 16 percent black and brown (199). Larger percentages of blacks and browns are found in districts in the periphery, where most of my survey interviews were conducted, making the survey useful in highlighting racial-opinion dynamics in such neighborhoods.

DESCRIPTIVE RESULTS OF THE 2006 SURVEY

Color and Race

Negro is a racial category. *Preto* is a color category denoting black, and *pardo* denotes brown or mixed-race people. *Moreno* is a term that Brazilians of all colors may identify as, and includes dark-skinned and light-skinned people with tans. Respondents were asked to identify their color in an open-ended and closed-ended question. In the open-ended question, they could identify in a color category with no choices given. In the closed-ended question, they were asked to choose a census color category. The census categories in the 2000 census were white (*branco*), brown (*pardo*), black (*preto*), yellow (*amarelo*), and indigenous (*indígena*). Yellow denotes people of Asian descent. Considering the open-ended color categories in both cities, 2 percent of Afro-Brazilians identified as white, 62 percent as black (*preto, negro, negão*), and 36 percent as brown (*mulato, moreno, pardo, moreno claro, marrom*). In my surveys, in both cities, more Afro-Brazilians chose a "brown" color or racial category in the open-ended question than interviewers classified them as (see table 1). In Salvador, interviewers classified

TABLE 1. NUMBER OF AFRO-BRAZILIAN RESPONDENTS SELF-IDENTIFIED IN CENSUS AND OPEN COLOR CATEGORIES; AND RESPONDENTS CLASSIFIED IN CENSUS COLOR CATEGORIES BY INTERVIEWERS

Salvador

CENSUS CATEGORY	OPEN-ENDED COLOR CATEGORY	INTERVIEWER CLASSIFIED CENSUS COLOR CATEGORY			
White (*branco*)	12	White (*branco*)	8	White (*branco*)	2
Black (*preto*)	208	Black (*negro, negão,* *preto*)	210	Black (*preto*)	230
Brown (*pardo*)	104	Brown (*mulato, moreno, pardo, moreno claro, marrom*)	121	Brown (*pardo*)	102
Other	6	Other		Other	0

São Paulo

CENSUS CATEGORY	OPEN-ENDED COLOR CATEGORY	INTERVIEWER CLASSIFIED CENSUS COLOR CATEGORY			
White (*branco*)	21	White (*branco*)	20	White (*branco*)	4
Black (*preto*)	141	Black (*negro, negão,* *preto*)	150	Black (*preto*)	191
Brown (*pardo*)	131	Brown (*mulato, moreno, pardo,* moreno *claro,* moreno *escuro,* moreno *jambo marrom*)	143	Brown (*pardo*)	119
Other	0	Other	3	Other	3

*Negão literally means big black or really black. In Brazilian Portuguese, one can emphasize that an object or person is large by adding ão to the word: thus negro becomes negão.

102 respondents as brown (*pardo*), whereas 121 respondents identified themselves as brown (*mulato, moreno, pardo, moreno claro, marrom*). In São Paulo, interviewers classified 119 respondents as brown and 143 respondents identified themselves as brown (*mulato, moreno, pardo, moreno claro, moreno escuro, moreno jambo, marrom*). There is a tendency to identify as brown because it acknowledges racial mixture, part of Brazil's national identity. I consider *marrom, moreno,* and *pardo* brown color categories. *Moreno claro* translates as light brown. The English translation of *moreno escuro* and *moreno jambo*

TABLE 2. MONTHLY FAMILY INCOME IN SALVADOR AND SÃO PAULO (%)

	SALVADOR	SÃO PAULO
No income	3	3
< 2 times the minimum salary* (R$700)	40	26
2 to 5 times the minimum salary (R$700–1,750)	44	46
5 to 10 times the minimum salary (R$1,750–3,000)	12	22
10 to 20 times the minimum salary (R$3,500–7,000)	1	3
Total	*100*	*100*

*The minimum monthly salary is R$350. Rather than an hour minimum wage, in Brazil one considers minimum monthly salary.

is dark brown. *Mulato* is mixed-race. Table 1 gives the results in absolute numbers of respondents identifying in the open-ended and close-ended questions and how they were classified by the interviewer. I focus on respondents' self-identification in the open-ended question.

Overall, the color and racial category most claimed was black (*preto* and *negro*). Considering the open-ended color categories, the Afro-Brazilian sample in Salvador is made up of 2 percent of Afro-Brazilians who identified as white, 62 percent who identified as black (*preto, negro, negão*), and 36 percent who claimed some type of brown (*mulato, moreno, pardo, moreno claro, marrom*) identification. Considering the open-ended color categories in São Paulo, 6 percent of Afro-Brazilians self-identified as white (*branco*), 47 percent identified as black (*preto, negro, negão*), 45 percent identified as brown (*mulato, moreno, pardo, moreno claro, moreno escuro, moreno jambo,* and *marrom*), and 2 percent identified as "other." In both cities, the number of blacks (*pretos*) interviewers classified as such exceeds the number of self-identified blacks (*pretos* and *negros*). Afro-Brazilians identifying as brown have fundamentally different political behavior than those who identify as black (G. Mitchell 2009). This leads to my conclusion that Afro-Brazilians identifying as black may be more likely to support affirmative-action policy than those who self-identify in nonblack categories. I note these are the categories respondents chose for the survey and in everyday life; color categories can change by the minute depending on a person's social situation.

Gender, Education, Income, and Age

In Salvador, 52 percent of respondents were male and 48 percent female. In São Paulo, 57 percent were female and 43 percent were male. In both cities, the average age was 33. In Salvador, respondents ages ranged from 17 to 67, and in São Paulo, from 16 to 83.

Educationally, 45 percent of the sample in Salvador and 36 percent of the sample in São Paulo had some high school education or had finished high school. In Salvador, 15 percent did not complete middle school, and in São Paulo, 24 percent did not. There were 19 percent of respondents in Salvador and 14 percent in São Paulo who were pre-college. In Salvador, 40 percent of respondents had a monthly family income of two minimum salaries or R$700 (approximately $350 USD).[2] I consider this low-income. About 44 percent of the sample had an average family income of R$700 to R$1,750 ($350 to $875 USD) per month. Only 13 percent of the sample had a high monthly family income, ranging from R$1,750 to R$7,000 ($1,875 to $3,500 USD) (see table 2). In São Paulo, 26 percent of respondents had a monthly family income of approximately R$700 (approximately $350 USD), 46 percent had a monthly family income between R$700 and R$1,750 ($350 and $875 USD), and 25 percent had a monthly family income between R$1,750 and R$7,000 ($875 and $3,500 USD). Although the sample in São Paulo was less educated than the Salvador sample, they earned more money—likely due to it being a more developed city. Now that I have examined descriptive statistics of relevant variables of the data, I turn to my analysis.

LOGISTIC REGRESSION ANALYSIS

Hypothesis and Variables

My hypothesis is that Afro-Brazilians who believe blacks (*negros*) face difficulties in society due to racism and discrimination, claim a black identification, and are highly educated are more likely to support affirmative-action policy than those who believe blacks' problems are due to social or class inequality, claim nonblack identifications, and are less educated. As stated earlier, previous research shows that Afro-Brazilians who identify as black are more likely to vote for black candidates. For this reason, it is likely that blacks would support racial policies for blacks. Presumably, Afro-Brazilians with higher incomes do not face class discrimination; thus it is plausible that when facing discrimination, they will attribute this to racial discrimination rather than class discrimination. Angela Figueiredo's (2010) work on middle-class Afro-Brazilians in Salvador show that they face racial discrimination but do not confront the per-petrators, because they simply believe these people have bad manners, and they do not want to cause problems for people less well off than themselves. Nonetheless, Figuereido's work is illustrative of the fact that middle-class Afro-Brazilians face racial discrimination. It is likely that Afro-Brazilians with lower incomes will at-tribute discrimination to their class rather than race. Gladys Mitchell (2010b) finds that Afro-Brazilians who self-identify as *negro* and *preto* are more likely to claim they have experienced racism than those claiming nonblack identities. For this reason, it is possible that self-identifying as black will positively correlate with support of affirmative-action policies.

The alternative hypothesis is that Afro-Brazilians with higher levels of educa-tion are not more likely to support affirmative-action policies than those with lower levels of education. As noted earlier, Telles and Bailey (2002) find that among all color groups, support for affirmative action decreases as education increases. It is noteworthy that the survey they use was restricted to the state of Rio de Janeiro and was conducted in the year 2000, before the implementation of affirmative-action policies in universities.

To test my hypotheses, I use a logistic regression model. The dependent variable is support for affirmative action in employment and university admissions, and the independent variables are racial/color identification, gender, age, income, education, city, and opinion of the major problem of blacks (*negros*). The survey question regarding affirmative action states: "Affirmative action is a program that focuses on the problem of discrimination against blacks (*negros*) and browns (*pardos*). It encourages universi-ties and workplaces to have a higher percentage of blacks and browns. Do you believe affirmative action programs are important?"[3] Respondents could answer yes or no. In the sample, 70 percent of respondents support affirmative action and 30 percent do not. Thus an overwhelming percentage of Afro-Brazilians in the Salvador and São Paulo samples support affirmative action.

Respondent ages were grouped in the following cohorts: 16–25; 26–40; 41–55; and 56 years and older. The variable city is a dichotomous variable and includes Salvador and São Paulo. The color/racial identification variable is how the respon-dent self-identifies in an open-ended question asking about their color or race. The categories are: white (*branco*), light brown (*moreno claro*), mixed-race (*mulato*), brown (*moreno, pardo, marrom*), dark brown (*moreno jambo*), the racial category black (*negro*), and the color category black (*preto*). The education categories are: did not complete middle school, completed middle school, some high school or completed high school, pre-college, in college or completed college, and graduate level education. The monthly family income categories are: zero; up to two minimum salaries or $350 USD; between two and five minimum salaries or between $350 and $875 USD; between five and ten minimum salaries or between $875 and $1,750 USD; and between ten and twenty minimum salaries or between $1,750 and $3,500 USD.

The independent variable, "major problem of blacks," is operationalized with the question "What do you think is the major problem of blacks (*negros*)?" I grouped these responses into eight categories. Those categories are (1) racism/discrimination/prejudice/exclusion; (2) lack of opportunity/lack of opportunity to study; (3) racism or discrimination from blacks themselves/blacks do not vote for blacks; (4) lack of education, lack of money/low education/poverty/hunger/lack of places to live/not prepared; (5) before they did not have space, now they do; (6) social inequality; (7) lack of unity, lack of knowledge about black people, lack of consciousness; and (8) blacks are not interested/accustomed to their situation/blacks do not like to study/lack of courage. These responses are quite telling, as some respondents blame blacks (*negros*) for their situation, while others blame racism or social inequality for the obstacles blacks face. Because of the open-ended format, answers are useful for examining if a respondent is sympathetic with blacks. Empathy can be demonstrated by acknowledging structural obstacles blacks face, rather than blaming victims of discrimination, or attributing difficulties blacks face to social inequalities.

Noteworthy is that most (50 percent) of the self-identified white Afro-Brazilian respondents cited a lack of education, lack of money, or poverty as the major problem of blacks. Most blacks and browns cited racism or discrimination as the major problem of blacks. About 36 percent of browns cited racism as the major problem of blacks, while 40 percent of *negros* cited racism. Roughly 43 percent of *pretos* cited discrimination as the major problem of blacks. Afro-Brazilians self-identifying as white were more likely to attribute black problems to class inequality, whereas most black and brown respondents discussed blacks' problems as racialized problems of racism and discrimination.

PRETOS VERSUS *NEGROS*, AND THE MAJOR PROBLEM OF BLACKS (*NEGROS*)

John Burdick (1998) noted that *pretos* as compared with *negros assumidos*, or Afro-descendants who later in life identified as black, more often recalled personal experiences of racial discrimination. Slightly more *pretos* cite racism and discrimination as a major problem of blacks. About 43 percent of *pretos* cite discrimination and racism, and 40

TABLE 3. "MAJOR PROBLEM OF BLACKS" CITED BY SELF-IDENTIFIED *NEGRO* AND *PRETO* RESPONDENTS IN SALVADOR AND SÃO PAULO, BRAZIL.

MAJOR PROBLEM OF BLACKS	NEGRO	PRETO
Racism/discrimination/prejudice/exclusion	40	43
Lack of unity, lack of knowledge about black people, lack of consciousness	5	7
Social inequality	1	0
Before they did not have space, now they do	7	7
Lack of education, lack of money/low education/poverty/hunger/ lack of place to live	28	32
Racism or discrimination from blacks themselves/blacks don't vote for blacks	5	1
Lack of opportunity/lack of opportunity to study	11	6
Blacks aren't interested/accustomed to their situation/blacks don't like to study; lack of courage	3	3
Total	*100%*	*100%**

*Rounding affected the tally in this column.

percent of *negros* cite racism and discrimination as the major problem of blacks (see table 3). Some 32 percent of *pretos* cite either a lack of education or money, or poverty as the major problem of blacks, while 28 percent of *negros* cite these same problems. Thus there are slight differences between *pretos* and *negros* in explaining the difficulties blacks (*negros*) face, but they are not overwhelming differences. It is noteworthy that 1 percent of *negros* claimed that the major problem of blacks is social inequality, and no *pretos* cited social inequality. It is also noteworthy that 5 percent of *negros* claimed that the major problem of blacks is racism from blacks, while only 1 percent of *pretos* claimed this.

LOGISTIC REGRESSION ANALYSIS RESULTS

I have discussed general trends of the independent variables. I now turn to my analysis. In the logistic regression model, support for affirmative action is the dependent variable, and the independent variables are age, city, gender, education, income, and the "major problem of blacks." In the logistic regression analysis, where support for

TABLE 4. LOGISTIC REGRESSION OF SUPPORT FOR AFFIRMATIVE ACTION (N 613)

INDEPENDENT VARIABLE	COEFFICIENT	STANDARD ERROR
Age	−0.97	0.31
Gender	−0.20	0.18
City	−0.52	0.19
Color	0.22	0.38
Education	−0.32	0.45
Income	1.21	0.50
Black problems	0.74	0.28
Constant	0.60	0.42

affirmative action is the dependent variable, age, city, and opinion of the major problem of blacks are all statistically significant at the 99 percent confidence interval (see table 4). Income is statistically significant at the 95 percent confidence interval. As age increases, the likelihood a respondent will support affirmative action decreases. Afro-Brazilians in the age cohort of 16–25 years old are 78 percent likely to support affirmative action, holding the independent variables income, gender, city, education, color identification, and major problem of blacks constant (see table 5). Those in the age cohort of 26–40 years old are 73 percent likely to support affirmative action, holding income, gender, city, education, color identification, and major problem of blacks constant. This likelihood decreases to only 58 percent for those 56 years or older. Thus a respondent in the youngest cohort is 1.3 times more likely to support affirmative action than a respondent in the oldest cohort, holding income, gender, city, education, color identification, and major problem of blacks constant. It is likely that younger cohorts support affirmative action more than older cohorts because of their

TABLE 5. PROBABILITY OF SUPPORTING AFFIRMATIVE ACTION BY AGE COHORT (INCOME, GENDER, CITY, EDUCATION, COLOR IDENTIFICATION, AND "MAJOR PROBLEM OF BLACKS" CONSTANT)

AGE	YES	NO
16–25	0.78	0.22
26–40	0.73	0.27
41–55	0.66	0.34
56+	0.58	0.42

accommodation to the discourse of racism and the need for redress through racial policies. As noted earlier, the discourse of race in Brazil has significantly changed from denying racism to acknowledging racism in Brazilian society, and younger cohorts have been more exposed to the rhetoric of acknowledging racism than older cohorts.

Respondents in São Paulo are more likely to support affirmative action than respondents in Salvador. Holding the independent variables education, income, gender, age, color identification, and major problem of blacks constant, respondents in São Paulo are 77 percent likely to support affirmative action, as compared to those in Salvador, who are only 67 percent likely to support the policy. I believe Afro-Brazilians in Salvador are less willing to support affirmative-action policies than respondents in São Paulo because the percentage of Afro-Brazilians in Salvador is more than double the percentage in São Paulo. As a result, racial dynamics in the two cities are different. There is a much larger white population in São Paulo. Because Salvador is overwhelmingly Afro-descendant, respondents may believe racial policies aimed at blacks (*negros*) are not needed in a city where they compose a majority of the population. In contrast, Afro-Brazilians in São Paulo are a minority, and thus may be more likely to acknowledge the need for racial policies for Afro-Brazilians. Much Black Movement activism began in São Paulo (Hanchard 1994), and São Paulo is home to South America's only university geared toward Afro-descendants. Thus activism has played a significant role in São Paulo despite the smaller percentage of Afro-descendants when compared to Salvador.

In this sample, education is not statistically significant; thus the alternative hypothesis that higher-educated respondents are more likely to oppose affirmative-action policy than lower-educated respondents is rejected. Although education is not statistically significant, income is. As income increases, the likelihood of support for affirmative action increases. Respondents who claim the major problem of blacks is discrimination are more likely to support affirmative action than respondents who believe the major problem of blacks is that they are accustomed to their situation, or that problems are due to social inequality. Thus my hypothesis is in part correct, but not entirely. Color or racial identification is not statistically significant. This is surprising, yet one explanation is that the survey question asks if respondents support affirmative action for blacks (*negros*) and browns (*pardos*). In the mainstream media and among Black Movement activists, the term *negro* is used to denote blacks and browns. Using the term *negro* includes browns, in addition to their specific mention with the term *pardo* in the survey question. Using the term *preto* or *negro* without the mention of *pardo* would likely have yielded different results. In a similar vein, Bailey (2008) finds that simply mentioning a racial policy for blacks results in an increase

TABLE 6. PERCENTAGE OF RESPONDENTS CITING RACISM AND DISCRIMINATION AS A MAJOR PROBLEM OF BLACKS (*NEGROS*), BY MONTHLY FAMILY INCOME BRACKET

INCOME	PERCENT
No income	4
Up to $350 USD	38
$350 to $875 USD	44
$875 to $1,750 USD	13
$1,750 to $3,000 USD	2
Total	*100%*

in respondents identifying as such. Thus the racial or color terminology in the survey question can influence survey results.

As predicted, those with higher incomes are more likely to support affirmative action than those with lower incomes. I posit that Afro-Brazilians with higher incomes are more likely to interpret challenges in the workplace or in society as challenges due to their race or color, rather than their class, because class is less of an issue. In fact these data show that of those stating the major problem of blacks is racism, 44 percent have a monthly family income between $350 and $850 USD, or two to five times the minimum salary. Thirteen percent of those citing racism and discrimination have a monthly family income between $875 and $1,750 USD, or five and ten monthly salaries. Education is not statistically significant. This finding is in contrast to Bailey and Telles's (2006) finding that education has a negative impact on support for affirmative action. This could be due to sample differences. A key difference is that my sample is restricted to Afro-Brazilians and limited to neighborhoods in Salvador and São Paulo. Telles and Bailey's data includes white, brown, and black Brazilians and is based on a state survey.

Fifty-nine percent of respondents who admit the major problem of blacks is racism and discrimination have monthly family incomes in the middle income category ($350 to $850 USD) and two highest income categories (see table 6). Only 4 percent of those claiming racism is the major problem of blacks come from the lowest income bracket of no earnings. However, 38 percent of those admitting racism is a major problem of blacks come from the next to lowest income bracket.

As predicted, respondents who cited racism or discrimination as a major problem of blacks, rather than blaming blacks or citing class inequality, had a higher predicted probability of supporting affirmative action (see table 7). Because many in the sample support affirmative-action policies, the predicted probabilities are high for

TABLE 7. PREDICTED PROBABILITY OF SUPPORTING AFFIRMATIVE ACTION CONSIDERING RESPONSES TO "MAJOR PROBLEM OF BLACKS" (AGE, GENDER, INCOME, EDUCATION, COLOR IDENTIFICATION, AND CITY CONSTANT)

MAJOR PROBLEM OF BLACKS	PREDICTED PROBABILITY OF SUPPORT OF AFFIRMATIVE ACTION
Racism/discrimination/prejudice/exclusion	0.80
Lack of unity, lack of knowledge about black people, lack of consciousness	0.75
Social inequality	0.73
Before they did not have space, now they do	0.71
Lack of education, lack of money/low education/poverty/hunger/lack of places to live	0.69
Racism or discrimination from blacks themselves/blacks don't vote for blacks	0.66
Lack of opportunity/lack of opportunity to study	0.64
Blacks aren't interested/accustomed to their situation/blacks don't like to study; lack of courage	0.62

all responses; yet there are some differences. Examples of responses that blame blacks are: racism or discrimination from blacks themselves, or blacks are not interested and are accustomed to their situation. In the first case, holding the variables age, gender, income, education, color identification, and city constant, the predicted probability of support for affirmative action for a respondent who believes the major problem of blacks is racism from blacks themselves is 0.66. Similarly the predicted probability for a respondent who claims blacks are not interested or are accustomed to their situation is 0.62. This is the lowest predicted probability of support for affirmative action of all responses. In contrast, holding the variables age, gender, income, education, color identification, and city constant, the predicted probability of support for affirmative action for a respondent who claims the major problem of blacks is racism and discrimination is 0.80. This lends credence to my hypothesis that respondents sympathetic to blacks (*negros*) by admitting the barrier of racial exclusion are more likely to support affirmative-action policies than those blaming victims of discrimination for the problems they face. Similarly, the predicted probability of support for affirmative action for a respondent who claims that blacks' problems are due to social inequality is 0.73, while the predicted probability of support is only 0.69 for those who claim blacks' problems are due to poverty or a lack of education. These results are demonstrative of the role that acknowledging racism as a problem of blacks, or claiming these problems are simply class-based problems play on support for affirmative-action policies.

AGE, CITY, INCOME, MAJOR PROBLEM OF BLACKS, AND SUPPORT FOR AFFIRMATIVE ACTION

To highlight the interaction of the independent variables age, city, income, and the major problem of blacks, which are all statistically significant in a logistic regression model where support for affirmative action is the dependent variable, I examine predicted probabilities. Holding the variables gender, color identification, and education constant, the predicted probability of supporting affirmative action for a respondent in the oldest age cohort (56 years and older) in Salvador with no income who believes the major problem of blacks is that blacks are not interested or are accustomed to their situation is only 0.28 percent. In contrast, holding the independent variables gender, education, and color identification constant, the predicted probability of support of affirmative action by a respondent in the youngest age cohort (16–25 years old) in the city of São Paulo, in the highest income bracket that admits the major problem of blacks is racism, is 0.92. This is a difference of 0.64. Thus the respondent in Sao Paulo in the youngest age cohort, highest income bracket admitting the major problem of blacks is racism is 3.3 times more likely than a Salvador respondent in the lowest income bracket who blames blacks for their problems to support affirmative action.

CONCLUSION

In this chapter, I find that Afro-Brazilian respondents in São Paulo are more likely than respondents in Salvador to support affirmative-action policies. I also find that younger respondents are more likely to support the policy than older respondents, and that as income increases, the likelihood that a respondent will support affirmative action increases. Beyond these demographic variables, an important finding is that Afro-Brazilian respondents who cite racism and discrimination as a major problem of blacks are more likely to support affirmative action than those citing social inequality or who blame Afro-Brazilians for their problems by claiming they are accustomed to their situations.

Scholars studying political opinion and racial attitudes of Afro-Brazilians cannot assume that racial solidarity leads to overwhelming support of affirmative-action policy. Yet it is important to consider that changing racial politics in Brazil may influence Afro-Brazilians to acknowledge racism in Brazilian society. While Brazil is a multiracial society seeking redress for the ills of racism, it is important to note how potential beneficiaries of policies aimed at them interpret these programs. It is ultimately up to individual Afro-Brazilians to interpret exclusion against them in society. As Afro-Brazilians increasingly acknowledge the role of both racial and class discrimination rather than simply class discrimination, it is likely they will support and seek the implementation of such programs.

NOTES

1. The author thanks the following for their assistance in Brazil: Edson Arruda, Paula Barreto, Magda Lorena, Cloves Oliveira, Leon Padial, Rosana Paiva, Jacqueline Romio, Kledir Salgado, Thabatha Silva, Gislene Santos, Darlene Sousa, Ricardo Summers, Jaqueline Santos, Gabriela Watson, Neusa, and Gloria Ventapane.

2. For an idea of the class standing of respondents, I report average monthly family incomes for various occupations. My statistical analyses concern monthly family income, which combines all incomes of those working in the household. A maid has a monthly family income of 386 *reais*, a bus driver of 964 *reais*, an engineer of 5,246 *reais*, and a construction worker 637 *reais* (www.worldsalaries.org/brazil.shtml).

3. Ação afirmativa é um programa que enfoca o problema da discriminação contra negros e pardos. Ela tenta incentivar que nas universidades e no trabalho tenha uma porcentagem maior de negros e pardos. Você acredita que programas de ação afirmativa são importantes?

REFERENCES

Bailey, Stanley R. 2008. "Unmixing for Race Making in Brazil." *American Journal of Sociology* 114(3):577–614.

———. 2009. *Legacies of Race: Identities, Attitudes, and Politics in Brazil.* Palo Alto, CA: Stanford University Press.

Bailey, Stanley R. and Edward E. Telles. 2006. "Multiracial vs. Collective Black Categories: Census Classification Debates in Brazil." Ethnicities 6(1): 74-101.

Brubaker, Rogers, and Frederick Cooper. 2000. "Beyond 'Identity.'" *Theory and Society* 29.

Burdick, John. 1998. "The Lost Constituency of Brazil's Black Movements." *Latin American Perspectives* 25:136–155.

Castro, Mônica. 1993. "Raça e comportamento político." *Dados* 36:469–491.

Covin, David. 2006. *Unified Black Movement in Brazil, 1978–2002.* Jefferson, NC: McFarland & Company.

Fernandes, Florestan. 1965. *A integração do negro na sociedade de classes.* São Paulo: Dominus Editora.

Figueiredo, Angela. 2010. "Out of Place: The Experience of the Black Middle Class." In *Brazil's New Racial Politics*, ed. Bernd Reiter and Gladys Mitchell. Boulder, CO: Lynne Rienner Publishers.

Francis, Andrew, and Maria Tannuri-Pinto. 2009. *Using Brazil's Racial Continuum to Examine the Short-Term Effects of Affirmative Action in Higher Education.* Unpublished manuscript.

Fry, Peter, Yvonne Maggie, Marcos Chor Maio, Simone Monteiro, Ricardo V. Santos. 2007. *Divisões perigosas: Políticas raciais no Brasil contemporâneo.* 1st ed. Rio de Janeiro: Civilização Brasileira.

Guimarães, Antonio Sergio. 2001. "The Race Issue in Brazilian Politics (The Last Fifteen Years)." Fifteen Years of Democracy in Brazil Conference. University of London, London, England, 15–16 February.

Hagopian, Francis. 1996. *Traditional Politics and Regime Change in Brazil.* New York: Cambridge University Press.

Hanchard, Michael. 1994. *Orpheus and Power: The Movimento Negro of Rio de Janeiro and São Paulo, Brazil, 1945–1988.* Princeton, NJ: Princeton University Press.

Hasenbalg, Carlos. 1978. "Race Relations in Post-Abolition Brazil: The Smooth Preservation of Racial Inequalities." PhD dissertation, University of California, Berkeley.

Hooker, Juliet. 2009. *Race and the Politics of Solidarity.* New York: Oxford University Press.

Johnson III, Ollie. 1998. "Racial Representation and Brazilian Politics: Black Members of the National Congress, 1983–1999." *Journal of Interamerican Studies and World Affairs* 40:97–118.

———. 2006. "Locating Blacks in Brazilian Politics: Afro-Brazilian Activism, New Political Parties, and Pro-Black Public Policies." *International Journal of Africana Studies* 12: 170–193.

Mainwaring, Scott, et al. 2000. "Conservative Parties, Democracy, and Economic Reform in Contemporary Brazil." In *Conservative Parties, the Right, and Democracy in Latin America*, by Kevin Middlebrook, 164–222. Baltimore: Johns Hopkins University Press.

Mitchell, Gladys. 2009. "Black Group Identity and Vote Choice in Brazil." *Opinião Pública* 15(2).

———. 2010a. "Politicizing Blackness: Afro-Brazilian Color Identification and Candidate Preference." In *Brazil's New Racial Politics*, ed. Bernd Reiter and Gladys Mitchell. Boulder, CO: Lynne Rienner Publishers.

———. 2010b. "Racism and Brazilian Democracy: Two Sides of the Same Coin?" *Ethnic and Racial Studies* 33(10).

Mitchell, Michael. 1977. "Racial Consciousness and the Political Attitudes and Behavior of Blacks in São Paulo, Brazil." PhD dissertation, Indiana University.

———. 2007. "Race and Democracy in Brazil: The Racial Factor in Public Opinion." Paper presented at the National Conference of Black Political Scientists, San Francisco, CA, 21–24 March.

Mitchell, Michael, and Charles Wood. 1998. "The Ironies of Citizenship: Skin Color, Police Brutality, and the Challenges to Brazilian Democracy." *Social Forces* 77:1001–1020.

Nobles, Melissa. 2000. *Shades of Citizenship: Race and the Census in Modern Politics.* Stanford, CA: Stanford University Press.

Oliveira, Cloves. 2007. A Inevitável Visibilidade de Cor: Estudo comparativo das campanhas de Benedita da Silva e Celso Pitta às prefeituras do Rio de Janeiro e São Paulo, nas eleições de 1992 e 1996. PhD dissertation, Instituto Universitário de Pesquisa do Rio de Janeiro (Iuperj).

Oliveira, Cloves Luiz P. 1997. *A Luta por um Lugar: Gênero, Raça, e Classe: Eleições Municipais de Salvador-Bahia, 1992.* Salvador: Serie Toques Programa A Cor da Bahia-UFBA.

Paixão, Marcelo, and Luiz M. Carvano. 2008. *Relatório anual das desigualdades raciais no Brasil, 2007–2008.* Rio de Janeiro: Editoria Garamond Ltda.

Pardue, Derek. 2004. "Putting Mano to Music: The Mediation of Race in Brazilian Rap." *Ethnomusicology Forum* 13:253–286.

Pereira, João Baptista Borges. 1982. "Aspectos do comportamento político do negro em São Paulo." *Ciência e Cultura* 34:1286–1294.

Prandi, Reginaldo. 1996. "Raça e boto na eleição presidencial de 1994." *Estudos Afro-Asiaticos* 30:61–78.

Racusen, Seth. 2010. "Affirmative Action and Identity." In *Brazil's New Racial Politics*, by Bernd Reiter and Gladys Mitchell. Boulder, CO: Lynne Rienner Publishers.

Reiter, Bernd, and Gladys Mitchell, eds. *Brazil's New Racial Politics*. 2010. Boulder, CO: Lynne Rienner Publishers.

Sansone, Livio. 2004. *Negritude sem Etnicidade: O Local e o Global Nas Relações Raciais e na Produção Cultural Negra do Brasil*. Salvador, BA: EDUFBA.

Santos, Gislene A. 2008. "Racism and Its Masks in Brazil: On Racism and the Idea of Harmony." In *Race, Colonialism, and Social Transformation in Latin America and Caribbean*, ed. Jerome Branch, 91–115. Gainesville: University Press of Florida.

Santos, Sales Augusto dos. 2000. *A ausência de uma bancada suprapartidária afro-brasileira no Congreso Nacional (Legislatura 1995/1998)*. 2 vols. Brasília: Centro de Estudos Afro-Asiaticos.

———. 2006. "Who is Black in Brazil? A Timely or a False Question in Brazilian Race Relations in the Era of Affirmative Action?" *Latin American Perspectives* 33:30–48.

———. 2010. "Black NGOs and 'Conscious' Rap: New Agents of the Antiracism Struggle in Brazil." In *Brazil's New Racial Politics*, ed. Bernd Reiter and Gladys Mitchell. Boulder, CO: Lynne Rienner Publishers.

Sheriff, Robin. 2001. *Dreaming Equality: Color, Race, and Racism in Urban Brazil*. New Brunswick, NJ: Rutgers University Press.

Soares, Glaucio, Ary Dillon, and Nelson da Valle Silva. 1987. "Urbanization, Race, and Class in Brazilian Politics." *Latin American Research Review* 22:155–176.

Souza, Amaury de. 1971. "Raça e política no Brasil urbano." *Revista de Administração de Empresas* 11:61–70.

Telles, Edward. 2004. *Race in Another America: The Significance of Skin Color in Brazil*. Princeton, NJ: Princeton University Press.

Twine, France Winddance. 1998. *Racism in a Racial Democracy: The Maintenance of White Supremacy*. New Brunswick, NJ: Rutgers University Press.

Valente, Ana Lúcia E. F. 1986. *Política e relações raciais: Os negros e às eleições paulistas de 1982*. São Paulo: FFLCH-US.

Von Mettenheim, Kurt. 1986. *The Brazilian Voter: Mass Politics in Democratic Transition, 1974–1986*. Pittsburgh, PA: University of Pittsburgh Press.

Afro-Descendant Peoples and Public Policies: The Network of Afro-Latin American and Afro-Caribbean Women

Altagracia Balcácer Molina and Dorotea Wilson

The very definition of racism, "the superiority of some people over others because of their membership in a particular ethnic or racial group,"[1] leads us to assume a position of rejection and rebellion against its many expressions. This alleged superiority has only been possible to establish through the use of force by groups who unilaterally built a hierarchical social structure based on discriminatory criteria such as poverty, ethnic and racial differences, sex, sexual orientation, and age, among others. In this structure, the highest place is occupied by the dominant groups, and people who do not share their traits are subjected to exploitation and discrimination.

Distinctions are made on the basis of ethnicity and race, which are aspects that have marked the history of humanity. In the continent of the Americas, they have been central in the construction of the collective imagination and social narrative from the time of colonization, which began in the fifteenth century.

Though the particular expressions of discrimination and exploitation have changed over time, Afro-descendant groups continue to experience these practices even today. At the same time, many sectors of society repudiate discrimination and continue to struggle for the recognition and validation of the rights of excluded groups, and for the kinds of conditions that will allow Afro-descendant people to develop on equal terms.

The exclusion of Afro-descendant people is expressed in many ways and has multiple consequences: "The injustices experienced by the victims of racial discrimination and other related forms of intolerance are well known: limited employment possibilities, segregation, and endemic poverty are just a few of them."[2]

.   .   .

We are speaking of racism—the negation of African origin—something that makes social and political positioning difficult given the implications of racism in the life of the Afro-descendant population in the country. It also has an impact on the organization of citizens to defend their interests and achieve respect for the rights that belong to all men and women equally without regard to race or sex, as the U.S. Constitution establishes.

- In 2005, the population of Latin America and the Caribbean was estimated at 543 million people.
- No specific censuses exist for the Afro-descendant population in each country, but studies estimate that we number between 88 and 197 million.
- Some studies indicate that there are at least 150 million Afro-descendant people in Latin America and the Caribbean—approximately 30 percent of the total population. About half of these (around 70 million) are women.

In addition to the disadvantages experienced by these excluded groups, women face other disadvantages in every society in the world because of their gender. The kinds of inequalities they encounter are well-known: they receive less remuneration for work of equal value, they have high levels of illiteracy, and they have limited access to healthcare services. Inequality based on race is different than gender inequality, but these forms of discrimination are not mutually exclusive. On the contrary, experience shows that far too often they are experienced together in a kind of aggravated or double discrimination that occurs for reasons of both gender and race.

Factors related to social identity—such as race, color, and ethnic and national origin—end up being enormously important factors for women. They create problems that may affect only certain groups of women, or may affect some women disproportionately as compared to others.

In this context, black women experience a double discrimination both as blacks and as women. They have been excluded and their plight has been made invisible in ways that still affect us today. *Invisibilization* occurs in many ways: for example, no statistics are gathered about this population in censuses, surveys, and various studies. There is no information that is disaggregated by ethnic and racial origin, in spite of the significant number of Afro-descendant people in the region.

WHERE ARE WE?

The majority of the Afro-descendant population of Latin America and the Caribbean are in Brazil, Colombia, Venezuela, Peru, on the Caribbean Islands, and on the Caribbean coast of Central America. Every country in the region has an Afro-descendant population except El Salvador. In some countries, we Afro-descendant people represent a high percentage of the population; in others we are a minority group.

In the case of the Dominican Republic, we are the majority. There, it is estimated that 80 percent of the total population is Afro-descendant.

POVERTY AND ITS IMPACT ON WOMEN

Many human-rights reports make the point that racism is a significant component of poverty, and that gender inequality added to racial discrimination places black women in a situation of greater vulnerability to the hardships of poverty.

Black women's experience of exclusion due to racism has been marked by poverty and by the lack of access to employment and to health and education services. Thus, black women are among the most vulnerable groups in society and occupy the lowest levels of the socioeconomic strata. This situation is as common in the rural areas as it is in the urban areas.

Having lower levels of education means that job opportunities are fewer and obstacles to achieving an acceptable quality of life are greater. Consequences include lower income, malnutrition, and unhealthier environments in the places where these women and their families live.

The economic marginalization of black women is also expressed in the fact that it is difficult for them to participate fully in their countries' investment in human capital and productive employment. Structural limitations also exist in terms of their ability to gain access to resources for production.

In countries where blacks are more than one-third of the population, they are the largest group of people who live below the poverty line, and the largest percentage of those who live in conditions of extreme poverty. Afro-descendant people are concentrated in the lowest levels of society. For example, in Brazil, they represent 70 percent of the poorest sector but only 15 percent of the wealthiest sector.[3] In Uruguay, only 8 percent of the black population are part of the middle class; 92 percent are in the most disadvantaged classes of society.[4]

When women are the heads of households, it is more likely that the household will be poor. In the Dominican Republic, 36 percent of households were female-headed in 2008, and while the data is not disaggregated by ethnicity and/or race, since we know that about 80 percent of the population is Afro-descendant and that they are in the lowest strata of society, it can be assumed that most women heads of households are Afro-descendant. According to data from the latest poverty study—*Dominican Republic Poverty Assessment: Achieving More Pro-Poor Growth*, written by the World Bank and the Inter-American Development Bank (2006) with the collaboration of various institutions of the Dominican government—the poverty rate for female-headed households (20.1 percent) is significantly higher than it is in other households. Single-parent households headed by men and all other households have much lower poverty rates, about 12.9 percent on average.[5]

Though women's participation in the labor force has increased almost to a point of parity with men, women still represent only one-third of all employed persons, and the unemployment rate is almost three times greater for women than it is for men. The differences are even more severe in the case of black women.

Unemployment has increased significantly for all population groups, but it has affected the less educated groups the most (including Afro-descendant men and women). Female unemployment has tended to grow at a faster pace than that of men. This is due to a continuing labor-market preference for employing men, a result of social conditioning in a society that continues to be *machista*.

EDUCATION

The education variable has a significant impact on the poverty levels experienced by the population in general and by women in particular. The fewer the years of schooling a woman has had, the higher the probability that she will be poor. In other words, education continues to be a primary factor for predicting income. In our countries, while the average level of education has increased for both Afro-descendants and whites, the inequality gap between the two groups has remained relatively constant. Illiteracy among whites is lower than among blacks. Studies in some countries like Ecuador and Honduras also show that there is greater illiteracy among the black population, and particularly among black women.

Work/Labor

While an increasing number of women are represented at all the various educational levels, however, this gain has not been accompanied by greater employment opportunities. Unemployment is greater among women than it is for men. The wage gap also remains—less remuneration for similar work—something that seems to point us once again to the inequalities that have been present since time immemorial and have kept gender-based discrimination in place. The situation is even more serious when women are discriminated against for racial or ethnic reasons. If you are a woman and you are black, you are doubly vulnerable to discrimination and to social, political, and economic exclusion.

Afro-descendant women are in the lowest strata of society and are therefore the poorest. They work in the lowest-paid jobs—primarily in the free-trade zones, as domestic workers, and in the informal economy.

While the laws of our countries do protect the right to equality, "states are not adopting efficient measures to keep people from being segregated in either the public or private spheres."[6]

While the laws of the country prohibit discrimination, it is clear that racial discrimination exists, as does discrimination based on gender, age, and sexual orientation, among other things.

The discrimination that black women experience in terms of their access to employment is sometimes justified by saying they do not meet the requirements of a "good presentation," but this is often based on a model of beauty that idealizes the white race. In fact, employment advertisements published in the newspapers often require the applicant to include a photograph, which violates the applicant's right to equal opportunity. This is another expression of racism in our societies, and it contributes to increasing the likelihood of poverty among black women in general.

Health

In most countries of Latin America and the Caribbean, the Afro-descendant population is located in the poorest strata of society, which means they are the primary users of public health services.

Maternal death cases often have to do with the fact that there are an insufficient number of public health centers. Women may lack the resources to travel to one of the health centers or to purchase the medicines that are prescribed for them.

Young women and adult women sometimes have undesired pregnancies, and this leads to abortions in unsanitary conditions that in many cases result in the death of both the mother and the child.

In some places, Afro-descendant women and children do not have access to any type of health service, and when a black woman does go to a hospital, she may be mistreated. Even if she arrives first, she is the last one to be called. As women wait for care in hospitals, they die, or they see their children die, because of systemic discrimination.

In terms of the social security law, a difficult situation has been created for Afro-descendant women workers because many of them do not have identity documents. This is true for all of the reasons already presented in this report describing the situation of poverty in which they live. A lack of documentation means that they may be excluded from some or many of the benefits they might receive from the social security system. It reduces their opportunities for accessing basic health services and the pension plan.

VIOLENCE

Today, many studies have documented the fact that violence against women is a phenomenon with multiple causes. The women who are most likely to be victims are women who live in urban areas; those who work in service jobs like manual labor or domestic work; those with less than twelve years of education; the less-informed; those who belong to religions other than Catholic; young adults; separated and divorced women, and women in consensual unions; the wives or ex-wives of men who work in sales or are manual laborers; and the wives or ex-wives of men who consume It is notable that women in many countries continue to denounce the fact that they are nine times as likely to be attacked in their own homes by their children's father, their ex-husbands, or their current partners than they are to be attacked violently on the streets or in a workplace.

Violence against women is invisible and silenced, occurring primarily behind the closed doors of a woman's home. It is a way that power relationships have played out over generations. Men are shaped by this violence and use it as a way to express power over a woman.

Violence deprives women of their rights and has a negative impact on women's health (physical and mental health, and an impact on suicide and homicide rates).

Where children are involved, violence impacts the child's educational performance and health and is related to the intergenerational transmission of violence. For women there is also an economic impact; violence leads to lower labor productivity and, therefore, lower income.

In terms of domestic violence against Afro-descendant women, the following aspects must also be taken into consideration:

- There is a sexual erotic myth that associates black women with pleasure and turns them into sex objects. Because of that, they are used and exploited commercially.
- Violence is cross-cutting in the case of black women; they are discriminated against because they are women and because they are black.
- In many cases, black women are not seen as citizens, who are entitled to rights of citizens.

POLITICAL PARTICIPATION

In 2008, women were 50.4 percent of the nearly 5.6 million people who were eligible to vote in the Dominican Republic and registered by August 16, 2007. In absolute terms, this means that 37,918 more women were registered to vote than men.

There has been both an absolute and a relative increase in the number of women voters who have exercised their right to elect their government representatives. Between 1970 and 2006, women went from 44.6 percent to 50.4 percent of total voters in the Dominican Republic. In absolute terms, this means that 21,476 more women voted than men in 2006.

The increase in the number of women voting for their public officials is not mirrored, however, by an increase in women being elected to the presidency of the Republic or to congressional or municipal seats. Women's participation at this level has not seen any steady progress. Rather it has been a zigzag pattern of advances and setbacks without any permanent gains.

The right of women citizens to be elected on a parity with men has faced many obstacles. While the region has had several women presidents, none of them have been Afro-descendant. The truth is that to have a real impact, a group must have access to power, and in most countries we women have little or no political power.

Formal political participation is low and/or very weak. The social and political participation of black women is not significant, though they do participate around their specific concerns in social movements, and in particular the feminist or women's movement. Black citizens almost never figure among the political and economic elite, or in the media of our countries. This happens even in those countries whose populations are primarily black.

In Latin America and the Caribbean, there are no black women presidents, and almost none who are government ministers, congresswomen, directors of autonomous organizations, mayors of large cities, or leaders of political parties. We are not in power, and it is necessary to access power to make the changes that our societies need in order to reach real, not just formal, equality.

PUBLIC POLICIES

A number of groups who represent the Afro-descendant population have achieved high organizational levels, and this has made it possible to develop initiatives to pressure governments and call attention to race-based inequalities in our society. As a result, some measures have been taken. However, the response to date is still weak and insufficient. One significant problem is the fact that this sector of the population has been made invisible by not being taken into account in national statistics. If we do not officially exist in this sense, it is impossible to design policies to work towards closing the inequality gap that permeates all areas of life for Afro-descendant people.

It is important to pay attention to the progress that is being made in the area of human rights, and to require complete compliance with the recommendations of international organizations and the decisions of the Inter-American Human Rights Court. International agreements and covenants must continue to be signed and ratified, and national legal frameworks must be adjusted to reflect these agreements.

The state has a responsibility to pay attention to racial and ethnic discrimination, which is often compounded by discrimination for reasons of gender, HIV/AIDS, disability, age, and sexual orientation, among others. The lack of state policies and measures in general in this area reveal that racial discrimination is not a major point of interest on the government work agenda.

In terms of poverty reduction, it is necessary to have quantitative data on the total number of Afro-descendant women in the country in order to design public policies that can contribute to creating opportunities for development and reducing poverty among this group.

The creation and implementation of public policies for the workplace, assistance with access to credit and land, and specialized programs to support enterprises headed by Afro-descendant women are positive measures that can contribute effectively to poverty reduction.

In terms of education, it is vital to provide documents to women and their children in order to guarantee them access to education. There is also a need to create literacy and technical education programs for Afro-descendant adults in order to provide them with tools for the labor market.

The majority of the Dominican population is Afro-descendant, and therefore so are the majority of women. In terms of political participation, however, if women do not work with a consciousness of their racial or ethnic identity, those who do reach decision-making spaces will not do so with an agenda of defending the interests of Afro-descendant people. It is imperative, therefore, that policy work includes work to raise people's awareness of their identity.

In the area of sexual rights and reproductive rights, it is essential to have clear information about Afro-descendant women and their socioeconomic and territorial placement. This information can be used to promote programs to support the issue in question, and to establish sexual and reproductive health programs that respond to the particular needs of this group.

The conclusion, then, is that the struggle must continue until we achieve the changes we need in every area—social, economic, political, and cultural—so that we can build a more just, inclusive, and supportive society.

NOTES

1. Real Academia Española, *Diccionario de la lengua española* [Dictionary of the Royal Academy of Spanish Language], 2008.

2. David Howard, *Coloring the Nation: Race and Ethnicity in the Dominican Republic* (Oxford: Signal Books, 2001).

3. *Informe sobre la situación de las mujeres Afro en Colombia* (RMAAD, 2009).

4. *Informe sobre la situación de la población Afro en Uruguay* (Montevideo: MundoAfro 2009).

5. World Bank and Inter-American Development Bank, *Informe sobre la pobreza en la Republica Dominicana: Logrando un crecimiento económico que beneficie a los pobres.* ["Dominican Republic—Poverty Assessment: Achieving More Pro-Poor Growth"] World Bank and Inter-American Development Bank, (Washington, DC, USA, 2006). Available at http://www.worldbank.org/reference/ (accessed 21 June 2011).

6. *Alternative Report to the Committee on the Elimination of Racial Discrimination*, United Nations, 2008.

7. Cáceres Ureña and Estévez Then, G. (2004). *Violencia Conyugal en la Rep'blica Dominicana: Hurgando tras sus Raíces.* Asociación Dominicana Pro Bienestar de la Familia (PROFAMILIA). Santo Domingo, República Dominicana.

PART 4

Migration, Diasporas, and the Importance of Local Knowledge

Decolonizing the Imaging
of African-Derived Religions

Amanda D. Concha-Holmes

In the vein of Harrison's (1991) call to "decolonize anthropology," I respond with a challenge to decolonize the imaging of African-derived religions. I attempt to expound on this process through a three-fold path. First, in order to de-colonize, one must comprehend some of the historical processes and implications of colonization. In this case, I delineate how racialized modes of scholarship and legislation have created derogatory and commodified representations and images of Afro-Cubans in Cuba. Then, once this historical foundation is set, I endeavor to reframe Lucumí (Yoruba practitioners in Cuba) religio-ecological knowledge,[1] specifically that of Osain. Finally, this paper contributes an explanation of the import of this knowledge, and more accurately, embodied ways of knowing, not only for the disciplines of anthropology and religion, but also for conservation and development in Cuba and beyond.

The academy has often understood African-derived knowledge (even that which has been transformed by its migration and novel syncretic formations, as is the case in the Americas) within an evolutionary hierarchical model denoting inferiority (and even criminality) (Harrison 1991; Rodriguez-Mangual 2004). To exemplify this occur-rence through a Cuban anecdote, I will begin by recounting a revealing story. Visiting my grandparents at their retirement home in Melbourne, Florida, in 2010, I met a Cuban couple who lived in Cuba during the early 1900s when the sugar mills were still in mass production mode, and many of the Afro-Cubans who worked in Cuba were still feared. I spoke with the gentleman of the couple, who recounted the following story:

> I was working for my father's sugar mill as a young lad, when it was rare for much intermixing to occur, and the black workers hardly ever invited white workers to their ceremonies. Those rituals were veiled in secrecy. This concealment was especially necessary because the religious ceremonies were illegal, and with good reason. [*With raised brow and lowered voice he continued:*] Africans [who lived in Cuba] were *known* to steal white babies and sacrifice them during these ceremonies.

In response to my inquiry, "Do you think that was really true?" he stated definitively, "Oh yes, it absolutely was" (personal communication 2009). This story is emblematic of one of the major issues that this paper addresses: the images chosen to construct a representation (or what I am calling the imaging) of African-based systems of knowing—particularly religious forms—often have been demeaning and denigrating. Thus, African and African-derived religions become collapsed with traditional and primitive in contrast to a Western modern and progressive. This pejorative contrast was happening in colonialist times as well as contemporary ones. Wirtz, author of the article "Santeria in Cuban National Consciousness," describes how her collaborators revealed similar stories in 2004: "Santeros [were] purportedly arrested for sacrificing children in rituals" (2004, 430). This stereotyping of Africans according to preconceived derogatory notions is a type of racism that has been enacted by scholars of Africans and African-derived religions, as well as performed through the introduction of conservation to the African continent and beyond.

Critical to a book on reexamining the Black Atlantic—particularly in terms of development issues—scholarship as well as conservation and development projects, I argue, must decolonize the imaging of African-derived religions. In that endeavor, I proffer the following account set primarily in Havana and Matanzas, Cuba, where I conducted field research during several distinct periods from 2003 to 2006.

My research relies on what I call evocative ethnography, which is organized around the principles of ethnography, using visual and cognitive techniques along with archival research to explore how Lucumí conceptualize nature and how I can translate these embodied epistemologies. Additionally, since some of these Lucumí ways of understanding nature encourage, according to certain practitioners, "respectful" environmental behaviors, I hope that this research will aid future studies and, more importantly, improved collaborations between Lucumí practitioners, scientists, and policymakers.

Due to the high number of both enslaved Africans and, importantly, *free* Afro-Cubans in Matanzas and Havana, the retention of African traditions is especially strong there (Reid 2004). Lucumí is practiced in Cuba by integrating Yoruba beliefs with Catholic icons, tenets of Kardecian spiritism, along with other African-based religions like Palo and Abakua. Often, Yoruba practitioners in Cuba will follow more than just one tradition. Thus, they allow for overlap that to a Western eye may appear contradictory. On the contrary, Yoruba "tradition" implies not only change but also integration of other belief systems. Instead of a closed-system philosophy that allows but one way, Yoruba tradition is based on dynamic transformation and process. Additionally, when I refer to Yoruba or Lucumí (which I use interchangeably) practitioners, I am referring to the people who are involved with the religion; they may or may not be descended from Yorùbáland, West Africa. This is an important distinction since neither Afro-Cubans nor Yoruba practitioners denote a homogeneous group.

The following example may help illustrate contemporary Afro-Cuban religion as it more realistically becomes performed in Cuba. This scenario involves a woman who holds multiple, seemingly contradictory roles in society, and as such is emblematically Cuban. She is an active member of the Communist Party, a soils scientist, a wife of a soils scientist, a mother to a college graduate who is about to leave the island, and a daughter of rural family origins. She helped build her home and many others so that she could have her own. She would be considered white—probably descended from Canary Island heritage. And at the time of my visit in 2006, she was suffering from a deep depression, and seeking help in the multiple forms that are commonly available in Cuba—biochemical, psychological, and religio-spiritual. This woman's situation helps illustrate some of the complexities of contemporary Cuban life and the intersections of various identity politics, scientific knowledges, and religious knowledges that form a cultural "hybrid" postcolonial identity (Bhabha 1994) known as Cuban.

Cuba's alternative modernity (Appadurai 1991) embraces complexity and nuance in myriad ways. Cubans are proud of a literacy rate higher than most United States cities at 99.8 (2002) percent (World Health Organization 2008). This statistic includes Cuba's rural, inner-city, and other typically marginalized areas. Thus, the majority is a very text-educated and cultured populace. Additionally, Cuba's accomplishments through its development policies as well as its scientific achievements rival industrialized nations' triumphs. In all of these respects, Cuba is an unquestionably modern country. Hence, Cuba challenges dichotomous notions of modern and traditional, West and non-West, science and non-science. Due to the excellent education that Cubans enjoy, the country boasts over 11 percent of the scientists of Latin America (including a cadre of professional foresters, and wetland and soil scientists)—even though they make up only 2 percent of the population. Moreover, Cuba's alternative modernity relies on the formative role that Lucumí and other African nations (like the Congo-based Palo Monte and the Carabalí Secret Abakúa Society) have played in defining its character and culture, which have important ramifications for scholarship on Afro-descendants as well as development and conservation studies. Accordingly, scholars and scientists must not only question the paradigm of creating an "other" whom "Western" scientists and scholars must teach, but also determine with whom they should share a conversation to more fully understand decolonialized imaging of African-derived religions.

Stephan Palmié in *Wizards and Scientists* affirms the modernity of African Diaspora cultural contexts in Cuba:

> For what I aim to demonstrate is that, far from designating even only typological opposites, the meanings, associated with the terms *Western modernity* and *Afro-Cuban tradition* represent mere facets of perspectival refractions of a single encompassing historical formation of transcontinental scope. . . . *Whatever else Afro-Cuban religion is, it is as modern as nuclear thermodynamics, or the suppositions about the nature of our world that underlie DNA sequencing, or structural adjustment policies, or on-line banking.* (Palmié 2002, 15, my italics)

The thrust of my work, then, is to rethink how Black Diaspora histories have been conceived and written, and to begin to conceptualize alternatives. My work focuses on highlighting what may be more locally relevant—yet often more discounted within academe—vehicles of knowledge production and transmission such as *music* and *movement*. In this endeavor, I hope to call attention to how (as Harrison 2008, 10 explains) a "specific subjugation of knowledge lead[s] to the marginalization of" certain perceptions, which have been historically devalued and shunned in the academy. Instead, I support the "transforming," "reworking," and "decolonizing" of anthropology (Harrison 1991 and 2008). In that vein, I seek to eschew an essentialized interpretation of the traditional, particularly as it refers to ecological knowledge, and hope to outline an example of an alternative and modern interpretation of nature and human/nature relations that may be more accurate and relevant for Lucumí practitioners, as well as pertinent for anthropologists and environmentalists.

AFRICAN KNOWLEDGES ARE MARGINALIZED WITHIN ACADEME AND CONSERVATION

In order to understand colonialized imaging of Lucumí practitioners, scholars must acknowledge how African-derived knowledge systems have been conceived and represented by those in positions of academic and governmental power. Academe prominently displays a retention of its colonial history through its tendencies to hierarchialize the validity of Western (read European and United States–based) knowledge systems over others (e.g., Harding 1998; Spivak 1988; Foucault 1971). In this vein, African-derived knowledges and scholars have been marginalized, misinterpreted, and (mis)understood (Harrison 1991). Harrison (2008) and Harrison and Harrison (1999) also have addressed this politics of knowledge as it is manifested in a colonialist anthropology, especially an anthropology of African-descendants in their numerous locations, phenotypes, and cultural predilections. Mudimbe (1988) lucidly points out in his book *The Invention of Africa* that scholarship is explicitly colonial when it is limited to "categories and conceptual systems . . . [that] depend on a Western epistemological order" (Mudimbe 1988, x in Yelvington 2006, 35). As such, the categories and therein the scholarship become an instrument for control within a European colonial project. I emphasize this point that the categories and conceptual systems of many academic disciplines, along with conservation and development projects, depend on a Western epistemological order.[2] And "[a] decolonized anthropology requires the development of 'theories based on non-Western precepts and assumptions'" (Jones [1988] 1970, A classic historical example of how a study of African religions is forced to fit within a colonial invention that serves to denigrate and enforce a hierarchy of knowledge and power is E. B. Tylor's nineteenth-century concept of animism ([1871] 1920). Tylor's term is based within an evolutionary construct of a hierarchy of civilization types from primitive and barbaric to civilized. Tylor, and other scholars, placed Africans and their religions squarely at the bottom, or the primitive side of this evolutionary hierarchical model denoting inferiority for those who did not follow a European system of knowledge production. This hierarchy of knowledges has been especially evident in how scholars have conceptualized nature, and in the rhetoric and practice of tropical conservation and development (Bassett and Zuéli 2003; Neumann 2003; Chambers 1997; Escobar 1995).

The conceptualization of internationally enforced conservation began around the same time as the colonial expansion of the 1800s and early 1900s (Neumann 2003). For example, one of the first systems of national parks was created in 1931, when the London-based conservation organization the Society for the Preservation of the Fauna of the Empire (SPFE) was established. In 1933, the Convention for the Protection of the Flora and Fauna of Africa was held in London, which resulted in an agreement that aligned itself closely with the SPFE's proposals. European preservationists embraced notions of Africa as wild nature, a primeval wilderness akin to "Eden" that would be lost if the efforts were not organized and implemented to preserve it (Anderson and Grove 1987).

Ironically, the reserve was in stark contrast to the efforts of the Europeans to colonize and "develop" the land of this East African region through intensive agriculture and ranching along with an incorporation into the global economy (Neumann 2003, 251). When the preservationists were challenged with the reality that African societies were already living within the proposed boundaries of the national parks, they opted for a binary solution. If the inhabitants conformed to a European imaginary of primitive, then they could stay. If they were imaged as "authentic," meaning unchanging and wild-like, the residents were able to stay as part of nature to be protected "as another native species" (ibid). For instance, in Parc National Albert (Belgian Congo) the "Pygmies are rightly *regarded as part of the fauna*, and they are therefore left undisturbed"[3] (in Neumann 2003, 243). If they did not adhere to this plan, then they were forcibly removed—sometimes to be put to work in the development projects on the adjacent lands.

This inherent racism was not limited to scholarship and policy implementation regarding conservation and religion in Africa; it was also fundamental to the beginnings of scholarship on African descendants in the Diaspora as well as many conservation projects (Barborak et al. 2002). The marginalization of African knowledge systems becomes especially pronounced when coupled with an analysis of African-derived religions. In this line of colonialist scholarship, the initial imaging of Lucumí practitioners demonstrates a palpable marginalization of African Diaspora peoples: Afro-Cubans were initially studied through a lens of interpreting African deviance and criminality.

BEGINNINGS OF AFRO-CUBAN SCHOLARSHIP

Fernando Ortiz, who originally coined the term "Afro-Cuban" and was one of the preeminent scholars of Afro-Cubans, offers a clear instance of African-descendants being studied to understand their inherent criminality. Specifically, in his early work, when he began to study their practices, religions, and cultural traits, he did so looking for reasons to explain their criminal behavior (Ortiz 1906). Based within the theoretical trajectory of his professor, the Italian criminologist Cesare Lombroso (1835–1909), Ortiz investigated what he labeled *el hampa afrocubana*. *El hampa* in Spanish is "the criminal underworld." Thus, not only did European scholars studying African-derived religions regard them as inferior in a hierarchy of development, but also Cuban scholars began their studies under a racialist approach that, with little distinction, criminalized practitioners of African-derived religions.

Furthermore, the Cuban government criminalized African activities in Cuba—particularly religious ones—through enacting a campaign against *brujería*, or sorcery.

The Cuban government of the early 1900s sought to diminish this behavior, deemed deviant, of residents who were labeled as practicing an "atavistic" religion—according to the 1870s work by Lombroso. African-derived religious practitioners were identified with a physiology that was associated with criminal behavior and related them to "throwback" or "primitive" practices. This campaign included outlawing *bembé* ceremonies like the one that was mentioned in the opening vignette. Hence, in efforts to "rid the island of 'degenerate' cultural practices and purge the African elements from national expression, the police confiscated countless percussion instruments" when they raided these forbidden gatherings (Carbonell 1961, 12 in R. Moore 2006). Furthermore, Cuban scholars like Jesús Castellanos (1879–1912), Fernando Ortiz (1881–1969), and Alejo Carpentier (1904–1980) initially gained access to the musical instruments they studied from these police stations.

In the 1800s in Cuba, an anti-African value system pervaded not only scholarship and legislation, but also access to education and cultural references. For instance, the Cuban Anthropological Society in the late nineteenth century "suggested that blacks and mulattos belonged to an inherently inferior race and questioned whether it was worth the trouble to educate them" (León 1966, 5–6 in R. Moore 2006, 3). During the mid-nineteenth century, Afro-Cubans represented less than 10 percent of all university graduates in every field, despite the fact that they represented almost one-third of the total Cuban population (de la Fuente 1995, 151 in R. Moore 1996, 5).

Also, newspapers like *La Prensa* "stated in the 1910s that the nation was doomed to failure as long as it tolerated, among other things, rumba and African-derived dances (Pappademos 2003, 1 in R. Moore 2006, 4). Moreover, little Afro-Cuban drumming or song could be heard or seen in the mass media prior to 1959, and few courses on Afro-Cuban history or culture were offered.

CHANGE AND TRANSFORMATION

Nonetheless, Cuba, like all nation-states, has been the site of a great deal of change and transformation throughout its long historical trajectory. Despite the lack of acclaim or monetary support for research on Afro-descendants in Cuba, a few scholars (at their own expense) initiated and continued their research. Fernando Ortiz, Lydia Cabrera (1899–1991), and Rómulo Lachateñeré (1909–1951) are the three most hailed figures in early Afro-Cuban ethnographic research. Each contributed greatly to the field in distinct ways: Ortiz with his concept of transculturation (in a moment dedicated to acculturation), Cabrera with her focus on participant-observation (before it was called that) and acknowledging practitioners for their vast knowledge—though unpublished and not derived from classroom-based education. Lachatañeré, the only scholar of color of the three, emphasized the diversity within Afro-Cuban religions, including the roles and knowledge of the practitioners. With his influence, the scholarly literature began to comprehend that many kinds of Afro-Cuban religions exist, and each has distinct roles, ideologies, and practices that pertain to the individual religion. For instance, this paper focuses mostly on Lucumí, and specifically the role of *Osainista*—the herbalist and healer—who by virtue of his job and role in the religion holds critical ethnobotanical knowledge.[4] Often, *Osainistas* are also practicing *paleros* since they work with nature (Rodríguez-Reyes 2004).

In addition to the recognition that many Afro-Cuban religions existed, scholars theorized the notion of not only Afro-Cuban identity, but the meaning of being Cuban with its inherent hybrid history and identity. As Fernando Ortiz's anthropological studies of Afro-Cuban culture and the hybrid nature of Cuban nationality matured, he became well-known for his emphasis that the African contribution "did not come to be injected into a pre-existing Cuban culture, but on the contrary the Cuban was born out of the marriage of primarily Spanish and African, through a long process of transculturation" (as quoted by Martínez Furé 1993, 111–112). Transculturation is, as Nancy Morejón, a Cuban poet and literary critic, explains, the "constant interaction, transmutation between two or more cultural components whose unconscious end is the creation of a third cultural whole" (1993, 229).

A metaphor Ortiz popularized to signify this mixture of Cubanness, or *Cubanidad*, is the *ajiaco*, a typical Cuban soup. They highlight the process of *making* the soup as the most important element, not the soup per se (Stubbs and Perez Sarduy 1996). In other words, "This process of synthesis is as yet incomplete, but can be accelerated in a revolutionary fashion" (Martínez Furé 1993, 112). This synthesis of races and cultures became iconic for Cuban national identity building. Later in his career, Ortiz emphasized more culture than race, and supported the state trend toward nationalism that attempted to publicly erase boundaries of race in the effort to recognize a raceless society of mixed Cubans. In this light, Ortiz championed the idea of transculturation, imagining Cuba as mixed racially and culturally. National rhetoric and identity building are critical to examine, especially notions of racial uniformity and equality.

In Cuba, this idea of uniformity began in the 1800s when Jose Martí (1853–1895), the Cuban poet, patriot, and martyr, defined Cuba as a raceless society. In the Republic of Cuba, he argued, the color of skin should not matter. Instead, Cuba should be a unified nation of Cubans regardless of skin color. Fidel Castro followed in Martí's footsteps when he led a revolution in 1959. As Jean Stubbs and Pedro Perez Sarduy explain, the 1959 "revolution moved rapidly to dismantle institutionalized racism"

(1996, 6). Castro made public assertions to define Cubans as not only a Latin American people but also a Latin African people. One of the major agendas of the 1959 Revolution was to dissolve differences of socioeconomic income and privilege based on ethnic divisions or racial divides, so that Cuban people would have equal access and rights. This includes issues of race, gender, religion, age, socioeconomic class, and job opportunities, to name a few of the most prominent and interconnected.

Fidel Castro (1953) addressed the issue of race, after being captured by government forces following the failed attack on Batista's military barracks at Moncada, in the speech now known as "History Will Absolve Me." Point number twelve of the speech asserts that the 26th of July Movement would implement "adequate measures in education and legislation to put an end to every vestige of discrimination for reasons of race [or] sex, which regrettably still exists in our social and economic life" (quoted in Sawyer 2006, 52). Furthermore, on 22 March 1959 Fidel Castro announced what has come to be known as the Proclamation against Discrimination: "We shouldn't have to pass a law to establish a right that should belong to every human being and member of society. . . . Nobody can consider themselves to be of pure race, much less superior race. Virtue, personal merit, heroism, generosity, should be the measure of men, not skin color," Castro then declared. He denounced racial discrimination and racial prejudice as "anti-nation" (Stubbs and Perez Sarduy 1996, 6). In 1959, revolutionary legislation required the desegregation of all neighborhoods, parks, hotels, cabarets, and beaches (Serviat 1986, 164 in R. Moore 2006, 5). In 1960, the Ministry of Labor monitored employment activities to guarantee fair allocation to blacks and whites. Many of the private homes that were abandoned by exiles, the government passed on to poorer, often black and racially mixed families. These and other substantial state mechanisms, such as the lowering of utility bills and rent amounts, enacting the national literacy campaign, and creating the numerous free medical clinics, helped reduce racial inequality further by increasing life expectancy, lowering infant mortality, and improving educational levels more equally for all Cubans—regardless of skin color, rural or urban residence, or age.

In this attempt to create a unified Cuban cultural group, public discussions on race were nearly nonexistent. Interest groups based on race were forbidden. People were allowed to gather only based on affiliation to occupational or student organizations. Moreover, few Afro-Cubans were employed in the revolutionary government. However, differences based on race—though expunged from the census and politically correct discussions—have not been erased from everyday realities. The members of a group meeting that I attended once made that quite clear. They were gathered to dispel the misinformed myth of racelessness, and dispute the racial inequalities that are manifested in terms of less income, less access to resources, and less access to upper-management jobs. The participants of this workshop were incensed and were disputing the glass ceiling that people of color endure.

As Stubbs and Perez Sarduy assert, "It would be shortsighted to think racism is eliminated" (1996, 7). The revolutionary gains aimed at disadvantaged Cubans do not always get translated into daily experience as such. Several scholars from the Havana-based National Union of Writers and Artists of Cuba (UNEAC) criticize Cuba for the persistent differences in opportunities, which the scholars deem are racially based. Sawyer statistically analyzed differences in professional opportunities to occupation holding education constant, and showed that although blacks and whites are about equal in administrative jobs (13.8 percent black, 13.9 percent white, and 9.3 percent mulatto), blacks and mulattos disproportionately hold labor jobs (30.8 percent black, 25.8 percent mulatto and 11.4 percent white) while whites disproportionately hold professional jobs (27.8 percent white, 18.5 percent black, and 15.5 percent mulatto) (Sawyer 2006, 139).

Yet, in Cuba, as in many Latin American nations, race remains a convoluted and complex notion that is influenced strongly by European and U.S. imaginaries and interventions. The dynamic difference in how race is understood in pluralistic societies is significant.

AFRO-CUBAN KNOWLEDGE OFFICIALLY IDENTIFIED AS FOLKLORE

The official, historical trajectory of African-influenced knowledge systems illustrates a marginalization from academe, as this paper has shown, yet a slight acceptance into areas of folklore. In Cuba, "nationalist discourse since the late 1920s has described African-influenced music as representative of everyone" (R. Moore 2006, 3). As such, folklore in Cuba becomes synonymous with African folklore (not Chinese, Spanish, or Jewish). Hence, in the process of imaging Cuba as a creolized nation (1920s–1940s), sorcery became folklore.

Instead of eliminating racism, this folklorization has provoked more marginalization, the commodification of cultural knowledge, and the reification of racialized categories rather than a true valorization of Afro-Cuban knowledge. For instance, "officials [had] referred to Afrocuban folklore as '*atrasada*' or 'backward,' primarily because of its associations with 'primitive' West African societies and their 'superstitious' beliefs. Composer Gonzalo Roig, interviewed in 1961, described traditional rumba as marginal, even barbaric, and having no place in 'true' Cuban culture" (Orejuela Martínez 2004, 127–128). Middle-class audiences continued to abstractly appreciate their country's mixed ancestry, yet dismiss African-derived traditions as primitive (R. Moore 2006, 7).

Nonetheless, change and transformation continue. In 1959, Castro's government created "more opportunities for folkloric ensembles and establishing centers for the study of Afrocuban heritage," offering greater national exposure (R. Moore 2006, 7). Despite African drumming encountering a great deal of prejudice in the 1960s, the Institute of Ethnology and Folklore was created in 1961, which showed the government's valorization and promotion of Afro-Cuban arts (R. Moore 2006). In 1965, Pedro Izquierdo (1933–2000), better known as "Pello El Afrokán," asserted that "only now, within the revolution, has Cuba given the drum its rightful place" (in R. Moore 2006, 7).

One of the most famous folklore ensembles is the Conjunto Folklórico Nacional (CFN), founded in May 1962 in Havana by Rogelio Martínez Furé and Rodolfo Reyes Cortés. This ensemble, like others, was founded with a fundamental goal to educate the public on the beauty and complexity of Afro-Cuban expression, which had too often been hidden from public view. Regardless, the promotion and folklorization were based on the secularization and commercialization of Afro-Cuban religions. In other words, the drumming event was covered only in the contained space of a formal, staged context. The traditions must be secular rather than sacred to obtain legitimate exposure. Noncommercial drumming and African-derived religious music were met with a notable colonial legacy of prejudice through decisions on cultural programming.

Eugenio Matibag asserts that this folklorization represents a "strategy of containment" and that "folklorization serves to relegate a vital, lived cultural form to the category of the artistic and picturesque, thus neutralizing its ideological power" and therein its cultural power (Matibag 1990, 247). Carlos Moore argued that folklorization was simply a form of "whitening" and "de-Africanization":

Dances and music which are part of the ceremonial complex of creeds and tenets of these adherents—considered, quite reasonably, as sacred . . . and bearing a functional meaning in their practices—are being prostituted and presented in theaters as "people's folklore." Why isn't the same applied to the sacred practices of the Judeo-Christian faiths? The subtle motives beneath this outrage are simple: (a) to emasculate the faith, through a prostitution of its most cherished religious values and a demoralization of its followers as a result; (b) to systematically destroy what are considered to be "pagan" and "savage" religious "cults" by means of "civilizing" them into a palatable "people's" folklore (C. Moore 1964, 220).

While discounting critical insight into the academy (e.g., religious studies, anthropology, or conservation), when African-derived religions are identified as folklore, critical knowledge systems are reduced to cultural commodification for tourists and nationals in different yet similarly detrimental ways. With regard to Afro-Cuban religions, Brandon clearly argues that folklorization is detrimental: "In the context of contemporary Cuban society such performances serve not to publicize religious practices but rather to desacralize them. In a sense they have been tamed. The entire world which they create in the life and imagination is reduced to an entertainment" (in Ebrahim 1998).

For example, Hagedorn argues that "the criminalization of sacred practice was gradually replaced with 'spectacle-iza-tion'" (Hagedorn 2001, 197). And Wirtz (2004) adds that the suspicion aspect never disappears. Regardless, the global flow of people, ideas, and practices, which is glossed as African Diaspora, deserves improved attention, particularly African-derived religio-ecological knowledges.

YORUBA RELIGIO-ECOLOGICAL KNOWLEDGE IS EMBODIED KNOWLEDGE

Ways of knowing through invocations, praise poetry, music, and dance are essential to nearly all Yoruba ritual in which spiritual forces are actualized—evoking and thus invoking spirit into physical form. Yoruba employ these embodied techniques to transcend boundaries and open communication among spirit, material, temporal, and spatial worlds, particularly to understand and work with what in the conservation world are called "natural resources." In contrast to the way many positivist scientists and Marxists may interpret nature, my study of Lucumí religion and Osain (deity of the sacred forests, herbs, and healings) reveals an embodied understanding of nature through which the boundaries of subject as well as material and spiritual elements become collapsed and traversed through specialized communication techniques. This embodied knowledge is, as Yvonne Daniel argues in her book *Dancing Wisdom*, "rich and viable and should be referenced among other kinds of knowledge" (2005, 4).

Lucumí is based on personal, embodied experiences incorporating the material and the spirit(ual) worlds into an integrated cosmology of conversations. The entire process is one of learning through embodied communication techniques. The community includes dead ancestors, *orishas* (subjective, divine beings who embody a natural element like rivers and a human pursuit like love), and the religious family; consequently, communication is achieved through embodied performances such as possession, divination, and initiation. Through dance, rhythm, and storytelling, the process of learning is bodily informed:

> When we as a Yoruba people have embodied the [drum's] return beat at an early
> age a whole virtual terrain opens up . . . it becomes embodied knowledge . . . in
> the process of communication. (Taiwo 2005, 184)

Raul Canizares explains that the divine can be accessed through the melodies produced in the throats and the complex rhythms of each of the six hands of the three drummers. Thus, highly trained singers and drummers, especially *batá* drummers, develop an ability to create a confluence of sounds and rhythms that bridges the seen and the unseen, the material and the spiritual, God and humankind. According to practitioners, the *orishas* were able to cross the waters from Africa to Cuba in these songs' rhythms carried by their devotees.

Initiated drummers called *alaña* hold the secret to unite humans with the *orishas* via specifically executed vocal melodies and phrases. If the songs are precise, they may achieve the desired effect, neither missing a beat nor mispronouncing a word, and the *orishas* descend from their heavenly abode and temporarily possess their devotees, initiating a mystic state of communion between the *orishas* and the participants (Canizares [1993] 1999, 69). As African theologian John Mbiti explains: "African music . . . is that aspect of life which provides the repositories of traditional beliefs, ideas, wisdom, and feelings" ([1969] 1999, 67). Hence, *santeros* consider properly consecrated *batá* drums to be living, powerful entities, the materialization of the great spirit Aña.

Verger (1976) explains how the *ofò* or chants for the Yoruba enact life, since sound creates live vibrations. Utterances through music and through the mouth embody power as Ayoade elucidates: "To the initiated the sound of the words is the audible manifestation of its innate force" (1979, 51). Prince notes that among the Yoruba, "to utter the name of something may draw that something into actual existence . . . not only within the mind and body of he who utters and he who hears the word, but also in the physical world as well" (1960, 66). Hence, Verger (1976) uncovers how Yoruba incantations that are chanted during the preparation of medicines summon the *ashé*, or dynamic essence, of the plants. The chant comprises monosyllabic action verbs from each plant and ingredient in the formula. Additionally, Drewal explains that the sound quality of verbs, nouns, adverbs, and adjectives in Yoruba incantations acknowledge a dynamic relationship between speech and action (1998, 257–259).

Not only do Yoruba practitioners acknowledge a strong correlation between power (*ashé*) and oral performance, but also movement in terms of dance and possession is a key tool in the process of communicating religious and environmental information. Dance is a critical tool to interpret Yoruba religion, access the divine, and understand nature in the process. As Drewal (1998, 259) details:

The phrase *kíkan* simulates verbally the effort quality of the dance, that is, one in which a dominant motif is raising (*kí*) and percussively dropping (*kàn*) the shoulders repetitively, i.e., *kíkan kíkan. Kí* is quick, sharp, and high (or up) in tone; *kan* is forceful, full, and heavy, dropping in tone. The dance further evokes, in its speed and thrust, the dynamics of lightning and thunder—in that order— associated with Shangó. In fact, from this perspective, the image of lightning and thunder can be seen, like the analogy to rainfall illustrated above, to derive meaning from its actual dynamic qualities, qualities which in turn reflect the nature of Shangó's power.

Yvonne Daniel, in her study on *Dancing Wisdom: Embodied Knowledge in Haitian Vodou, Cuban Yoruba, and Bahian Candomblé*, reveals that the "movement sequence and motifs for the divinities conform to identifiable patterns that are recognizable across the African Diaspora" (2005, 63). Ogún's dance exemplifies these common patterns since his dance has "explicit, literal meanings and implied, abstracted meanings that are common in all three ritual communities" (ibid). Aggressive warrior stances, kicking through tough terrain, and sharply using some sort of metal like a machete to cut through the thicket or through an opponent are predominant movement themes that demonstrate the warrior nature of this spirit. Thus "ritual dance performance was a repository of remembered movements and musical components [and] also a repository of complementary legends, beliefs, and attitudes, with contrasting and alternative resolutions for temporal problems" (2005, 64). These alternative resolutions may be constructive for conversations on tropical conservation and development, and they are precisely what I hope to more fully uncover with an improved insight into Yoruba religion and its practitioners' conceptualizations of the environment.

Nature Reconceptualized: Translating Osain

Fundamental to Lucumí religion is a conceptualization of nature that is both physical and spiritual. Instead of a cognitive model of the spirituality of religion as distinct and separate from physical nature, Lucumí religious knowledge interprets nature as repositories of *ashé*, or divine essence, and as *orishas*, or spirits. *Ashé* is power that is not only rhetoric, but spirit made tangible. This spiritual power, with the proper knowledge and incantations, can be infused into material objects as well as accessed from appropriate plants. *Orishas* embody multiple layers of reality: metaphysical, physical, spiritual, and material worlds; they are both an aspect of nature and a human pursuit, and much more. The way to access the power, the *ashé*, of the plants is to communicate appropriately—through very specific rhythms, chants, and movements that address individual *orishas*. These are also the techniques through which the transmission of this knowledge occurs. These ways of knowing and learning about nature are examples of what I refer to when I say "embodied epistemology." By this I mean that humans are able to communicate and receive guidance, ask permission, interact, and even embody the *orishas*. "While others pray to an invisible god hoping someday to see him," Canizares explains, "the Divine is manifested in Santería as living, breathing beings one can touch, kiss, and love" ([1993] 1999, 14). In order to understand Lucumí eco-religious knowledge, one begins to recognize that nature is constructed not merely as an ecological system of natural resources depleted of spirit or subjectivity of their own, as is the norm in Western epistemological models. Instead, the environment becomes replete with specific beings whom those initiated into the knowledge can communicate with, listen to, interact with, and even embody.

OSAINISTAS, EMBODIED KNOWLEDGE, AND RESPECTFUL ENVIRONMENTAL BEHAVIORS

"Without Osain, there can be no religion," state numerous practitioners emphatically. As Canizares explains, "Because the wilderness is the true repository of all of Santeria's secrets ... plants, especially herbs are essential to every Santeria ritual" ([1993] 1999, 101). Indeed, essential to Yoruba religion in Africa, and in all of its diasporic manifestations, is an *orisha* who may be understood as the embodiment of nature and medicine, including herbs, plants, trees, and the forest. Osain (spelled Osanyin in Yorùbáland) is the deity of the herbs, the wilderness, the sacred forest; he resides in the woods and along any path where lie herbs and precious weeds. Additionally, each individual plant has its own *orisha* to whom a practitioner must appeal in order to access the healing essence of that stalk or leaf's potency.

Furthermore, when attempting to comprehend Lucumí ecological knowledge, one must refer to the specialists of this knowledge: the *Osainistas*. These followers of Osain are trained with the specialized, embodied techniques of how to communicate with the spirits in the forest, and are thus most intimately connected with this religio-ecological knowledge and its contingent practices. These herbalists and healers are particularly trained in the embodied techniques that allow for direct communication with the plants through using specialized movements, music, and salutations to communicate with the *orisha*. For instance, Osvaldo Villamil, a seventy-two-year-old man who is the head of one of the few *cabildos* that has existed since the 1800s in Cuba, explained:

> You must learn the mystery of Osain. This comes through the sounds of Osain's prayers. They know at what time you can go and collect the plant that you need and you must tell this plant why *she should give you the authorization* so that you can collect from her what she gives you. And, this is material.[5] (personal communication 2004, my italics)

Material is not separated and contrasted in binary opposition to spiritual. Instead the material and the spiritual worlds are interconnected; they become embodied in each other, and experienced through ritual. "Plants have their mystery," Osvaldo explains, and the Lucumí religion combines both scientific and spiritual methods to know the natural elements: "We understand her [nature] in a scientific-spiritual way" (personal communication 2004). Thus, spiritual and material, religion and ecology merge to form an interdependent, intersubjective community within which humans must learn to communicate not just through naming, but also through experiential ways of knowing.

One of the most important aspects of communicating with the plants, and a fundamental element of this collaborative relationship, deals with listening. Communicating with the spirits of the plants does not appear to be equivalent to how some people envision "talking to God" in the form of prayers (e.g., asking that personal needs be met). Instead (though also in addition to), communication takes the form of listening to the spirits of the plants: "Osain speaks . . . according to tradition, Osain speaks" (personal communication 2005). Listening to nature is a vital principle inherent in intersubjective communication. One way to listen is heightening one's perceptions to environmental clues, yet that is not the only way that practitioners listen. Additionally, practitioners must ask permission from the owner of the plant, from the spiritual owner. As one *Osainista* explains, "So, you cannot arrive and take any material that is not yours if you do not ask permission from the owner" (personal communication 2006). Hence, intersubjective communication implies the need to ask permission in an appropriate way, listen to the response, and respond accordingly. The knowledge of how to interact, then, comes through learning specific Yoruba ecological knowledge.

I assert that this element of not only requesting but listening helps to cultivate a relationship of respect that then nurtures environmental practices that are more aligned with conservation. For example, Javier, a thirty-two-year-old male Yemaya follower who goes to the forest daily to request and collect herbs for healings and rituals in the temple of Xiomara (dedicated to Oshun), commented that "religious practitioners respect, take care of, and listen to the plants! I know how to communicate with the plants," he exclaimed (personal communication 2004). He made it clear that not only does he know how to communicate (speak and listen to the plants), but that this knowledge helps inform environmental practices that are respectful and caring.

Through understanding the physical world as spiritual, Osvaldo suggests that *Osainistas* have less harmful practices. Specifically, he details how environmental behaviors like herb collection are based on practices of respectful behaviors. The exact practices that he details are echoed by all of the *Osainistas* with whom I spoke, and are based, they say, on a pattern of respecting life. As one renowned *Osainista* reports:

> We don't damage/hurt/tamper with the forest. For example, if right now we go to the forest and we need to collect a plant, we always respect this plant's roots. Already, this is a form of helping the forest. You take the branches that you need but you respect the roots. If you pull out the roots, you are killing it. She could have reproduced but you are radically killing her. Because you didn't leave any part of her so that she can survive. This is to say that, she will reproduce, do you understand, the birds on one side, the owners of the forest who are the animals, also make their trails . . . humans make one and the animals make another. Now, the careful person knows that a little plant that is sprouting, you don't step on. . . . In this aspect, we respect. Because we do not need to practice this, what we do comes from learned knowledge. And the herbs for the orisha, we don't use absolutely anything like a herbal tea, nor anything like that. It is natural, natural nature of the herb itself. . . . But, that's where you have to be an Osainista, so that you know what you are asking from these plants, these plants can offer you. (Personal communication 2006)

Osainistas are the herbalists of the Yoruba practitioners, and they are the primary ones in Matanzas, Cuba, who go to the woods to communicate with the plants, and return with them to make the powerful concoctions necessary for any initiation, healing, and/or ritual. Thus, these practitioners are the specific ones who should be integrated into conversations on conservation.

IMPORT TO CONSERVATION AND DEVELOPMENT: CONVERSATIONS AND CONTEMPORARY COMPLEXITIES

In the previous section, I briefly covered how Lucumí ecological knowledge is based on traversing the divide of material and spiritual in their conceptualization of, and interaction with, the environment. Nature is conceptualized as more than simply a group of objects available for exploitation at any time. Instead, the cognitive map is comprised of multiple subjects, called *orishas*, who have bodies, wills, and desires. Not only does each of the different plants have its *orisha*, each plant also has its specific form of power. This *ashé*, with the right religio-ecological knowledge, can be accessed and utilized for healings and initiations. The embodied knowledge that is necessary to transcend the material/spiritual divide relies upon specific chants, movements, and drumming rhythms to invoke the deities and thus communicate with the plants. Using ethnographic data, I assert that this knowledge and its application cultivates relationships based on respect—particularly for the *Osainistas*, who are the herbalists and healers of the Lucumí community who interact most with the plant world. As Snodgrass et al. (2008, 309) find in Phulwari ki Nal, where certain individuals (that is, the herbalists and healers) "consciously limit resource overharvesting and environmental damage to their lands," the *Osainistas* report pro-environmental behavior in Cuba. Thus, these "religious specialists with knowledge of healing plants" may be more likely to share interests in common with organizations promoting ecologically sustainable development.

Lucumí religious practitioners' and particularly the *Osainistas*' ability to communicate between worlds and negotiate respectful relationships with the plant world holds implications for conceptualizing ecology, and also has relevance to conservation conversations. Here, I invoke Bakhtin's dialogic ([1930] 1981) and the metaphor of dialogue that Matory (2005) prefers to suggest: not that we should see opposing worldviews, but instead that we should create spaces for conversation, thereby comprehending power as productive and generative, not only repressive (Foucault 1979; Spivak 1988; Escobar 1995). In that vein, I propose a more "ethical relation"[6] that "embrace[s] . . . impossible differences and distances—indispensable for any movement toward decolonization" (Landry and MacClean introduction to Spivak 1996, 5). As Shiva (1989) details the comprehensive ecological knowledge of the women in India that she seeks to integrate into scientific analysis and environmental policy, I hope to encourage a more open dialogue between Yoruba practitioners, scientists, and scholars so that they may learn from each other in open conversation.

The need is apparent. As Escobar (1998, 61) emphasizes in his article "Whose

Knowledge? Whose Nature?" discussing inequities of rhetoric in conservation, "It is clear ... that there is a fundamental asymmetry in biodiversity texts between modern science and economics and local knowledge and practices of nature." He continues to assert that the attention that is given is "insufficient and often misguided to the extent that local knowledge is rarely understood in its own terms" (ibid). Hence, discussions of the environment, which inherently include projections for development, must include locally significant ways of knowing. Otherwise, the act of viewing and representing other peoples through a Western epistemological order sustains this colonialized imaging that homogenizes myriad distinct African-derived cultures as the same, and as inferior within an imaginary hierarchical system that places the white European, Christian male at the pinnacle. This arrangement only serves to reify a colonial system that scholars and legislators use to create a category of race (e.g., Smedley [1993] 2007; Baker 1998; Harrison 1995), along with categories of religion, culture, and nature. These categories have direct implications for development and conservation visions and projects.

From my experience as a scholar and as an intern working in the conservation field (e.g., Barborak et al. 2002), I notice that this element of improving scholarly understanding of local conceptions of the environment is critical. As Spivak (1988) poignantly reminds us in her article "Can the Subaltern Speak," it is not the speaking that is missing, but the listening. Subalterns cannot be truly heard by the privileged of either industrialized or the less industrialized worlds. Can development practitioners and conservationists listen carefully enough to "hear" alternative visions of the world that do not share, or only partially share, a similar ontological and epistemological foundation?

By translating Osain, the Yoruba deity of healing herbs and the sacred forest, I hope to improve the understanding and representation of Yoruba ecological knowledge and ways of knowing nature in Cuba to make a theoretical and methodological intervention in the field of tropical conservation and development, as well as African Diaspora studies. Thus, I agree that to gain collaborative conservation and less-colonialized representations of African-derived religions, scholars, scientists, and policymakers should become better listeners, and to achieve that, we must broaden the scope of our methods to include embodied knowledges and ways of knowing such as music and dance. These forms of knowledge transmission (particularly the kinds of environmental knowledge that the *Osainistas* embrace) should not be relegated to mere folklore for commodification and tourist consumption. Instead, *Osainistas* and their ecological knowledges should be valued for their own merit and on their own terms. By this I mean that Cubans with multiple perspectives, including scientists, policymakers, and practitioners together with those people who are two or all three at once, come to the table to discuss their viewpoints, concerns, and visions for development, conservation, and the future. In this way, I hope to support more equitable partnerships.

In Cuba, this means that international organizations like the UNEP (United Nations Environmental Programme), government organizations like CITMA (Ministerio de Ciencia, Tecnología y Medio Ambiente [Ministry of Science, Technology and the Environment]) and nongovernmental organizations like FUNAPRO ("Antonio Núñez Jiménez" Foundation for Nature and Humanity) could work more directly with specific *Osainistas* to understand Yoruba ecological knowledge, as well as to work toward more open conversations (*pace* Spivak 1988) that attempt to listen as well as explain. Thus, *Osainistas* specifically, along with *santeros* and *santeras* and *Babalawos* and *Iyalawos*, may offer more culturally appropriate leadership, and can offer their role as religious leaders and knowledge transmitters to guide their religious kin in environmentally friendly environmental knowledge, attitudes, and behaviors that are informed by a decolonialized imaging of African-derived religions. In this way, some of the sacred forests and plants that religious practitioners require for their work can be saved.

As two sacred grove experts, Nyamweru and Sheridan (2008, 289), explain in a recent journal volume dedicated to sacred groves in Africa:

> Sacredness does not equal conservation, instead social, political, and economic arrangements mediate cosmology and ecology, and it is in these institutional arenas that Africans negotiate both spiritual values and pragmatic material goals.

Moreover, scholars interested in conservation must particularly understand the role of the *Osainista*, who seems to follow what Snodgrass et al. refer to as "an herbal healer's conservation" (2008, 309). This distinction is critical, because it highlights the diverse roles, practices, and knowledges of different religious practitioners by focusing on the *Osainistas*' roles and relationships with herbs in the Lucumí religion.

I hope to attend to Snodgrass et al.'s call to move "the argument of anthropological and political ecological debates from a simple discussion of whether [certain people, particularly indigenous] are conservationists to the issue of cultural variation," and I add in roles, identities, values, and knowledge (2008, 309). Just as Cubans should not be considered homogeneous, Yoruba practitioners in Cuba (and beyond) should not be considered monolithic in their values or their practices. Though Lachatañeré began to explain to audiences that Afro-Cuban religions were several and varied, and Canizares indicates a range of practitioner association and involvement within the Yoruba religion, neither of these scholars and few others mention the role of the *Osainista*. Regardless, *Osainistas* perform a special and crucial function in understanding and enacting Yoruba ecological knowledge.

CONCLUSION

In conclusion, this paper has highlighted marginalized epistemologies in the academy by reframing Afro-Cuban ecological knowledge. In unpacking a historical legacy of colonialism along with a decolonizing trajectory to more fully understand African-derived religions, my point has been twofold: one, to show a different way to illustrate certain black histories and experiences, particularly those that enjoy a keen sense of embodied ways of understanding the environment; and two, to encourage more equitable partnerships among Cuban scientists, Lucumí practitioners, practitioners of other religions, the Cuban government, and international organizations to be able to work together to envision and co-create a Cuban future.[7]

NOTES

1. Lucumí or *Regla de Ocha*, as it is also known, is most widely known as Santería (literally, Way of the Saints). In the first quarter of the twentieth century, Santería replaced *brujería* as the name for Yoruba religion as practiced in Cuba. Yet, similarly to how *brujería* denoted working with witchery, or wizardry, and thereby was to a Catholic, colonial mind associated with evildoings that were understood in terms of crime and criminality, Santería also came to reference the religion with a pejorative image—connoting the deviancy of worshiping the saints rather than God. Currently, many practitioners refer to their religion as Yoruba, and to themselves as *santero/as* or *religioso/as*.

2. Although I question the dichotomous division of Western and non-Western, particularly when dealing with Cuba, I still defer to the terms to acknowledge a difference between dominant epistemological aspects that are European in origin and form, and those that are African.

3. Report on the Delegates of the International Congress for the Protection of Nature, Paris, June 1931, to His Majesty's Government.

4. *Osainistas* in Cuba are predominantly male. Only postmenstrual women are allowed to be initiated.

5. "Tiene que aprender el misterio de Osain. Eso viene a través de metafonico de conversaciones de resos de Osain saben en que tiempo puede ir y recoger la planta que tu necesitas que le tienes que decir a esa planta para que te de la autorizacion para tu poder recojer de ella lo que ella te de. Vaya. Y eso es una material."

6. "Thinking of the ethical relation as an embrace, an act of love, in which each learns from the other, is not at all the same thing as wanting to speak *for* an oppressed constituency" (Landry and Maclean 1996, 5).

7. One scientist I interviewed said that what she wanted was "a Cuban future"—meaning those Cubans who have remained and continue to live on the island (Holmes 2008).

REFERENCES

Anderson, D., and R. Grove. 1987. "Introduction: The Scramble for Eden: Past, Present and Future in African Conservation." In *Conservation in Africa: People, Policies and Practices*, ed. D. Anderson and R. Grove, 1–12. Cambridge: Cambridge University Press.

Appadurai, Arjun. 1991. *Global Ethnoscapes: Notes and Queries for a Transnational Anthropology.*

———. 1996. *Modernity at Large: Cultural Dimensions of Globalization.* Minneapolis: University of Minnesota Press.

Ayoade, J. A. A. 1979. "The Concept of Inner Essence in Yoruba Traditional Medicine." In *African Therapeutic Systems*, eds. J. A. A. Ayoade, Z. A. Ademuwagun, I. E. Harrison, and D. M. Warren, 49–55. Waltham, MA: Crossroads Press.

Baker, Lee D. 1998. *From Savage to Negro: Anthropology and the Construction of Race, 1896–1954.* Berkeley: University of California Press.

Bakhtin, M. [1930] 1981. *The Dialogic Imagination: Four Essays.* Edited by Michael Holquist. Austin: University of Texas Press.

Barborak, James, Amanda Holmes, Gerald Mueller, and Jocelyn Peskin. 2002. "Community Involvement in Managing Protected Areas of the Meso American Barrier Reef System—How Real Is It?" *Policy Matters* (10):107–109.

Bascom, William. 1969. *Ifa Divination: Communication between Gods and Men in West Africa.* Bloomington: Indiana University Press.

Bassett, Thomas J., and Karl S. Zimmerer. 2003. "Approaching Political Ecology: Society, Nature, and Scale in Human-Environment Studies." In *Political Ecology: An Integrative Approach to Geography and Environment-Development Studies*, ed. K. S. Zimmerer and T. J. Bassett, 1–28. New York: The Guilford Press.

Bassett, Thomas J., and Koli Bi Zuéli. 2003. "The Ivorian Savanna: Global Narratives and Local Knowledge of Environmental Change." In *Political Ecology: An Integrative Approach to Geography and Environment-Development Studies*, ed. K. S. Zimmerer and T. J. Bassett, 115–136. New York: The Guilford Press.

Bhabha, Homi K. 1994. *The Location of Culture.* New York: Routledge.

Cabrera, L. [1954] 2000. *El monte, igbo finda, ewe orisha, vititinfinda: Notas sobre las religiones, la magia, las supersticiones y el folklore de los negros criollos y del pueblo de Cuba.* Miami: Ediciones Universales.

———. 2004. *Afro-Cuban Tales.* Lincoln: University of Nebraska Press.

Canizares, Raul. [1993] 1999. *Cuban Santería: Walking with the Night.* New York: Original Publications.

Chambers, Robert. [1983] 1995. *Rural Development: Putting the Last First.* Essex: Longman House.

———. 1997. *Whose Reality Counts? Putting the First Last.* London: Intermediate Technology Publications.

Curtin, P. 1964. *The Image of Africa: British Ideas and Action, 1780–1850.* Madison: University of Wisconsin Press.

Daniel, Yvonne. 2005. *Dancing Wisdom: Embodied Knowledge in Haitian Vodou, Cuban Yoruba, and Bahian Candomblé.* Champaign: University of Illinois Press.

Drewal, Margaret Thompson. 1998. "Dancing for Ogún in Yorubaland and in Brazil." In *Blackness in*

Latin America and the Caribbean: Social Dynamics and Cultural Transformations, vol. 2, eds. J. Arlene Torres and Norman E. Whitten, 256–281. Bloomington: Indiana University Press.

Ebrahim, H. 1998. "Afrocuban Religions in Sara Gómez's *One Way or Another* and Gloria Rolando's *Oggun*." *Western Journal of Black Studies* 22(4).

Escobar, A. 1995. *Encountering Development: The Making and Unmaking of the Third World.* Princeton, NJ: Princeton University Press.

———. 1998. "Whose Knowledge, Whose Nature? Biodiversity, Conservation and the Political Ecology of Social Movements." *Journal of Political Ecology* 5.

Foucault, M. 1971. *The Order of Things: An Archaeology of the Human Sciences.* New York: Pantheon Books.

———. 1979. *Discipline and Punish: The Birth of the Prison.* New York, Vintage Books.

———. 1980. *Power/Knowledge: Selected Interviews and Other Writings, 1972–1977.* Edited by Colin Gordon, 52–62. New York: Pantheon.

Grove, D. A. R. 1987. "Introduction: The Scramble for Eden: Past, Present and Future in African Conservation." In *Conservation in Africa: People, Policies and Practices*, ed. D. A. R. Grove, 1–12. Cambridge: Cambridge University Press.

Hagedorn, Katherine. 2001. *Divine Utterances: The Performance of Afro-Cuban Santería.* Washington, DC: Smithsonian Institute.

Harding, S. 1998. *Is Science Multicultural? Postcolonialisms, Feminisms, and Epistemologies.* Bloomington: Indiana University Press.

Harrison, F. V. 1991. *Decolonizing Anthropology: Moving Further toward an Anthropology of Liberation.* Arlington, VA: Association of Black Anthropologists.

———. 2005. *Resisting Racism and Xenophobia: Global Perspectives on Race, Gender, and Human Rights.* New York: AltaMira Press.

———. 2008. *Outsider Within: Reworking Anthropology in the Global Age.* Urbana: University of Illinois Press.

Harrison, Ira E., and Faye V. Harrison. 1999. *African-American Pioneers in Anthropology.* Urbana: University of Illinois Press.

Holmes, Amanda D. 2005. "Osain in Translation: Yoruba Religion and Ecology." Film.

———. 2008. "Cuban Voices on Being Cuban and the Future in Cuba." *Transforming Anthropology: Journal of the Association of Black Anthropologists* 16(1):70–71.

Lachatañeré, R. [1939] 2005. *Tipos étnicos africanos que concurrieron en la amalgama cubana: Actas de folklore.* Edited by R. Acosta, 72–82. Havana: Fundación Fernando Ortiz.

Landry, Donna, and Gerald MacClean. 1996. "Introduction: Reading Spivak." In *The Spivak Reader*, eds. Donna Landry and Gerald Maclean, 1–13.

Latour, Bruno. 2004. *Politics of Nature.* Translated by C. Porter. Cambridge, MA: Harvard University Press.

Martínez Furé, Rogelio. 1993. "Imaginary Dialogue on Folklore." In *AfroCuba: An Anthology of Cuban Writing on Race, Politics and Culture*, eds. Pedro Perez Sarduy and Jean Stubbs, 109–116. Melbourne: Ocean Press.

Matibag, E. 1996. *Afro-Cuban Religious Experience: Cultural Reflections in Narrative.* Gainesville: University Press of Florida.

Matory, James Lorand. 1994. *Sex and the Empire That Is No More: Gender and the Politics of Metaphor in Oyo Yoruba Religion*. New York: Berghahn Books.

———. 2005. *Black Atlantic Religion: Tradition, Transnationalism, and Matriarchy in the Afro-Brazilian Candomblé*. Princeton, NJ: Princeton University Press.

Mbiti, J. S. [1969] 1999. *African Religions and Philosophy*. Oxford: Harcourt Education Limited.

Moore, Carlos. 1964. "Cuba: The Untold Story." *Présence Africaine: Cultural Review of the Negro World (English Edition)* 24, no. 52 (1964): 177 229.

Moore, R. 2006. "Black Music in a Raceless Society: Afrocuban Folklore and Socialism." *Cuban Studies* 37.

Morejón, Nancy. 1993. "Race and Nation." In *AfroCuba: An Anthology of Cuban Writing on Race, Politics and Culture*, eds. Pedro Perez Sarduy and Jean Stubbs. 227 237. Melbourne: Ocean Press.

Neumann, Roderick P. 2003. "The Production of Nature: Colonial Recasting of the African Landscape in Serengeti National Park." In *Political Ecology: An Integrative Approach to Geography and Environment-Development Studies*, ed. Karl S. Zimmerer and Thomas J. Bassett, 240–255. New York: The Guilford Press.

Nyamweru, Celia, and Michael Sheridan. 2008. "African Sacred Ecologies." In *Journal for the Study of Religion, Nature and Culture* 2(3):285–291.

Orejuela Martínez, Adriana. 2004. *Castro's Final Hour: The Secret Story behind the Coming Down of Communist Cuba*. New York: Simon and Schuster.

Ortiz, Fernando. 1906. *Los negros brujos*. Havana: Ediciones Cardenas y Cia.

———. 1950. *La africanía de la música folklórica de Cuba*. Havana: Ediciones Cardenas y Cia.

———. 1951. *Los bailes y el teatro de los negros en el folklore de Cuba*. Havana: Ediciones Cardenas y Cia.

Palmié, Stephan. 2002. *Wizards and Scientists: Explorations in Afro-Cuban Modernity and Tradition*. Durham, NC: Duke University Press.

Prince, Raymond. 1960. "Ife." *Annals of the Institute of Cultural Studies* 2:47 64.

Reid, Michele. 2004. *Negotiating a Slave Regime: Free People of Color in Cuba, 1844–1868*. Dissertation: University of Texas at Austin.

Robbins, P. 2003. "Fixed Categories in a Portable Landscape: The Causes and Consequences of Land Cover Categorization." In *Political Ecology: An Integrative Approach to Geography and Environment-Development Studies*, ed. Karl S. Zimmerer and Thomas J. Bassett, 181–200. New York: The Guilford Press.

Rodríguez-Mangual, Edna M. 2004. *Lydia Cabrera and the Construction of an Afro-Cuban Cultural Identity*. Chapel Hill: University of North Carolina Press.

Rodríguez Reyes, Andrés. 2004. "Illness and the Rule of Ocha in Cuban Santeria." Translated by John DuMoulin. *Transforming Anthropology* 12(1–2):75–77.

———. 2005. *El Cabildo Lucumi de Santa Teresa en la ciudad de Matanzas*. Matanzas: República de Cuba Centro Provincial de Superación para la Cultura.

Sawyer, Mark Q. 2006. *Racial Politics in Post-Revolutionary Cuba*. Cambridge: Cambridge University Press.

Shiva, Vandana. 1989. *Staying Alive: Women, Ecology and Development*. London: Zed Books.

Smedley, Audrey. [1993] 2007. *Race in North America: Origin and Evolution of a Worldview*. Boulder, CO: Westview Press.

Snodgrass, Jeffrey, et al. 2008. "Witch Hunts, Herbal Healings, and Discourses of Indigenous Ecodevelopment in North India: Theory and Method in the Anthropology of Environmentality." *American Anthropologist* 110(3):299–312.

Spivak, G. C. 1988. *Can the Subaltern Speak? In Other Worlds: Essays in Cultural Politics.* New York: Methuen.

Stubbs, Pedro, and Jean Perez Sarduy. 1996. *AfroCuba: An Anthology of Cuban Writing on Race, Politics, and Culture.* New York: Ocean/Latin American Bureau.

Taiwo, Olu. 2005. "The Orishas: The Influence of the Yoruba Cultural Diaspora." In *Indigenous Diasporas and Dislocations*, eds. Graham Harvey and Charles D. Thompson, 105–120. Surrey, UK: Ashgate.

Thornton, John Kelly. 2002. *Africa and Africans in the Making of the Atlantic World, 1400–1800.* New York: Cambridge University Press.

Tylor, Edward. [1871] 1920. *Primitive Culture.* New York: J. P. Putnam's Sons.

Verger, P. 1976. "The Use of Plants in Yoruba Traditional Medicine and Its Linguistic Approach." Seminar Series 1976/1977, ed. O. O. Oyelaran, 242–295. Nigeria: University of Ife, Department of African Languages and Literature.

Wirtz, Kristina. 2004. "Santeria in Cuban National Consciousness: A Religious Case of the Doble Moral." *Journal of Latin American Anthropology* 9(2):409–438.

World Health Organization. Http://apps.who.int/whosis/database/core/core_select_process.cfm.

Yelvington, K. A. 2006. "The Invention of Africa in Latin America and the Caribbean: Political Discourse and Anthropological Praxis, 1920–1940." In *Afro-Atlantic Dialogues: Anthropology in the Diaspora*, ed. K. A. Yelvington. Santa Fe, NM: School of American Research Press.

Neoliberal Dilemmas: Diaspora, Displacement, and Development in Buenos Aires

Judith M. Anderson

The development of organizational capacity is key for the advancement of African diasporic people in any nation. Structural racism can thwart such efforts, as already marginalized individuals find themselves further isolated by the same policies that were designed to assist them. Dominant Argentine society, like that of many Latin American and Caribbean nations, insists that racism is imported from other nations, specifically the United States. Argentina, the reputed "European nation in Latin America," does recognize discrimination against some racial and ethnic minorities, yet denies the existence of anti-black racism. The perceived absence of black people is interpreted as eliminating the possibility of anti-black racism. The existence and persistence of black organizations refutes this, as does increased immigration of blacks from Africa and Latin America and the Caribbean.

Anti-black racism as a global phenomenon is a product of colonialism and certainly not unique to the United States. Colonialism has ensured that while racial terminology might differ from country to country, those racialized as black are consistently located at the bottom of the global racial hierarchy. Africans and Afro-descendants in Argentina fall within this category. Though the Argentine state appears to be addressing racial inequalities through the creation of policies that target the poor, these neoliberal practices have only buttressed the existing racial infrastructure.

This paper helps illustrate how neoliberal multiculturalism functions on the ground in Argentina. I specifically explore how it impedes the process of organizing around black identity. A small number of blacks have attempted to negotiate these challenges through the creation of their own antiracist organizations to access the resources the state provides. Some government policies have facilitated the upward mobility of Africans and Afro-descendants in Argentina, yet the same policies have also led to increased marginalization, socioeconomic displacement, and impoverishment for others. Understanding how to interpret local race relations is crucial for those working in the field of development. A significant element of many development initiatives is economic change and advancement. Based on field research conducted from 2007 to 2008, I provide the context for neoliberal socioeconomic policies that were executed in the lives of blacks residing in Buenos Aires during that time.

THE FOUNDATIONS OF ORGANIZED ACTIVITIES
AROUND BLACK IDENTITY

For many, it is difficult to imagine modern-day Argentina as a nation with a thriving black population, and even more so as a politically active one that mobilizes around black identity. In Argentina, as in many other nations with the presence of the African Diaspora, there has long been resistance to dominant society's notion of pure European origins. This is evidenced in the existence of the black press, mutual aid societies, and many other black organizations (Andrews 1980; Lewis 1996), as well as African-based cultural practices that contribute to Argentine popular culture (Lanuza 1942).

In Argentina, there were several organizations involved in the public politics of race,[1] which I define as organized public efforts to mobilize individuals around black identity. The Argentine government created the National Institute against Discrimination (NIAD) in the late 1990s, and the recently established Refugee Assistance Organization, to help combat the problems that plagued black ethnic blocs at a state level. International governments also played an important role with the embassies of South Africa, Brazil, and the United States, all actively participating in public racial politics. The most active black organizations in Argentina included the Nigerian Organization, the Afro-Indigenous Coalition, and the African Diaspora Working Group. To contextualize the role of these black organizations in the expression of modern-day racial politics, I focus on a moment that served as a concrete marker of organized black political activity on a national scale, one that originally incorporated a pan-Africanist vision.

The Afro-Argentine at the helm of black political organization was Martin

Escobar, who began his activism in his late thirties. Many local blacks, as well as nonblack allies, recognized Escobar as the founding father of their most recent activities centered on black identity. Escobar was a handsome, dark-skinned man with a distinct presence that drew people in. He had the look of Hollywood royalty and the dynamism of the greats, in the United States context, like Malcolm X and Martin Luther King Jr. He remained well respected by everyone as a man who tried to raise consciousness among blacks as well as unite them. On the other hand, in more recent years, he has been remembered as a man who had some very harsh criticisms of his fellow Afro-Argentines, and especially of those who have presented themselves as leaders of organized coalitions of Africans and Afro-descendants. This did not make him any less respected of a figure, but it did make some black leaders reluctant to introduce me to him.

Unfortunately, Escobar had a debilitating stroke in 2002, which left him with limited mobility and speech capacity. His son Dominique, a reggae artist with a strong Rastafarian ideology, shared his father's history, legacy, and vision with me. This vision led Escobar to go into exile for twenty years in Switzerland during the Proceso de Reorganización Nacional or the military dictatorship that influenced the nation from the mid-1960s to the early 1980s. Escobar was a major activist and is now idolized by local blacks and their nonblack allies.

A cofounder of early black activism in Argentina and a close friend of Escobar was Paul, an eloquent, intelligent, middle-aged Nigerian man who arrived in Argentina in the late 1970s. Paul continued to be respected among local blacks and was the president of the Nigerian Organization of Argentina. He revealed that in 1982 he and six other black men of different national origins including Afro-Argentines formed an organization to discuss black politics and mobilize blacks in Argentina, but it dissolved after personal conflicts could not be resolved.

Argentina's Africans and Afro-descendants are still in the initial stages of forming unified political activities. In the past fifteen years, several black organizations have been created, but few have engaged in public politics, or even had this as a goal. A small delegation of black activists from Argentina attended the 2001 United Nations World Conference against Racism, though the effects of their participation in this international dialogue had yet to be seen. As several local and foreign blacks have noted, things happen very slowly in Argentina. Escobar and Paul helped plant the seeds of political mobilization, but along the way, the activist drive really lost momentum. By contextualizing these and other efforts of mobilization within the realm of Argentine racial politics, we can better understand how this process has unfolded historically.

RACE, PERONISM, AND THE *CONFLICTO CON EL CAMPO*

Through their research on the U.S. healthcare system, H. E. Page and Brooke Thomas remind us that spaces inside the city, like those within institutional walls, can be racially marked as white. They identify this white public space, noting,

> Either in its material or symbolic dimensions, white public space is comprised of all the places where racism is reproduced by the professional class. That space may entail particular or generalized locations, sites, patterns, configurations, tactics, or devices that routinely, discursively, and sometimes coercively privilege Euro Americans over non-whites. Its material resources are formidable institutions that include the territories they claim or the markets they control. (Page and Thomas 1997, 94)

We can broaden this characterization to understand the racial landscape in Argentina. By *Porteños* defining the capital city of Buenos Aires as the "Paris of Latin America" and themselves as "Europeans," they have in a way marked that entire landscape as white public space. In Argentine folklore, *Porteños* are lighter in skin color, have straight hair, and have a greater knowledge base of elite European cultural practices than the rest of Argentina's population. Guano notes that in the city of Buenos Aires, "whiteness and membership in the urban middle class tacitly establish who has the right to speak for the Argentine nation" (2003, 161). This notion of whiteness as an indicator of belonging not only to the city but also the nation only intensified after the 2001 economic crisis, at which point Buenos Aires's middle-class residents tried to rationalize their own disenfranchisement by creating a discourse of how the city's "modernity was being eroded by the presence of a *mestizo* lower class" (Guano 2004, 69). Through a series of formal and informal cultural practices, there is a distance maintained between dominant society and racial "others."

The literal physical marginalization of blacks, as manifested in their relocation outside the city of Buenos Aires, was reflective of their location on the periphery of the Argentine imaginary. Inside the city limits, black goods, services, and bodies were consumed, but not otherwise integrated into Argentine life. Mimi Sheller's work on consumption, though situated in the Caribbean, is useful in understanding these types of historic racial/spatial relationships and how they reveal the legacy of slavery through patterns of economic exploitation. Sheller broadly defines consumption as "a way of understanding a broad set of relations that are at once economic, political, cultural, social, and emotional" (2003, 5). This paradigm of consumption can be adapted from a transnational scale to the national level to better apprehend the relationship between the residents of *villas miserias*[2] and low-income housing and the members of dominant Argentine society who do not acknowledge them as belonging to the nation or even contributing to its development. The consumption framework is mobilized to comprehend relationships between dominant Western societies and the formerly colonized who remain disenfranchised. Sheller notes that slavery "is not only an economic relation; it is also a cultural, symbolic, spiritual, bodily and affective relation, thus its legacies are manifold" (2003, 4). These marginal racialized bodies are consumed in the form of unpaid or underpaid labor by dominant societies. All the while a spatial distance is maintained between these laborers and those that consume them.

The cheap labor of *negros* has been critical to the production of Argentina's most precious commodity—beef. Fresh beef has been consumed practically on a daily basis by the average Argentine, and it has held a high cultural value. It has been considered a dietary staple and widely accessible across income levels. You commonly would see makeshift grills perched on the sidewalk of a construction site or behind houses in the *villas miserias*, in addition to professional models in the backyards and balconies of the upper classes. The most popular restaurants anywhere served *asado* (grilled cuts of beef with its accompanying sides of entrails, sausages, chicken, pork, and salads) along with other menu items. The *asado* has been the king of Argentine cuisine, a regular weekend activity that would involve an entire day of socializing, and of course a mandatory part of all special occasions from birthdays to Christmas. The 2008 Agricultural Strike or *Conflicto con el Campo* put an abrupt pause in this important everyday cultural practice. The price of beef increased astronomically, leading to dramatically reduced consumption and rapidly increasing discontent with the newly elected government.

The issues of race and racism in Argentina for the most part had managed to escape national media attention until the *Conflicto con el Campo* captured the headlines for months. The stage was set in October of 2007 when Cristina Kirchner went from being first lady to being the president of Argentina. Though she represented the same political party as her husband and predecessor, this change, combined with global economic shifts, helped foment a major conflict between the government and agricultural producers. The *Conflicto con el Campo* quickly evolved into a discussion about race and class, as poor *negro* farmers claimed to be the target of racial and economic discrimination while their wealthy, lighter-skinned *criollo* colleagues would be less affected by the strains of new tax policies.

In Argentina the label of *negro* most often has been used as a marker of subordinate status. Though the anthropological dialogue on the role class has played in the lives of Afro-descendants in Latin America has a long history (Yelvington 2001), we can reexamine class-based discourse as a neoliberal expression of racism. As Faye Harrison elucidates, race may sometimes be displaced or refracted upon other vectors of inequality, like class, in public discourses, especially those that deny race's relevance (2002). But class discourses may be mobilized in ways to discount the salience of race, which has long been common in Latin America. There has been significant overlap in the two categories of *negro*, though class-defined *negros* might not acknowledge that they have also been racially marked as "other" by the hegemony. The discussion of *negros*, darker-skinned individuals who self-identify as having indigenous ancestry, and discrimination was all over the media during the *Conflicto con el Campo*. But the other *negros*, the Africans and Afro-descendants, did not present themselves in these public debates in spite of common concerns and parallel histories of subjugation. Argentine society, though highly racialized, is one in which issues of race have been suppressed, contributing to denial of racism and the "disappearance" or diminished visibility of Afro-Argentines.

The *Conflicto con el Campo* represented the complexity of ideas about blackness in Buenos Aires, Argentina, where an emerging Black Movement has been slow to develop. The latest manifestation of the Peronist government began a year of political changes and rough transitions that translated into private conflicts. Tensions were already high within the local black ethnic blocs, which had long been heavily factional-ized, as well as outside of them.

Those public racial debates had their origins in the policies of the Peronist government (1940s–1950s) that championed the working class and mobilized it to support their political agenda (Svampa 1994). Both blacks and nonblacks noted that the Peronist government popularized the practice of giving free handouts to the lower class in exchange for political support, creating a noncritical constituency that easily could be manipulated with cheap bribes. Historically, blacks have disproportionately been some of the most economically and socially marginalized members of Argentine society, positioning them as benefactors of Peronist policies.

Lupe and Pedro were Afro-Argentines in their thirties whose family lines dated back to the colonial period. They noted that Peronism was a movement of laborers in the 1940s and 1950s to help the working class and the nation's poorest. The Peronists did not make any explicit effort to recognize or assist any racial or ethnic minority, including Afro-descendants who would identify as such, as in the case of some Afro-Argentines. They created free public hospitals, built affordable housing for the lower class located just outside of the city of Buenos Aires, and provided paid vacation leave for all workers. Of all of these benefits, the housing offered the greatest opportunity for Afro-Argentines. One of the most well-known neighborhoods that was created out of these housing initiatives is Barrio Perón, which was created in the 1940s and has continued to have a high percentage of Afro-Argentines as its residents. It is not known if the removal of Afro-Argentines and other racialized blocs from the capital city was a subversive part of the Peronist agenda or just a "fortuitous" side effect, but it has been an undeniable contributor to their lack of visibility. These policies were the next phase in the nation-building project following the whitening policies that were enacted in the early 1900s.

Though neoliberalism is a more recent policy framework, consolidated in the last thirty years, its ideological foundation may have rationalized the benefits of certain Argentine policies in more contemporary terms. Specifically, the construction of Barrio Perón, which relocated all *negros* outside of the capital city and away from the highest-quality goods, services, and resources of the nation, demonstrated this exercise of cultural hegemony. Perpetuating a colonial pattern, blacks would have to continue to go through whites to have their basic needs met, as quality hospitals, schools, and businesses were not a part of the new neighborhood designs. These types of policies were created to benefit *negros*, yet maintain their position at the bottom of the economic strata. On the surface, Peronists had finally incorporated the too often forgotten *negros* who had historically been excluded from Argentine polity, but they did so in a manner that did not upset the status quo.

Recent accounts of Argentine history justified the creation of Barrio Perón by revising it through the lens of neoliberal multiculturalism. In this retelling of history, Afro-Argentines have been well provided for by the government, and thus have had no reason to empathize with the concerns of other black ethnic blocs. This helped foster what Hale defines as racial ambivalence (2006) among Afro-Argentines towards other black ethnic blocs that have had a different position in the racial hierarchy established by the dominant society. Because of the intersections of race and class through these types of practices, some Afro-Argentines even have had the "privilege" of not being marked as black. Racial ambivalence as a political sensibility provides a firm foundation for neoliberal multiculturalism.

Paul offered a different perspective on the *negro* in Argentine society. His viewpoint was indubitably influenced by his subjectivity as a Nigerian who emigrated to Argentina in the 1970s, briefly served in its military, and served as an adviser in the 1984 Peronist Caucus of the Argentine House of Representatives. He later joined the Radical Caucus, which was more in line with his political ideology. Paul initially attended Peronist rallies where he was accepted as *negro*, but at the time, he was unaware of the meanings of that term within the Argentine context. He explained that, for the Peronists, *negro* is a synonym for poor, rather than referring to any specific ethnic origins or phenotype. Argentina's historical whitening agenda has contributed to the redefinition of the term *negro*, which before the rise of Peronism had referred to skin color, though the term often was avoided because of racist ideas about blackness.

According to Paul, racial mixing in Argentina has generated a new category of *negros* that fell between the classic categories of white and black. Argentine society has not differentiated between the new class-defined *negros* who were popularly despised for their laziness and dependence on the state, and the *negros* who were the descendants of enslaved Africans and African immigrants. The new *negros* were notably very poor and worked as farm hands or factory workers, or in other low-paying unskilled labor positions. Perón mobilized the class-defined *negros* along with his wife Eva, who popularized the term *cabecitas negras*, which has now been considered a slur. In Paul's opinion, the conflation of terms combined with the absence of a strong black identity among Afro-Argentines has permitted poor, non-Afro-descendants to usurp the identity of *negro*.

Ivan, a nonblack ally of the politically organizing blacks in Argentina, a state employee, and an African studies professor, added that the Peronists were notoriously corrupt. He agreed that they introduced race into the Argentine political dialogue, but the Peronist class-defined *negro* as the darker-skinned person of indigenous descent. Argentines of known African descent possibly could have contributed to the Peronist discourse on the *negro*, especially in the interior of the country, where historically many industries were dependent on slave labor.

Ivan acknowledged that it was not clear why Peronists chose that term over others in circulation, such as *mestizo* or *criollo*, both of which imply a mixed heritage. *Negros* of African descent participated in modernity through Peronist policies that benefited the working class, though race itself, as a ground of discrimination, was never specifically focused on, for unknown reasons. Ivan suggested that perhaps it was easier to exchange their concerns for racial equality for the benefits of the Peronist agenda. Part of the legacy of the Peronists has been that they are the only visible non-Afro-descendant organization in Argentina that uses *negro* as a synonym for a political identity.

Then the smoke came. It was mid-April 2008, and the city had been wrapped in a never-ending curtain of smoke for almost two weeks. It was one of those rare moments in history when politics literally took one's breath away. For days, there was no sun, no moon, no wind, no rain, and all people could do was pray for the ability to hold their breath just a little bit longer. Several subway lines were closed, congesting already packed street traffic even more. The usually buzzing city sidewalks were empty at night, as no one wanted to be exposed to the smoke unless they had to be, and during the day, people abandoned the outside tables to eat crammed inside tiny restaurants. In some neighborhoods of Capital,[3] individuals had to be hospitalized for smoke inhalation. City officials recommended that people wear masks in those areas to filter the smoke.

The news media claimed that the smoke derived from just some misdirected farmers in the bordering province of Entre Rios who decided to slash and burn their fields to fertilize them, but the explanation was very suspicious. The timing was just too perfect, and nothing like this had ever happened in the history of the Rio de la Plata region.

One of the black leaders, who was also an engineer, explained that this was "political smoke." Some 290 different fires were set in areas bordering Capital Federal, causing the toxic waves of smoke. This was an intentional and well-planned political protest against Cristina Kirchner's government. If an agreement were reached between the agriculturalists and the state, then the smoke would disappear. About a week later, the smoke finally cleared. The people who set the fires were not punished, because in Argentina real justice is rare.

THE ARGENTINE STATE'S INTERVENTIONS

National Institute Against Discrimination

The Argentine state made very few direct interventions in issues related to race. The main medium for transmitting its political position while maintaining a desirable public image has been NIAD. The organization's literature cited several pieces of international human-rights legislation as its model, listed a 24-hour hotline, and detailed copious recommendations for legislation. Two research consultants familiar with the organization told me what they knew about its composition and history.

NIAD was created in 1992 primarily by a coalition of Jewish Argentines, with the help of the non-Jewish Arab interest bloc, but did not start functioning until 1994. Jews and Arabs immigrated to Argentina at the end of the nineteenth century during a massive wave of European immigration and have since been aligned in the city of Buenos Aires through common business ventures, mainly related to providing credit for new businesses (Klich 2006). These blocs by far have been the most powerful and well-organized minorities in Argentina, and the only ones that can successfully compete with nonblacks for political and economic power. They have had the most clout in these realms and have had some of the most powerful leaders of the nation associated with them. Former president Carlos Menem, of Lebanese origin, funded a prominent, opulent mosque in the city of Buenos Aires.

The president of NIAD was elected by a special committee rather than a popular vote. One of the directors of the organization was Arab, and the other two were Armenian Jews. The board came from an NGO and not the state, though NIAD was a state agency. No blacks figured on the board of directors, and of its approximately 120 employees, only five were black (all Afro-Argentine). Only one of those was an actual state employee. The principal agenda of NIAD has been to protect the interests of its founders, who were also its donors.

The public could access the resources of NIAD through filing a formal discrimination complaint. Lupe, NIAD's only Afro-Argentine state employee, explained that it typically took two months for the organization to respond to complaints because of their heavy caseload. They had five lawyers and two advisers that helped review the cases and made recommendations for how they could be resolved. Those involving racially motivated violence were not the responsibility of NIAD, but of the police force. The popular opinion of the majority of Argentina's residents has been that the police are notoriously corrupt, discriminatory, and violent. Most people preferred simply to avoid contact with them to prevent incurring problems.

To file a complaint with NIAD, a grievant had to show tangible proof of discrimination, such as an application that specified it would not consider blacks for the position. This was especially necessary for more subtle cases of discrimination when other explanations could be valid. Afro-Argentines of colonial heritage have filed more than five hundred complaints since the organization was founded. When minors were involved, NIAD legally could not handle the case, as it only dealt with adults. NIAD had no jurisprudence, so it could not create legislation, and under the office of the secretary of the interior, it has had little influence in lawmaking. Ultimately, the organization had no purview over legal processes.

NIAD as an institution has been viewed widely by blacks and nonblacks as ineffective and only serving a symbolic purpose, rather than affecting policy and enacting real change. The organization sponsored numerous events and gave away expensive full-color publications about itself, but ultimately it helped maintain the status quo by ensuring that social inequalities remained, while the marginalized individuals who were most likely to complain about them were appeased with colorful certificates and cocktail receptions.

Among the symbolic actions of NIAD was a funding competition it held for underrepresented groups (Afro-descendants were specifically listed, among others) to win $15,000 pesos to put towards a project. The ad for this competition appeared in the *Buenos Aires Herald*, an English-language newspaper primarily read by foreigners, who were among NIAD's wealthy donors. The ad, which was completely in Spanish, did not appear in the two most widely read national newspapers, *Clarín* and *La Nación*, nor did it appear in the popular *Página 12*. It was highly unlikely that any of the ethnic blocs the ad purportedly targeted actually saw it, but NIAD could claim this minimal effort as part of its community outreach. The previous year's African Diaspora Working

Group applied to fund an event, but an employee of NIAD won the competition, and for unclear reasons still had not executed the project for which she had received the funds. This only fueled the rumors and contributed to the divisions among black blocs.

NIAD has been seen as only responding to crisis situations in which the government's image was at stake. Then, it basically played the role of the public-relations department of the state. This was best illustrated during the *Conflicto con el Campo* when the president of NIAD, Graciela Hernández, appeared on TV holding the hand of a poor *negro* (class-defined) farmer and walking through the halls of the NIAD building. Graciela was a nonblack Argentine popularly identified as a *criollo* or person of mixed origins, which included indigenous and European. As a government organization, NIAD could not and would not address the role the state played in perpetuating discrimination. A research consultant who worked on the test census project to count Afro-Argentines believed that NIAD would not directly support the project because it conflicted with the state's discourse on a nonexistent black population. NIAD refused to address the messy issue of race, and privileged other categories like "immigrant" or "woman," ignoring the specialized issues that accompanied racial discrimination.

An Afro-Brazilian research consultant recognized that NIAD, like most state institutions, did not want to teach people how to defend themselves. In reality it was just a mechanism for the state to monitor and control national and foreign marginal populations. It has been a paternalistic organization comprised of whites who liked to rescue blacks in their free time. I witnessed evidence of my consultant's observations at the Woman's Day event sponsored by NIAD. Women from varying social, economic, and racial backgrounds were lumped together, with a representative from each bloc speaking briefly. A woman with AIDS, who lives in a *villa miseria*, made an emotional, heart-wrenching plea for help. President Hernandez announced that she would put her in immediate contact with the Minister of Health office, a gesture that received thunderous applause. This was one of the rare occasions in which NIAD was forced to intervene, but one had to sacrifice her dignity and beg in a public, televised forum before the state would vow to take the actions it had already promised.

The creation of NIAD was in itself a function of neoliberal multiculturalism. As a neoliberal expression of racism, it could serve as "a progressive response to past societal ills that has a menacing potential to perpetuate the problem in a new guise" (Hale 2006, 12). The funding competition for underrepresented groups illustrated this quite well. NIAD choosing to only recognize Afro-descendants as one coherent, singular group had several purposes. First, it set the disparate ethnic blocs against each other to compete to represent all Afro-descendants through the project. Consequently, it ensured they would not work together to challenge the underlying power structures that constituted the racial hierarchy. That further promoted individual opportunism and corruption among already marginalized people while reconfirming racist myths about blacks being disorganized, unintelligent, and untrustworthy. Through that practice, Afro-Argentines in particular remained invisible as they were lumped together with immigrant blocs that had very different histories and relationships with the state. Though NIAD did not directly support the test census, the census helped confirm the state agenda and national mythology that "there are no blacks in Argentina." Because of their geographic location outside of the capital city, Afro-Argentines tended to have the least access to the state's resources and therefore were the least prepared to compete with more literate blocs that have a better understanding of how state bureaucracies function. Thus, in accordance with the neoliberal multicultural ideology, distinct boundaries were maintained between cultures under the guise of promoting social cohesion (Hale 2006).

Black ethnic blocs in Argentina have had a great amount of respect for the Jewish blocs, whom they considered extremely well organized, with a political agenda they had fought successfully to implement. Though blacks were less familiar with the Arab community, they were viewed in a similar manner. Several consultants even noted that Jews, Arabs, and blacks all faced ethnic and religious discrimination in Argentina. The animosity blacks have displayed in NIAD is not directed towards the other ethnic minority blocs but towards other black blocs. NIAD had become a battleground where the different blocs of blacks faced off and competed for minimal resources. Many blacks recognized that these public confrontations in front of an important potential donor have only hurt the black cause. Afro-Argentines felt that they should be the only blacks receiving aid from the state, because of their history in the nation. On the other hand, the other black ethnic blocs saw the Afro-Argentines as not sufficiently politically active, disorganized, divided, and undeserving of assistance. One positive contribution of NIAD was that it recognized the colonial heritage of Afro-Argentines, helping make them more visible.

Refugee Assistance Organization

The Refugee Assistance Organization was a recently created government intervention that dealt primarily with African refugees in Argentina. The Buenos Aires branch of the organization had been open less than a year when I met Vicente, an Argentine of European descent in his late twenties, who explained its history and duties. Vicente and an older colleague created the organization under a government initiative presented by the Minister of the Public, an autonomous sector. The Refugee Assistance Organization was not its own government ministry. In late 2006 the organization heard of several violent episodes of attacks involving African refugees in Rosario, Santa Fe (a province in the northwest of the country). Vicente, a law student interested in human-rights issues, spent more than a year visiting African refugee camps. The seven employees of the organization included psychologists, a social worker, and a biologist with anthropological training who also had spent time in African countries.

There were a few NGOs in Argentina that have included African refugees as part of their projects, but most of them were affiliated with a Christian church. The majority of African refugees who arrived in Argentina come from Muslim countries. The main problem that the Refugee Assistance Organization had with the other organizations is that they blanketed all refugees together, instead of addressing the specific needs of African refugees. One of the Catholic organizations, through funding from the United Nations High Commissioner for Refugees, paid for the hotels that African refugees lived in, provided that they proved they were in the process of soliciting refugee status. They also gave the refugees $80 pesos per week (about $25 U.S. dollars) and free Spanish classes. Another Christian organization provided them with free clothing.

The Refugee Assistance Organization had 116 registered refugees all under the age of twenty-one. Of these, only five were female, one of whom was African. Almost all of the refugees sold jewelry and lived in poorly maintained motels with Argentines and immigrants from other countries. At the time African refugees were spread across more than twenty-five motels in different parts of the city. They often had Argentine friends (even girlfriends), and friends from other countries that were not African. In Buenos Aires the interactions between refugees and locals was usually not violent, but infrequent. In Rosario, the interactions with refugees had been more violent, but the general public tended to interact more with them.

The Refugee Assistance Organization had an extremely limited budget and difficulty finding people who would volunteer their time to help. Vicente said that no black organization had come forward to create links with his organization. He admitted to seeing a lot of divisions among the Africans and Afro-descendants in Buenos Aires. On the other hand, Vicente made it clear that the refugees did not want to be used for any organization's or individual's personal gain, so they were very skeptical and cautious about the existing black blocs. Generally, the African refugees did not even want to work with other Africans, even those from their homeland, because they thought they would exploit them as well. They preferred to live alone, and attempts to unite African refugees under one roof have all failed.

INTERNATIONAL EMBASSY INTERVENTIONS:
SOUTH AFRICA, BRAZIL, AND THE UNITED STATES

The Embassy of South Africa has been the most prominent embassy supporting local black politics. Their representative William, under an African Union initiative to reach out to the Diaspora, was involved closely in many programs targeting blacks in Argentina. William, a dynamic, personable, and insightful individual, had been called from his law practice to work in the Mandela administration as a diplomat. As a black South African, he understood anti-racist struggles firsthand. He was raised by a single mother in a poor working-class family, so he could empathize with the problems facing blacks in Argentina. He had a sincere pan-Africanist vision, which he shared with the many friends he had made within the local black ethnic blocs. He and I quickly became friends, and he served as a father figure to me and many other blacks who resided in Buenos Aires. His wife and he were looked to for guidance and were considered exemplars of good African values, which they extend to all members of the Diaspora regardless of origin.

The Embassy of South Africa, via William's urging, recently has enacted concrete measures to support Africans and Afro-descendants in Argentina. They provided a large donation to reimburse the organizers of the previous year's Africa Week. The event was not a great success and ended up serving as a background for publicizing personal conflicts among the black leaders rather than drawing them together. The embassy also sponsored a small coalition of delegates from Argentina who attended a pan-African conference in Brazil in 2006. Unfortunately, that conference was so disorganized and lacking in direction that the representatives could not even produce a report of their activities there. Finally, the Embassy of South Africa provided scholarships for two black female students enrolled in the African studies master's program at a local university. William seemed disappointed that one of the students had not finished the program in a timely manner in spite of being fully funded. The embassy kept investing in projects though it did not see the fruits of its labor. This was a source of growing frustration for William, as it became harder to justify supporting organizations that did not respond in a way that promoted their own advancement.

William also helped create a library in the Southern Cape Verdean Alliance building, located just south of the capital city in the province of Buenos Aires, where large number of Cape Verdeans have lived historically due to shipping industry ties. Additionally, William was trying to negotiate the purchase of an antique home in San Telmo, a historically black neighborhood, which contained remains of slave quarters in its basement.

As a part of its diasporic mission, the Embassy of South Africa extended an invitation to its events to all black organizations. The embassy rented out one of the most prestigious exhibit spaces in the country for a month-long celebration of African culture extending from Africa Day on May 25. It invited all of the black ethnic blocs to take advantage of this highly visible space and hold events there free of charge. Only one poorly planned and executed, but well attended, Afro-Brazilian event took place in the center. Guests had harsh criticisms of the sloppily assembled, disorganized commemoration of the abolition of slavery in Brazil. Many Brazilians even noted that black Brazilians do not participate in such commemorations because that adhered to the dominant discourse of helpless black slaves saved by the generous white princess Isabella. The event organizer, a black Brazilian named Horacio, did not have experience in organizing those types of events, nor was he knowledgeable about the historical background of the commemoration. He used the opportunity to promote himself and his individual projects. Horacio organized the event to commemorate the abolition of slavery in Brazil yet was seemingly oblivious to the criticism of the Brazilian holiday. This was consistent with the behavior of the majority of the black public figures—behavior that came under harsh scrutiny from those within black blocs and that contributed to their divisions.

By the end of my year-long stay, William had all but lost hope in unifying the black ethnic blocs. Key individuals made it clear that they would not work together under any circumstances. William decided that the blacks residing in Buenos Aires really did not know what they wanted to achieve, which was a significant obstacle. In Argentina, blacks, as a whole, did not have a sense of the global issues concerning the Diaspora. Initially, William thought the Argentine state did not care about blacks, but he soon concluded that it already had exhausted its efforts to reach out to local blacks. Ten years ago, the Argentine Department of Social Welfare held a meeting and asked Afro-Argentines what the state could do for them. No one knew what they wanted; consequently, they all just sat there and complained about general social injustices rather than presenting specific initiatives. They had no long-term objectives then, and they still had not solidified at the time of this writing. William, fatally optimistic, wanted to help the black blocs in Argentina revive that dialogue and approach the government with some concrete objectives. He noted that African embassies took a "wait and see" attitude when it came to supporting local black organizations since they wanted to see projects realized in a timely manner. The other African diplomats warned William when he arrived in the country almost two years previously that it was futile to try to work with local blacks, because they refuse to overcome their infighting. But William would not give up that easily.

In February 2008, the United States Embassy held its first Black History Month event in Argentina. The initiative was created by Kelley, an African-American foreign service officer whom I later befriended, and Rosa, a Latina from the United States who was a political officer and very familiar with African American history. Kelly had great interest in meeting Afro-Argentines and other blacks who resided in Argentina, as well as learning Argentina's black history. The embassy had two other black U.S. employees: Nadine, who was in the military, and Leonard, who was also a foreign service officer. Neither of them was involved in the planning and organizing of the event, but Leonard was in attendance with some of his colleagues.

Kelly, the principal organizer of the event, contacted Claudia, an Afro-Argentine of Cape Verdean descent, who after fifteen years was once again the president of the Southern Cape Verdean Alliance. Claudia, an academic studying in a master's program, was regularly featured in media articles about Afro-Argentines and was a self-appointed spokesperson for the blacks in the nation. She frequently traveled internationally to conferences in Europe, Latin America, and the United States. Claudia was a very well-connected woman, with networks that stretched internationally. The first time I met her was at my university in 2005, which was a stop on a U.S. university tour she did to present the documentary *Afro-Argentines*, in which she was prominently featured. Claudia, in her late forties, was a young scholar at Escobar's side when he helped lay the foundations for the latest political mobilization around black identity. She greatly admired and respected him, though it had been years since she had contact with him.

Claudia assured Kelly that she would bring a large group of about twenty to thirty Afro-Argentines to the event, as well as a group of five performers to dance on stage. Kelly was very excited as it would be the first time she would have contact with Argentina's native black population. She arranged for her busy colleagues to leave their offices and escort the guests of honor to the auditorium where the event was held. Kelly ordered abundant hors d'oeuvres and wine to make the reception that followed extra special.

I found out about the Black History Month event through a black U.S. expatriate who had been living in Argentina for a couple of years and put me in contact with Leonard. I arrived early and was introduced to the ambassador, his wife, and another diplomat. I sat in the front row with another African American woman and her Panamanian friend. Claudia arrived shortly afterwards and was sincerely surprised to see me at the event. She brought with her two elder members of the Southern Cape Verdean Alliance, a young female dancer of Cape Verdean descent, and an African drummer who performed with the dancer. No other local blacks came, and the organizers later told me that they were very unhappy with the turnout.

Claudia sat on stage with Kelley and a translator. Kelley gave an impressive presentation highlighting the history and significance of the event, as well as notewor-thy blacks in U.S. history and their contributions. Claudia was asked by the embassy organizers to speak about how the U.S. Civil Rights Movement had inspired the Cape Verdean community's activism. She provided a rather indirect answer to the question, so I asked her what the Cape Verdeans, as the most organized and visible blacks in Argentina, had done to unite black ethnic blocs in Argentina and promote activities that politically unified Africans and Afro-descendants. Claudia, in an indirect way, said they were working on that, but proudly noted her organization had been in existence for eighty years. After the presentation, the Cape Verdean dancer and the drummer performed a Nigerian *orisha* dance, which I found odd since the majority of the bloc are professed Catholics. Those types of activities have helped reinvent traditions that did not otherwise exist, and could help draw together distinct diasporic groups (Copeland-Carson 2004). By the way the two performed, it was apparent they had not rehearsed together. No explanation was provided about the dance, costumes, or its connections to local black culture, so it all seemed very out of context.

That was not Claudia's first encounter with the U.S. Embassy. Recently, the em-bassy had sponsored her to study issues related to civil rights at Spelman College. They asked Claudia to recommend others to participate in the program, but she had yet to provide them with any names. The organizers later requested the same from me, so I provided them with my contact information, and we had a private, informal meeting to discuss the state of Africans and Afro-descendants in Argentina.

I attended the African Diaspora Working Group meeting where at least twenty Afro-descendants were present, and Claudia announced that she had been invited to the U.S. Embassy event. She failed to mention that the embassy had requested the presence and participation of local black blocs. I spoke to several of my research consultants, with whom Claudia also has contact, about the event. Every one of them said they would have liked to attend, but were not even aware of the function.

That same evening of the embassy event, Kelley attended an African Diaspora Working Group fundraising dinner during which the drummer provided an inspired performance with two African dancers, also friends of Claudia, with whom he regularly performed. Kelley expressed her deep disappointment in Claudia for failing to come through for the embassy event when she had all of the resources to provide them with the best representation possible. Kelley also began to question Claudia's role in the various black collectives. This was the same criticism of Claudia that I would hear repeated by various members of local black ethnic blocs. While the U.S. Embassy event was successfully organized, the embassy was naive about the divisions between blocs, which prevented the participation of local blacks.

The Brazilian Embassy has been the most reluctant to support the black cause.

Argentines very strongly have associated blackness with Brazilianness. The embassy seemed to resent this and made clear efforts to divorce itself from its black image. The Brazilian Embassy has had a history of refusing to sponsor events that associated Brazil with black people. One research consultant from a well-established dance school designed a performance honoring the African cultural heritage of Brazil. When she went to the embassy to see what type of support they could offer, she was told by a representative that "Brazil has nothing to do with Africa." An Afro-Brazilian consultant who is a well-respected dance instructor presented a creative work to members of the embassy, who refused to sponsor her doing it. She later saw her project carried out by a nonblack individual associated with the embassy who did not give her credit for her ideas.

In 2007, the Brazilian embassy hired Catelina, an Afro-Brazilian professional, as part of its staff. Blacks realized that the presence of a black face in the embassy was not necessarily indicative of a change in vision regarding black populations. Catelina was a very friendly, diplomatic, soft-spoken individual who had usually taken a moderate stance on issues to maintain an open dialogue in tense situations. She participated in several of the African Diaspora Working Group meetings and was usually present at large events sponsored by black ethnic blocs, but as a guest and not an official representative of the embassy. This included several of the Afro-Brazilian sponsored events. Among those was a party held to showcase two local legends of Afro-Brazilian music. Catelina was present along with two nonblack diplomatic colleagues from the embassy who had never attended a black Brazilian–sponsored event. The nonblack women were presented with flowers, applause, and a long recognition speech thanking them for their support. The middle-aged Afro-Brazilian female host had a reputation for creating functions in the name of all blacks to increase her personal income. Critics of her overly gracious performance in front of the whites assured me that she was probably planning another money-making event with them where they would share the profits. Unfortunately, this pattern of behavior was all too common among blacks.

Both the United States and South Africa have come to define themselves as multi-cultural states, while recently Argentina has been superficially redefining itself in this manner to participate in popular global notions of modernity. The inclusion of local Africans and Afro-descendants in their activities can be interpreted as reflective of the neoliberal multicultural agenda of these nations. The recognition of these ethnic blocs—and their subsequent legitimization through participation in the activities of high-profile embassies of nations that are the international paradigms for understanding blackness—has had its positive attributes. On the other hand, it has been almost exclusively folkloric expressions that were embraced in these settings. In state-selected forums, including those of Argentina, blacks were occasionally allowed to publicly air their grievances to other minorities and nonessential state representatives. By the time these gatherings ended, little more has transpired than a cathartic group-therapy session organized by state officials. These embassies had successfully expanded their national political ideologies abroad to legitimate domestic struggles, but they had simultaneously helped sustain Argentina's neoliberal multicultural agenda.

THE REALITY OF A *NEGRO* NATION

Where were all the African and African-descendant *negros* when the *Conflicto con el Campo* was being played out very publicly on a national stage? Perhaps blacks did not want to be associated with those *negros* who were protesting in the Plaza de Mayo. Dominant society has considered the *negros* of the Peronists to be ignorant, lazy, and undignified masses that could be easily swayed by the few crumbs of bread thrown in their direction. As Guano notes, middle-class white Argentine residents in the city of Buenos Aires still upheld the discourse of Sarmiento, one of the founding fathers of Argentina and an architect of the project to refashion it into a European nation (Guano 2003). In the minds of those individuals, nonwhites were the barbarians who were responsible for the economic downturn of Argentina, and for stifling its advance towards modernity. Since the mid '90s, some black cultural expressions, such as different dance and music styles, have been publicly welcome in the city, though African-based religious practices were not (Frigerio 2001). Black people, on the other hand, have not been warmly received, as evidenced in the accounts of my research consultants, my own observations and lived experiences, and news articles documenting violence towards blacks. In spite of those realities, there continued to be a very strong denial of racism in Argentina, and anti-black racism in particular.

One major obstacle in uniting black ethnic blocs is that they did not truly embrace the Diaspora concept and had a difficult time seeing the commonalities between the different national factions. They most likely just needed some serious self-critique and introspection before being able to advance. Blacks from different blocs had varied opinions and positions, but let these get in the way of presenting a united front when necessary. William suggested that the leaders just needed an impetus to propel them forward.

There were enough Argentines of African descent and other blacks to have a unified critical mass of activists and a successful political movement in Argentina. The resources needed to make real change happen were already within the existing blocs. The main problem was that most of the individuals of African descent, both

Argentine and foreign, did not identify as such. Among Argentines in general, there was very strong resistance to having the racially defined *negro* included as part of the national identity.

The Argentine government should not be blamed as the villains in this modern-day racial drama, nor should they be expected to be the saviors or heroes of blacks. The state has made concrete efforts to recognize blacks and even offer them some resources. Additionally, Argentina has faced international pressure to adopt neoliberal multicultural practices so that it can be akin to the nations after which it models itself (the United States, France, and England) and truly participate in international politics. Policies, like those of the Peronist government, fall under the category of colorblind social reforms that set out to address issues of class inequality. Inadvertently they can address racial disparities, though racism has not been deemed a problem in the Argentine imaginary. As overt expressions of racism are no longer acceptable, the state has accepted a broader ideology of antiracism filtered through a neoliberal lens. Neoliberal policies have prevented the presence of blacks from truly being legitimized in Argentina. Those working in development with an interest in increasing the visibility of Africans and Afro-descendants have to understand the milieu in which such policies exist, and how these initiatives might, in fact, be sustaining the mythology that blacks have an insignificant presence in Latin American and Caribbean nations.

NOTES

1. Pseudonyms are used for organizations, individuals, and neighborhoods.

2. Shantytowns.

3. Capital Federal is the name Argentines commonly use to differentiate the city of Buenos Aires from the province of Buenos Aires. Sometimes it is simply shortened to Capital.

REFERENCES

Andrews, George Reid. 1980. *Los afroargentinos de Buenos Aires.* Madison: University of Wisconsin Press.

Copeland-Carson, Jacqueline. 2004. *Creating Africa in America: Translocal Identity in an Emerging World City.* Philadelphia: University of Pennsylvania Press.

Frigerio, Alejandro. 2001. "Cómo los Porteños conocieron a los Orixás: La expansión de las religiones afrobrasileñas en Buenos Aires." In *El negro en la Argentina: Presencia y negación*, ed. D. V. Picotti. Buenos Aires: Editores de América Latina.

Guano, Emanuela. 2003. "A Color for the Modern Nation: The Discourse on Class, Race, and Education in the *Porteño* Middle Class." *Journal of Latin American Anthropology* 8(1):148–171.

———. 2004. "The Denial of Citizenship: 'Barbaric' Buenos Aires and the Middle-Class Imaginary." *City & Society* 16(1):69–97.

Hale, Charles R. 2006. *Más que un Indio=More Than an Indian: Racial Ambivalence and Neoliberal Multiculturalism in Guatemala.* 1st ed. Santa Fe, NM: School of American Research Press.

Harrison, Faye V. 2002. "Unraveling 'Race' for the Twenty-First Century." In *Exotic No More: Anthropology on the Front Lines*, ed. J. MacClancy. Chicago: University of Chicago Press.

Klich, Ignacio. 2006. "Arabes, judíos y árabes-judíos en la Argentina de la primera mitad del novecientos." In *Árabes y judíos en América Latina: Historia, representaciones y desafíos*, ed. I. Klich. Buenos Aires: Siglo XXI.

Lanuza, José Luis. 1942. *Los morenos.* Buenos Aires: Emecé.

Lewis, Marvin A. 1996. *Afro-Argentine Discourse: Another Dimension of the Black Diaspora.* Columbia: University of Missouri Press.

Page, Helán E., and Brooke Thomas. 1997. "'Black Male' Imagery and Media Containment of African American Men." *American Anthropologist* 99(1):99–111.

Sheller, Mimi. 2003. *Consuming the Caribbean: From Arawaks to Zombies.* International Library of Sociology. New York: Routledge.

Svampa, Maristella. 1994. *El dilema argentino: Civilización o barbarie: De Sarmiento al revisionismo peronista.* Colección La Cultura Argentina. Buenos Aires: El Cielo por Asalto, Imago Mundi.

Yelvington, Kevin A. 2001. "The Anthropology of Afro-Latin America and the Caribbean: Diasporic Dimensions." *Annual Review of Anthropology* 30(1):227.

Pluralizing Race

Mamyrah A. Dougé-Prosper

On October 23, 2006, in response to the debilitating repercussions of the U.S. housing crisis, a group of activists and homeless people took over a vacant public plot of land in Liberty City, Miami, Florida, with the slogan and mission "Take Back the Land."[1] Having denounced the failures of the local and national governments in providing adequate and fair housing options to lower-income black people in Miami, Take Back the Land founded a shantytown it named Umoja Village, arguing that the village was an exercise of the black community's human right to self-determination and housing. On April 23, 2007, the village burned down leaving forty Umoja residents homeless. Take Back the Land members convened and decided to implement the new phase of its campaign: occupying public and foreclosed units. In January 2007, after having driven by the village and noticed the banner with the "Take Back the Land" emblem, I researched and approached the group with the desire to understand its political process and vision. Three months after the erection of Umoja village, after attending a few meetings, I became a volunteer organizer. In this paper, I want to present Take Back the Land's history and work, its analytical framework, and its discourse. I also aim to examine and discuss Take Back the Land's strategic use of race in its discourse, and its seeming neglect of other facets of identity and lived experiences, such as gender and immigration status, that also affect low-income people.

Critical feminist theorists call for the development of alternative epistemologies and methodologies that move beyond traditional positivist binaries, such as objectivity versus subjectivity, and knowledge versus politics (Collins 2000; Harding 1986; Haraway 1988). In this vein, for my project, not only have I drawn from theoretical frameworks emerging from indigenous experiences and typologies and critical thought produced by participants themselves, but I have also brought to bear Donna Haraway's (1988) concept of "situated knowledges." Haraway argues that rather than performing the "god trick" of claiming absolute objective knowledge, a more responsible and accountable knowledge admits to its partiality and situatedness. Rather than aiming for universalizing theories from "nowhere," situated knowledge aims for the localizing, historicization, and pluralization of knowledge claims. Thus, not only my awareness of my positionality as a Haitian diasporic woman who enjoyed "middle-class" privileges in Haiti and has been educated in U.S. American universities within a period of academic vacillations between modernism and postmodernism, but also my recognition of the heterogeneity of my sites of research have both informed the choice of my methodological process.

My primary methodological approach has been participatory action research wherein the participants in the study help to refine my research questions, modes of gathering information, analysis, and reporting. Hickey and Mohan (2004) envision participation to be a transformative process that yields political outcomes that benefit the group(s) included in the research or study. This paper has been shaped by my experiences with the Take Back the Land organization in Miami over a period of two years, from January 2007 to January 2009. I have employed Haraway's (1988) metaphor of dialogue, which emphasizes the exchange between myself, the researcher, and my "objects" of study—the participants rather than the metaphor of discovery, which invisibilizes the agency of those "objects." In the case of Take Back the Land, I functioned as both researcher and participant.

Tribalist Devon Abbott Mihesuah (2003) argues that knowledge and works produced on "indigenous" people should undergo a process of reflexivity during which the theorist or author allows his or her work to be critiqued by his or her "object" of study. Mihesuah's concept of reflexivity extends the traditional anthropological tool of simply keeping a diary in which researchers write down their thoughts, which they hope will assist them in achieving a semblance of objectivity. Mihesuah stresses accountability as a necessary component in scholarly work. The researcher must submit his or her work for review to his or her participants. This concept of reflexivity marries well with the participatory-action research method. However, my critical study of Take Back the Land is complicated by my position as both an organizer and a researcher. Reflexivity in this case is a convoluted process. I have attempted to produce a paper in which my positionality is not dissimulated—a paper, nevertheless, that provides a critical analysis of the group.

This paper is a recount of my activist work, and an analysis of the various findings of the Take Back the Land organization on the national housing crisis and its ramifications on the socioeconomic fabric of Miami. Take Back the Land was founded in Miami in October 2006 as the "black" response to the housing crisis and its subsequent erosion of the "black" communities of Liberty City and Little Haiti.[2] Liberty City is a neighborhood in Miami that has predominantly housed low-income African Americans, while Little Haiti is another that has been primarily inhabited by low-income Haitian immigrants (see Stepick et al. 2003). I joined Take Back the Land as a volunteer organizer with no intention of developing an academic report on my experiences. I entered the formation as a support volunteer and eventually became a decision maker. This transition allowed me to learn about the various layers that inform organizing work. I am currently still a member of Take Back the Land in Miami, even though most recently, since its graduation to a campaign of the national organization called U.S. Human Rights Network, I have been inactive (mostly due to my graduate school responsibilities). In this paper, through the exploration of the narratives produced by Take Back the Land, I am interested in demonstrating that a simple race analysis of the housing crisis and gentrification does not suffice, and instead a more complex and sophisticated approach needs to be applied that pluralizes race with the inclusion of other important experience—such as class, gender, and immigration status, among other factors.

TAKE BACK THE LAND

In June 2007, the *Miami Herald* published a three-part series exposing government involvement in creating one of the most devastating housing crises in the United States of America. The articles revealed the direct relationship between corrupt government officials and unscrupulous developers and investors. Both the city government of Miami and the county government of Miami-Dade had misused public funds to support housing projects that never materialized. More significantly, the city and county governments allowed developers to default on their loans, while the demolition of houses was ordered by the city's housing chief, consequently leading to an increase in homeless families. Among many cases, the *Miami Herald* exposed the City of Miami's neglect to follow up after $1.4 million was dispensed to construct forty new low-income homes, which were never actually built. This exposure of government ills, entitled the "House of Lies" series,[3] emphasized the need for a rectification of government corruption. Nevertheless, to date, most agents of gentrification have remained in office, and some have even been given the op-portunity to resign with impunity. On October 23, 2006, a group of self-identified "black" activists and homeless people took over a vacant public lot on NW 62nd St. and NW 17th Ave. in Liberty City, Miami, and founded Umoja Village, a shantytown that housed over 150 people over a period of six months.[4] With the protection of the Pottinger Settlement Agreement,[5] which entitles any homeless person to engage in life-sustaining activities such as eating, sleeping, and grooming on vacant public land if he or she is unable to obtain shelter in the city's homeless facilities, Umoja Village had the legal right to stand. However, on April 26, 2007, three days after having celebrated our six-month anniversary and announcing our plan to erect more sustainable and permanent housing fixtures, Umoja Village burned down under suspicious and inconclusive circumstances, leaving forty people homeless. We, Take Back the Land, had been planning to adopt the hexayurt[6] as the new model of housing for Umoja Village. This model would have been easily mountable (and consequently demountable) to be more appropriate to the hurricane-prone city. On April 27, 2007, twelve people were arrested attempting to reoccupy the land,[7] only one of which was an Umoja Village resident. The other arrestees were activists of Take Back the Land and allied organizations and individuals.

Take Back the Land, inspired by the Landless Workers' Movement in Brazil and the Western Cape Anti-Eviction Campaign in South Africa, is both a movement and an organization whose objectives are to house and feed people, assert the right of the black community to its land, and build a new society. The fundamental driving force of Take Back the Land is land. It contends that the United States exists as a result of the genocidal displacement of American indigenous and African peoples. Recognizing the historical erasure of American Natives' bodies and stories, and before taking over the plot of land, Take Back the Land sought and obtained the blessing of the American Indian Movement. Take Back the Land argues that the alienation of black people from their land is detrimental to their advancement. Rather than allowing the crafters of gentrification (the corrupt government officials and the developers) to control and determine the use of the land in low-income black communities, Take Back the Land had risen as an opposing force to the renewed, organized, and government-backed displacement of poor black people. Take Back the Land posits that people need to engage in self-determination and take control of their lives in response to government failures. Take Back the Land delineates the plight of poor black people in the United States by tracing the history of their oppression: from their kidnapping from the Afri-can continent and forced descent into slavery, to the declaration of their emancipation yet continuation in servitude through the system of sharecropping, to the segregation and denial of certain of their basic civil rights, and finally to their forced expulsion from the land upon which they had built their communities to make room for richer and whiter people.

Take Back the Land understands gentrification to be the forced removal of poor black people from urban areas to be replaced by richer whites. While the language used by Take Back the Land is inflammatory and provocative, its explanation mirrors the modern definition of the phenomenon, which describes gentrification as the result of market fluctuations that cause low-income people to vacate their neighborhoods to allow middle-income people to populate those areas. Scholars such as Hamnet (1991) and Bridge (1995) argue that gentrification involves both a change in the social composition of an area and its residents, and a change in the nature of the housing stock (tenure, price, condition, etc.), and Zukin (1987) stresses the role of the government and the real estate industry in shaping this change. These scholars, however, do not share Take Back the Land's political agenda, and their discourse is less emotional and emotive. Nevertheless, their basic arguments coincide with the political framework from which Take Back the Land produces its own narrative.

Take Back the Land seeks to radicalize the center of the spectrum of political beliefs and actions by shifting the dominant discourse that normalizes homelessness and poverty, and by reconstructing an alternative discourse in which housing is a human right. Take Back the Land extends the definition of homelessness to include not only those who live on the streets and remain unemployed, but also people who may be working, but live in housing crowded by multiple family members as a result of the unavailability of affordable shelter. Take Back the Land attempts to create a political space in which more reformist groups can directly negotiate their demands with the government. Take Back the Land understands its relationship with the state as adversarial, and consequently limits direct interaction with the government. However, Take Back the Land targets its action against the government in order to highlight and expose contradictions within the system, and in order to raise the consciousness of the people on whose behalf it fights, in addition to the general population. Take Back the Land's direct actions serve multiple purposes. In addition to opposing the government and shifting the dominant discourse, Take Back the Land seeks to provide housing and give the necessary support to homeless people. While Take Back the Land has demonstrated only nonviolently, it relies on adversarial tactics (such as the erection of a shantytown in the middle of Miami) that may provoke the state into violent response. Aware of the state monopoly on "legitimate" violence, Take Back the Land has not incited violence since its inception. Instead it refers to the methods and accomplishments of the civil rights movement of the 1960s in order to advance its cause. This reference is extremely important when enlisting the support and understanding of the population. Emphasizing the use of civil disobedience as did the Civil Rights Movement, Take Back the Land pushes people to think beyond the illegal nature of its actions and to challenge the unjust legal status quo, as did the leaders of the Civil Rights Movement when they encouraged people to desegregate public venues even though the law had prohibited such actions. By couching its message in terms of justice, Take Back the Land problematizes the law and instead invokes morality. It disturbs the binary that juxtaposes the legal against the illegal, and revokes the respective values of right and wrong that have been assigned to these dichotomous categories.

When Umoja Village stood, it was a manifestation of the need for the Liberty City community to respond to government abandonment. Take Back the Land explained that Umoja Village was a necessary reaction to a manufactured housing crisis that had provoked the displacement of already marginalized peoples vulnerable to their landlords' neglect, developers' aggressive manipulation, and politicians' corruption. The village was named Umoja, a Swahili word that means unity, as a result of the Afro-centric nature of the group. While the decision-making space was reserved for its black leadership, Take Back the Land enlisted the support of many white individual and group activists to help build the shanties and ensure the continual flow of food and other supplies (among other expectations). Take Back the Land envisions itself as a particular facet of the social justice movement and understands that cross-racial alliances are important for the advancement of the movement as a whole, in addition to its particular vision. Take Back the Land defines gentrification through a race and class lens, positioning the government and developers as producers of a housing crisis that has resulted in an overwhelming increase in homelessness.

Umoja Village residents were primarily single African American males. Many of the women with children who had sought shelter in the village were immediately approached by the city government and granted temporary and sometimes permanent housing. Concerned about its representation nationwide and internationally, the city wanted to protect its image and reputation. Most village residents were adults above the age of fifty who suffered from some form of undiagnosed mental illness, and often former drug abusers. The city could afford to ignore that segment of the population and even justify its denial of their right to housing. Village residents approved new shanty occupants during weekly meetings. There were a few homeless people voted in to live in the village who did not self-identify as black. While those additions were few, their presence and participation in the life of the village had already begun to problematize Take Back the Land's hard line on race. Moreover, while Umoja was supposed to serve as a representation of the effects of gentrification on low-income black people, it ended up representing a sample of the population that was not the most directly and immediately affected by the crisis. Single African American males over the age of fifty were also experiencing the deleterious effects of gentrification. However, the most vulnerable people were families with different immigration statuses, often headed by single mothers. Umoja Village did not capture this trend within the crisis. Nevertheless, its existence symbolized and effectuated the possibility of a change in the conceptualization of land ownership. Take Back the Land fought for the collective control of land and not for private ownership.

FROM UMOJA VILLAGE TO TAKE BACK THE HOUSING

After the fire, the commissioner of the Liberty City district, Michelle Spence-Jones, approached Take Back the Land to offer the Umoja Village land in return for its silence. The decision to engage the commissioner was not unanimous. Take Back the Land was faced with the choice of remaining politically rigid or ensuring some practical gains for the movement. The commissioner would provide some government funds to assist Take Back the Land, and a partner of its choosing to build low-income housing on the land. Take Back the Land would have to stop protesting against her, and more importantly, it would have to cease any efforts to rebuild the village at any other given site. Take Back the Land agreed to the terms and entered an extensive negotiation process with the commissioner. When the proposal was presented to the rest of the board of commissioners, it was voted down. The nonprofit low-income housing developer who had agreed to partner up with Take Back the Land had backed out of the deal. The commissioners could not approve the transfer of ownership of the land from the city to a political organization devoid of building skills. While Take Back the Land did not gain the rights to the land, it framed the deal as a victory. Umoja Village and the land negotiation had created the political space necessary for Take Back the Land to move its agenda forward.[8]

In the summer of 2007, the organization began its engagement in a new campaign called Take Back the Housing, which fulfilled the same objectives as Umoja Village. Take Back the Land was continuing its adversarial takeovers to provide housing for people on public land, and pursuing its attack and deconstruction of the notion that profit is of greater importance than people. Take Back the Housing consisted essentially of moving families into vacant public and foreclosed housing units and homes in the Liberty City and Little Haiti communities.[9] The demographics of the participants in the Take Back the Housing campaign significantly differed from that of the village. Umoja had housed over 150 people over a period of six months. Almost all of its inhabitants had been single African American men over the age of fifty. Take

Back the Housing housed a little over ten families with more than two children, for the most part headed by single mothers.

Additionally, in many of the cases, members of the families held varying immigration statuses. Through this campaign, Take Back the Land worked to uncover the other silenced victims of gentrification whose decision-making process around housing differed from that of Umoja Village residents. Take Back the Housing participants possessed a different set of concerns. They sought more permanent housing and remained concerned about their ability to stay together as a family, away from the police, away from the agents of the state, away from the media, and away from vulnerable structures. Another differentiating factor between the two campaigns was the decentralization of the Take Back the Land community of families. Each family occupied the houses that had been identified during the reconnoiter process as vacant and suitable for living. Through this method, the organization could not ensure that different families would be placed in the same area. Umoja had functioned as a village, with a common garden, library, kitchen, outdoor shower, and Porta-Potty. It was accessible due to its visibility and centrality. Take Back the Land created a network of connected homes scattered throughout different geographical locations in Liberty City and Little Haiti. It designed workshops, bringing the different participating families together to inform them about their legal rights and prepare them from potential attacks.

Take Back the Housing relied on the reputation of Take Back the Land through word of mouth and presentations at various local organizations. Many families approached Take Back the Land, sharing their fears and desperation around their housing situation. Few were willing to risk potential altercations with the police, even though the organization had taken measures to enlist the donation of criminal, immigration, family, and civil legal counsel and defense. Others needed additional assistance to pay utility bills such as electricity and water. The families that finally acquiesced to participate in the campaign varied. Some were willing to publicize their situation, while others were too ashamed and fearful of retaliation. Some were prepared to join the organization's activists in the defense of their home, and others were too alarmed at the possibility of violent repercussions from the authorities. Some participated in the campaign for over two years, while others were able to find alternative housing in under one year. Take Back the Housing revealed the complicated nature of gentrification in a pluricultural city and the oversimplification of a rhetoric of race in the discussion of this phenomenon. The campaign, consequently, demanded that Take Back the Land utilize multiple narratives around the housing crisis, gentrification, and its proposed solutions.

It's Not Just about "Race"

While the Take Back the Housing campaign continued to grow, and Take Back the Land prepared to expand into the national level, a simple race analysis was no longer sufficient, and a multidimensional approach was devised in order to successfully execute the next phase of the movement. In Take Back the Land's rhetoric, blackness had been homogenized. Umoja Village had permitted the dissimulation of other factors in the analysis of the housing crisis and gentrification. Strategically essentializing all peoples of African descent provided the organization with a uniform discourse to present to the larger public. Moreover, it allowed the organization to unify various groups of people under one political assemblage. This strategy was particularly effective during the existence of Umoja Village, a shantytown comprised of mostly African American men. Blackness is a globalized concept, constructed through the colonial project by which the West otherized its subjects and solidified Europeanness, and consequently whiteness (see Trouillot 2003). Blackness holds transnational meanings that were reappropriated in the nineteenth century by various movements, such as the Marcus Garvey and Negritude movements. These movements invoked a notion of blackness that was not confined by the borders of the respective nation-states of their authors. Take Back the Land's narrative re-territorialized blackness within the U.S. national historical context. The history of blackness it delineates is that of African America. Take Back the Land's strategic decision to strictly highlight that particular experience of blackness is not a result of its lack of understanding of what Mohanty (2003) terms "politics of location," which emphasizes the links between time and space as indicators of the hegemonic processes of colonialism and imperialism. Strategic essentialism is a method of organizing and resisting oppression through the deliberate presentation of a united front (see Spivak 1996). Take Back the Land presented this conceptualization of blackness through its choice of language. Nevertheless, the long-term use of strategic essentialism as an organizing tool can lead to obscuring the diversity and plurality of a constructed group. While the campaign had exposed the feminization of the gentrification crisis in Miami, Take Back the Land did not reframe its discourse to reflect this phenomenon. Approaching a gendered analysis of the housing crisis could marginalize Take Back the Land's voice. Race presented itself as a unifying category and a specific lens through which to analyze and retort against gentrification. An intersectional approach was not attempted, even though Take Back the Land incorporated in its messaging the particular experiences of single mothers within this crisis.

As Take Back the Land shifted completely into the Take Back the Housing campaign, its use of political language became more applicable to a citywide and nationwide context beyond the rhetoric of race and blackness. Take Back the Housing had become the dominating and sole campaign of the organization, and Take Back the Land had to emphasize a more inclusive message, that of housing as a human right. This modification in the discourse does not underline identity politics (see Smith 1998), but rather broadens the political scope under which a myriad of people with varying identities can demand housing as their human right. In this campaign, Take Back the Land again did not utilize intersectionality (see Collins 2000) as an organizing tool. Breaking down identity to the innumerable possibilities of intersecting experiences would paralyze the political process of developing organizing strategies that could actually move an agenda. Through the Take Back the Housing campaign, and particularly since the adoption of Take Back the Land as a national campaign strategy of the U.S. Human Rights Network, the emphasis on the human right to housing discourse has served as a response to the housing crisis in a national context, while the local language continues to be colored by the local conditions. The political rhetoric continues to adapt to particular facets of the setting and area in question.

CONCLUSION

In this paper, I have attempted to present my critical analysis of Take Back the Land's discourse, a housing-activist organization in which I served as a volunteer and later on as a decision maker during my active membership over the period of two years. As both the researcher and a participant of the study, I occupied a unique position that allowed me to experience the processes that engendered the political rhetoric of the organization. I chose not to recount in this paper the innumerable complex conversations and discussions that produced the discourse advanced by Take Back the Land. My primary and, at the time, sole purpose for participating in the organization had been the result of my own personal political leanings and beliefs. However, I have not refrained from providing a critical perspective of the organization, and more importantly the framework of its narratives. In this paper, I was not concerned about the individuals that constitute the organization. Rather, I wanted to analyze the discourses that accompanied and shaped Take Back the Land and its campaign. Perhaps, in a different paper, it would be interesting to explore the political and socio-personal makeup of the decision makers and other members.

I have attempted to demonstrate how Take Back the Land's political discourse was shaped by the conditions of the housing crisis and the particular campaigns it developed and engaged in. With the inception of the organization came the creation of a shantytown, Umoja Village. This village was inhabited by a specific demographic that did not reflect the larger composition of the people most directly affected by the housing crisis and gentrification. Umoja Village housed for the most part single African American men over the age of fifty. The second campaign, Take Back the Housing, revealed a different face of gentrification: families of two or more children, headed for the most part by single mothers and constituted of members with different immigration statuses. This shift in Take Back the Land's campaign obligated it to broaden its discursive scope from a strictly race-based message to a more inclusive rhetoric of human rights. While the slogan "Housing as a Human Right" had always been the underlying framework of the organization, it was not until the Take Back the Housing campaign that Take Back the Land began to emphasize it. It, however, reserved the right to use more specific language about race when relevant and appropriate. Just as it had strategically decided to homogenize blackness in order to render its message coherent and uniform, it also strategically decided to widen that language, particularly as it entered a national phase.

Nevertheless, Take Back the Land did not shift its rhetoric to highlight the feminization of gentrification and the housing crisis. While the politics of the members of the organization are radical and therefore include a critical analysis that challenges heteropatriarchy, they did not inform the discourse that was developed around Take Back the Land. Approaching the housing and gentrification crisis through an intersectional lens would have proved to be too difficult to convert into a national campaign.

NOTES

1. Take Back the Land is also the name of the group that founded Umoja Village.
2. Take Back the Land is now a national campaign of the U.S. Human Rights Campaign. However, Take Back the Land, the organization, still functions locally in Miami.
3. Http://www.miamiherald.com/multimedia/news/houseoflies/.
4. Almost all of the Umoja Village inhabitants were single African American men over the age of fifty.
5. Http://openjurist.org/40/f3d/1155/pottinger-v-city-of-miami.
6. Http://hexayurt.com/.
7. See Max Rameau, *Take Back the Land* (Miami: Nia Press, 2008) for more details. Activist members of Take Back the Land and supporting organizations attempted to rebuild the village by setting up tents on the land. All were arrested to prevent the reoccupation of the land.
8. See Rameau, *Take Back the Land*, for more details.

9. After the destruction of Umoja Village, Take Back the Land began its new campaign, which it named Take Back the Housing.

REFERENCES

Bridge, Gary. 1995. "The Space for Class? On Class Analysis in the Study of Gentrification." *Transactions of the Institute of British Geographers* (New Series) 20(2):236–247.

Collins, Patricia. 2000. *Black Feminist Thought.* New York: Routledge.

Hamnett, Chris. 1991. "The Blind Men and the Elephant: The Explanation of Gentrification." *Transactions of the Institute of British Geographers* (New Series) 16(2):173–189.

Haraway, Donna. 1988. "Situated Knowledges: The Science Question in Feminism and the Privilege of Partial Perspectives." *Feminist Studies* 14(3):575–599.

Harding, Sandra. 1986. *The Science Question in Feminism.* Ithaca, NY: Cornell University Press.

Hickey, Samuel, and Giles Mohan. 2004. *Participation: From Tyranny to Transformation? Exploring New Approaches to Participation in Development.* London: Zed Books.

Landry, Donna, and Gerald Maclean, eds. 1996. *The Spivak Reader: Selected Works of Gayatri Chakravorty Spivak.* London: Routledge.

Miami-Dade Housing Agency. 2007. *The Housing Element Report.* Miami, FL.

Mihesuah, Devon Abbott. 2003. *Indigenous American Women: Decolonization, Empowerment, and Activism.* Lincoln: University of Nebraska Press.

Mohanty, Chandra Talpade. 2003. *Feminism without Borders: Decolonizing Theory, Practicing Solidarity.* Durham, NC: Duke University Press.

Rameau, Max. 2008. *Take Back the Land: Land, Gentrification, and the Umoja Village Shantytown.* Miami: Nia Press.

Smith, Barbara. 1998. *Writings on Race, Gender, and Freedom: The Truth That Never Hurts.* New Brunswick, NJ: Rutgers University Press.

Stepick, Alex, Guillermo Grenier, Max Castro, and Marvin Dunn. 2003. *This Land Is Our Land: Immigrants and Power in Miami.* Berkeley: University of California Press.

Take Back the Land. http://www.takebacktheland.net.

Trouillot, Michel-Rolph. 2003. *Global Transformation: Anthropology and the Modern World.* New York: Palgrave Macmillan.

United States District Court Southern District of Florida. 1996. "Pottinger Settlement Agreement." Miami, FL.

Zukin, Sharon. 1987. "Gentrification: Culture and Capital in the Urban Core." *Annual Review of Sociology* 13:129–147.

Conclusion

The specificity of the modern political and cultural formation I want to call the Black Atlantic can be defined, on one level, through [a] desire to transcend both the structures of the nation state and the constraints of ethnicity and national particularity. These desires are relevant to understanding political organizing and cultural criticism. They have always sat uneasily alongside the strategic choices forced on black movements and individuals embedded in national and political cultures and nation-states in America, the Caribbean, and Europe.

—Paul Gilroy, *The Black Atlantic*

This volume is a unique collection of essays by scholars, activists, and representatives from funding agencies. The starting point is the Black Atlantic (Gilroy 1993). Our aim here is to use the idea as a way of presenting and discussing issues that have been, and still are, relevant to Afro-descendants in the Americas, even though we are aware that many of the communities discussed here do not fit neatly into the Atlantic region. In South America, many African American communities concentrate on the Pacific coasts of Colombia, Ecuador, and Peru. However, given its salience and notoriety, the concept of the "Black Atlantic" still is a highly evocative and sensitizing concept, offering a way of recognizing broader macro-level processes linking peoples of African descent who share historical circumstances created during slavery and its aftermath.

Several lessons can be drawn from the chapters assembled here. To many writers—scholars and activists alike—identity still remains a central issue and problem. What does it mean to be black in Latin America and the Caribbean? How does blackness fit into the national tropes of mixedness? What is the price to be paid for asserting one's difference? How, in the end, to achieve full membership in national communities while at the same time valuing membership in a different, broader community, that of the African Diaspora? Much is at stake here. On the one side full and equal citizenship, which continues to be upheld by national states. On the other, in the words of Faye Harrison, the struggle to become fully human, that is, to be respected, recognized, and accepted for all that one is—an equal member of the national community and also a member of the African Diaspora. Nation-states and citizens mobilized around ideas of nationhood have always had difficulties admitting and trusting those who have double, or multiple, allegiances. This is notoriously true when migration and transnationalism are the focus of discussion, but it is also apparent in the case of African (-) Americans. Double-consciousness is still the characterizing condition of African Americans, no matter what parts of the Americas they call their home. Their positions within national communities are typically negotiated with reference not only to the nonblack and non-minority members of their political community, but also—as the authors focusing on Haiti and the Dominican Republic have demonstrated—with reference to the neocolonial frameworks of other black communities in their own struggle to achieve status and recognition. Under conditions of globalization, one might say, Foucault's normalizing gaze has been universalized so that now the whole world, and all the communities within, can readily serve as yardsticks and measuring rods when comparing deviance and establishing normalcy and desirability. Biopolitics have become globalized.

The learning we can draw from these discussions is that before development strategies can successfully address the material needs of African American communities, those strategies have to support them in their struggle for recognition and respect so that they can become full members of the political communities that control the resources and destinies of the territories they control. This needs to happen without forcing black and other minority communities to give up who they are and what makes them "them." Universalist approaches to liberalism, which deny the recognition of particularities, will not be able to achieve this, because they are unable to take into account past injustices that have produced ingrained and normalized advantages for some groups. Historically privileged groups have benefited from affirmative-action policies for hundreds of years, which has allowed them to secure and consolidate elevated positions in the social hierarchies of their countries. Achieving justice and equity will thus take concerted and long-term government commitment, targeting historically excluded groups to offset the extreme power and status imbalances that were institutionalized and normalized over hundreds of years. The agency of historically excluded groups needs to be targeted with public policies and actively supported so that equal opportunities become a true reality.

African American communities have long recognized that they cannot win this battle for justice and equity without bringing governments and states at least partially onto their side. Black protest and mobilization repertoires have reflected this insight over the last years—backed by the almost surprising impact of the Anti-Racism Conference held in Durban in 2001. Many movements have indeed been successful in changing the legal frameworks and official national representations so that these now recognize the multicultural nature of their constituents. The cases of Colombia and Nicaragua provide ample examples of these victories. However, once legal frameworks and official rhetoric change, it becomes clear that laws do not create reality—social interaction does. Changing engrained patterns of discriminatory practice, and changing the ways historically privileged groups have been able to benefit from systems of injustice requires much more than simply changing a constitution (even if changing a constitution to recognize minorities and give them special rights and protections is important and far from easy). As the case of affirmative action in Brazil demonstrates, public policy needs to follow the change of legal frameworks—and it is then when most protests and resistance from historically included groups must be expected, because people and groups tend to fight over concrete privileges and access, not laws. Whatever the strategy, national states and governments remain central players in the game of allotting opportunities and structuring life chances, which is why so many of the chapters assembled here include an analysis of governments and government policies and how they interact and shape the politics of black organizing and activism.

Beyond governments, the works assembled here also leave no doubt that no adequate understanding of, let alone improvement for, African-descendants is possible without first recognizing the profound impact and significance of historical processes of racialization. Exploitation in the Americas has resorted to ideological legitimation by marking non-Europeans as different and stigmatizing them in a deep-seated historical process of racialization, thus creating "race." Once race was created, it served to further exploit and stigmatize, producing all the negative effects on racialized groups that psychologists and sociologists have long described. Yet racialization has also brought different people suffering under the same racial regime together and allowed for their networking, mutual solidarity, and political mobilization. This is the story of African Americans in the United States, where discrimination made anybody not entirely white "black"—thus bringing together people of far-reaching experiences, histories, and interests. "Race" in the United States thus became a positive political tool—one that has produced very significant political gains. The political effectiveness of race has to be recognized and appreciated—and not confounded with epistemological and identity claims about "who one is," or "to what group one belongs." Scholars have contributed much to confounding these two realms, and the mixing up of political claims with identity claims has created much friction, especially between North American and South American black activists. Not that these frictions represent any real dangers. The fear of racializing southern societies is a fear typically expressed by those who benefited from the status quo ante, allowing them to exploit without fear of retaliation. If anything, it expresses the continued paternalism of white South Americans, who fear for "their" societies. "Race" has taught U.S. African Americans significant lessons about the importance of cross-color alliances and the forging of communities of fate among all those suffering from similar forms of oppression. To many U.S. African Americans, the lack of black solidarity they witness in Latin America and the Caribbean thus appears as a lack of consciousness, and reflects a scenario that they have successfully overcome, where some still remember the times when colorism also had divided nonwhites in the North. The chapters by Kimberly Eison Simmons, Seth Racusen, and Gladys Mitchell all provide highly relevant insights into these dynamics.

As political lessons were learned in the United States, those lessons were also absorbed by black leaders in the South, made possible by intensified transregional communication and interchange, as well as through intensified migration and cheaper flights and phone calls. Nonprofit organizations played a role in the facilitation of black-to-black interchange, as the authors of the first part of this book demonstrate. The often-made accusation of "imperialism" is, however, entirely misguided, as such organizations as the Ford Foundation can only provide the channels to facilitate interchange. They cannot dictate or control the content of this interchange. Furthermore, the interchange among people of African descent, as Paul Gilroy and, before him, Melvin Herskovitz have demonstrated, had never ceased to exist. Slave trade ensured the continuous communication among different Diaspora communities, and as slaves were traded as goods and sometimes sold several times during their lifetime, communication among them never stopped. As Celia Maria Marinho de Azevedo (2004) has shown, slaves in Rio de Janeiro were well aware of the slave revolts happening in Haiti during the 1790s and were seen marching in the streets of Rio carrying portraits of Jean-Jacques Dessalines. Robert Stam (1997) provides another example of these transatlantic, or "Black Atlantic," community ties when relating the story of former Brazilian slaves living as free blacks in New York City, then still called New Amsterdam. According to Stam, "Afro Brazilians, also arriving with the Dutch from Brazil, were among the very first black people to arrive in New York City (Stam 1997, 27). The creation of this early Diaspora network was facilitated by the fact that during the seventeenth century, the Dutch had colonial possessions in parts of Africa, Brazil, and North America, easing commercial flows between these three continents and Europe, much in the same way the Portuguese and Spaniards had done earlier and the British and French would do later (Reiter and Mitchell 2008). The idea of neatly contained national communities is an illusion and an ideological tool similar to the one that suggests ethnic, or even biological, purity of national citizenries.

Communication among people of African descent is clearly not a twentieth-century novelty. However, processes commonly called "globalization" have sped up the pace and intensity of this communication, allowing for more immediate and direct contact among different black communities of the New World—and between those and Africa. This has led to an increased ability to get to know each other and share one's own experiences and learning—especially with regard to political mobilization around the idea of "race." The tropes of mixedness and *moreno* culture were not invented, disseminated, and integrated into national schoolbooks by or for blacks to begin with, and the fostering of Latin and Caribbean national identities was in most cases not undertaken for the sake of benefiting or integrating black communities, but to the contrary, to allow Creole elites to disassociate from blackness as far as possible when claiming whiteness was not a real possibility. While "white" at home, they were deemed "colored" by the whites from the North—be it the United States or Europe—in the perverse global game of justifying privilege through claiming whiteness and establishing global social hierarchies through such claims of "justified" privilege. One should thus not be surprised that *moreno* ideologies are coming under scrutiny by black activists and social movements, given that these ideologies, and the practices and policies they helped to legitimize, have not produced significant improvements for black communities. Asserting one's position within national *moreno/mulato/mestizo* communities thus represents an important struggle for African American communities throughout the hemisphere—one that aims to provide the very foundation upon which any development must rest, as it aims to rescue, assert, and delineate the human condition of black communities amidst other, nonblack communities. At this early stage, this struggle still aims to find a voice and make it count and be respected.

What several of the authors assembled here thus clearly demonstrate is the ongoing struggle of black communities to define themselves without neglecting the multifaceted aspect of their lives and destinies, while at the same time seeking to maintain, and if possible improve, their standing within potentially hostile national communities that look at them with suspicion, guilt, and fear. Latin American and Caribbean elites, of course, have much to feel guilty about and be afraid of when it comes to the black populations living among them—and sometimes constituting a numerical majority. They, the elites, through inventing their own whiteness, have been able to live comfortable lives by standing on the shoulders of their nonwhite fellow denizens. They had, and have, servants, maids, cleaners, porters, guards, washers, and other almost-slaves who continue to lift them up and allow them to think of themselves as bigger, taller, and higher up than they truly are, so that they can breathe the same "civilized" air of their European "brethren." They are, however, keenly aware that they do not stand on solid ground—morally as well as politically. Hence the fear of U.S. scholars, activists, and foundations "secretly" introducing U.S. racial hatred to what those elites have always perceived as "their" harmonious lands. What if yesterday's Dessalines becomes tomorrow's Farrakhan? The ground upon which the elites stand might one day give way entirely—or worse, it might swallow them up.

However, several chapters of this book provide us with a glimpse of how resilient, creative, generous, and patient African American communities have been to ensure their survival and carve out spaces for themselves within extremely hostile societies, under unthinkably inhumane conditions. The fragmented character of the emerging picture points to the need to continue to explore, explain, and disseminate the difficulties and barriers that African descendants in the Americas encounter today, and how difficult it is for them to narrow the gap that still separates them from nonblacks after hundreds of years of slavery, discrimination, exploitation, and disdain. In this, our study and development approaches have to be just as multifaceted as the realities we seek to unveil. Therefore, as reflected in this book, this is not an effort of cultural anthropologists alone. We also need to find more and better ways to quantify what racism does to limit a person's agency.

At the same time, while the production and dissemination of "hard evidence" is very important—even more so as most hard sciences have pretended for far too long that their work has no connection to issues of social justice, thus escaping their responsibilities as scientists doing science for a purpose—the social sciences and humanities have important insights and findings to contribute. This becomes evident when considering the important role of religion for African American communities. Religion has always played, and continues to play, a central role in this resistance. Different African religions, determined by specific ancestral lineages and thus specific to the regions of different ethnic groups and family clans, melted together in the New World to form new, pan-African religions, thus hinting at the great tolerance of African religions. The emerging pan-African religions, known in the New World as Candomblé, Santería, Vodun, Xango, Palo Mayombe, among others—once they constituted themselves, also incorporated other religions: indigenous, Christian, and Muslim, producing entirely new and highly amalgamated and syncretized religious practices that have influenced any and all religious activity of the Americas today. American religion, no matter which one, is different than religious practice in the Old World. It is more celebratory, less suspicious, and less ashamed of embodied rituals, and more connected to spiritism, possession, trance, and exaltation than anything the Old World could have produced by itself. New World religion also retains and combines much of the knowledge about healing, preservation, and community-building from the different communities that contributed to its creation, and as such, it offers opportunities for situated and context-conscious development. Development, as argued above, needs to be sensitive to, respect, and integrate the knowledge of those whose lives are being developed. If not, it continues to be domination.

The chapters assembled here also allow us to perceive the differences and similarities among the various African American communities of the New World—stretching from struggles over housing in Miami to the continuing fight against invisibility in Buenos Aires. It becomes clear that these struggles are all characterized by the need to fight on several fronts simultaneously. For African American communities, a struggle for better housing is never only a struggle to improve material conditions; it is always also a struggle to assert their dignity as a community, to fight back against racism, to lift up their own community members against the potentially devastating effects of continued stigmatization and disrespect. And while we have seen throughout these chapters that black females suffer from multiple burdens that tend to propel them to the very bottom of social hierarchies, we have also learned how young black males especially suffer from the multiple burdens placed upon their shoulders. How to be a man when one's manhood has been undermined for so long? How to live up to all the expectations of one's own community without having the necessary preparation and training? How to be humane and generous when one is looked upon with suspicion and fear, and thus routinely dehumanized? Several of the chapters assembled here allow us to take a deeper look into the gender dynamics by which any negotiation of belonging is necessarily conditioned.

Finally, this collection offers a way to better understand the struggles and plights of different African-descendant communities in the Americas, including the Caribbean. It is far from complete, but it seeks to connect to the other significant efforts already available focusing on this population. Indeed, the African Diaspora as a field of study has grown over the years. The University of Texas at Austin now has a department devoted to the study of the African Diaspora. In the 1990s, Michigan State University had the African Diaspora Research Project, under the leadership of the late Ruth Simms Hamilton. There is a professional organization known as the Association of the Study of the Worldwide African Diaspora (ASWAD). Ruth Simms Hamilton and Joseph Harris were two of the pioneers of early African Diaspora studies. Contemporaneously, within the context of the African Diaspora, scholars, researchers, activists, and everyday citizens identify and name similarities among African Diaspora communities and create strategic alliances based on common goals and objectives.

We started with the conviction that only a proper understanding of the specific problems of these groups and communities can lead to the design of effective development strategies able to support their efforts of overcoming the many obstacles, burdens, and disadvantages they inherited from the past. This collection thus ends with a call for situated and contextualized development strategies and appeals for efforts of collaboration between different communities, white and black, foundation and banking, scholarly and activist. Each of these communities has developed its own codes and internal logics, separating them from other, equally relevant systems of knowledge production, project development, and assistance. None of these communities can afford to be excluded from the joint effort to overcome racism and exclusion, because everybody is affected by it in some way. Openly attacking racism is not the sole task of those affected by it. Instead, it is the task of everyone, especially those who have and might continue to benefit from racialized exclusion, because besides the victims, racism undermines the morals of the victimizers by transforming them into monsters that benefit from the denigration of others. No true effort and gain is worth anything if it is achieved at such a cost. Fighting racism must thus become a mainstream effort and part of any sound and complete scholarly study, development project, or activism in and on the Americas—and we hope that this book helps push it there.

REFERENCES

Azevedo, Celia Maria Marinho de. 2004. *Onda negra medo branco.* São Paulo: Ana Blume.

Gilroy, Paul. 1993. *The Black Atlantic.* Cambridge, MA: Harvard University Press.

Reiter, Bernd, and Gladys Mitchell. 2008. "Embracing Hip Hop as Their Own: Hip Hop and Black Racial Identity in Brazil." *Studies in Latin American Popular Culture* (27):151–166.

Stam, Robert. 1997. *Tropical Multiculturalism.* Durham, NC: Duke University Press.

Contributors

Judith M. Anderson received her PhD in cultural anthropology from the University of Florida and is an independent scholar. She continues to research themes of identity and race among Afro-descendants in Argentina.

Amanda D. Concha-Holmes is a research associate in agricultural education and communication at the University of Florida. As a visual and ecological anthropologist, her interests are in the documentation of ecological and cultural resources through film and media that emphasize local perspectives and grassroots movements in a critical examination of African Diaspora knowledges, particularly embodied and applied pedagogical systems, representations and identity-formations, religion and ecology, and the ethics, praxis, and alternative partnerships of development and conservation.

Darién J. Davis is professor of history and international studies at Middlebury College, and director of the Latin American Studies program. His major areas of research are Brazilian and Spanish American social and cultural history, African and "Latino" Diasporas in the Atlantic world, and transnationalism.

Lauren Derby is associate professor of modern Latin American history at the University of California, Los Angeles. Her research focuses on politics and popular culture in the Dominican Republic, Haiti, Puerto Rico, and Cuba.

Mamyrah A. Dougé-Prosper is a doctoral candidate in the Department of Global and Sociocultural Studies at Florida International University. Her research focuses on social movements, postcolonial nation-states, gender, race, class, sexuality, and Haiti.

Faye V. Harrison is joint professor of anthropology and African American studies at the University of Florida. Her publications include *Resisting Racism and Xenophobia: Global Perspectives on Race, Gender, and Human Rights* (2005, ed.) and *Outsider Within: Reworking Anthropology in the Global Age* (2008).

Juliet Hooker is associate professor of government and African and African Diaspora Studies and associate director of the Teresa Lozano Long Institute of Latin American Studies at the University of Texas at Austin. Her research focuses on multiculturalism, race and nationalism in Latin America, and African American and Latin American political thought.

Leonardo Reales Jiménez is a PhD candidate in political science at the New School University in New York. He works as a content advisor for the Afro-Latinos Project. His research focuses on ethnic leadership, political participation, community development, human rights, and Afro-descendant issues.

Paula A. Lezama is assistant director and academic adviser, Institute for the Study of Latin America and the Caribbean at the University of South Florida. Her research interests lie in economic and social development, and the analysis of poverty and inequality, especially when pertaining to Afro-descendant populations in Latin America and the Caribbean.

Gladys Mitchell-Walthour is assistant professor of comparative politics at Denison University. She specializes in racial politics in Brazil.

Altagracia Balcácer Molina has been a Dominican activist for women and Afro-descendant rights for more than fifteen years. She studied economics in Moscow, and at Columbia University in New York. Ms. Balcacer is a professor at the Universidad Autónoma de Santo Domingo and has worked for the government and international organizations in the areas of education, gender, women, economics, and development.

Judith A. Morrison serves as the senior advisor for the Gender and Diversity unit at the Inter-American Development Bank. She is responsible for providing leadership to the bank for analytical and operational work related to African-descendant and indigenous populations throughout Latin America and the Caribbean. She previously served as regional director for South America and the Caribbean at the Inter-American Foundation, where she was responsible for managing staff and operations for the region. From 2005 to 2007, Morrison was a director at the Inter-American Dialogue and the executive director of the Inter-Agency Consultation on Race in Latin America (a consultative donor consortium established at the World Bank with the Inter-American Development Bank, Ford Foundation, Pan-American Health Organization, and Department for International Development–UK).

Tianna S. Paschel is assistant professor of political science at the University of Chicago where she conducts research on race, social movements, state policy, and globalization in comparative perspective.

Seth Racusen is associate professor of criminal justice and political science at Anna Maria College. His research focuses on the use of law and public policy to contest racial inequalities in Brazil, and the transnational constitution of identity and public policy.

Bernd Reiter is associate professor of comparative politics at the University of South Florida, where he holds a joint appointment with the Department of Government and International Affairs and the Institute for the Study of Latin America and the Caribbean. His research focuses on citizenship, democracy, and racialized exclusion.

Kimberly Eison Simmons is associate professor of Anthropology and African American Studies and director of the Latin American Studies Program at the University of South Carolina. Her research focuses on racial, gender, and identity formation in the African Diaspora, African American culture, and Afro-Latinos/as in the United States. She is the author of *Reconstructing Racial Identity and the African Past in the Dominican Republic* (2009).

Dorotea Wilson is a prominent leader in Nicaragua's "Atlantic Coast Autonomous Region," and a member of the Sandinista National Executive. The region is now recognized as semi-autonomous under the Nicaraguan constitution. Ms. Wilson played a prominent role in the establishment of the region and in fighting for the rights of the country's indigenous population. She has also served as the mayor of Puerto Cabezas, one of the major cities on the Atlantic Coast, and as a member of the National Parliament and the government of the Autonomous Region. She joined the Sandinistas in

1975 and was active in the underground movement against the Samoza dictatorship. She advocates for the rights of women of color in general, and those from rural areas in particular. She has written articles on the history of Nicaragua from the point of view of the oppressed.